The Michigan Historical Reprint Series

Reprints from the collection of the University of Michigan University Library

This volume is produced from digital images created through the University of Michigan University Library's preservation reformatting program. The Library seeks to preserve the intellectual content of items in a manner that facilitates and promotes a variety of uses. The digital reformatting process results in an electronic version of the text that can both be accessed online and used to create new print copies. This book and thousands of others can be found in the digital collections of the University of Michigan Library. The University Library also understands and values the utility of print, and makes reprints available through its Scholarly Publishing Office.

For access to the University of Michigan Library's digital collections, please see http://www.lib.umich.edu.

The Scholarly Publishing Office seeks to disseminate high-quality, cost-effective scholarly content through both print and electronic publishing. Information about the Scholarly Publishing Office can be found at http://spo.umdl.umich.edu.

The Scholarly Publishing Office
the University of Michigan
University Library

THE LIFE AND TIMES

OF

HENRY LORD BROUGHAM,

WRITTEN BY HIMSELF.

IN THREE VOLUMES.

VOL. III.

NEW YORK:
HARPER & BROTHERS, PUBLISHERS,
FRANKLIN SQUARE.
1872.

TO THE READER.

THE following instructions were given by Lord Brougham to me, as his executor:

"Before the Autobiography can be published, you must see that it is arranged chronologically.

"If (writing from memory) I have made mistakes in dates, or in proper names, let such be corrected; but the *Narrative* is to be printed *AS I HAVE WRITTEN IT.*

"I alone am answerable for all its statements, faults, and omissions. I will have no Editor employed to alter, or rewrite, what I desire shall be published as *EXCLUSIVELY MY OWN.*

"BROUGHAM, *November*, 1867."

In publishing Lord Brougham's Autobiography, the above explicit directions have been scrupulously obeyed.

BROUGHAM & VAUX.

BROUGHAM, *January*, 1871.

CONTENTS OF VOL. III.

CHAPTER XIX.

CHAPTER XX.

CHAPTER XXI.

CHAPTER XXII.

CHAPTER XXIII.

CHAPTER XXIV.

CHAPTER XXV.

PREFATORY NOTE.

Having in my possession much correspondence with King William IV. on public affairs, I applied for and obtained her present majesty's permission to publish the same.

Sent inclosed to General C. Grey.

"Brougham, October 8, 1867.

"Lord Brougham offers his humble duty to your majesty, and ventures to state that, having been for a few years past engaged in preparing his Autobiography, he takes the liberty of soliciting your majesty's gracious permission to publish those portions of the correspondence between his late majesty King William IV. and himself that bear upon the public affairs in which Lord Brougham took part while he held the Great Seal.

"Lord Brougham being in his ninetieth year, hopes your majesty will pardon him for employing the hand of another to write this letter."

To this the queen commanded General the Honorable Charles Grey to return the following answer:

"Balmoral, October 13, 1867.

"My dear W. Brougham,—I have this evening received your letter, and have lost no time in submitting that from Lord Brougham to the queen, who commands me to say that she has no objection to the publication of the correspondence by him which took place between himself and the king, while he was lord chancellor.

"Believe me yours very truly, C. Grey.

"William Brougham, Esq.,
"Brougham, Penrith."

THE LIFE AND TIMES

OF

HENRY, LORD BROUGHAM.

CHAPTER XIX.

Elected Lord Rector of the University of Glasgow.—Public Dinner in Edinburgh.—Henry Cockburn.—Scotch System of Education.—Ireland in 1828.—Question of the Repeal of the Roman Catholic Disability Laws.—The Wellington Cabinet.—O'Connell.—The War between Russia and Turkey.—Prospects of France.—Home Affairs.—The King and Denman.—Libel Prosecutions.—Opening of the Session of 1830.—Acceptance of the Offer of a Seat for Knaresborough.—Summary of Parliamentary Career.

Before I resume the subject of Ireland and the Catholics, I must mention an event of so much interest to me, that I can not avoid referring to it. In the spring of 1825, the students of the University of Glasgow conferred on me the office of rector of that university.* I was to be installed on the 6th of April, and some of my Edinburgh friends were desirous of giving me a public dinner upon my first return to that city, after an absence of nearly a quarter of a century. The 5th of April was fixed upon, and the dinner took place in the Assembly Rooms, Henry Cockburn being in the chair.

Highly as I prized the honor about to be conferred upon me by Glasgow, the Edinburgh dinner, unlike the ordinary run of such festivities, made so deep and lasting an impression upon me, that this period of my life would be incomplete without some account of it. Certainly it was one of

---

* See "Inaugural Discourse on being installed Lord Rector of the University of Glasgow, April 6, 1825."—*Lord Brougham's Speeches*, iii., 69.

the most striking scenes I ever witnessed, not only from the vast assemblage—nearly nine hundred people—but from the admirable arrangements and conduct of the whole proceeding; nor was there any thing more remarkable or more flattering to me than this fact, that notwithstanding my political opinions had been so strongly opposed to the party which for so many years governed Scotland, yet many distinguished members of the Tory party (Cockburn told me more than fifty) were present, forgetting their hostility to my principles, and cordially testifying their approval of my public conduct and character. Cockburn, as I have said, was chairman, and in proposing my health, naturally referred to my education in Edinburgh, and to the great influence the Scotch system had upon my achievements, which he described as greater than had ever been attained by the intellectual powers of a single and unaided man. He then referred to the queen's trial, particularly dwelling on the courage, greater, he said, than the ability, which I had displayed in standing up alone against all the power of a king and his subservient ministers. He then especially spoke of what I had done for the education of the people, which, he predicted, would be my most appropriate monument, and far greater and far more enduring than any statue, or any commemorative emblem in Westminster Abbey.

It is impossible to describe the enthusiasm which Cockburn's speech excited—the cheering of the vast assembly was such as I never before or since have heard, lasting for many minutes after the chairman sat down.

When I returned thanks, I could not resist touching upon what Cockburn had said of the proceeding against the queen, which was, I insisted, no *trial*, for every channel of defamation had been opened and poured upon the accused, who, borne down by the strong hand of unscrupulous power, had been saved only by her innocence, and by the force of that law, which the king and his ministers had combined to destroy.

Before I sat down, I seized the opportunity to declare my decided approbation of the Scotch system of education, as contrasted with the English. I said that I had never known any scheme so well adapted for forming and finishing a learned course as that pursued in the Old High School of Edinburgh and in the University. For that was the system so invaluable in a free State—a system which cultivated and cherished higher objects than mere learning, which inculcated a nobler ambition than the mere acquisition of prosody and the dead languages.

My English friends will cry aloud against this doctrine, which they will designate as rank heresy. Nevertheless, such was my opinion in 1825, and such it still is, after a lapse of forty years since I uttered the sentiments above stated.

During the whole of the year 1828, there was no political question of such importance as the state of Ireland. I do not remember any subject that ever excited such overwhelming interest; all public men were occupied in discussing it, and in speculating upon the possible intentions of the Government. Lord Grey held strongly to the opinion that there was but one way to settle the question, and that Wellington *must* be convinced of this; yet even up to the end of the year, the duke, as well as the leading members of his government, appeared to be as hostile as ever to emancipation, and as firm as ever in maintaining the principles on which they had always acted.

The duke seemed to be immovable. Peel, on Burdett's motion for a committee on the disability laws, declared *his* firm adherence to the opinion he had always held, and which had become more strengthened the more he considered the question.* So late as December, the duke, writing to Dr. Curtis, the Catholic Primate of Ireland, distinctly stated that, anxious as he was to see the question put at rest, he as yet saw no prospect of a settlement. Lord Anglesey, the lord lieutenant, because of the construction he publicly put upon this letter, was recalled, and replaced by the Duke of Northumberland. For this act Wellington was most violently attacked and abused by O'Connell and the Catholic Association.

I have before remarked upon the singular sagacity which Lord Rosslyn displayed, when, in the autumn of this year (1828), he truly conjectured the course Wellington would ul-

* See Hansard, 9 Geo. IV., xix., 579.

timately adopt, and the reason of his reserve: on the one hand there were the Brunswickers and rabid Orangemen, the aversion of the king, and the certain hostility of the House of Lords; on the other, the Catholic Association, with O'Connell capable of sacrificing every thing to gratify his own inordinate vanity. Then Peel was believed to be impracticable, and his refusal to join the duke in any measure of concession, must end in his resignation, which would upset the Government, and thus greatly increase the difficulties with the king. Yet Rosslyn insisted that Wellington would never run the risk of a civil war—leading to bloodshed in Ireland, and to the almost certain interference of France, which would be too glad of any opportunity to revenge the humiliation of 1815.

All these difficulties seemed to Rosslyn to account for Wellington's reserve, and led him to the conclusion that, supposing he meant concession, he would keep his intentions secret until the moment came for action.

Lord Grey was persuaded that, looking to the state of Ireland, Wellington *must* have arrived at the conviction that there was but one way to settle the question. Grey also knew that Arbuthnot, Hardinge, Murray, and even Lyndhurst had been talking in the same strain; so every thing was tending to the result which became known to the public, when Parliament met in February, 1829, and the king in his speech, after referring to the Catholic Association, recommended Parliament to consider whether the laws imposing disabilities on Roman Catholics could be safely removed.

Peel, having first resigned his seat for the University of Oxford, on being elected for Westbury, brought in the bill in the Commons; and actually within three weeks of its introduction it passed, and by a considerable majority. On the 10th of April, it was read a third time in the Lords, and immediately afterwards received the royal assent.

Among the opponents of the bill in the Commons, there was no one more hostile than Wetherell, one of the most honest and independent men I have ever known. He was especially bitter against Lyndhurst, whom he stigmatized as a miserable apostate, when he referred to the powerful speech made by the Protestant Master of the Rolls,* who had now within a little year become a Catholic lord chancellor.

Wetherell, as attorney-general, when directed to prepare what he described as the "atrocious bill," positively refused. This refusal, followed by his violent speech against Lyndhurst, led to his being dismissed. He had refused to *resign*, saying, "No, let them turn me out." Tindal was solicitor, but, sitting for the University of Cambridge, if he had been appointed attorney-general his seat would have been vacated, and his re-election most doubtful; so the office was allowed to remain vacant until June, when, on Best retiring from the Common Pleas, Tindal was appointed chief-justice, Scarlett, attorney, and Sugden, solicitor-general.

In the autumn of 1829, the following letters passed between Lord Grey and me:

"Lambton Castle, October 11, 1829.

"MY DEAR BROUGHAM,—I received your letter here this morning. I came on Monday to meet Lord Cleveland, and hoped to have met you also. I regret and condole with you most sincerely on the cause which has prevented it, as well as the still greater pleasure that I should have had in receiving a visit from you at Howick.

"Holland, in a letter that I had from him three days ago, makes the same mistake that you do about Angern. This was a Prussian possession, and was ceded back to Russia by the last peace. What they now get, are four fortresses on the Asiatic frontier, which were restored to Turkey by the treaty of Bucharest, kept, I believe, by Russia on the pretense that other parts of the conditions of that treaty were not fulfilled by the Porte, who alleged the same plea, till every thing was settled by the treaty of Ackerman, which we thought proper to open again by the treaty of the 6th July. The terms, upon the whole, are not such as ought to surprise us, considering that the Turks had no means of resistance, and were absolutely at the mercy of their conquerors. Nor, considering the steps by which things had been brought to this pass, and the active situation of affairs, had we either the

* He spoke a pamphlet written by Phillpotts, Rector of Stanhope, afterwards Bishop of Exeter.

right or the power to resist them. But I suspect that our ministers consider them as any thing but moderate in themselves, or creditable to the character and influence of this country, after the interest we have shown in the fate of our ancient ally.* As to myself, I hate the Turks, and should be glad to see them driven out of Europe, if it could be done without danger to the general peace; but we must give the devil his due; and looking at the origin of the war, I can not but think they have been the victims of the greatest violence and injustice. In this view, the terms can not be said to be moderate.

"The state of politics is undoubtedly not a little curious, and I feel very comfortable in my situation of spectator. I have no doubt that if the Duke of Cumberland, who will never forgive either the Duke of Wellington or the chancellor, and whose influence with the king is unbounded, could form a high Tory Administration, the thing would soon be done. But here is an impossibility which I do not see how they can surmount. Sadler, I suppose, would be their man, but this would be too ridiculous.†

"I have no doubt that Polignac's policy is taking a character not friendly to this country. It was the obvious and necessary consequence of his being supposed to have been made by our influence. For this, as well as for other reasons, I am willing to believe that the Duke of Wellington is unjustly charged with a measure which would not only have been wrong, but foolish in the extreme. Adair, from whom I have heard twice from Paris, gives a frightful account of the state of things there, and of the spirit which prevails against England.

"I had heard that Ellenborough had brought his action against George Anson; but your information is probably more correct.

---

* In reference to the treaty of Adrianople, concluding the war between Russia and Turkey in 1824.

† Mr. Sadler, returned for Newark, having, by help of the Duke of Newcastle's interest, defeated Sergeant Wilde, the Government candidate. Mr. Sadler made his maiden speech against the bill, and it was the best on that side of the question—not only great in argument, but wonderful as an effort of oratory.

"I have this morning a sad account from Lady Jersey of her child, whose situation appears to be now quite hopeless. From the last accounts, I had hoped that there really was at last some appearance of real amendment.

"I rejoice in the success of the University. I return to Howick to-morrow. Ever yours, GREY."

"November 10, 1829.

"MY DEAR LORD GREY,—Since I came to town I have seen hardly any body, being kept in court every day, except Saturday and Sunday. Last Sunday I saw one or two—as Sir Henry Parnell, Lord John Russell, etc.

"Parnell says nothing can be more clear than that things are going on well in Ireland, upon the whole; and though there are the *remains of agitation*, yet it wants support both from the priests and the Catholics of influence. He gave some remarkable instances—as of an Orange squire whom he had seen, a violent man, but who admitted that the priests were behaving well; and a Catholic gentleman of influence, who had joined *heartily* in putting down the disorders in his neighborhood, and durst as soon have been burnt as try such a thing a year ago, even if he had been so disposed, which he would not have been. Parnell thinks the law quite sufficient to do all that is wanted, and that Coercion Acts and such-like would be worse than useless.

"Lord John Russell had seen Pozzo at Paris, and found him astonished at our Government trying to lessen the Greek territory; because by so doing, as he justly observed, no kind of aid is given to the Turk. It seems to me very plain that *our* interest rather is to make as great a state (they say, a kingdom is resolved upon, and with a German prince, *not* being a Bavarian) as possible; for Russia may thus eventually be counterbalanced in the Mediterranean. Lord John gives the same account with every one else, as to Paris, and indeed France at large—that they all seem quite confident the present ministry can not stand, though the Chambers would support a *moderate* Royalist one. But they would (it is said) not *now* support one with Polignac at the head. Polignac told some one that he had ten millions placed at his disposal by the king. This was in answer to a question as to how he could meet the Chambers. You may recollect Villèle expected to carry the five per cent. question some years ago in the same way, and failed.*

"Our own Government is in some respects like the French, for there seems a universal opinion that it can not go on as it is. The rage (for it amounts to that) against Peel does not at all subside; and I have lately heard of calm kind of men, like Lord Harewood, speaking of him as they would of some one they had a personal quarrel with.

"I find Scarlett has no communication with any of them; and he knows no more of their judicial appointments than of what is going to happen in Japan. I doubt if the chancellor knows much more, though they say the new baron is fixed upon, but nobody knows who it is.

"Denman is gone to Windsor to-day, in room of the recorder, who is very ill. This is a bitter pill to the king, who has always greatly dreaded such an accident. He (the king) is not yet quite certain of going to Brighton. Mrs. Taylor† has been *dangerously* ill; but they think her safe now. It was severe inflammation. Yours ever truly,

"H. BROUGHAM."

Next day I wrote again to Lord Grey:

"November 11, 1829.

"MY DEAR LORD GREY,—When you see to-day that the recorder's report was put off yesterday, and lay that together with what I said of Denman going down, you will have your suspicions of the reason for the putting off. In fact, a countermand of the council arrived late on Monday evening. So none of them went down. The courtiers say it had nothing to do with Denman going; and was solely owing to the king having again changed his mind about going to Brighton; for they say the only reason for holding the council, was to let him go to Brighton this week. It may be so; but I own, knowing the king as I do, I have a strong suspicion that he put it off to give the *recorder* a chance of recovering, and thus avoid seeing Denman. For after summoning them all, what

* Jean Baptiste Comte de Villèle, Minister of Finance to Charles X.

† Mrs. Michael Angelo Taylor, sister to Sir Harry Vane Tempest.

harm could there have been in receiving the report, except the trouble to the people of going down, which his majesty is not likely to have cared for?

"All Westminster Hall is filled with astonishment at the chancellor's *boldness* in making Bolland the new baron. It is making the Exchequer by far the most incapable court that ever was known in Westminster Hall at any time, and that when they are about to try to open it and make it an efficient court! Bolland is so generally liked, that Copley seems to have presumed upon this; but it is very outrageous.

"Yours ever, H. B."

"London, December 21, 1829.

"MY DEAR LORD GREY,—Since I wrote, little has occurred till within the last day or two, when reports have been very prevalent that Knighton is out or going.* I some time ago had heard of his being tired of it, and a man who knows him lately said that he thought he had lost favor by not humoring the king; but now I understand that Alvanly has written to Lord Sefton as a thing he believed certain, that Knighton is out, and succeeded by Sir Herbert Taylor.

"I take it, from all I can see, the French Ministry is out too, or as good as out. I hear Lady Tankerville has been saying this; and I find Scarlett believes it, probably from what his son writes, who is at Paris with Stuart.

"Here things are much in the same state; the ultras are as violent as we, and Wetherell tells me there is not the least foundation for the stories of any of them being conciliated. On the contrary, they threaten much from the ensuing session. The strange thing is, that some of them who are actually in office hold the same hostile language. Beckett, I know from undoubted authority, talks exactly as if he were in avowed hostility to the Ministry. They assert in Cumberland that he and Sadler have bought the 'Leeds Intelligencer'—a violent ultra paper; and it is a known fact that the Lowther editor of a similar paper at Carlisle has been sent to conduct it at Leeds. But my information of Beckett's language

* Sir William Knighton, Physician and Keeper of the Privy Purse of George IV.: created a baronet January, 1813, died October, 1836.

comes from those who know and have talked to him.* The Duke of Cumberland's apartments at Windsor are ordered to be got ready, and I much doubt Lord Rosslyn's opinion that he is losing ground there is not correct.

"Yours ever, H. BROUGHAM.

"The Hollands are come to Saville Row. He quite well—she only middling; and poor Miss Vernon very ill indeed.

"I saw Mrs. Taylor yesterday: she has had a relapse, though without inflammation, and is very unwell. Taylor is going about as much as ever."

"Howick, December 24, 1829.

"MY DEAR BROUGHAM,—I can not believe that Knighton's retirement from Windsor, if it be true, is voluntary. I never heard of any body, who had once got fairly within the atmosphere of the Court, being able to live out of it. It becomes as necessary to the life of a courtier as water to that of a fish. For some reason or other, I suppose, therefore, the king wishes to get rid of him, and I shall not be surprised to hear that he retires with poor Tucker's place.

"The Tories may talk as loud as they please, but opposition is too ungenial a climate for them. They will attorn when they see nothing better to be done. In the mean time, pray leave them a clear stage, and see what they are up to, and sing,

"'Suave mari magno.'

"Rosslyn was here for three days, in his way to Scotland, and I expect him again in his way back. I learned nothing from him that I did not know before. As you have seen him, I need not add that there is no foundation whatever, and never has been, for the reports which have been circulated about me.

"Ponsonby's last letter is from Paris, and I think he is a good observer, though not without a strong bias against the Liberals; speaks of them as being governed by their violence, and thinks Polignac more likely to stand than he was some time ago. I, too, I confess, am not without fears of these said Liberals; not on account of their revolutionary views, if such

* Right Hon. Sir J. Beckett, member for Haslemere.

they have. On that point I am no alarmist. On the contrary, my wishes would naturally be for a free government in France, but on account of their avowed hostility to this country (which I am not such a dupe as to believe to be confined to the Duke of Wellington's administration), and of their propensity to war.

"We have at last winter—frost and some snow; but the snow only a sprinkling, and the frost not severe.

"Ever yours, GREY.

"Does Denman go with the recorder's report, which I see is to be received to-day? Pray tell me if there is any thing worth remarking in the king's demeanor, or in these trials for libel."

At no time was party feeling more bitter than while the Catholic question was in agitation, and after Wellington had, by passing the bill, estranged so many of his Tory supporters; nor was the press behindhand in the violence of its invective.* One of the most virulent was the "Morning Journal," a newspaper that had been established by some of the most angry opponents of the Government: it was conducted by a Mr. Alexander, a clever man and a good writer. His articles became so outrageous, that the attorney-general (Scarlett) considered that it was his duty to take steps to put a stop to them. One of his first attempts was against an article which plainly enough insinuated that Lyndhurst had made Sugden solicitor-general, in consideration of having received from him a large sum of money, either as a gift or as a loan. Scarlett accordingly moved for a rule for a criminal information against Alexander, and the proprietors of the paper. Alexander, in opposing the motion, made an affidavit in which he swore that Lyndhurst was not the person alluded to in the article. The Court of King's Bench evidently did not believe him, for it granted the rule. Scarlett, however, instead of proceeding, abandoned the rule, and filed an *ex officio* information. He also filed others for libels against the king and his ministers, and one for a libel on the Duke of Wellington.

* The "Act for the Relief of his Majesty's Roman Catholic Subjects" had received the royal assent on 13th April, 1829.

Scarlett was perfectly justified in attacking the newspaper, but nothing could excuse his proceeding by *ex officio* information, after he had, from Alexander's affidavit, ascertained the line of defense, and had also by his change of tactics secured for himself the right to reply.

I expressed my opinion on this subject in the following letter to Lord Grey:

"Brougham, January 10, 1830.

"My dear Lord Grey,—Your letter followed me here yesterday, I having left town late on Thursday, and got here on Saturday, through much snow, till I got into the north of Yorkshire.

"The recorder made a great exertion to relieve *his sovereign*. The Ministers were quarrelling with the latter in such a way, that there was no saying where it might have ended. It is very absurd not to make Denman a judge, which would be a most perfect and highly popular appointment, and get rid of their difficulty at once. But really, if personal *exclusions* are to be allowed, and *personal caprice* to weigh, as in Wilson's and Denman's case (I say nothing of my own, because I defy both king and ministers to injure me in any manner of way, and it would be well for them perhaps if they could say as much of me), and if the king is to be humored in these things, we might as well live in Algiers.

"The libel prosecutions are of two kinds. Copley's* were clearly right, and indeed necessary, though Scarlett, changing one of them† into an *ex officio* information, was quite wrong, and might have been fatal to his verdict, had the blockhead of a man not defended himself. The others, except the one holding up the king as bullied, were very injudicious, in my opinion, and that one only right as making mischief between the king and ultras. Alexander has been convicted four times, and will receive no more punishment than if he had been convicted twice; but will receive much pity, and the press will rally in his favor. To be sure, never had a Government more favorable circumstances for convictions, with so

---

* Lady Lyndhurst had been charged with selling chancellors' livings.

† In which Lord Lyndhurst was charged with corruption in making Sugden solicitor-general.

weak a set of cases. The man's folly and baseness gave them (I should say us, for I was for the prosecution, and therefore ought not to be quoted) verdicts, where a good defense ought to have got acquittals, at least in the second. As for the Duke of Wellington prosecuting the mad parson's letter, it is inconceivable.

"Alexander repeatedly quoted a 'noble friend who is intimately connected with the Government' as advising him so and so. This was clearly Lowther. Can any thing be more humbling than the situation the Duke of Wellington is contended to place himself in, allowing the men who hold his best places to take open part against him? I *know* that Beckett talks openly against the Government, and they say one [night] Lowther will be found voting on one side, and another on t'other. It seems to be thought that the duke will try to go on as he is, trusting to the disunion of his adversaries, and relying, above all, on *our* dislike of the Duke of Cumberland. But he will find it quite impossible to carry on the government in the House of Commons on that bottom alone, unless, indeed, he has got some great and popular measures, as he had last session. I still can't help thinking the Polignac concerns will be out. A more unhappy folly never was committed, however, than the Liberals are guilty of in taking this warlike tone, which, I fear with you, is against England, and not merely against Wellington. Indeed, they seem to be for war because the Court is for quiet, and not to mind much with whom, only that war with us would, they think, please the French mob.

"I hear a pleasant thing happened t'other day with Aberdeen. When Madame Lieven was saying, 'They never can keep their places after the meeting, without a man of any talents among them' (she meaning, of course, Polignac and Co.), he said, 'Do you mean our Cabinet?' very innocently.

"Yours ever truly, H. B."

"January 24, 1830.

"MY DEAR LORD GREY,—I have seen nobody but lawyers of various sorts (*civilians* and commoners) since I came, except Lord Holland for a few minutes a week ago. But every one—including king's advocates, registrars, doctors, and proctors, generally the most loyal of men—has the same cry —'Something must be done; this Ministry can never go on as it is.'

"All the reports one hears from hour to hour of Peel being out, Huskisson negotiating, etc., may be idle fancies; but, that there is the greatest confusion at head-quarters from the approach of the session coming on them unprepared, I believe. You may depend upon it, the king was in great danger. I had believed not, from what Halford told Lord Holland, having for the moment forgotten what long experience should have taught me of Court physicians. I have since *ascertained* that he was in real danger. I suppose you have heard from Lord Holland that Leopold's Greek crown is of his own getting, chiefly at the Tuileries, and not at all of our giving. The king and rest of the family are all very angry at it.*

"I find, among other counties, Cumberland is to meet, and I have got a copy of Lord Lonsdale's letter, approving the meeting, as the Duke of Wellington denies the distress, but recommending them to confine themselves to stating that, and not vote on the much-controverted matter of the remedies. I hear his language is stronger than his letter.

"In haste, yours ever, H. BROUGHAM."

"I write this at Guildhall, where we are kept half the night."

"Howick, January 31, 1830.

"MY DEAR BROUGHAM,—I have long been in your debt for two letters, and have had, almost daily, the intention of acquitting myself of that debt, ever since I received the last. I found, as usual, a ready excuse for putting it off, in having nothing material to say. In truth, I am too apt, in all things, to act upon the converse of the old adage, and never to do to-day what I can put off till to-morrow. I have now an obvious interest in writing, for Parliament is on the point of meeting, and I do not wish to deprive myself of all chance to hear from you any thing of importance that may occur.

* Before Otho of Bavaria was chosen as King of Greece, there had been negotiations with Prince Leopold of Saxe-Coburg to accept the crown, but in the end he declined it.

"Never, to be sure, did a meeting take place under more extraordinary circumstance—distress so general and intense as was never before experienced; the public, without much distinction of party, calling out with one voice, and in a tone that must be heard, for relief; and a ministry, except in the energy of its chief, possessing in its general composition none of the qualities calculated to meet with a crisis. I have long been convinced, and I think I said so in my last, that no attempt would be made to give it strength, in such a way as we could approve. I believe I also said that the Tories would be found mitigable and purchasable, if they saw no better hope: and accordingly we see in the only appointments that have taken place, and more particularly in that of Lord Chandos (which, the way in which it is mentioned in the papers, seems to entitle to belief), a strong confirmation of that opinion. Yet it is under such circumstances that Lord Cleveland has come forward as an avowed and decided supporter of the Administration. I suppose that you, of course, have had some explanation with him on this subject. He wrote to me explaining the grounds of his conduct, and desiring Howick's and my opinion. I told him that, with the very best personal disposition towards the Duke of Wellington, and the most anxious wish to give him my support, I could not pledge myself as a declared adherent of the Government; that the most I could promise was a friendly neutrality—and that I must continue, on the seat which I have so long occupied, to support or oppose the measures of Government according to my opinion; that I should leave Howick to himself (as Lord Cleveland also proposes to do), but that his conduct would probably be the same as mine; and that, if he should find himself compelled to take a line which might detract from the full and sufficient support that Lord Cleveland wished to give to the Administration, Howick's seat would of course be, whenever he required it, at his disposal. So the matter stands, as I have not heard from him since.

"Poor Tierney! I am sure you would feel his loss, as all who knew him must do.* I have had a much longer and more

* George Tierney, who had been long conspicuous as a Parliamentary supporter of the Whig party, died on the 26th of January.

intimate connection with him, and my regret must be deep and lasting.

"What do you say to Leopold's appointment, and to the feeling which solicited it? I hear the king has given up his opposition to it, which does not place him in a very dignified situation. Kings ought not to proclaim resolutions which they may find themselves unable to keep.

"Ever yours, GREY."

The Duke of Devonshire was quite aware of the difficulty I was in at this time as regarded the amount of support I was disposed to give to Wellington's Government, while I retained perfect freedom at any time to oppose it if I saw fit. All this was inconsistent with the full support given to it by Lord Cleveland.

The Duke of Devonshire in all things coincided with my views and opinions; and upon Knaresborough becoming vacant by Tierney's death, he in the handsomest way proposed that I should accept the seat, and thus be perfectly free to act as I pleased with respect to the Government. I gladly accepted his offer, and wrote accordingly to Lord Cleveland.

"Hill Street, January 31, 1830.

"MY DEAR LORD CLEVELAND,—I feel great uneasiness in now writing to you—indeed more than I almost ever felt before upon any other occasion, because I am afraid you will dislike what I have resolved to do. But after the fullest consideration, I am quite convinced that the resolution I have come to is the best, and that you will, upon a little reflection, perceive it to be so. I shall by to-morrow's post accept the offer of a seat from the Duke of Devonshire (Knaresborough); and I have resolved to do so before writing to you, in order to avoid the possibility of giving you any embarrassment, either with respect to myself or the Government, by consulting you beforehand. For I well know that your very great kindness towards me would, if I had done so, have led you to desire that I should continue to sit for Winchelsea, and to go my own way when we unfortunately might differ.

"It is very possible, in the present state of things, that we may not be found to differ materially. Indeed I should say this is more than probable. But it can not be doubted that as you are giving the Government your avowed and regular support, and as I could not take that course, this difference would be embarrassing; and would, besides, lessen the importance of your assistance to the Government.

"It is impossible for me not to feel most severely the pain of any thing that has even the appearance of a separation of our long political union, to me so gratifying in every respect. But as nothing ever can alter the sentiments of gratitude and friendship which I have for you and yours, or lessen my sense of the very singular obligations under which I and mine are laid to you, I feel quite confident little more than the form even of our political intercourse will be altered, and any other change is wholly impossible, let politics take what course they may. Believe me ever most truly yours,

"H. B.

"P.S.—I did not write yesterday, because I could not make up my mind without further consideration. I now feel convinced that, had I determined otherwise, I should not have done right, and should have been wanting in what I owed to you."

"Hill Street, February 1, 1830.

"My dear Lord Grey,—I write a few lines to inform you of my having accepted the Duke of Devonshire's very kind offer of the unfortunately vacant seat for Knaresborough.

"I owed my connection with Lord Cleveland entirely to you, and I have not announced this resolution to any one else except Lord Cleveland himself, to whom I have just written (or rather sent the letter I wrote last night), and the Duke of Devonshire. I took a day or two to consider of it, for Lord Cleveland's most handsome conduct, and the entire freedom he left me as well as Lushington in, made it very difficult to decide. There had been a correspondence lately, which showed how little he ever thought of controlling any one in regard to political conduct.

"I shall send you a copy to-morrow of my letter to him, as it will explain the grounds of my decision, and I shall add other matters which I have not time now to write. I wish I could see Howick immediately on his arrival, and I shall endeavor to do so. Yours ever truly, H. Brougham."

"Osterley, February 2, 1830.

"My dear Lord Grey,—I now inclose the copy of my letter to Lord Cleveland, which I will thank you to return, as I have no other.

"Some things he will understand by an allusion which it would require long explanation to make intelligible to those who had not been aware of things that have passed. The most material of these are the following:

"After bringing me in at your request in 1815, when I started in 1818 (or rather was put up without my knowledge) for Westmorland, he wrote to state that his connection with the Lowthers would make it impossible for me, if the contest went on, to come in (should I be defeated) for his seat. I saw the propriety of this clearly, but I thought I was committed in honor, and I adopted what had been done without my knowledge, and stood. Lord Thanet immediately said he would return me for Appleby, and did so in effect; that is, he returned Concannon, and I continued for Winchelsea, he explaining to Lord Cleveland that it would be hurtful to the contest then going on if I were chosen at Appleby the very day before the county election began.

"At the dissolution in 1820 he (Lord Cleveland) at once returned me, not caring whether the Lowthers liked it or not. In the spring of 1822 I was very anxious to have him bring John Williams into Parliament, and we had some correspondence about it. On going the circuit I saw him at Raby, and he spoke of it in the kindest manner, saying he wanted to have an opportunity of showing his regard for me. I said he had abundantly done that already, but that I was glad he had thought of Williams, supposing he meant that. To my great surprise he said he meant to bring in one of my brothers, a thing of which I never had dreamt. But I said, as to William, it was quite out of the question on account of his profession; and as to James, I never had fancied such a thing. He said I might choose which, but he meant to offer a seat to one of them. I said I had no right to refuse for James, without letting him know; and Lord Cleveland sent a kind message to him. Of course he accepted, and afterwards declined to stand for Petersfield for many reasons. Lord Cleveland, however, brought him in for Tregony, and he also brought Williams in. Now all this detail was necessary to show you that there probably never was one man under more obligations of this kind to another than I to Lord Cleveland.

"All this made our differences in 1828 very painful to me, and nothing could be more handsome than his whole conduct then. I can not enter into it without going over the ground of my refusal even to receive the propositions made to me by the Government through him, which would detain you too long. I believe he was extremely hurt, and not less so when last summer I took a line so opposite to his; nevertheless, and though he always frankly declared to me his own opinions and feelings on party and politics, nothing could exceed the delicacy with which he uniformly treated both my brother and myself as to our conduct.

"We have been in correspondence lately, and so have he and Lushington, and it was impossible that any thing could be more satisfactory; for though he never asked me any question as to whether I approved and could join in the course he had taken or not, yet he asked Lushington this, and on being informed he could not, but was ready to leave him unembarrassed by going out of Parliament, Lord Cleveland in the handsomest way said he never thought of such a thing, but only wished to know Lushington's sentiments, and said every thing that could set him at ease. He had declared his opinions and intentions to me, but knowing mine from my letters and conversation t'other day at Newton House, he did not ask any question. However, I told him what I thought, and ventured to give him my opinion as to the course he was taking, it seemed to me, in the dark, both with regard to measures and men; hoped he would at least wait till he was asked by the Government—and stated, or rather restated, my own determination; remarking the wide difference between a disposition to find the measures of Government such as deserved support—a great and even extreme reluctance to attack Peel after the dreadful sacrifices he had made, a wish that this might not become necessary, a fixed determination in opposing the Government, not to play the game of the common enemy, etc., etc.,—*and* giving the Government the avowed and regular support he seemed disposed to lend them. I also gave him my notions as to the way in which both master and man seemed inclined to treat those who did now and then support them, referring to Peel's unaccountable conduct when Lushington defended him last year; and observed, that never did I know two people so deplorably in want of help behave more insolently to those who gave it. I have not any copy of my letter here, but I have given nearly the substance. It was written last Friday week, and I have had no answer; but it required none, after what had passed for some weeks before, both with Lushington and myself.

"You will now perceive clearly how very unpleasant it has been for me to take the step I have done. For after the full explanations we had come to, and the perfect liberty at which I was left, the occurrence of a time when I might desire to go out was possible indeed—nay, was very likely to happen in my case (not certainly in that of any of his other members), but had certainly not arrived; and I knew that, were I to mention the Duke of Devonshire's offer, and consult him about accepting it, it would be only (and in a very indelicate way) asking him to give me, or rather to renew to me, a request that I should remain in his seat on my own terms, for he might be said in substance to have done so already. I therefore determined to decide first, and then let him know what I had done.

"I have *bored* you with a long detail; but, as you *won't* come to town (which you certainly ought), it is one of the evils you expose yourself to.

"Ever yours truly, H. BROUGHAM."

"Howick, Febuary 5, 1830.

"MY DEAR BROUGHAM,—I received your letter yesterday. Its length required no apology. On the contrary, I was much obliged to you for so full an explanation.

"My letter, which must have crossed yours on the road, will already have informed you how entirely the view I have taken of Lord Cleveland's determination, and of the conduct which I shall myself pursue, agrees with yours. I sincerely wish to support the Duke of Wellington's Administration, but every day adds to my doubts; more especially when I consider the sort of recruits that are sought for, and the manner of enlisting them.

"I am no less obliged to Lord Cleveland than you are, nor am I less sensible of the kindness and liberality of his conduct. But I can not disguise from myself that Howick now stands in a very awkward situation, and that the time may not be distant when he may find it necessary to relinquish his seat.

"The only doubt I could have as to the step you have taken* arises from your previous explanations with Lord Cleveland, from which he may not unnaturally have conceived that you had no thought of any change. But you will of course suit your time of vacating to the convenience of any arrangements that he may have to make for Winchelsea, so that it can not prove really embarrassing to him. The only other remark that occurs to me is that, by changing your seat at this moment for the Duke of Devonshire's, it may be inferred that your disposition towards the Government is more hostile than it really is. These are only doubts, however; and upon considering the whole matter, I think I should have acted as you have done.

"Though you are already acquainted with the substance of what has passed, I have desired Howick to show you the copies, which he has, of Lord Cleveland's letter and mine. There has been no answer to the last.

"I am anxious to hear what has passed yesterday, and any thing else that may show the line that the hundred squads of politicians are likely to take. Ever yours,

"GREY.

"I return the copy of your letter to Lord Cleveland."

The following letter will show how very much Lord Cleveland was annoyed by my determination, so unexpectedly made known to him, and yet how steady and unvarying was his friendship:

"Cleveland House, Febuary 4, 1830.

"MY DEAR BROUGHAM,—I have suffered many grievances and disappointments in the course of a long political life, but I never experienced one which created me so much sorrow as

* Coming in for Knaresborough, on Tierney's death, on the Devonshire interest, instead of Winchelsea on the Cleveland.

that which you communicated to me last night, conveying the very hasty and unexpected decision of your no longer continuing for Winchelsea.

"I can not charge myself with having said or done any thing unkind to you, and I sincerely lament that you should so suddenly have adopted such a resolution which, with personal communication, I think you would not have done.

"You have undoubtedly chosen a much younger and a far more consequential patron than myself, but I deny that you can find one who is more sincerely attached to you than, yours very faithfully and truly, CLEVELAND.

"It will be a great satisfaction to me to see you."

The following letter to Lord Grey explains the unfortunate delay which had happened to prevent Lord Cleveland receiving my letter, and his consequently hearing what I had resolved to do, most unexpectedly, and only as a piece of gossip, which he refused to credit:

"February 8, 1830.

"MY DEAR LORD GREY,—Lord Cleveland was very deeply grieved, even more than I had expected, and at first could not at all reconcile himself to it, perceiving many evils, I believe, as likely to arise. To render the matter worse, he had never let me know he was coming up, so my letter went to Newton House, and he came to town wholly unknown to me, and heard it, *quite incredulous*, the evening he arrived. I first heard of his being here that evening from Lambton, and instantly wrote to him. He got my letter on coming home from Meyrick's, where he dined, and where he had heard it and denied its being possible. All this for a day or two was extremely annoying; but the arrival of my letter from Newton House proved that I had communicated it to him before I even wróte to the Duke of Devonshire, and I showed him that I had been doing all I could to make the duke bring in Denman, for some months back. Not the least difficulty arose as to Winchelsea, or indeed any thing else, and he has been quite relieved by the interviews we have had. All is now right, and he *already* must see, and I think he admits, that I could do no otherwise.

"He has brought in John Williams, a most excellent

choice, and which prevents much of the effect apprehended from my going out at such a moment.

"Ever yours truly, H. BROUGHAM."

"February 17, 1830.

"MY DEAR LORD GREY,—The state of the Ministry of which I had been predicting, from what happened last session, is if possible more deplorable than I had expected. They literally are at the mercy of any one or two men of weight among our people who may choose to make a run at them; and this is very likely to happen. In truth, it was very difficult *not* to turn them out, the first night. After what they did last year, and the sacrifices Peel made, it is impossible not to wish them well. But who *can* support such a set? Then they take a cipher, and add to their list as often as a place falls vacant. What think you of Frankland Lewis for treasurer of the navy? The duke is still blind to his situation, and seems resolved to have nobody about him of any weight.

"The division of t'other night proves nothing. All the ultras and Huskissonians (except Huskisson himself) voted with them. Hume spoke of eight and a half millions being reduced. Our people were sorry for having divided with him, and I dare say the next time you see a division it will be very different.

"The Speaker, t'other day at his dinner, talked most decidedly and openly of the impossibility of this state of things going on.

"The Tories (and it is not the least merit of the Government) are enraged beyond measure at the appointment of Abercromby.* That act was fighting the ultras in their stronghold, and in the way most hateful to them. It is an excellent symptom. Peel's speech on Graham's motion was also good in this point of view.

"Lord Lansdowne bringing in young Macaulay and passing over Denman, has given us all much pain, and me more than any one. It is partly owing, however, to a misunderstanding, for he did not like to offer Denman a seat as *locum*

* James Abercromby, afterwards Speaker, appointed Chief Baron of Scotland by the Duke of Wellington's Government.

tenens for Kerry. I don't believe any apprehension of Windsor entered into it. Lansdowne's usual *love of a novelty* perhaps did, though it certainly ought not; but you know his weakness. Yours ever truly, H. BROUGHAM."

"Howick, February 29, 1830.

"MY DEAR BROUGHAM,—I have long owed you a letter, but I had nothing to say. The same cause might make me continue silent. But I must express the pleasure I have felt in reading your speech on Lord John's motion.* Howick tells me it was admirable—one of the best, if not the best, he ever heard from you. The division was very great, considering the question. The Tories, I hear, divided against you, and a good many of Huskisson's friends, as was to be expected. This tends to confirm the opinion I have had from the beginning, that, when convinced of the unprofitableness of opposition, they will return to their natural places in the rear of the Government. And symptoms, too, do not appear to be wanting that the minister, when he finds it necessary to strengthen himself, will look to this quarter rather than to any other, as that which will afford him the requisite numbers, the readiest instruments, and the best means of satisfying the Court.

"From hence you can expect no news. Our weather is now delightful, and most favorable to the operations of the planter and the farmer.

"If any thing occurs worth writing, and you can spare a moment from your numerous and important avocations, I shall hope to hear from you.

"I see you have got an opposition at the London University. Ever yours, GREY.

"Nothing could be better than Abercromby's appointment, and I rejoice in it sincerely. But, with all its merit, it shows no disposition to give any political office to any person of that description. These seem to be reserved for Chandoses and Wortleys and Frankland Lewises—excellent men, no doubt, but who do not add to my confidence in the Administration."

* 23d February. For leave to bring in a bill to enable Manchester, Leeds, and Birmingham to return members to serve in Parliament.—*Hansard*, vol. xxii., 11 Geo. IV.

CHAPTER XX.

Accession of William IV.—Motion on Colonial Slavery.—Invitation to stand for Yorkshire.—The Canvass.—The Triumph.—Congratulations.—Althorp.—Durham.—The French Revolution of June.—Opening of Parliament.—First Reform Project.—State of Parties.—The Whig Projects and the Radical.—Influence on Britain and the Continent of the Revolution in France.—The Duc de Broglie.—The Death of Huskisson.—Question of the Intentions of the Wellington Ministry.—Decided by the Declaration against Reform.—The Ministry in a Minority.—Their Resignation.—Lord Grey sent for.—Formation of the Whig Ministry.—Intention to support it, but not to take Office.—Offer of Attorney-generalship and Great Seal declined.—Prevailed on to accept the Great Seal and a Peerage.—Influenced by the Assurance that continued Refusal would break up the Ministry.

In June, 1830, George IV. died. Soon after the House met, on the accession of William IV., I gave notice that I should take an early opportunity of bringing forward the question of Colonial Slavery. This I did on July 13th. I freely admitted the difficulties that stood in the way of any government in legislating on such a question. I myself proposed no plan, but asked the House to resolve that the state of slavery in our colonies should be taken into consideration at the earliest practicable period of the next session, with a view to the present mitigation and final abolition of slavery. Peel, after suggesting some feeble palliatives, urged me not to press my motion to a division. To this I refused to agree, and was defeated by a majority of 29.*

I have referred to the motion and to my speech, which certainly was fully appreciated in the country, because that speech, as much as any thing I had ever done, exercised a notable influence on the coming Yorkshire election.

Before the end of July Parliament was prorogued, and, immediately afterwards, dissolved.

The representation of counties, as a general rule, is confined either to great land-owners, or to persons so connected

* Speeches, ii., 129.

with the large properties as to represent the landed interest, rather than the body of small freeholders; moreover, to contest or even to stand for a county involves no inconsiderable expense. In merely preparing for the possibility of a contest, Mr. Marshall, in 1826, found it necessary to spend nearly £20,000, as his son John afterwards told me.

To select as candidate a man totally unconnected with the county, either by property or family ties, was a proceeding so unheard of, that, when I received an invitation to stand for the great county of York, I was beyond measure astonished. So impossible did it appear to me that the proposal to return me should succeed, that, before I gave my answer, I consulted some intimate friends of great position in the county, and of high authority on the subject in question. I am bound to say that some of the answers were far from encouraging. This I attributed to the peculiar local feeling, stronger in Yorkshire than in any other county in England, that only a Yorkshireman would be acceptable; and the assurance that any candidate quite unconnected with the county would, almost to a certainty, be opposed, and put to great expense, was set down by me to the same cause.

The invitation I had received was coupled with an assurance that I was to be put to no expense. I was thus so far relieved from having to consider the question my landed friends had more than hinted at, and had chiefly to look at the circumstances under which the offer was made, and which had led to my being selected. Something, no doubt, was owing to my successful efforts in the repeal of the Orders in Council, still gratefully remembered in many parts of Yorkshire. Next, I was conscious that I had acquired popularity in the queen's case; but, beyond all these reasons, I was certain that the part I had taken on the question of slavery and the slave-trade had been recognized with such marked approbation by the constituents of my friend and illustrious fellow-laborer, Wilberforce, that I felt secure of their support against any opponent. This body of friends included all the religious sects who had been Wilberforce's main strength. So, all these things considered, I felt perfectly justified in cordially accepting the invitation to stand, and at once began my canvass. All this took place during the Assizes. It so happened that I had an unusual number of briefs, some in very heavy cases. It was not possible either to give them up or to turn them over to my juniors. I was obliged, after a night of hard reading and preparation, to be in court every morning by half-past nine o'clock; then I had to address the jury, to examine and cross-examine witnesses—in short, to work for my various clients just as if there had been no such thing pending as an election. Then, as soon as the court rose, indeed sometimes before, I jumped into a carriage, and was driven, as fast as four horses could go, to the various towns—many of them twenty or thirty miles from York; at each town or considerable place I had to make a speech, never getting back to York till nearly midnight, and then I had my briefs to read for next day in court. This kind of life lasted nearly three weeks. It was by much the hardest work I ever went through; but good health, temperance, and the stake I was playing for carried me through. I not only survived, but, during the whole of this laborious time, I never in my life felt better, or more capable of even further exertion, had such been called for.

The nomination was on the 29th of July. The ultimate candidates were Lord Morpeth, Duncombe, Bethell, Stapylton, and myself.

My canvass was over on the 30th. On returning that evening, I found at my lodgings the following very encouraging letter from George Strickland:*

FROM MR. STRICKLAND.

"York, Friday, July 30, 1830, 4 o'clock.

"DEAR B.,—As far as a meeting can settle a question previously to an election, you are to be member for the county of York. I send a copy of the resolutions. We had much debating. But your party from the west is powerful and de-

* One of my oldest friends, and also my brother James's, they being nearly of the same age. We were all three together students at the University of Edinburgh. He was the eldest son of Sir William Strickland of Boynton, in the county of York. At his father's death in 1834, he succeeded as Sir George Strickland; and afterwards, through his mother, heiress of Catharine Cholmley, of Whitby and Howsham, acquired those estates, and took the name of Cholmley.

termined. Old Marshall proposed you. Dan Sykes seconded. . . . I was the first country gentleman who spoke in your favor. The others were united in opposition; some came over, seeing the necessity of the case. Ramsden was named and brought forward by Charles Wood and Tom Dundas, but no person ventured to second the resolution in his favor; and after many speeches in recommending unanimity, and pointing out its necessity, Ramsden was dropped and the meeting broke up. You are secure, though Martin Stapylton is in the field, and there may be much confusion. All the sects (religious) are united for you, and abolition of *slavery*, which is your stronghold; all who supported Wilberforce—excepting the *Evangelical Church*, who appear to be against you. If I understand them, *they* oppose you upon the principles of the *London University*, which they set forward. There is no pledge given that you will not be opposed at the election by the country gentlemen. But if you are firm they may start some new man, and they may throw out one of the present candidates, *but you will not be the one.*

"The proposal is, though the question has not been publicly discussed, that you should pay your share of the sheriff's bill for the hustings, *but no more.*

"I shall be in York on Sunday evening to endeavor to see you and James. I write in haste, because I return twelve miles into the country (to Howsham), where I shall remain till Sunday. Ever yours, GEORGE STRICKLAND."

I have said before that the repeal of the Orders in Council was my greatest achievement*—I say now that my return for the great county of York was my greatest victory, my most unsullied success. I may say, without hyperbole, that when, as knight of the shire, I was begirt with the sword, it was the proudest moment of my life. My return to Parliament by the greatest and most wealthy constituency in England was the highest compliment ever paid to a public man. I felt that I had earned it by the good I had done—that I had gained it by no base or unworthy acts. I am bound to add, that the feeling of gratification was general and strong in the party, both towards me personally and with a view to the

* Vol. ii., p. 7.

good of the cause. Not only outlying members of the party, but those who were in the strictest sense party men, shared in the triumph. The following letters are, one from a "watcher" during the junction, Althorp; the others from Lambton. Grey's joy, of course, was as great as any one's.

"MY DEAR BROUGHAM,—If I have not written to you before, it is not from my feeling less pleased in your triumph than any other of your friends. It is the highest honor and the greatest reward that ever was bestowed upon a public man, and the greatest that can be; and what is more, it is well deserved. I should not have written to say this, if I had nothing else to say; but as it becomes one of your duties, as member for Yorkshire, to attend Doncaster races, I write to say that you had better come here. I shall be most happy to see you, and I will find you a conveyance to the races as many days as you like to go there. I conclude this will find you at Brougham. Yours most truly, ALTHORP.

"Wiseton, near Bawtry, August 26, 1830."

"Lambton Castle, Friday.

"Well done, thou good and faithful servant! Go on and preach the word everywhere. Of all the great public triumphs and rewards, certainly yours is the greatest, and I am sure you will use it for the best of purposes. Among the foremost ought to be the downfall of this odious, insulting, degrading, aid-de-campish, incapable dictatorship.

"At such a crisis, is this country to be left at the mercy of barrack councils and mess-room politics?

"But thou art patience to go on; only be yourself again when Parliament meets, and it must end.

"Shall you come to these or Newcastle Assizes? If so, don't forget us. Ever yours, D.

"Little O* and lesser O† come to-day, and Lord Grey to-morrow. What glorious beings the French are!"

* Ossulston, then actually Earl of Tankerville, his father having died in 1822. He was still frequently called by old friends "Little O," the name given to him during his father's lifetime. He laughed much at some of Lambton's weaknesses (love of arms, pedigree, and the like), and used to say, "By God, sir, if Lambton calls upon you, he thinks he has a right to quarter your arms!"

† His son, then Lord Ossulston, now Lord Tankerville.

"Lambton Castle, September 1, 1830.

"MY DEAR YORKSHIRE (which I trust will be the title you will take when chancellor),—I agree with you entirely and absolutely as to the necessity of being fully prepared and organized before the meeting; it would be an act of suicide not; and nothing can save the incapables but our customary bungling and want of concert.

"There should be some preparatory meeting of a few shortly (when your circuit is over), and a general muster the week preceding the meeting of Parliament, between the 20th and 24th of October. For God's sake, don't let us exhibit the deplorable exhibition of olden times, when, to use Castlereagh's figure, we always 'turned our backs on ourselves.'

"The unfitness, nay impossibility, of any cordiality existing between the liberal Government of France and Aberdeen, the representative of the Metternich school, ought to be shown in every possible way.

"No efficient government, in my opinion, can be formed without Palmerston, Grant, and Huskisson; and I am sure Lord Grey is of the same opinion. Shall we succeed most effectually in ousting the present imbecile crew by an open junction? or by cordial co-operation, without any ostensible junction, until the enemy is defeated? Let me have your opinion; the open junction might deprive us of the aid of the ultra Tories in the assault when the town is taken; the garrison may then be formed according to our best judgment of its expediency and efficiency.

"(When we have to combat a field-marshal, it is necessary to use military terms.)

"But I should like to have your ideas, pro and con, before I see Lord Grey; and tell me if we are likely to meet before you go to town. I have heard that you are to be at Doncaster races. Is that so? or shall you remain at Brougham until you go south?

"By the way, should you think it advisable—if a meeting of Durham and Northumberland could be procured—to have some resolutions and petitions carried in favor of your beer bill? which, if I remember right, is confined to our two counties.

"I don't know that it can be done; but if you approve, I can talk to Loch and Headlam about it.

"Yours ever, DURHAM."

In the canvass for the county, the chief stress was laid upon the slave-trade and slave-emancipation; education, and general improvement, and reform in all its branches, were the subjects on which my supporters put forward our claims; and the opposition to tyranny abroad, as well as the advocacy of peace, was strongly insisted on, and obtained additional weight, as well as a lively present interest, from the revolution which happened at Paris while the canvass was going on —the revolution in many respects resembling our own, a century and a half before. Indeed, our triumph at this election was by the opposite party much ascribed to the "three days" at Paris, and the use we made of that event in attacking the ministers of Charles X. and their violent measures; while some of our most zealous friends, as Dan Sykes, ascribed it to my speech on slavery in the Commons on the 13th July; but Sykes, being brother-in-law of Henry Thornton, and a great abolitionist, was, with Wilberforce, very naturally inclined to regard our victory in the county so long represented by him as an anti-slavery triumph. Whatever opinions may be held on this point, it is quite certain that Parliamentary Reform had been almost a kind of local question with Yorkshiremen, ever since the days of Sir George Saville and Wyvill; and the part I had taken in the question when it was brought forward after the Walcheren inquiry, and afterwards in 1812, was often referred to in the canvass, as well as in the castle-yard of York. I was therefore pledged to take the lead in that question, now that I had become member for the county. It was a great mistake of Lyndhurst and others to represent (in the debates in 1831) that little or nothing had been said on reform the year before in Yorkshire, but only on slavery and the French Revolution, though there was some color of truth in the statement as regards slavery. No doubt the accounts, if not confined to these subjects, at least dwelt chiefly upon them, because Yorkshire was peculiarly interested in the slavery question; so that subject, as well as the news from Paris, were topics of the day, and the papers therefore dwelt more on them. But that reform both in Yorkshire and elsewhere occupied men's minds exceedingly, is certain; and I well remember Abercromby's regret that Lansdowne should have given in to the mistake of supposing it a dead secret. I both on my canvass and after my return pledged myself formally, feeling it incumbent on me to stand forward as the leader of Parliamentary Reform, which may be said to have taken its rise in Yorkshire. I announced this at a great Leeds dinner, one of the many which Morpeth (my colleague) and I attended on our progress at the end of autumn, to thank and to meet our constituents. I gave similar pledges at Hull, Sheffield, Saddleworth, and elsewhere. That matter, therefore, might be considered settled; and it only remained to agree with the Whigs on the particulars of the plan. Having been returned for Knaresborough as well as for the county, I had to declare, when Parliament met, for which I chose to sit. On declaring for Yorkshire, I gave my notice, and it stood for Tuesday, the 16th of November.

I had previously summoned the party to meet me at Althorp's chambers in the Albany, because he had a large room there; my dining-room in Hill Street being too small to receive so numerous a body. They came. I unfolded my plan, the details of which I shall presently refer to. It gave satisfaction. I told them it was all I could hope to carry while out of power, but that if ever armed with office, I should be disposed to go farther. I had given notice of my motion on the first night of the session, before even the speech from the throne was read. Therefore all men saw I was in earnest, and all knew I should redeem the pledge I had given in Yorkshire.

In November, 1830, when Parliament met, it was found that the Duke of Wellington, having neglected the use of Crown influence at the general election, had been sorely disappointed of a favorable House of Commons. To the three parties of ultra Tories, Radicals, and Whigs, were united the remains of the Canning party, which, though small, were important, notwithstanding the irreparable loss sustained by Huskisson's death; but Palmerston's official habits and abilities, and the power of debating, as well as the respectable character of the two Grants, together with Spence (a barrister of some weight), in the Commons; with Melbourne, Ripon, Granville, Canterbury, in the Lords—gave the body a weight beyond its size. The ultra Tories had never forgiven Wellington and Peel the Catholic Emancipation; and the Dukes of Richmond and Newcastle, with Knatchbull, Wetherell, and Vyvyan, so entirely formed part of our force, that, in corresponding with Lord Rosslyn on the results of the general election, we both set all that class down as members of the combined Opposition; and such they continued to the end of the short campaign which overthrew the duke. As members of our party, many of them continued after we came into power, Richmond being their representative in the Cabinet, and as such would they have remained still, but for the Reform Bill.

The state of the Reform question was now so entirely different from what it had been in former times, that the principles were wholly different from those which guided the rational and considerate reformers thirty or even twenty years before. In those days there had been a complete schism in the Reform party. At the head of the extreme or Radical branch was the old Major Cartwright, called the venerable, who held moderate to be, what he always termed it, mock reform; and even the Burdett party soon grew tired of him.* He, and those who continued to side with him, raised their notions to such an excess of unreasonable intolerance, that long after both Romilly and I had incurred their contempt, and indeed hostility, by declaring for rational measures, they made to each of us, when we had lost our seats in 1812, and before we were brought in for other places, a serious proposal to bring us in for Middlesex, on condition that we pledged ourselves to support annual Parliaments, universal suffrage, and the ballot. We both gave the same answer to this very friendly address, which was presented to each of us by a deputation—namely, that we greatly doubted their power to return us, but that if it were ever so certain, their conditions could not be agreed to on any account.

---

* John Cartwright, born 1740, died 1824. He was an object of great political notoriety in the early part of this century, and was the author of an octavo volume called "The British Constitution Illustrated." His "Life and Correspondence," edited by his niece, was published in 1826, in two volumes.

I had, moreover, in those days incurred their dislike or pity (for they often treated moderate or mock reformers as objects of compassion), by circulating a letter, after the loss of Brand's motion in 1810, remonstrating with those who insisted upon a general measure which they had not a chance of carrying, while by singling out some of the most manifest abuses in the system, the removal of which would be highly beneficial in improving the constitution of Parliament, they might either succeed, or bring the adversaries of Reform into disrepute—such as giving votes to real land-owners in Scotland, and putting an end to the glaring evil of the whole of that country having not a single real election, either for counties or boroughs. My opinion was in favor of gradual proceedings, unable "to see any reason for moving most swiftly on the most slippery ground where the precipice is nearest and the gulf deepest." So I regarded the dangers of rash experiments on the frame of our constitution, adding, that a sincere and zealous reformer—one who wishes to do good, and has a higher ambition than to make a noise—one who wants to have a reform and not a clamor—would avoid whatever might bring his cause into contempt. Every thing was now changed, so as to make the practical application of my principle to its full extent impossible, but not to preclude its guidance and government of our proceedings. The strong and universal feeling in the country, made it necessary to propound a plan embracing most of the essential points, but that might be framed in general accordance with the principle. Pledged to bring forward an effectual, though moderate and safe plan, I was guided by that principle in the details which I proposed.

In forming this plan, I considered the deep-rooted feeling which prevailed in favor of an effectual reform, the manifest defects in the existing system, and the progress made by the question of late years—so great as to extract from Canning an avowal that the question was as good as carried on John Russell's motion in 1826 being defeated by a small majority. There were even indications of a division among the supporters of Government on this question, or a great tolerance of dissent from them, in some of their important office-bearers; thus Scarlett, attorney-general, held his office upon the express condition of being allowed to vote for Parliamentary Reform. From these undeniable facts, I drew the conclusion that my motion had a fair chance of being carried. It was therefore absolutely necessary to frame the plan such as to be adopted against the more strenuous supporters of the Government, and the less open resistance of some of the Opposition.

It must therefore be moderate. But there is always this difficulty, that if you make a measure much less effectual than the bulk of its friends desire, it loses their support, besides leaving defects in the system attacked, which are very material. In steering my way between these opposing considerations, I proposed at our meeting at Althorp's what I reckoned an effectual and yet a temperate reform; not as much as we should require had we the support of the Government, or even its neutrality, but as much as we could hope to carry by our own force through the country's support, and which, above all, should remove the more gross and practically felt defects. These were—the exclusion of so many of the greatest towns, or rather cities—as Manchester, Birmingham, Leeds, Sheffield, Brighton, etc.—from all share in the representation; the treating copy-holders as if they were still like their predecessors, the serfs of the Middle Ages, so that the owner of a customary tenement of thousands a year had no vote, while his neighbor voted for a forty-shilling freehold; the taking no account whatever of lease-holders, whether in town or country; the putting borough representatives in the hands of freemen, the class of inhabitants, generally speaking, the least to be trusted either for honesty or independence; the allowing these to vote without regard to the place of their residence, so that at every contest scores of absent voters, carried at the candidate's expense, might turn the election against the votes of resident freemen; the number of close or nomination boroughs returning members—in other words, the proprietors choosing representatives of the people without any check or control; the number of boroughs, not close, but having so few voters that they were the nests of corruption, while larger places sent no members: these were the principal evils and abuses which I proposed to remove.

I did not propose to condemn all close boroughs, because there would have been great difficulty in carrying a measure for their entire extinction; and also, because there was a manifest convenience in keeping certain seats open for men who had no chance of being returned by populous places, and because these boroughs were far less corrupt than those having a few voters. I therefore proposed that while the great towns should have members, the places for them should be found as was most necessary, without increasing the members of the House, by limiting many of the smaller boroughs, and all the close boroughs except five or six, to the return of one member; and those five or six I proposed to disfranchise altogether. The right of voting in all towns sending members was to be household suffrage; a strict system of registration was prescribed both for counties and boroughs; all non-resident voters were disfranchised; the election for each contested seat confined to one day; and the duration of Parliaments limited to three years.*

A very important event had occurred after my plan was framed, which induced me to extend it in several essential points. At the opening of the session, the Duke of Wellington made his celebrated declaration against all reform. We leaders of the Whigs had heard, during the four weeks after the election, that the Tories had become alarmed by the returns. I was in correspondence with Lord Rosslyn upon these, he maintaining that we had not gained so much as our calculations showed, and that they (his party) would make a much better show than I expected—but he still would not deny the fact of some important elections having gone against them; and Lord Wallace and William Dundas, whom I happened to meet, considered, as well as Rosslyn, the Yorkshire election to be the worst for them.

The following letter from Rosslyn illustrates what has been said of his feelings and Lord Grey's; and, with my answer, shows the position of parties, and that an attack on the Ministry *had been resolved:*

---

* See the account of Mr. Brougham's intended plan of Parliamentary Reform, in the "History of the Whig Ministry of 1830 to the Passing of the Reform Bill," by John Arthur Roebuck, M.P.; i., 420.

[*Private and confidential.*]

"St. James's Square, August 28, 1830.

"MY DEAR BROUGHAM,—I thank you most sincerely for your confidential communication, and particularly for the expressions of kindness towards myself, which I can never allow myself to doubt under any circumstances. Your estimate of the result of the returns to Parliament differs widely from the report made up by those connected with Government, whose business is to look narrowly into the subject.

"You say that you have gained, as compared with the last Parliament—

				Gain.
In England, 42,	and lost	9	=	33
In Ireland, 16,	"	2	=	14
				47
In Scotland, 0	"	3		3
				44

"Now the account on the other side is—

England	gained 41,	lost 25	=	16
Ireland	" 9,	" 6	=	3
Scotland	" 4,	" 1	=	3
And Government gains on the whole,				22

making a difference of 66. In estimating the numbers, the ultra Tories and Huskisson's adherents are all given to you, as the declared head of the combined Opposition.

"In considering this question, I do not overlook the result of some county elections, and least of all undervalue the election of Hume for Middlesex, or the importance which you justly attach to the vote which placed you in the representation of the county of York.

"I give you full credit for your desire to maintain the peace and quiet of the country, an object for which I am sure the Duke of Wellington would make any sacrifice; and, in passing, I must say that I know nothing that justifies your opinion that he has ever shown any repugnance to a fair connection with the Whigs, if any opening had been left to him to believe such a thing feasible. With respect to liberal policy, the phrase is so vague and general, that I can only answer that the king has acknowledged the new King of France and his Government as frankly as possible, and as promptly as the notification of the change permitted; and that, in consequence of the step taken by the British Cabinet, the same course will be pursued by the other Powers of Europe, who are all (as I believe) prepared to follow and adopt our policy in that matter.

"I am much mistaken if you will not find the duke's Administration determined to do all that is possible to preserve the peace of Europe, as essential to the security and interests of this country, and to abstain from all interference whatever in the internal arrangements of any other nations, leaving them to choose their own institutions and their own governors, and to manage their internal concerns as they like, provided only they don't meddle with their neighbors. I rejoice in your desire for peace and tranquillity, and I regret that the extreme nature of the opposition which you announce seems to leave little hope that we may be in a situation to co-operate as cordially as I could have wished in the pursuit and attainment of those valuable objects in which we feel a common interest, and which we equally profess to desire.

"Yours faithfully, ROSSLYN."

"Lancaster, Tuesday.

"MY DEAR LORD R.,—I have just got your calculations as to numbers, and I fear you and your friends reckon sadly without your host. I have not time to dissect it, but I only take your number of twenty-five, which you say are the seats in England on which Government gains. Look at the following, which I set down without any lists, from memory, while I was at breakfast, and now copy over from the back of a letter on which I had marked them:

"Of the forty above written, at least twenty-seven are Whigs or Radicals, about three Huskisson's, and the rest ultras. I assure you I can with difficulty put down fifteen (and that is making great allowances), where we have lost and Government gained. This includes all Lord Cleveland's changes, as Howick and Tregony, where I know that Gordon is rather a Whig than any thing else. It includes two doubtfuls, as Reading, and I make no kind of allowance of such places as Bristol and Boston, where we gain steady votes every night, instead of men like Bright and Heathcote, who, three times in four, voted against us, or went away. I have at home nearly a dozen changes of this sort (including such as Lord William Russell), who are always abroad. Then I don't quite reckon that such as Williams and Bruce will be very fond of voting against me on all questions, and even Vesey is better than such fixtures as the Tollemaches, who never were absent, and always voted with Government.

"What you say of the opportunity for junction being past is *now*, I fear, too true. I always thought the duke had forfeited every title to Lord Grey's forbearance, and that of his friends, when he first put his exclusion on the late king's personal prejudice; and then the king dying, had no excuse to offer. However, he has taken his line, and I believe he will find Lord Grey has taken his.

"The worst of a weak government, which can't stand alone, is, that it invites aggression and endangers the peace. Here is all Europe in a state of movement. I daily expect news from Spain. I am almost equally confident of some change in Belgium; and I can never believe, till I see it, that the people there will not follow the French example, and end by becoming a French province. Then what chance is there of France, or any one else, caring a straw for a Government which has against it all the country, half of the House of Commons (and nearly all the leading men in it), and neither the aristocracy nor Church for it? It won't do; and my only prayer is that the impossibility may be discovered before mischief is done abroad or at home.

"I wished to state these things before we take our positions. Mine is not of my own seeking, or to my liking, when it places me with the ultras (perhaps the Lowthers even), and against you, the duke, Peel, and Copley. Ever, H. B.

"P.S.—The lists as to Ireland are *quite clearly* different from your account, but I have not Duncannon's returns."

The thoughts which the recent Revolution in France gave rise to led to my writing the following letter to my great friend, the Duc de Broglie:

TO THE DUC DE BROGLIE.

"Brougham, August 16, 1830.

"My dear Duke,—I have only delayed offering you my most hearty congratulations on the greatest event for liberty in modern times, because I did not wish to interrupt, for even half an hour, the share, so useful to the country and to all countries, which you have in it. But I can now no longer avoid troubling you, because I owe it as a debt of gratitude to say how deeply all the friends of freedom and sound principle feel the weight of their obligations to the great virtue and courage of your people. I fear we should not have done so well; but I know we shall now follow your glorious example, if—which God avert—it should ever become necessary. The promptitude shown by the Parisians in resisting; their sagacity in feeling, as it were by instinct, that it was a case for arms, and not for courts of law; but more than all, their signal temperance, and even humanity, in victory—are the finest lesson to other countries that any people ever afforded in any age. I look back with delight, and even with pride, on the zeal with which I have always, in Parliament and out of it, declared my hopes of French liberty, at seasons when it seemed most in jeopardy, and did all I could to encourage your great chiefs with the feeling that we felt for them in England during their glorious struggle.

"All, however, that you can gain of solid good, and all that we and the rest of Europe can hope from your example, must depend upon the *sobriety*, and *wisdom*, and *moderation* of your conduct in settling the State. And this fills me with anxiety. To expel the guilty; to hear of no terms with the branch of Charles X.; to exact severe punishment from the Polignacs, etc., who have shed so much blood, and meanly run away from danger; to limit the power of the Crown, and effectually prevent a recurrence of the dangers you have lately repelled; to strengthen your elective system by making its basis much broader—all this I am clearly a friend to. But I dread a too weak executive—a republic, in which it will inevitably end, is better than that—for the transition to it is full of cruelty and of danger to freedom as well as peace. But I am sure no man in his senses thinks a republic can safely or beneficially be attempted in France, any more than in England. Then let me entreat you, do not make the crown a mere name.

"My next alarm is about the aristocracy, because I perceive some idea of making the peerage for life only. This is a very crude idea. It gives the Crown far too great power, and the aristocracy too little—it makes the latter dependent on the Crown. Then why dread a nobility in France, where they are all, or nearly all, of such moderate fortune? Your law of succession keeps you safe from our overgrown grandees, and even we find, in spite of their wealth, that in these days the people is more than a match for them—nay, would be, with a reformed Parliament, quite too strong for them. The peerage is of excellent use with us in preventing violent and rash changes. All who have much influence in our House of Commons know and feel this. They feel, too, that the peerage is a great screen on many occasions to the people as against the Crown. It would be an improvement if we had some means of lessening their influence in the House of Commons. All mischief would then be at an end, and the good only remain. But of this improvement I do not despair, for the diminished patronage of the Crown is gradually doing part of it, and the increased influence of the people is doing the rest. I assure you that this last general election has made a great step in this direction. Had the fine example of Yorkshire been set to other counties earlier, many more peers would have lost their hold over counties. As it is, they have lost it in many places, thanks to Yorkshire, and also to the extreme unpopularity of the Duke of Wellington's Administration, which unites all parties against it. I anxiously hope that you and we shall go hand in hand with our improvements; and I am certain that the less widely you depart from the sound principles of what ought to be our constitution, the better will it be for us both, and the better security will be gained for the peace that now happily unites us, and keeps all the world quiet.

"My greatest alarm, however, is from what I was shocked to see mentioned—the National Guards to choose their own officers! I can not describe my alarm at such a project. It is laying the seeds of revolt and civil war in the foundations of the constitution. It is making a future revolution almost certain. It is establishing the worst of all revolutions and tyrannies—a deliberating army—and almost insuring a military government. I am sure the wise and excellent prince whom you have justly raised to the throne never can approve of this, and that if he assents to it he can only do so by compulsion. For God's sake, reflect on the certain effects of beginning with a king whom all must distrust, if you place him in a position necessarily false! I need not say more to you. I almost felt disposed to run over to Paris, to warn our friends against such rocks, which they seemed not to see, though touching them. I hope I have been misinformed, but I could not rest till I had written to you. My best respects to the duchess; and believe me ever yours,

"H. BROUGHAM.

"P.S.—The utter weakness of our present Ministry you can hardly form an adequate idea of. In Parliament they have no power—no debaters who can be heard, no certainty of carrying any question; and in the country all parties are against them. They were weaker than Polignac was before the elections, and the general election has lessened their numbers by above thirty. Every one sees that they can not go on, and they dare not attempt a *coup d'ètat.*"

On the then engrossing subject of the French Revolution, I had the following letter from Lady Charlotte Lindsay:

FROM LADY CHARLOTTE LINDSAY.

"47 Green Street, August 25, 1830.

"DEAR MR. BROUGHAM,—I had the pleasure of finding your letter on my arrival in London the day before yesterday, and I am delighted to find that you take so much interest *in my* revolution. I feel really as one does about a favorite child—so afraid of *its behaving ill,* and becoming unpopular. My child, I am happy to say, was very good all the time I was with it, though it sometimes showed symptoms of its youth and inexperience, yet it has hitherto, though conscious of its strength, been easily brought round by reason. There was a little disturbance one day, occasioned by some work-people who were out of employment; but they were soon set to rights, and work will be provided for them. The most dangerous idea some have got into their heads is a wish to dissolve their present Chamber of Deputies, in order to have a new one elected, according to the new law of elections. Now, perhaps I am wrong, but it appears to me that an immediate dissolution of the Chamber, after the important act it has achieved, would weaken the king's title, and be running the risk of much confusion. I said this to Benjamin Constant, a night or two before I left Paris, and he agreed with me, and said that he hoped to be able to get it deferred. Constant has much weight with the people at present, and has made a very proper use of it, but it will not last very long, poor man! for he is dying: his physicians say that he can not live six months. His disorder is a disease of the spine—the same, as he told me, that put an end to Madame de Staël.* I was at the Chamber the day before I left Paris, and heard Guizot, the ministre de l'intérieur, make a very good, business-like speech, and Martignac an eloquent one. De Tracy moved for an early discussion upon abolishing the punishment of death, which was seconded in a short but affecting speech by Lafayette. This is evidently in the humane intention of saving the lives of the Ministers who are taken. As to Polignac's head, it is so little worth taking, it can now do no harm by remaining upon his shoulders.

"Philippe I. has acted with great prudence and good sense. I have no doubt of the sincere liberality of his sentiments. His *personal* courage is unquestionable, and I hope his *political* courage and decision may prove equal to his situation; he certainly will have great occasion for these qualities. His son, now Duke of Orleans, is a very popular young man, rather an *ultra Liberal,* as all *very* young men of high rank ought to be; and they say that he is modest, and willing to listen to the advice and opinions of his elders.

"Yours ever, "C. L."

With reference to Melbourne's position in connection with the Canning party, it must be observed that he was the only regular Whig, or Foxite; but he had, besides, an intimacy of long standing with Huskisson, who was married to a near re-

* He died on the 10th of December following.

lation of his mother, and had always been on terms of familiar intimacy with his family, even at times of the greatest party violence, as 1806 and 1807. All the men in question were zealous and enlightened friends of liberal policy on commercial subjects, and firm friends of the Catholic cause; and its success next year, to which they materially contributed, made our alliance with them more close. Indeed, the concert was so perfect on that question, that the announcement which I made of our fixed determination not to take office, on the alarm given of the king under the Duke of Cumberland's guidance being about to threaten the duke's Cabinet and to call in the Opposition, was made in concert with Huskisson. The addition to our party of such men as Palmerston, Grant, Melbourne, and Huskisson himself, was most important; and our combination next year was still further completed by the results of the general election. It was with Melbourne that I communicated on the present state of affairs. I had expected to meet Huskisson at Liverpool, on the opening of the railway. I had written to him, and inclosed a letter to Melbourne. The following was Melbourne's answer:

"Panshanger, September 19, 1830.

"My dear Brougham,—I should long ago have answered your letter, which poor Huskisson sent to me here, had it not been for the stunning event, of which the account succeeded so immediately.* You can easily conceive the affliction it has caused me; and, in a public point of view, it is unnecessary to expatiate upon the loss, particularly at this moment. I have been obliged to have the operation performed for a carbuncle, which has succeeded perfectly, but which prevented me from travelling. This saved me from being a witness of the melancholy catastrophe; otherwise I should have regretted that it lost me the opportunity of having a full conversation with you upon the present most important and critical state of public affairs. They are at once too wide and too extensive to be entered upon in writing, and still more, they are liable to so much change and fluctuation, that

* The death of Huskisson on the 15th of September, by an accident at the opening of the Liverpool and Manchester Railway.

the conclusions to which one might come now, might perhaps be totally unsuitable to the state of things a month hence, at the meeting of Parliament. Before that time, I hope I shall have an opportunity of talking with you. In the mean time, as the recent reports which have appeared in the newspapers might lead you to suppose that there have been renewed overtures, it may be as well to assure you that, as far as relates to myself, there has been nothing of the kind since those of last July or August (I forget which), and with which and their results you are acquainted. Of course I can not answer for others with the same certainty, but I do not believe that they or any of them have received any further communication. If any should be made, all the motives which induced us to decline the former proposal would, in my view, be rather strengthened and increased than weakened and diminished, by the loss which we have just sustained. It we hesitated to trust ourselves to the duke and his followers with the assistance of Huskisson, we should, of course, be still more unwilling, now that we are deprived of him, and the weight which he carried with him. Of course, the Ministry in France has a most difficult task. A new Ministry in England which comes in in the natural and constitutional course, we have always seen, finds obstacles almost insuperable, in the bitterness of its enemies, in the unreasonable expectations of its friends, and in the general distrust which always attends upon new men, to whom the public are unaccustomed. But all these difficulties are aggravated tenfold to a Ministry which is placed in this situation by a revolution. However, I have a feeling that they will come through in some way or another; there seems to be a certain portion of good men in the world, and general unwillingness to go to war, from which I augur good results, at any rate. We should hold cheerful language at the same time, without breaking out into extravagant encomium, which is awkward if the whole thing ultimately goes to the devil, as it did before. Adieu. Yours faithfully, MELBOURNE."

Many of our party were always ready to accept what little measures of moderate reform they could get, such as were now and then conceded, sometimes by Peel, and sometimes by Robinson (afterwards Goderich), to whom they paid some court; but to the duke they looked with no little hope. They recollected 1829 and the Catholic question, which they ascribed, and justly, entirely to him, and conceived that he would bring Peel more easily over on Reform, against which he had never been pledged, as he was so deeply upon that question. The profound secrecy which he had kept upon it to the very last, and in which Peel had entirely joined, made those of our moderate and placable Whigs whom I have referred to persuade themselves that he had planned some concession upon Reform, in order, if not to satisfy the country, at least to appease the prevailing feeling of discontent; and no small number of those men were believed by us leaders to be prepared to accept a very small measure from his hands.

We were alarmed at this prospect, which would not only have been most disastrous to the party, but, independent of all factious views, we really believed that it would have been fatal to Reform; because any measure which the duke could give must have been so very trifling as to be of little value, and it would, by dividing the real reformers, have deprived us of almost all the advantages of our present position, destroyed the effects of the general election, and postponed indefinitely the real reform, as well as our obtaining the government, and thus carrying so many other great measures. While these apprehensions and doubts continued, I was at Brighton for a few days about the end of October, and I there saw William Harrison, who was confidentially employed in preparing the Government bills. Calling upon him one morning, I found with him his brother Sir George, who held office in the Treasury. Of course I could not expect them to tell me if there was any Reform measure in contemplation; but the manner in which they received the question, the broad and unrestrained ridicule which they cast upon such a supposition, as of an utter impossibility, really made me and those of our friends to whom I communicated what had passed, believe that our alarm had been groundless. The conversation with the Harrisons, of course, was any thing but confidential, from the nature of the case; but I said, "I suppose I may tell our friends that you deny the prevailing report;" and they said they had not even heard of it till I told them, and that I might quote their authority to contradict it. The only thing that took away from the weight of this testimony was the possibility of the duke having carefully kept the secret even from those most natural to be employed. But the success of the plan ascribed to him depended upon the measure being introduced ready to be pressed through, else he had upon his hands the borough proprietors, and other strong enemies of all reform, the Eldons and Wetherells of his own party; and unless the Harrisons were employed, he had little chance either of having the work done or the secret well kept. We were, therefore, pretty sure that no measure was intended. But this was only on the eve of the session opening, and all that we could expect was the whole question being left in our hands. Our gratification, therefore, was not inconsiderable when the Duke made his declaration that, so perfect did he consider the system, he should, had he a new one to propose, only attempt the nearest approach to the old one which was possible. It is observable in the letters of Lord Grey and Lord Rosslyn how great a disposition existed in these and other chiefs of the Whig party to join with the Duke of Wellington, had that been met with a like disposition on his part. Indeed he had held the Duke of Bedford's proxy ever since the junction Ministry.

The same circumstances continued during the session (1830), and the events of the session added strength to them. The dissolution then came; and nothing could be more exemplary than the duke's forbearance—only exerting the influence of office when he could not avoid it. The result of the election was altogether favorable to the Opposition; but still there was no indication of change in the duke's disposition as to the party, Lord Rosslyn's case the year before having been succeeded by no other. The declaration against all reform left no longer any doubt or hesitation.

That declaration plainly gave us a very great advantage in every way, and made it quite safe to extend our plan with the hope of carrying it through. The meeting at Althorp's had discussed, or rather conversed upon, what I laid before them; and, after some slight changes, it was agreed that I should bring it forward on the 16th of November. On the day before, we somewhat unexpectedly, on a motion of Parnell's respecting the Finance Committee, beat the Government after a debate of no great interest, in which, indeed, neither Peel nor I took any part. Next morning I went to the Court of King's Bench and made my arrangements, so as to allow me to get home early, to prepare for the evening. However, as I had some suspicion the Government might break up on the division of the previous night, rather than go out on my motion being carried, as we knew it would be, I did not care to go through the trouble of getting my speech all ready until I had asked a question of Jersey, to whom I wrote a note, begging, if it was no secret, to know whether they were out or not. He replied that they *were* out. I therefore was not surprised at the announcement made by Peel, that the Ministry had resigned; and I was pressed to postpone my motion, which I did, stating that I should certainly bring it on upon Thursday, the 18th.* On that day I was again pressed, but answered that as I had no concern whatever in the political arrangements which were supposed to be going on, and intended to have no concern with them, I should not delay my motion above a few days, but bring it forward, of whatever materials that Ministry might be composed. *This was loudly cheered.* As I left the House, I met Arbuthnot, and asked him how the carrying a committee on the expenditure should be deemed a sufficient ground for breaking up the Government. He said that the

* On the 15th November, on the motion of Mr. Goulburn, Chancellor of the Exchequer, that the House go into Committee on the Civil List, Sir Henry Parnell moved as an amendment, "That a select committee be appointed to examine the accounts presented to the House by order of his majesty, connected with the Civil List, and to report thereon." This was carried by 233 to 204. It is stated that, "while the members who went for the amendment remained in the lobby, Mr. Brougham addressed them, and requested them not to go away after the division; for that, if they were defeated on that amendment, it was the intention of the honorable member for Dorsetshire to move another for the appointment of a committee to inquire into all the items of the Civil List after the first three. This notice was received with cheers."—*Hansard.* On the 2d, Mr. Brougham had given notice that on that day fortnight he would bring on the question of Parliamentary Reform. This would have been on Tuesday, the 16th, and on that day the resignation of Ministers was announced.

true ground was their expecting to be beaten on my motion; and that if a Government were brought in upon Reform, the duke felt it would make the measures proposed much more extensive than if their predecessors went out on any other ground. This was a course dictated by his wonted sagacity and practical good sense. I may add that my declaration of having no intention to take office, afterwards so much commented upon, was a statement of my positive and well-considered resolution *at the time*, and that I then firmly believed my taking office to be impossible.

When I returned home that evening (the 16th) from Lincoln's Inn, where I had as usual gone after dinner, I found the following note from Lady Grey:

"MY DEAR MR. BROUGHAM,—Lord Grey desires me to tell you that he has this moment been sent for by the king.

"Sincerely yours, M. E. GREY."

I found also several letters referring to what had passed in the House, and deprecating my supposed intention to refuse office; and as it had been said that I should certainly refuse the attorney-generalship, when I went to Brooks's in the evening of Wednesday, the 17th, and the day after, I was surrounded by leading men among our friends, who strongly urged upon me the duty of not refusing it. Afterwards others joined in the exhortation, and one or two came from Grey with the same advice (Duncannon certainly), because I had all along said that I would take nothing, or that if I *must* take office, it should only be the Rolls; for if there were no other reason against taking the attorney-generalship, the certainty of a Yorkshire contest on taking an office, which I might quit in a month and lose a large portion of my professional income by the circuit (to which I could not return, owing to the rules of the bar), would be enough to decide me—but that the same objection did not apply to the Rolls; and I know that Leach, too anxious to have the Great Seal, would at once make way for me.

On Wednesday the 17th, just as I was getting into the carriage, and going to Chambers for the evening, Lady Glengall, a friend of Leach's as well as of mine, called with a view of ascertaining whether I was a candidate for the Great Seal, as Leach was bent upon it, and feared I might stand in his way. I told her to relieve his mind from any such alarm, for I never certainly dreamed of such a thing.

On that same day, Grey asked me if I would accept the office of attorney-general. I said, "*Most certainly not.*" And being again pressed, I said that I wished to have no office whatever. I was member for Yorkshire, and desired to keep by that and by my profession. This, I found, threw them into much difficulty. However, I remained firm till Thursday night, always assuring them of my hearty support out of office; and they as constantly saying that such support would not be sufficient for carrying on the Government, considering my position in Parliament and in the country. At length, late on Thursday evening, I was told that the negotiation must go off, on account of my persistent refusal. I repeated that I would take the Rolls, but nothing else, as I was resolved to remain in the House of Commons, and that I would not take a subordinate place like attorney-general. I was then told the Rolls was impossible; and this, from something I had just heard, did not surprise me.

Late on Thursday evening, I received the following note from Lord Grey:

"My dear Brougham,—It is necessary that I should see you as soon as possible to-morrow—*i. e.*, as soon as possible after I am up, which, worn out as I am, can not, I fear, be much before ten o'clock. Pray name the hour when you can be with me, and let me again repeat that it must be as soon as possible. Ever yours, Grey.

"Thursday night, November 18, 1830."

I answered as follows:

"Friday morning.

"My dear Lord Grey,—Your note alarms me, as I had thought affairs were going on quite smoothly. I am in this difficulty, that I must begin an argument in the House of Lords at ten exactly, and shall be kept to reply, which can not well be over before half-past one; and were I, in these times of reports, to try to put it off, I should be much and seriously injured by it.

"But I can be with you before two. I could call at half-past nine on my way to Westminster, but that would rouse you, and you are much better in bed.

"All I saw yesterday were in great spirits, and most perfect good-humor and disposition.

"In haste, ever truly yours, H. B."

He answered as follows:

"I can see you now in your way to Westminster if you can come. If not, I shall expect you at two, or as much before as may be possible. I shall not go out till I have seen you.

"Yours, G.

"Friday, November 19, 1830."

Accordingly I called on my way to Westminster, and he at once said that he had been desired by the king to ask if I would take the Great Seal. I stared, and said it was utterly out of the question—that I could not give up the bar, and take the chance of being turned out of office in two or three months—that my fortune was not sufficient to support a peerage—and that I would not on any account give up Yorkshire and my position in the House of Commons. He said he had received the answer I gave to Duncannon and Althorp, positively refusing to be attorney-general, and that I would support the Government as zealously as possible without office; or that, if I must take office, the Rolls was the only place I could take. He added that, when he first saw the king and mentioned it, the king answered that the Rolls was quite impossible, and dwelt upon the attorney-generalship, which that day Lord Grey had told him I positively refused, though I knew that his taking the Government depended upon my consenting. The king then asked, on his (Lord Grey's) saying that the negotiation must go off, as Mr. Brougham was inflexible, if he had offered me the Great Seal? and on Lord Grey's saying he had not, because he supposed there was the same objection to that as to the Rolls—"Oh no," said the king, "there is no one I would rather have for my chancellor." He afterwards once or twice alluded to this when in particularly good humor, and called me *his* chancellor, as named by himself and not by my colleagues. In fact, I more than suspect that the Tories, on going out, warned him not to leave me in the Commons, member for Yorkshire, chief of the popular party, and irremovable Master of the Rolls. In fact, I *know* that Huskisson told a friend of mine that he did not see how any Government could go on were I without office, and only member for Yorkshire; but that if I had the Rolls too, I was absolute for life.

The suspicion I have just stated was founded on more than a mere guess; for on Thursday evening, the 18th, I received from an intimate friend, who happened also to be much connected with the Duke of Wellington, the following note:

"Thursday evening.

"It will be interesting, and possibly may be important (while all this Cabinet-making is going on), to you to know, *on the authority of Alava*, from whom I had it, that the duke, on leaving the king on Tuesday, thus spoke to him: 'If I may be permitted to give your majesty one piece of advice, it is —on no account to allow Mr. Brougham to be Master of the Rolls; for such a position, coupled with the representation of Yorkshire, would make him too powerful for *any* Government.' You well know that *I* could not venture to ask the duke if this were true; but you know also his habit of talking to Alava. I only add, that *I* believe it."

I told Lord Grey that I had every kind of objection to quit the House of Commons and the bar for a promotion so very precarious; and I showed him how absurd such a sacrifice would be on my part. I made no objection to the construction of the Cabinet as he described it, only I remarked that Graham's place was prematurely high; observing that he was a kind of pocket-vote of Lambton's. Grey begged I would see Althorp before I rejected the office of the Great Seal; assuring me the whole treaty was up if I refused to concur. I then left him, having to go to the House of Lords at ten. There I argued a long, dull, dry, and complicated appeal case, chiefly turning on accounts and figures. I sent for Althorp, and for Sefton, whom I often used to consult on my private concerns, having the greatest confidence in his soundness and judgment. They arrived separately before the time came for me to reply, and I made my junior take the reply off my hands; so I went to the consultation-room, where I found Althorp, Sefton, Duncannon, and my brother James, whom Althorp had desired to come, as thinking he would be in favor of my acceptance. I stated my reasons fully, and put it to them whether I could make such a sacrifice in common prudence, independent of the position in the Commons which I was called on to abandon, and the representation of Yorkshire. There was a good deal of discussion, but it ended in Althorp saying he saw no answer to my objections. They all went away except Althorp, and he said, when we were left alone, "Well, I have not a word to say against your reasons and your feelings, and therefore there is an end of the matter; and you take upon yourself the responsibility of keeping our party for another twenty-five years out of power, and the loss of all the great questions which will follow, instead of their being carried." I again denied this, because I was willing to devote myself to the party, and with greater influence, from being a supporter out of office. He said, "That is a totally different thing from official support, because every now and then there comes a question on which you really differ, and have not the excuse for supporting the Government against your opinion, which you consent to waive in order not to break up the Ministry. However, there is no use in arguing the matter. Grey is determined, and will let the king know to-day, when he goes by appointment at two o'clock, that there are such difficulties in the way that the Government can not be formed; and you take upon yourself to let our friends all know that *you* are the cause, and the only cause, of the attempt failing."

I said I must have an hour to consider; and I sent for my brother and Denman, with whom I had a conversation upon the way in which Althorp had put the matter. They both said the same thing had occurred to them, and also to Sefton and Duncannon, after the meeting an hour ago. It ended in my letting Grey know that I yielded to their remonstrances. I ought to add that the only person who saw the subject in the same light as myself, was my mother, who, in a very remarkable letter, warned me against giving up the substance of power for a name.

Thus she wrote: "If, as is probable, office is offered you in the new Government, pause before you accept it; do not be tempted to leave the House of Commons. As member for Yorkshire, backed by all you have done for the country, you are more powerful than any official that ever existed, however high in station or in rank. Throw not away the great position you have raised yourself to—a position greater than any that could be bestowed by king or minister."

The step, however, was taken; and the only justification of it, in common prudence, was that the party would have been next thing to ruined had I refused. But the folly of the step, as a selfish one, was abundantly evident. I took a peerage and £4000 a year for life, without the chance of making my income greater, however inadequate I might find it. I had been accustomed to spend a great deal more, without any rank to support; and I gave up an income of more than double, and which the first change at the bar would raise to above £10,000 a year. I also gave up a profession of which I had become extremely fond; and I gave up the finest position in the world for an ambitious man like me—a man who loved real power, cared little for any labor, however hard, and less for any rank, however high. But I made this sacrifice, for which the gratitude of the party at first knew no bounds, and afterwards was reduced to less than nothing.

So much has been said by the Whigs of my anxiety for office, and so often have they denied the benefits I conferred on the party, that I am tempted to refer to the late Duke of Bedford's opinion on the subject.

In the winter of 1859 I had occasion to write to him, to ask him to help me in an application I was about to make to Palmerston. Among the various grounds on which I rested my claim, I mentioned to the duke incidentally how much I had done for the party, but I chiefly urged the great sacrifice I had made for their sole benefit by taking the Great Seal; and I reminded him of the circumstances in these words: "You may recollect the extreme difficulty they had in overcoming my objections; that I first refused the attorney-generalship, then the Great Seal, because it would take me out of the House of Commons. I had no objection to the Rolls; but the king would not let Lord Grey offer it to me, and himself proposed the Great Seal, which I positively refused, till Grey made Althorp, Duncannon, and Sefton overpersuade me, by declaring that the Government could not be formed if I persisted. I told them, at the same time, and probably yourself also, that my mother joined in my strong objection to quit the House of Commons for the chancellorship and the Lords. However, there was no help for it, as Grey and Althorp refused to accept my hearty and constant support out of office, when the Rolls was refused by the king. So I gave up my profession, which was secure, and took a precarious office. I think all this gives me a claim. In 1830, John* was not in the Cabinet, and is not acquainted with the particulars known to Althorp, as well as yourself, to whom I appeal, now that Althorp is unhappily gone. Believe me ever most affectionately yours, H. B."

To this I had the following reply:

"Woburn Abbey, Christmas-day, 1859.

"MY DEAR BROUGHAM,—My first letter this morning shall be to you, to send you my best and sincere wishes, and to tell you that yours of the 19th, received yesterday, could not fail to *gratify me*, as a mark of your old friendship and confidence.

"I well remember all you refer to in 1830—my communication with Althorp on the subject, and what you said to me at the time, and your own feelings, and your mother's sentiments. I know also that you have devoted the best days of your life to the political service of the public; that you alone have done much more for the party than any man, and for which they owe you a debt they never can repay; that your labors to do good to the community in various ways have been unceasing, and latterly, at your period of life, wonderful.

"If towards the close of such a career any thing could be done to reward such services, and to gratify you, it would give me much pleasure. What more can I say? You do not ask me to take any step, and mark your letter as 'private and confidential.'

* Lord John, brother to the duke.

"I shall therefore say nothing of it to any one. I have a very accurate recollection of all that passed about you in 1830, and of the part I took in it with Althorp, unknown to you at the time, and unnecessary to repeat now.

"I just missed you in London, having gone upon the day or the day before you left. I hope, however, to see you on your return, in good health and full vigor. Till then, adieu.

"Ever sincerely yours, BEDFORD."

When, preparatory to taking my seat in the Court of Chancery at Westminster, on Thursday, the 25th of November, 1830, I was sworn in by the Master of the Rolls, I had a very large attendance to witness the ceremony and to do me honor; the Dukes of Sussex and Gloucester, Prince Leopold, all the Cabinet ministers, the Duke of Devonshire, the Bishops of London, Carlisle, and Gloucester, and many other distinguished persons, whose names I can not now recollect.

It so happened that a Chapter of the Garter was held that day to make the Duke of Bedford a knight, so that many who gave me their support and countenance were in full court dress, and this made the whole affair look very gay.

The only thing which I have left out in the preceding pages is, that a Cabinet had been held at Lansdowne House on Thursday, when Grey stated to them all that had passed. This was not known to me till Lansdowne afterwards told me of it; his recollection in every particular agrees with mine as to the attorney-generalship, the Rolls, and the king's refusal of the Rolls and offering the Great Seal, all which Grey had told the Cabinet, and had their unanimous concurrence in his proposal.

On the morning of the 20th, I received the following letter from Lord Grey:

"Friday evening, November 19, 1830.

"DEAR BROUGHAM,—Althorp has already a commission from me to offer the treasury to Nugent.

"Sefton I love as much as you do, but I do not see any thing that I could offer him just now. But of this when we meet to-morrow. I do not think he expects it. I will also talk with you about Horne to-morrow.

"The king, when I announced your acceptance to him this evening, was most gracious, really quite cordial and hearty in approving the appointment. I must say that from the beginning to the end I have met with nothing but the utmost confidence and kindness. It is this that has enabled me to arrange a new Government in four days. I see no reason why we should not all be sworn in on Sunday evening, or at latest on Monday. Ever yours, GREY."

Early in December, Alexander, the chief baron, was taken ill enough to make his resignation probable. This led to Grey suggesting to me that Lyndhurst might succeed him. This proposition was rather startling to me, because I knew that Lyndhurst's hostility would in no degree be lessened, that he would oppose us as bitterly as ever, and that the only justification for appointing him was his undeniable fitness for the office. On this subject I received the following letter from Lord Grey:

"Berkeley Square, December 6, 1830.

"MY DEAR BROUGHAM,—I have just heard that the chief baron (Alexander), too ill, as you know, to go upon the special commission, is disposed to resign his seat altogether on the bench, and to take the retiring pension.

"Lyndhurst, I have also reason to believe—though I have had no communication with him of any kind, and have this from no direct authority, but I believe, on what appears to me good grounds—would accept the appointment of chief baron.

"I lose no time, therefore, in expressing my anxiety, if the opening should occur, to make this arrangement. It would be creditable to the Government in placing a most effective judge on the bench; it would contribute materially to our ease and comfort in the House of Lords; it would be gratifying to my feelings of personal kindness to Lyndhurst; and it would save Lyndhurst's pension to the public—no immaterial consideration in these times, and more particularly when we shall be under the necessity of granting two, to make the law arrangements in Ireland. I therefore must again express my earnest hope that you may feel no objection to this arrangement. Ever yours, GREY."

After reading this letter of Lord Grey's, before I answered it, I had to consider the sound and long-established practice of a chancellor making judges without any communication to any of his colleagues. That course was, first to take the king's pleasure, and then to tell the minister. I know this practice has been complained of. It is right—it is necessary —it is the only safeguard the public can have against jobbing and political intriguing for judicial places. It throws all responsibility on the Great Seal undivided. When Grey suggested to me Copley as chief baron, there could be no doubt, judicially speaking, of the fitness of the appointment; this might have made it a proper exception to the rule. Eldon, however, sent me a message on the chief baron (Alexander) retiring, to remind me that "no minister had any right whatever even to open his mouth to me on the subject." I suppose he had heard that Grey was moving in Lyndhurst's behalf. Eldon added, that the minister had no right to interfere in the appointment either of a puisne judge or of a lord chief baron. I was well aware of this, and ever after made a point of acting upon the sound old practice. However, in the instance of Copley, I felt that, in consulting with Lord Grey on his appointment, I might deviate from the rule, because I was doing a great thing for the profession and the country, and, Grey hoped, for the party—a hope which Lyndhurst's conduct in the House of Lords soon showed to be grievously fallacious. I believe, however, that Grey thought not a little of flattering Lady Lyndhurst, to whom both he and Lambton had been paying most assiduous court; and whom I verily believe they had even flattered with the hopes of the Great Seal. After having given the question full consideration, I answered Lord Grey as follows:

[*Private.*]

"December 7, 1830.

"My dear Lord Grey,—I can only say on this, as on any other occasion, whether ecclesiastical or civil, I shall always consider the patronage of the Great Seal as most usefully exercised when it is exercised for the common benefit of the Government; and I shall always be ready to give up every private and personal inclination, or even to deviate from the usual and correct practice on such a subject, and that, too, even where I might have any wishes of my own inconsistent with it. But Lyndhurst is an old and valued friend of my own, so that nothing could more gratify me than doing any thing he may like; and though I place a rival near me, and enable him to make a great judicial reputation, that is all the better for the country and the Government.

"Ever yours, H. BROUGHAM.

"P.S.—I see I have assumed you know the doctrine of Westminster Hall about the chief baron being the *property* of the Great Seal, which I give up, in this instance, at your request."

"Downing Street, December 30, 1830.

"MY DEAR BROUGHAM,—I was prevented answering your letter, as I intended, yesterday.

"All you say about O'Connell, his motives and his conduct, is quite true. His abuse of me I care little about, though full of falsehood and injustice. You have an equal right to complain of him, but I don't think the notice of it which I see in to-day's 'Times' was worth while.

"That such agitation should proceed from such causes, is indeed lamentable—or rather, I should say, should succeed after such pretenses. If the Doherty grievance had not existed, another would have been found. The truth is, the long delay of the Catholic question gave O'Connell a power with which he was unwilling to part; we provoked him by making the Relief Bill offensive to him personally, and by not giving him a silk gown; and he now aims at being what he styles himself, the Liberator of Ireland, at whatever expense of mischief, or even of ruin, to the country.

"The accounts from thence are as bad as possible. Anglesey is persuaded that an explosion will take place, and there is a great deal of secret information by which it appears that the [illegible] are in active communication with this country, and if true in the tenth part of it, it proves that the danger is most formidable and imminent.

"We have done all we can to have a disposable force for any emergency, in rendering the militia efficient with the least possible delay; in sanctioning the employment of yeomanry corps, as recommended by Anglesey; and, at the same time, in directing the attention of the Irish Government to any measures which may attend the prospects of relief, or be useful in diminishing the causes of dissatisfaction.

"At home every thing is better. I have a letter from Jeffrey to-day, in which he tells me he is to be with you at Brougham on Saturday. Among other subjects, I conclude you will have some communication with him on the subject of a Parliamentary Reform in Scotland. We are already in possession of the solicitor-general's opinions on this subject, and have the outline of a plan formed, on which I am most desirous to have an opportunity of communicating with you. Indeed I should have done so before, but for your constant occupation in court and subsequent absence from London, though I was hardly prepared to say any thing upon this subject before you left us. Any communications you may have on this subject should be communicated to as few people as possible, and to these under an intimation of the strictest secrecy. You are sufficiently aware of the inconvenience attending reports before the measure is ready, as was experienced in the case of [illegible], though completely without foundation.

"I wish you would think of some plan for furnishing employment for the laborers who are in want of work, by subscriptions, which might be assisted by a grant of money, after the meeting of Parliament. When do you come back? I am going to-morrow for three days to Panshanger and Hatfield, unless something should occur to bring me back sooner.

"Ever yours, GREY."

CHAPTER XXI.

The Grey Cabinet.—Parliamentary Reform the immediate Object.—The Reform Bill.—Schedule A.—History of the Construction of the Measure.—Personal Anecdotes.—The King.—Earl Grey.—Sir Herbert Taylor.—Sir Francis Burdett.—Lord John Russell.—Lord Althorp.—Sir John Hobhouse.—The Duke of Richmond.—The Bill announced in the Commons.—The Policy of the Opposition.—The Question of refusing Leave to bring in.—The Policy of Resigning or Dissolving.—The Dissolution.—Necessity that it should be by the King in Person.—Account of the Interview with Him.—Scene in the House of Lords.—The Elections.—Correspondence with Lord Grey.—The Measure lost in the Lords.

As soon as the Government was formed, Reform was the first question, after taking the pressing measures for the repression of riots, and securing the peace of the disturbed counties. Our position as to Reform was now entirely different from that in which we were when I announced my plan at the party meeting; and it was no longer possible to bring that forward, as I had intended. A measure which we might hope to carry while in opposition, if kept within certain bounds, and which the country would thankfully accept from a party out of office, would most probably disappoint the zealous friends of the question, if it were all that a powerful Government, with the people's support, chose to give. The changes which the Government plan of Reform made in the scheme which I had proposed to the party at Althorp's room in the Albany, were consequently considerable, from the difference of our position as a Government. But the most important by much was the entire extinction of nomination boroughs—Schedule A. And I am bound to admit that it was Schedule A that finally carried the bill. Although I had a great tendency towards retaining one member, I could not resist Grey's view of how impossible it was upon principle to give a single person, because he happened to be the proprietor of a borough, the power of naming a representative of the people. I gave up with reluctance my household suffrage for the ten-pound franchise, because, in fact, this sum meant different amounts in different places, and all plans for adjusting the right so as to keep some proportion to the real value were found impossible, besides the inconvenience occasioned by the diversity. But I succeeded in altering the twenty pound, which was the sum the committee had fixed. I was certain that this would create many small constituencies; and on this being stoutly denied by the committee, I obtained returns, which proved it to demonstration. One town with 17,000 or 18,000 inhabitants had not twenty persons who would have been entitled to vote. In that town there were not even three hundred rated at ten pounds. I must do my colleagues the justice to say that this at once changed their opinions, and reduced the sum from twenty to ten.

After many preliminary discussions, we agreed that the whole subject should be referred to a committee, consisting of Graham, Durham, Duncannon, and John Russell, who was not then in the Cabinet, but Paymaster of the Forces. They examined carefully the various plans which had at different times been proposed, and drew up in minute detail a series of provisions, which were to form the substance of the bill, after we should have considered and discussed them in Cabinet. The outline of the proposed plan was taken by Grey to Brighton, where the king then was, and laid before him. He gave a general approval, which Grey communicated to me by the following letter, written the day after his discussion with the king:

"Brighton, January 31, 1831.

"My dear Chancellor,—My interview with the king took place immediately after my arrival here yesterday. It lasted too long to allow of my sending you an account of the result by last night's post. The king entered into every part of the proposed plan of Reform with great care, and, I must add, with great acuteness; and, in the end, understood it completely. The result is, that it has his full and entire approbation.

"He has been equally satisfied with the new arrangements of the Civil List, which have been laid before him by Althorp this morning.

"With such claims upon us, it hurts me to the greatest degree to find that Grant can not be reconciled to the proposal for an outfit for the queen. His opposition to it goes the length of inferring his resignation, if it should be persevered in. I could not expose the king, and more particularly the queen, to all the disagreeable consequences of a breach in the Government on such a question; but I must repeat I feel very much *hurt* at the obstacle which stands in the way of a grant, sanctioned by precedent, reasonable in itself, and consistent with, as I think, or rather conducive to, a well-understood economy. I wish any thing could be done to make Grant hear reason on this subject, and I wish it the more anxiously as the king is quite ready to give up this claim.

"Ever yours, GREY."

Grey afterwards told me that the king said he should consider the subject of Reform more fully, and give the Cabinet his opinion in writing. This he did very minutely, prefacing it by an observation that it would be more satisfactory for us to learn on what points he had doubts, and on what points objections, because we should thus be satisfied that he had fully considered the subject.

Many attempts were made to have it believed that he had not given his concurrence; and these were aided by the bad habit which he had of conversing on all subjects with the peers to whom he gave audience, and some of whom were in opposition to the Government. I had to explain this to him, and to show him that, as no responsible minister was present, he ought, as the rule was, only to hear, and not to speak. Knowing how much he regarded his father's example, which he was always desirous to follow, as I well knew, from having had several communications with him before we were in office, I cited this, and gave him several instances of George III. following the rule most strictly—among others, that of the late Duke of Norfolk (the Jockey), as told me by himself, and also left in a written memorandum. He had an audience to complain of his dismissal from the lord-lieutenancy of the West Riding, on account of his having given the toast at a public dinner, "The majesty of the people," and entered at great length upon the subject. The king said not a word, but, on his taking leave, told him he thought more of him as Howard of Greystoke than as Duke of Norfolk; this being a strong feeling of the duke himself, which George III. had heard of. When the king, William IV., fully understood the rule, he became much more select in the persons to whom he said any thing, and for the most part followed the rule; but still there were things said on various subjects which got about, and did us great mischief in our very difficult position, with a House of Lords in which the majority was very decidedly against us.

Generally speaking, it must be said he was an excellent man of business—unlike his brother, who would ask no questions for fear of showing his ignorance—or his father, who ran on with too many, and would not wait for answers. He asked as many as were required to let him fully understand whatever was brought before him, and gave his own views with perfect candor and fairness; nor was he the least impatient of contradiction, but, on the contrary, rather courted it, in order that he might come to a full understanding with his ministers.

One circumstance of a trifling nature was yet very characteristic of his honesty: he generally sat opposite to the light, so that you might see the expression of his countenance, he never having any thing to conceal, or any part to play. We had but few serious differences during the first ten months. One was about the dissolution in April, to which he objected, but came round upon a Cabinet minute being sent that, if refused, we should resign in a body. Another was on the illuminations which that dissolution occasioned, because he felt that the measure was taken as an act offensive to the Parliament, to which he felt much gratitude for their liberal endowment of the queen. The Admiralty having been illuminated was what he most complained of, because he conceived himself professionally involved in it. The assistance he derived on all occasions from Sir Herbert Taylor was of the greatest value both to him and to his ministers, from the excellent and useful talents, the high honor, and the strict integrity of that worthy man, who at critical moments did not hesitate to do acts which involved him in great responsibility; on one occasion especially, when he wrote a kind of circular to some of the most violent opposition peers, informing them that Grey and I had received in writing the king's promise of an unlimited creation of peers to pass the Reform Bill. He named no names, but said the power existed in writing, and was in such hands as he knew would use it.

At this period I received many letters written by Sir Herbert Taylor, but at the king's dictation, relating to his private affairs, and the grievances he was suffering under from his children: these relate to matters too private to be published; I therefore pass them by, and go to a letter I received in January, 1831:

[*Private.*]

"Brighton, January 19, 1831.

"MY DEAR LORD,—I have not delayed to read to the king the letter which I had the honor to receive from your lordship this morning, and I need scarcely assure you that his majesty expressed in the strongest terms his approbation of your proceeding upon the occasion of swearing in the new chief baron, as worthy of yourself, and a mark of respect well merited by Lord Lyndhurst.

"The further particulars which you have been so good as to give of the constitution, of the magistracy, etc., of Scotch cities, have appeared to his majesty very interesting, and well deserving of attention.

"But the part of your lordship's letter which chiefly engaged the king's mind naturally is that wherein you enter upon the important question of Parliamentary Reform, which has been, and continues to be, a subject of so much anxiety. His majesty rejoices that Lord Grey has mentioned to you the correspondence which has passed upon it; and his majesty expressed himself pleased with the manner in which you have entered into it, and pleased also to find that you agree with him in the wish that the question could have been postponed for this session, and even for a longer period; at the same time, that his majesty agrees with you and with Lord Grey—and is satisfied by the reasons assigned by both—that it may not be possible or even advisable to defer *being ready* to bring it forward as a measure of Government. His majesty is, however, satisfied also that those who are thus placed under the necessity of bringing forward, at such a period as this, a measure 'which, to be well and wisely handled, ought to be handled at a time when there is little else to disturb the attention,' will endeavor so to frame it and so to ascertain the feeling of the majority upon it, as to secure themselves against the possibility of a defeat, which might produce consequences which no person would dread and deprecate more sincerely than his majesty. Supposing these even to be confined to a dissolution of Parliament, it must be obvious to the Government, as it is to the king, that such a result of the agitation of the question would be injurious to the general interests of the country, and would hazard its peace and its security, to a greater degree than at any period of its history at which it could possibly have occurred.

"His majesty can not contemplate without the greatest apprehension the possibility of a general election, and of contests in every part of the kingdom, at a moment when so much excitement prevails; when the disposition to violence and outrage, to the almost indiscriminate and unprovoked destruction of property, has with difficulty been checked by the strong hand of the law; when the measures decided upon to strengthen the hands of the executive and the civil power, which this state of things had called for, are yet in preparation. His majesty naturally looks to what passed at Preston for the example of a popular election under such circumstances, and for the exclusion of men of character and respectability, not in consequence of any abuse or defect in the system of representation, but in consequence of the populace taking the law into its own hands, and defying all rule and its enforcement by constitutional authority. He looks with still greater anxiety to the state of Ireland, and to the possible results of popular elections, while Mr. O'Connell's influence, and the excitement his seditious proceedings have created, still prevail—one effect of which might be, the return of a large proportion of the Irish members who would be advocates for the Repeal of the Union, and perhaps for the full measure of Mr. O'Connell's designs. All these are circumstances which have engaged his majesty's attention, and have been the subject of his conversation; and he has given me full authority now to express them to your lordship. There yet remains another not less important circumstance, though it would not arise till after the successful issue of the attempt in the House of Commons—namely, the possibility of a serious and *protracted* difference between that House and House of Lords, which is to be deprecated on every account; for, to use your own words, 'the Constitution could no more stand without Lords than without Commons.'

"I have troubled your lordship with a long letter, upon a subject on which I should not have presumed to write without his majesty's sanction. I have felt, however, that you will be glad, and that it might be useful to you, to be in possession of his sentiments; I think I may venture to add that they will not be urged in a manner that can embarrass his Government.

"I have the honor to be, with great regard, my dear lord, your lordship's very obedient and faithful servant,

"H. TAYLOR.

"THE LORD HIGH CHANCELLOR."

When all had been agreed upon as to the substance of the bill, it was very important to have it carefully drawn, because we well knew the injurious effects or faults or obvious blunders in a measure that had to undergo such opposition from so many kinds of objectors. Wilde was of great use in advising me on the question as to whom the details of the drawing should be committed, that I could not do better than employ a very skillful draftsman, Peacock, who afterwards rose to great eminence in the profession, and who was then an able pleader, but not much known. He was afterwards appointed to a judgeship in India, where I believe he died. It was absolutely necessary to have a trustworthy person in this as in every other department connected with the bill, because we felt the necessity of keeping the most absolute secrecy on the whole of its provisions. This was not easy, from the number of persons who of necessity were acquainted with the whole plan, and from the extreme curiosity that prevailed to know something, at least, of what was proposed. Yet we were quite convinced that, to give the measure any chance of success with the country and with Parliament, it must be brought forward at once, without any single part of it being previously known to the public. A week or ten days would have sufficed to raise objections in all quarters, even among its friends, and discontent would have prevailed among many because of the reform going too far; among many more, because of its not going far enough; besides that every one would have had a plan of his own, and not a few must have rejected it from ignorance of the subject, and being led by no weighty authority. To those in Parliament and not in office, the most tempting occasion would have been afforded of urging or of feigning their discontent. In short, the keeping the whole of the measure secret until the moment of promulgation, with the full weight of Government, appeared absolutely necessary, if the bill was to have fair play.

There never was a secret more perfectly kept. But we all felt anxious to ascertain beforehand how the measure was likely to satisfy our friends, and we conceived it best to sound those of the most extreme opinions. My brother James was then living with us in Berkeley Square, and he had always been what was called a Burdettite—at least he leaned strongly to that section. Of course it was a subject on which he never came with me, although I was aware of his great anxiety to know what we were about, both on account of the subject and on account of the Government, which, though in no office, he strongly supported. But I avoided saying a single word of any kind (as he did), because inferences might be drawn from whatever I said, and it is a sound rule for keeping a secret never to utter a word upon the subject of it, even so far as to say you intend to conceal it. I thought, however, I would sound him, after we had resolved to satisfy ourselves in that way; and I asked, suddenly, one morning, "What should you say if we intended to disfranchise half the rotten boroughs, or to leave them only one member each, giving the votes abolished to the great towns?" "Oh, that is quite romantic; you never will be able to do that." I told him that he might confide it to Burdett, but with a positive injunction against its going farther. He told me at dinner that Burdett, like himself, thought it far too good news to be true, and that he could not believe it, but would say nothing till he heard more. We resolved the same evening, in Cabinet, to make Burdett our confidant under seal of secrecy, and the outline of the plan was next morning communicated to him. He was overjoyed, but greatly doubted if we did not go too far. He made one or two suggestions both as to the measure itself and our mode of proceeding, some of which we took advantage of.

His friend and ally, Hobhouse (now Broughton), has plainly intimated in the House that his opinion, after full consideration, continued to be, that the measure went rather too far.

Our final discussion was held in the Cabinet just before the 1st of March, when the bill was moved in the Commons by John Russell. We had from the first resolved that he should bring it forward, from the subject having of late years been in his hands; no doubt, also, because, having no Cabinet office, this was reckoned a kind of compensation. There were many reasons why Althorp, our leader in the Commons, should have charge of it. Among others, his not bringing it in was held to show a slack support of the measure by the Government. Our conduct soon gave a refutation to that argument; but Althorp's minute acquaintance with the details, exceeding that which I ever knew any one to have on any measure, and his ready answer to all objections, or explanation of all doubts, with his unexampled temper throughout, led both Grey and myself to doubt if it would not have been better in his hands. However, it was too late now to make any change, and we talked over our prospects under the present arrangement, and considering the measure as finally settled. The Opposition, and the adversaries of Reform generally, had had nearly four weeks to reflect upon their course, as the notice was given in both Houses immediately on the meeting after the Christmas recess. I told my colleagues that there was nothing so foolish as not being prepared for the enemy's movements; and that on fully considering what these were likely to be, and having only one guide to answer the question—namely, what I should myself do in their place — I had no doubt whatever, that on the plan being opened, I should at once say (and here I made the speech I expected Peel to make), "This is not reform, but revolution; we can not suffer the bill to be brought in as if it were a plan of improvement; it is a measure of destruction. I move that it be rejected at once, and that we refuse leave to bring in the bill." Goderich said he did not believe Peel was up to this, though he admitted there was no better way of meeting it before the country could be excited in its favor. I said, There is a better general than Peel in command of the party; the duke will assuredly take that course. Of this I felt the more certain, because I knew how meanly he thought of Peel's leadership on the last occasion, when Parnell's motion was carried. On the announcement to him at his house, where he had an evening party, he expressed no regret, but considerable surprise, especially at Peel having left the Government almost undefended. Here the duke was quite wrong; Peel could have done no otherwise than he did.

We should have been in the greatest difficulty if the course which I described had been taken. The country was not in the least prepared for so large a measure; and the excitement in favor of it would not have been greater than the alarm on the other side. Besides, we had been warned by the king, that though he entirely approved the bill, and would give it all the support in his power, he did not engage to dissolve on account of it—indeed he plainly had indicated that he would not. All, therefore, depended upon time being given for the country to take part with us strongly and generally.

Le Marchant,* my principal secretary, was as usual under the gallery, and sent me, from time to time, a short report of what passed. These accounts were always so admirably clear in all respects, that Grey used to say he seldom looked at the newspapers next morning. On the evening of the 1st of March he was there, of course; and I had two or three of the Cabinet to dine with me—Melbourne and Richmond. We were at table, and waiting with anxiety the bulletin from Le Marchant. We said, Let us drink success before we know our fate. The first accounts, between five and eight o'clock, were only that the House was full, and the surprise at the plan very great. The third was that some one, I think Sir Robert Harry Inglis, a stout opponent, had followed John Russell, and had gone at large into the question—in short, that Peel had missed his chance, and that all was safe. On

* Sir Denis Le Marchant, Bart., second son of Major-General Le Marchant, who was killed at the battle of Salamanca.

conversing afterwards about the conduct of the Opposition in debating the bill for some nights, and their not dividing against the leave to bring it in, it appeared that some of the staunchest supporters of the Government had declared generally their intention to vote for leave, though strongly opposed to the bill; and Richmond happened to have letters which were put into the post that day, after the plan had been opened, written from the House of Commons, and posted without any address—as happens much oftener than might be supposed, and even with letters containing bills or money. They were therefore, in the regular course of the office, brought to him as postmaster-general, and opened by him. They shortly expressed alarm at the measure, but said they could not vote against bringing in the bill. These letters were from two of the staunchest friends of the Opposition, written to two great borough-owners. I have often discussed with the Duke of Wellington the same subject, and asked him how he could let such a manifest error be committed. He entirely agreed as to the course they ought to have taken, but said Peel was not so much to blame as he appeared to be, for some of the greatest adversaries of the Government and of the bill had taken a very strong objection to refusing leave. My answer was, that I had over and over again found even important members of our party deciding against what I intended to do; but if it was clearly right, and was of much importance, when I persisted, notwithstanding their objections, they all, or almost all, fell in with the rest—and so would the objectors in Peel's case. My statement applied, of course, to measures and conduct in Opposition.

The effect of the announcement of our plan was beyond any thing I can recollect. The most sanguine were astonished at a measure so much larger than they had hoped would be brought forward. The feeling of astonishment was the same in the House on both sides, as I heard from James the next day; and out-of-doors it was as strong and as universal. The duke had a party that evening, and before the account reached him, he had been expressing his disbelief of the report he had heard of what was said to be our plan, and a moderate measure as more than he thought we should venture to propose; and he inclined to disbelieve the reports; but when the first news of the bill came, he said that it was utterly impossible, and must be a mistaken account. Rosslyn, when I met him at the House, considered our policy as ill conceived, and sure to fail; but I gathered from him, that if mistakes had been committed, especially the duke's declaration, and the suffering the bill to be brought in, upon which he entirely agreed with me, there would be no more errors or oversights; and he gave me to understand that the duke was taking matters into his own hands as to their tactics, both in the Commons and Lords. I asked him what they meant to do in the country, and he said they must wait to see the impression made. On this, as on every occasion, I expressed our regret at not having him with us. He had been strongly pressed to join the Government when it was forming; the communication was through my brother, as their intimacy made a consideration of the reasons for and against the new Ministry more easy. He had at first said it was impossible, but James begging him to take a few hours for consideration—whether he was so bound to the duke that he could not return to his friends who had regarded his taking office with the duke as highly proper and as agreeable to them—next day he said that, independent of other considerations, he felt bound in honor to the duke, and—though without the least doubt the duke had released him and desired him to join us—he felt that he could not; and the duke's most handsome behavior only made it the more impossible. Afterwards, when the bill was brought in, he said there were new reasons that made it out of the question; for he had always been against Parliamentary Reform, even of the most limited description, and to join in this wholesale measure was out of the question. He was one of the North party, and at the coalition they had always differed with the Whigs on this subject.

The second reading was carried by a bare majority of one. Some days before, we had sustained a defeat in the Commons upon the timber duties,* and our friends thought we

* In committee on Customs, 18th March, on the motion of Lord Althorp for an alteration in the duties on certain kinds of timber imported from the Baltic, there was a division of 236 against 190, being a majority of 46 against Ministers.

were bound to dissolve, or resign — as foolish a notion as could enter into their heads, especially considering that the excitement was spreading daily wider and wider, but had by no means reached its height. I found expectation of our taking this course extended even to calm and reflecting persons; for I had a letter from Abercromby, at Edinburgh (where he was sitting as chief baron), in which he said—"I conclude that this letter will cross one announcing a dissolution."

Although dissolving on the timber-duty defeat was out of the question, yet that defeat, and the narrow majority of one by which the second reading was carried, made it quite clear that we must take the earliest opportunity which our adversaries might give us of appealing to the country, and of having a Parliament chosen under our Government, as this had been under the duke's, who, I must say, had exercised as little Crown influence in the late election as any one at the head of the Government could. Just about this time, it appeared to me quite possible that the king might refuse to dissolve, for I well knew how adverse he was to take that step. Hence, as our resignation would have followed such refusal, I quite laid my account with shortly being out of office; and as there were some important matters connected with the Court of Chancery that I had much at heart, I wrote the following memorandum, which I intended should be given to my successor:

"Court of Chancery, April 20, 1831.

"As it is very probable that the Great Seal may not be held by me beyond a few days, I think it proper to leave to my successors this intimation respecting the office of accountant-general.

"Mr. Harvey* has for some time tendered me his resignation, and before Easter I begged he would retain his office for a few weeks, because I had an important arrangement in preparation. That arrangement requires a bill to be carried through Parliament, for which there has not been time.

"I intended to abolish the Scotch Court of Exchequer, for reasons unnecessary to be stated, but chiefly because it is

* Springett Harvey, Accountant-General of the Court of Chancery.

wholly superfluous, not trying more than one defended cause in a year. I then intended to give the chief baron the office of accountant-general, which would have saved his retiring pension. My reason for not beginning with giving him this place was, that he had a perfect right to claim his period of retirement as chief baron, with the pension belonging to that office, instead of waiting till he had completed his period as accountant general (twenty years), and the smaller pension of £1500. This could best be done by his resigning under the bill.

"My wish is to see this arrangement carried into effect, whoever is chancellor. It is highly beneficial to the country by saving money, and still more by rescuing the Bench and profession from the evil consequences of there being any thing like sinecure judges.

"Some arrangements of detail will be necessary for this plan, because certain revenue business is very improperly committed to the Scotch Exchequer.

"BROUGHAM, C."

For three weeks we had been deliberating on this question of dissolving, and when we had resolved, and were waiting anxiously for a fair ground, Gascoigne's motion against lessening the numbers of the House for England and Wales (which the bill proposed to do) was carried by a majority of eight; and two nights after, by a majority of twenty-two, he carried an adjournment on a Liverpool bribery case, which prevented our going on with Supply. This was deemed a fair ground of dissolving; and having held communication with the king on the subject for some days, and obtained his reluctant consent, we took the step next day, 22d April. These motions of Gascoigne's, especially the first, were always complained bitterly of by our more practised adversaries. Croker, the ablest opponent of the bill, and whose only error was the furnishing us with a statement of all his objections, by reducing them to one form of motion, said that Gascoigne had shipwrecked their opposition to the bill by his motion to alter the only good thing in it, the reduction of the numbers.

These were the greatest difficulties in our situation during the whole month, after the narrow majority on the second reading which had led to our determination, and which, indeed, clearly showed that the bill was lost if we did not dissolve. The chief difficulty was the king's great reluctance. Indeed he at first refused, and reminded us of the reserve under which he had given his approval of the bill. After much discussion, both in conversation and by correspondence, in which I of course took part, addressing a very full and anxious letter to him, as well as having an audience, it ended in our determining all to resign unless the request was granted. We had a Cabinet on the subject, and all signed a minute to that effect. Fortunately the king had made up his mind to refuse no longer, before our minute could reach him, and he could refer to something that had passed with me as showing this, which it did when fairly considered, though it had not so appeared to us. Nevertheless, our minute was framed conditionally, and did not exclude the supposition of his previous change of mind.

Another difficulty was the probability of the Commons addressing against dissolution, in which the Lords would certainly have joined. Our secret was so well kept, that the Commons did not believe the danger so near, and adjourned on the 21st without supposing we could make the vote on the Liverpool Bribery Bill a reason for dissolving. If the joint address had been carried, with the king's reluctance, he of course would have retracted the consent given, as he would have had a perfect right to do in the change of circumstances produced by the address; and the more so because a dissolution, though it might change the Commons, could have no effect whatever on the Lords.

Here, indeed, was another of our difficulties: the Lords might address, even if the Commons did not; and that they would take this step, soon appeared more than probable. On the morning of the 21st of April, William Courtenay,* whose position in the House and great intimacy with the peers gave him great opportunities of finding out what was going on, told me that Shaftesbury, who was decidedly against us, had declared that, if the king came down in person to dissolve, a

* Afterwards Earl of Devon, but at this time Clerk of the Parliament in the House of Lords. He had been a Master in Chancery.

motion of adjournment must be made *pro formâ* "to receive the king, and that their lordships retire to robe;" and Courtenay added that Wharncliffe was to move an address; and the same evening, after asking Grey whether the ministers had advised the king to dissolve, on Grey refusing to answer a question so unusual, Wharncliffe gave notice that he should next day move an address praying the king not to exercise his prerogative.

Now nothing can be more certain than that such an address, if carried, would in no respect have deprived the king of the power he has by the constitution to dissolve Parliament; but it is no less certain that, had such an address been carried, the king would too gladly have taken advantage of it; for although he approved of the bill, and said he would give it every support in his power, he left it with the existing Parliament to determine, and would do no act by which that Parliament should be set aside and another appealed to.

Every thing, therefore, depended upon the dissolution being effected before any thing intervened to prevent it. The greatest efforts were made in every department to expedite the writs, and the speech, which was at first framed to be delivered by commission. To prevent the mischief which the carrying of an address would to a certainty have occasioned, it was absolutely necessary that the king should dissolve in person.

I lost not a moment in communicating all these circumstances to my colleagues, and it was accordingly resolved that very early next morning we should have a Cabinet before the Speech Council, which was to take place at half-past eleven, and finally resolve on the mode and manner of proceeding. We met accordingly, and almost all agreed to go on, though one or two, appalled by the many increasing difficulties, asked if it was too late to reconsider the whole matter. Here I appealed to the Duke of Richmond, and asked him if he had ever seen a council of war held on the field just before going into action. He said, "By God! never; neither I nor any one else." Then, said I, let us go in to the king. Grey and I went in, and stated our clear opinion that it would be necessary for him to go in person, though we were most unwilling to give him that trouble. I took care to make him understand the threatened proceedings of the Lords, and the effect the proposed motion for an address was intended to have on his majesty's proroguing Parliament. He fired up at this —hating dissolution, perhaps, as much as ever, but hating far more the interference with, or attempt to delay, the exercise of the prerogative; and so he at once agreed to go, only saying that all must be done in the usual manner; and he mentioned several things which he said could not be got ready in time, for it was little more than one hour off, the House meeting at two o'clock. The sword of state and cap of maintenance were mentioned by him; and we told him that Lord Grey would carry the one, and somebody else the other. But, said he, the troops—there is no time for ordering them, and it is impossible to go without them. I had foreseen this difficulty; and on ascertaining that the Life Guards—the regiment usually in attendance on such an occasion—were quartered at some distant barrack (I think it was Knightsbridge), sent to the Horse Guards for such men as happened to be there. On the king making the observation about the troops, I said, "I hoped his majesty would excuse the great liberty I had taken; but being quite certain he would graciously accede to our request, I had sent to the Horse Guards for an escort to be ready at half-past one." He said, "Well, that was a strong measure," or "a strong thing to do." I believe I had prepared him for this by a little more apology and explanation than is mentioned above; but he ever after, when in very good-humor, used to remind me of what he called my high treason. He then spoke of the Lord Steward as being required; but we had sent to summon him. Then Albemarle, the Master of the Horse, was out of the way, and when found, said it would not be possible to get the state carriages ready in time; but the king said he was determined to go, and that any thing would do. There was a story about London that he had said to Lord Albemarle he would go in a hackney-coach rather than not go at all. I can not say whether this is true or not—all I can say is, that I do not recollect hearing it; but this I do know, that he had become so eager to go, that no trifle would have stopped him. The draft of the speech was then submitted to him, and approved, with a sentence which I prefixed with my own hand; and as I had a secretary in the adjoining room, a fair copy was made for the Council which was then held, that it might be read and approved in form.

Having to go home in order to dress, the gold gown being required, I got to the House soon after two o'clock, the hour to which we had adjourned; and after prayers I left the wool-sack, in order that I might be in readiness to receive his majesty. Lord Shaftesbury, on the motion of Lord Mansfield, then took the wool-sack, and Wharncliffe rose to move the address of which he had given notice. Then began a scene which, as it was represented to me, was never exceeded in violence and uproar by any bear-garden exhibition. The Duke of Richmond, interrupting Wharncliffe, moved that the Lords take their seats in their proper places; for, said he, I see a junior baron (Lyndhurst) sitting on the dukes' bench. Lyndhurst, starting up, exclaimed that Richmond's conduct was most disorderly, and *shook his fist at him.* This brought up Londonderry, who did not speak, but screamed that the noble duke, in his attempt to stop Wharncliffe, had resorted to a wretched shift. Wharncliffe then began by reading the words of his motion. I was here told by Durham what was going on, and that unless the king came soon the Lords would vote the address, because Wharncliffe meant to make no speech; so I rushed back into the House, and began by exclaiming against the unheard-of doctrine that the Crown ought not to dissolve at a moment when the House of Commons had refused the supplies. This was loudly denied, but I persisted that the vote I referred to had, in fact, that effect. I went on purposely speaking until we heard the guns. Then came great interruptions, and cries of order, which continued until a messenger summoned me, when I said I had the king's commands to attend him in the Painted Chamber. Shaftesbury again took the wool-sack, and they continued debating until the procession entered. When the door was thrown open, the king asked me, "What noise that was?" and I answered, "If it please your majesty, it is the Lords debating." He asked if we should stop, but was told that all would be silent the moment he entered. The Commons were summoned in the usual way; and, having received the speech, he read it with a clear and firm voice. I doubt if any part of it was listened to beyond the first sentence, prefixed to the draft, and which I alone had any hand in writing: "I am come to meet you for the purpose of proroguing this Parliament, with a view to its *immediate* dissolution." He dwelt upon immediate. While we were waiting for the rest of the Commons, beside the speaker and the few who accompanied him, the king asked me many questions, as to who such and such peers were, and what were the names of the commoners who stood behind the bar. I remember Cobbett was one, whom he had never seen before.

The consternation which the dissolution produced among our adversaries I never could understand, for it seemed to take them by surprise; and yet every one must have seen, from the resistance in the Commons, and the strength of the Opposition upon every question, that we had but one course to take. Many relied upon the king refusing; but as soon as the universal feeling of the country became manifest, which it did at least a fortnight before we dissolved, they had no reason to doubt that the king would yield to us; and they must have been quite assured that they could not take the Government in the only way in which the duke could have agreed to take it—upon the ground of his declaration absolutely to resist all change.

It was on the 4th of July that the debate had begun in the Commons on the second reading of the bill, which was carried by a majority of 136. The bill soon after went into committee, where the Opposition exhausted every resource of debate and obstruction. The committee finished on the 7th of September, having been occupied nearly two months on the clauses. The third reading passed without any discussion; but on the question that the bill do pass, there was a final debate which lasted three nights. The subject was well debated by the Opposition, and by no one better than by Croker, who had throughout the whole discussions shown himself *facile princeps.* On the 21st of September, the bill passed by a majority of 109, and next day was brought up to the Lords with an important clause, added in spite of our great majority, known as the Chandos clause, or leasehold franchise, to which we had, after being beaten, submitted. The bill was read a first time without debate, and the second reading fixed for an early day in October.

The Lords continued as hostile as ever. Our position was extremely embarrassing. Personally it was still more unpleasant to such of us as were in the Lords. Grey felt it more vexatious than I did, he being charged with the conduct of measures in any one of which, or in any part of any one, we had a majority against us; but I felt it also, and our position was all the more hopeless that nothing could exceed the skill of the duke's management, and his candor and firmness made him more formidable.

I had now sat one legal year in the Court of Chancery. I had cleared off all the arrears; and when I sat for the last time in the beginning of September, I had to leave the Court and walk home at twelve o'clock, there being nothing to do. I deemed it my duty to submit the following statement of this fact to the king:

"Berkeley Square, September 1, 1831.

"MOST GRACIOUS SOVEREIGN,—I humbly crave permission to lay at your majesty's feet the report that your majesty's High Court of Chancery has this day been adjourned to Michaelmas term. It is, sire, a matter of unspeakable satisfaction to me that I have been enabled to dispose of every cause and every kind of business which was ready for hearing, and that, except one or two things in which all the parties desired time, being unprepared to proceed now, every matter brought into the Court before the first of July last has been fully heard. All the cases, too, except a single one upon the construction of an obscure will, heard the night before last, have been decided as well as heard. I have, therefore, the gratification of reporting to your majesty that there is an end of all arrears in Chancery, and that a continuance of the same system, aided by the extreme diligence and perseverance of their honors, the Master of the Rolls and the vice-chancellor, will effectually prevent any arrear from again accumulating.

"I humbly crave your majesty's pardon for thus presuming to lay these particulars before your majesty. But I know your majesty's paternal care of the best interest of your subjects will plead my excuse; and I have further to express my sense of your majesty's great goodness in dispensing for three weeks with my attention upon your majesty's Court, which has materially aided my efforts in Chancery.

"All which is most humbly submitted by your majesty's most dutiful subject and servant, BROUGHAM, C."

To this statement I received the following most gracious answer from his majesty:

"Windsor Castle, September 2, 1831.

"The king has received with much satisfaction the report made in the lord chancellor's letter of yesterday, that the High Court of Chancery had been adjourned to Michaelmas term, and that he had been able to dispose of every cause and every kind of business which was ready for hearing. His majesty believes this to be the first instance on record, or at least within the memory of any legal person now in practice, of there being no arrears in Chancery; and his majesty is quite sensible how much credit is due to his present able and industrious lord chancellor for the indefatigable zeal and the perseverance which have led to so desirable a result, one for which the country ought to feel so grateful to him and to those who have co-operated with him in the discharge of duties so important and arduous. WILLIAM, R."

Up to the dissolution of April, 1831, the king had been steady in his support, and never more firm than when he went in person to dissolve; but soon after that, it became obvious to us that he was beginning to show an amount of lukewarmness likely to be very embarrassing. He made a vigorous attempt to induce Lord Grey to modify the measure. A very few days after the dissolution, he sent him a strong representation urging the expediency of delay, in order to give time for calm deliberation, after the then state of excitement had passed away. He described the measure as a "perilous experiment," which he did not dare to risk, and urged upon Grey, notwithstanding his pledge to carry the *whole* bill, the necessity of some modifications. This document was considered by us in Cabinet, and Grey answered to the effect that solemn pledges could not be abandoned. The king, as already mentioned, was very angry at the illuminations that followed the dissolution. Then he disliked the violence of the elections. Next he saw we were having a very great majority, which no king ever likes; and he also thought the Lords were likely to be more obstinately opposed to us than ever.

All this laid, in my opinion, the foundation of his subsequent change of opinion. He also, while heartily supporting us—for instance, making Grey K.G. during the elections, to show his favor—persisted in seeing Tory peers, and in having at his table chiefly our adversaries.

After the Lords had thrown out the bill in October, the king remained firm to us, but reminded us that he had always foreboded this, and showed no disposition to get us out of our difficulty. The Bristol riots alarmed him much. In the autumn of 1831, the following letters passed between Lord Grey and me:

TO LORD GREY.

[*Private.*]

"August 5, 1831.

"MY DEAR LORD GREY,—I can't help feeling most anxious about France, and a little about Russia. One thing is clear, if *we* move one inch, we give both a pretext to enter Belgium or Holland (the latter they won't do).

"Surely we could put it to Prussia that the best policy is to be firm, and make France abstain from entering Belgium; for if once, *on any pretext*, she gets possession, no French Government is strong enough to withdraw.

"But as to France, I must say I feel most strongly the necessity of sending a most powerful and important special ambassador, to let the king and ministers know our feeling, and that of the country, against war. *You* would do it with most effect, but I fear could not be spared. Then Lansdowne seems the next best, he having no department here.

"The resident minister always goes on in a jog-trot way, and what he says by way of warning has very inferior effect. As for those endless conferences, they are mere cloaks for chicane. Pray consider of this.

"Ever yours, H. BROUGHAM."

TO LORD GREY.

"September 1, 1831.

"MY DEAR LORD GREY,—The king was extremely gracious about the old seal, and has ordered Rundell to make a fine salver to put it in. He had Rundell's partner with him yesterday evening, whom he sent to me this morning before eight. I insisted on giving Copley half.

"The weather is enough to give any body lumbago, even those who, like us, have done nothing to deserve it.

"I closed the Court to-day, and have only left one thing (entered before 1st July) undecided, and that a cause heard on Tuesday night, and on which I have not yet made up my mind. I announced the end of the vice-chancellor's court.

"Yours truly, H. BROUGHAM."

TO LORD GREY.

"September 2, 1831.

"DEAR LORD GREY,—The inclosed is from a Canada paper: they have let you off well, as being priggish and having a Newcastle burr, and *also* as not being like D. O'Connell.

"Yours ever, H. BROUGHAM."

Now began the consideration of a question which occupied the minds of all the Cabinet—I mean, what steps were to be taken, or what preparations were to be made, to meet an event which we could not but anticipate—the rejection of the bill by the Lords. The following letters relate to this important subject. The first, from Lord Grey, is in answer to what I had written proposing a large creation of peers:

FROM LORD GREY.

"East Sheen, September 2, 1831.

"DEAR CHANCELLOR,—Thank you for your prescription. I am nearly well without calomel, which I always wish to avoid unless absolutely necessary.

"Your dose of peers is rather too strong for my stomach. I mean to prepare a good batch, according to precedent, for the coronation. If men are to be made with a view to the Reform Bill, it must be afterwards, and must be a Cabinet measure. I doubt whether even the largest of your numbers would make the thing sure, and failure after a large creation would be ruinous.

"I rejoice in the successful termination of your labors in the Court of Chancery. I should like to extend my holidays till Monday. Could you attend a Cabinet on that day—in the morning?

"Pray look over the inclosed paper, and let me have your opinion upon it as soon as possible. Ever yours,

"GREY."

FROM LORD GREY.

"East Sheen, September 3, 1831.

"MY DEAR CHANCELLOR,—As you desire to have your paper sent you to-night, I have not time for comments upon it. Nor are they necessary. The case must be brought under the consideration of the Cabinet, which is summoned for Monday at twelve, when I hope you will make a point of attending, and when the whole matter may be fully discussed.

"In much of your reasoning I agree, on some points I doubt — on one or two, not very material ones perhaps, I differ; but on the general statement of the frightful consequences of a rejection of the bill, any man who has the gift of reason must agree. To obviate such a danger, every thing that does not add to uncertainty of success great evils of another description, ought to be risked. But here there arise some very important and very difficult considerations.

What would be the result of a large creation of thirty or forty peers, and failure after all? I am inclined to believe that the mischief of such a result, both to ourselves personally and to the public, would be found greatly to exceed any other that can be imagined. And here I must state that I have great doubts whether thirty or forty additional peers would give us a majority. Then, you will say, create fifty. But will fifty do? I think it uncertain, or perhaps more than uncertain, if the bishops, as I hear, will vote for a postponement of the measure for some months, to give time to the country for calm consideration. This, I believe, is certainly to be the measure, and the Duke of Wellington speaks confidently of a majority of sixty, though I can not understand the grounds of his calculation.

"I say nothing of the king's consent. I think he would do a great deal, but he would be startled at what you require.

"I lean very much to the coronation batch, in the first instance. The second creation need not be deferred till after a vote, but may take place when the bill comes up, and when we may be able to form a more accurate estimate of our future prospects.

"But this and every other part of the question will be better discussed among us on Monday. In the mean time, it will occupy my thoughts night and day; and I am sorry to say that I feel myself very unequal to the exertion, and to the resolution which the crisis requires.

"Ever yours, GREY."

Althorp took a different view of the question, and a little further consideration served to bring Lord Grey nearer to the plan suggested. Althorp's view will appear from the following letter, which he wrote to me in October:

FROM LORD ALTHORP.

[*Private and confidential.*]

"Downing Street, October, 1831.

"MY DEAR BROUGHAM,—The effect of Friday's debate upon the Bankruptcy Bill is to render it impossible to force the measure forward. It was very ill opened, both as to the plan of the speech and as to its execution. Denman ought not to have attempted any detail of the clauses to be introduced in the committee. If he touched upon them at all, it ought to have been in the lightest manner possible. But he went into the whole detail, and executed it abominably, from the very simple cause that he evidently did not in the least understand it, and could hardly have read the provisions which he undertook to explain. On the other side, Wetherell made a very effective speech—one of the best I ever heard him make. He passed by the whole of the material provisions of the bill, and fastened upon the unexplained but opened money clauses. If you carry the second reading of Reform in the House of Lords, and we consequently continue sitting, there will be no great difficulty in putting the matter right; but if the Reform Bill is thrown out, and we consequently prorogue as soon as we can, it will be impossible to attempt to carry the Bankruptcy Bill. At all events, if the bill is to go through a committee in the House of Commons, you must not trust to the lawyers. Some of us laymen must be instructed so as to fight it. I am very much obliged to you for what you have said in the 'Edinburgh Review.'* If praise is able to recompense a man for sacrificing every thing he likes, I certainly ought to feel myself quite recompensed. I am come over to your opinion as to what ought to be done in case the House of Lords reject the Reform Bill. We ought, I think, to endeavor to make *peers enough to carry it.* This, in my opinion, is a question of principle, and not of degree. The number to be made should depend only on the number required.

"Yours most truly, ALTHORP."

Before this I had written to Lord Grey as follows:

[*Private.*] TO LORD GREY.

"September 27, 1831.

"MY DEAR LORD GREY,—I have been considering this matter of Lord Anglesey's arrival, and think, from all that passed at Windsor these two days, that he ought not to go to the levee—where he can not possibly have much, if any, time to do good—but that he should say he can not, from indisposition after his journey, attend the levee, but will wait on the king, at Windsor, on Thursday.

"My belief is that *his* seeing the king will be very useful. I can see him in the morning and talk over matters with him, and he can see you at Sheen, on his way.

"Pray consider of this. Lord Holland takes the same view, but you of course must decide.

"Yours ever, H. BROUGHAM.

"The Russians come Friday, so he should go Thursday."

At this time I received the following letter from Parnell:

FROM SIR HENRY PARNELL.

"September 29, 1831.

"MY DEAR LORD BROUGHAM,—Pray do not delay seeing

* See "Edinburgh Review," September, 1831, p. 308.

O'Connell. He is very much changed these last few days. In every thing he says, he displays great irritation and anger. Late on Monday night he made a furious attack on Stanley, on account of something that offended him about Maynooth, and quite without any just cause for the attack. I have tried to discover the cause of this change, and I am told it arises from O'Connell's seeing the session approaching to a close, and nothing doing for him.

"Since I dined with you, I have spoken to Brownlow, Sheil, and several other Irish members, and I find but one opinion among them, quite concurring with my own, as to the Union and the connection between England and Ireland being in great jeopardy. They all say that a regular plan is arranged for renewing agitation on a greater scale than at any former period. All O'Connell speaks about is what he will do in this way when he returns to Ireland.

"There is really no time to be lost in making an arrangement with him. Only see what a handle he will make of the throwing out of the Reform if this shall happen. He will say there is no other hope for Ireland but the repeal of the Union, and you will have just as universal a demand in Ireland for its repeal as there is in England for Reform.

"It is now quite evident that all that is wanted to secure such an arrangement is more courage in the Cabinet. I never heard a reason given against doing what ought to be done, which could not be traced to some ill-founded apprehension. The difficulty which sprang from ignorance of the state of Ireland is now almost entirely removed; and no one can any longer doubt that all danger as to Ireland may be done away, and the peace of it established, by making a friend of O'Connell.

"As the putting of him into the office of attorney-general would accomplish the business in the most effectual manner, this should be done, and done immediately.

"Mr. Sheil might be made resident under-secretary in London for Ireland, by giving him Sir Charles Flint's office. In this way it would become an efficient office.

"Mr. Wyse and Mr. O'Farrel should be made Lords of the Treasury.*

* Mr. (afterwards Sir Thomas) Wyse, member for Tipperary, and Richard More O'Farrel, member for Kildare.

"As to the Catholic clergy, it would be sufficient for paying them to enable the parish vestries, if they thought proper, to give salaries to the priests, according to the size of the parishes. I am quite certain that this plan would work very well.

"Now that Lord Anglesey is here, of all things keep him here, even, if it must be so, in the office of lord lieutenant. He could, I believe, agree to every thing I have suggested, if he were encouraged to do so by you and others. Believe me yours very truly, H. PARNELL."

It was about this time that the king's original liking for popular exhibitions of himself became extinct, and was succeeded by a great repugnance to all such appearances. He would go to prorogue or to meet Parliament, because he reckoned that a regular part of his duty as sovereign; but all other exhibitions he hated; and he never failed to pity or to blame — according to the humor he was in — Louis Philippe for being "a puppet in the mob's hands," which "he was resolved never to be." I never argued this matter with him but once, on the question of his going in person to give his consent to the Reform Bill, and he, both in an audience and on my writing to him, flatly refused.

On the 3d of October began the debate on the second reading of the bill, moved by Lord Grey in a most admirable speech.* After five nights' debate we divided, and were defeated by a majority of 41.

Before leaving town for ten days' rest, having been in hard work without any interruption for twelve months exactly, I talked seriously to Melbourne as a friend, and as head of the police department. I told him that *I* was prepared to make a stand and refuse being dictated to by the mob, or the Radicals, or even the party—that I would make up my own mind and take my own course, and that I would look for my protection to the returning good sense of the people, and for my reward to my own approval if they should fail me. He generally agreed with me, but he was alarmed. I was supported

* On the 21st of September, the bill, in its second shape, had passed the Commons by 345 to 236. It was sent up to the Lords next day.

by some of the great bodies, and by all Scotland, whose confidence in me continued unbounded and unbroken.

I returned to town the 2d of November, having left it the 19th of October. I found the Cabinet divided on the great point of meeting Parliament now or after Christmas. Grey determined for the latter course. I stood firm for the former. I gave intimations of being determined, and carried the majority with me. Durham was abroad, but wrote that he looked only to me for saving them.

Early in October I had the following letter:

[*Private.*] FROM SIR HERBERT TAYLOR.

"Windsor Castle, October 8, 1831.

"MY DEAR LORD,—I was with the king when I had the pleasure of receiving your lordship's letter of this evening, and therefore had an opportunity of *immediately* reading it to his majesty, who was extremely interested by its contents, and ordered me to thank you for the communication of passing events, your remarks on the state of affairs, and on parts of last night's debates in the House of Lords.

"His majesty has not heard of any concourse of people about the House of Lords and Downing Street, but had been assured that all was quiet and peaceably inclined, and he was glad to receive so satisfactory a confirmation of this from you. Upon these occasions, and more especially on a sloppy day, it is doubtless more agreeable to be in the good graces than in the bad graces of a mob; but I question whether your lordship would not readily have dispensed with the mark which you received of this favor, and whether it might not remind you of the danger to which the candidates for fame at the Olympic games were occasionally exposed.

"His majesty was much concerned to hear that the failure of the bill had affected the funds and created mercantile alarm; and he will be anxious to know on Monday to what extent this has been carried, and what may be the course taken by the bankers and merchants. The shutting of shops upon such an occasion is surely a new symptom of the times, or at least a very unusual and extravagant demonstration of feeling upon a political and constitutional question, upon which it is reasonable to allow, and has been heretofore allowed, that there may be difference of opinion.

"Indeed I observed, in reading the report in the 'Times' of your lordship's splendid and admirable speech, that you for one do not subscribe *to all* parts of the bill, and were prepared to state your objections to certain provisions of it, if it were allowed to go into committee; and from what you write to me, I had not mistaken your meaning, even as to your desiring it to be understood that the bill had gone rather farther than suited *your* views of Reform. The debate in general must have been most interesting, and, with one exception, appears to have been carried on without personality and acrimony. It must have been satisfactory to all those who feel the necessity of upholding the constituted authorities, to observe that those who were the most strenuous advocates for what is considered the popular cause were as decided as their opponents in condemning and reproving any attempt of the people to carry their point by infractions of the peace or of the laws of the country.

"In short, the general tone of the discussion appears to have been good, and I can not think that we shall in the end have reason to regret that it has taken place, or its possible results in such amendments as may reconcile to it opinions which are entitled to some deference and respect. I conceive also that your declaration and Lord Grey's, made in such forcible language against the refusal to pay taxes, can not fail to make a useful impression. It is indeed highly important that the people should be admonished by those whom they consider their advocates, that they are not warranted in taking the law into their own hands because their legislators differ upon a question which has so long been that of a difference of opinion in the great councils of the nation.

"Lord Grey's reply, and particularly the concluding part, struck me, as I read it, to be admirable, and full of spirit and feeling, and I was not a little pleased to augur from it that his majesty would not be disappointed in the hope and the wish he had earnestly expressed (before any thing of the nature of the debate could be known to him), that what had occurred would not occasion the retirement from his councils of Lord Grey and his colleagues. This would, indeed, be to be most seriously lamented on every account, and, if I may judge from some of the speeches, is an event dreaded and deprecated even by the Opposition.

"I observed the expression of the Duke of Wellington's change of sentiment, or rather his admission that the change of times called for a different view of things, which you notice; but we are as yet ignorant here how the bishops, and others whose intentions were considered doubtful, have voted.

"I hope the House of Commons will not come to any resolutions hastily; they had much better be passive—let the thing work quietly, and give you time to consider dispassionately what is best to be done. Their interference with respect to any vote given by a member of the royal household would be quite unwarrantable, and Lord Ebrington would ill consult the interest of the cause he espouses if he was to propose any thing so obnoxious, and which must be repelled as an encroachment on the prerogative. The times, the temper of all concerned, require palliatives, not stimulants. I wish, indeed, that Parliament could be prorogued with the understanding that another bill should be introduced as soon as it again meets.

"Pray forgive my taking up so much of your time, and believe me to be ever, with great regard, my dear lord, your lordship's most obedient and faithful servant,

"H. Taylor.

"P.S.—Have you read the speech of Colonel Napier at the Devizes meeting? You will find it in the 'Globe' of the 7th instant.

"The Lord High Chancellor."

The speech Sir Herbert refers to was made by Sir William Napier at a Reform meeting held at Devizes. The king was furious. He instantly wrote to Lord Grey, complaining of Napier having used expressions which were manifestly intended to excite the people to rebellion, for the purpose of supporting a measure then under the consideration of Parliament. He regarded this proceeding of Napier's as so factious, that all his previous gallant conduct as a soldier could not excuse it. He regarded it as a most revolutionary act, proving him to be a bitter enemy to all constituted authority.

My impression is that the king went so far as to suggest to Lord Grey that Napier ought to be dismissed the service. I forget what Lord Grey did or what he wrote to the king on this subject. I certainly so far sympathize with the king's strong feeling, that I may say I well know my esteemed friend William Napier was quite ready to go all lengths to save the bill.

CHAPTER XXII.

State of Public Feeling. — Pressure for the Creation of Peers. — Lord Brougham has an Interview with the King.—Narrative of what passed.—Correspondence with Earl Grey on the Creation.—State of Trade.—Public Feeling in Scotland.—Letter from Lord Durham pressing the Necessity of a Creation on the Cabinet.—Sir Henry Parnell on the Condition of Ireland.—Necessity of the Creation pressed on the King.—His Repugnance to it.—Postponed till the Second Reading.—This carried by a Majority of 9.—Suspense.—Large Public Meetings.—Negotiations with Lords Harrowby and Wharncliffe.—The Bill in its new Form through the Commons.—First Contest in the Lords.—Necessity for the Creation stated to the King.—The Grey Cabinet resigns.—Lord Brougham requested to form a Ministry.—Declines.—The Duke of Wellington attempts to make a Cabinet.—Its Failure.—The King consents to the Creation.—His Authority required in Writing.—How made known to the Opposition.—Question if the Power would have been used.—Passing of the Act.—Question of the royal Assent in Person.—Given by Commission.

THE great difficulty of all now pressed upon us—the House of Lords. The long and earnest debates in the Commons had increased the enmity of the Lords, and there was even a prevailing belief among them that reaction had begun in the country, the debates having been conducted with great ability undeniably. This hope had no real foundation, and our support in the Commons continued undiminished. Our only risk of hostile divisions arose from the great security of our supporters in relying on so large a majority, that even those who most dreaded any reverse which should lead to a change of Ministry now and then lent themselves to motions which we disapproved. In short, party discipline was somewhat relaxed by the too great confidence of our friends in our strength. The bill being thrown out in the Lords raised so great a ferment in the country, and made such a rally round us in the Commons, as plainly showed how ill-grounded all the Tory hopes of reaction were. But now began the craving of our most staunch supporters, and of others rather belonging to the Radical party, for the creation of peers. First, we were required to have a nominal prorogation in order that the bill might be again brought in. A deputation of Westminster Radicals waited on Grey, with a kind of threat that they would oppose the Government if this course were refused. I had the same threat served upon me by the same parties. They received the most unqualified refusal, though in civil terms, from both of us.

The shortening of the recess was the next object of these parties, and in this desire they were joined by our supporters generally. A Cabinet was held early in November, at which the day of meeting was fully considered. This was one of the very few occasions on which we had any difference of opinion, and it was with great reluctance that I found myself unable to take the same view with Grey. Indeed, in the present state of the country, I held an immediate termination of the agitation occasioned by the bill to be absolutely necessary, to prevent the spread of such riots as had taken place at Nottingham and Bristol; and I felt sure that the more discreet portion of our adversaries would take the same view of the matter, such as the duke and the *waverers*, as Harrowby, Wharncliffe, and others were called, who desired a compromise, which was impossible, when the country had taken up the cry of "the bill, the whole bill, and nothing but the bill." When we had fully discussed the subject of meeting Parliament, I felt obliged, and Althorp was of the same mind, to divide, and we had a considerable majority for immediate meeting. Grey was so kind and amiable about our proceeding that Althorp said it made him quite regret what we had done. Our reasons, however, were quite conclusive.

But all this time the great difficulty remained of the Lords. There were constant reports of changes since October, and names were given; but upon inquiry we found the reports had no foundation. The feeling that we must have more strength by creating peers, had been strong at the prorogation; and all my correspondence during the fortnight (my whole vacation) that I was at Brougham showed the anxiety and even impatience of our friends, not merely the violent party, but the more reflecting and considerate, to be increasing daily. I had occasion to write to the king (through Sir H. Taylor, of course), on my way to town, and I thought it right to prepare him for a request that he would help us in this respect; and when I got to town I received a doubtful answer, which some of us thought rather favorable, but I only considered it as showing that he (the king) had thought very much on the subject, and had not been able to consider the suggestion favorably.

In November I went to Brighton, where I saw the king, and on the 28th I had a conversation with him, of which the following is a very full minute written by me at the time:

I was at the Pavilion from half-past eleven till two, and about two hours of that time with the king. I found him extremely well, and in peculiarly good spirits. He sat opposite to the light, as he generally does, and I opposite to him.

After a few words upon the Bankruptcy Court appointments, and approving of Erskine for chief judge, and Rose for puisne, on Baron Bayley's giving up—and also approving the grounds in which the terms of the latter (an Act of Parliament for his salary) had been refused—his majesty himself began upon the Reform Bill—a thing I have hardly ever, perhaps not ever, known him do before. Indeed he has often avoided the subject, and never more than when I passed two days at Windsor on the eve of its coming on in the Lords. To-day he was very desirous to discuss every thing relating to it, and the whole conversation was occupied with it.

He repeatedly expressed his great regret and astonishment (strongly marked) at the conduct of those who had prevented it from going to a committee. He said there was nothing they might not have debated there—even Schedule A (qualifying this remark by saying, "Suppose I agreed with them—as I certainly do not—in regard to Schedule A, even that question might have been raised in the committee"). He asked me how I could account for such a proceeding, which seemed so great an error even upon their own views, and supposing they only wanted most safely for themselves to alter the bill. I said I always looked to an adversary as acting upon some views of his own advantage which might be more or less judicious, but seldom supposed any gross blunder; and that I imagined they had reckoned upon a better division with proxies, and were distrustful of their forces attending, especially should there be any excitement in the people as the committee went on. He said, still he thought this a blunder, for they could, after being beaten in the way alluded to in committee, throw it out on the third reading. He had alluded to Lords Wharncliffe and Harrowby, and I set him right as to the former's degree of influence, drawing a distinction between the two; and I also endeavored to prevent any idea of negotiation with Wharncliffe so as to modify the bill, representing his communications with Lord Grey in their real light (which he seemed to have understood). He expressed his wonder at Lord Harrowby's opposing the second reading, and asked how I explained it. I said that he had certainly either changed his intention within a week before the debate began, or at least had become fixed in his latter resolution, which I accounted for by the irresolution of their party, and their various opinions all ending in referring the matter to the decision of a firm man—viz., the Duke of Wellington—who had insisted on the step being taken, and they complied. He said, still he could not account for the Duke of Wellington doing so, for it seemed unaccountable in any view of his policy. (This introduced the former part of the conversation, which I have transposed.)

We conversed on various parts of the bill—and he dwelt on the London districts—the qualification varying in different places, and the want of seats for Ministers and Crown lawyers. I alluded to the change of my own opinion as to the qualification, and explained about the state of the small and even many large towns (as Leeds) in respect of [*illegible*] houses, and the difficulties at all times, and impossibility now, of having the varied qualification. I reminded him how strongly I had expressed myself in the debate on the second reading on this part of the subject, admitting my original leaning towards the varied qualification. (This reference to what I said as to the qualification was twice made in the course of the conversation—both at the present part of it, and when conversing on what might have been discussed in committee; but I then also repeated that all I could have done was to secure a discussion of the subject, and that I had said I could not honestly hold out any hopes of my coming round to them on the matter.)

Upon the seats for Government I also referred to my speech, where I had confessed this difficulty; but I said that though I should be well pleased the other parties, either Tory or doctrinaire, broached it, we never could; indeed he agreed that it was a far more violent innovation than any thing we had ever been charged with. When I said that I understood the doctrinaire party were not all averse to it, he inquired all about Bentham and others, which I explained. But I showed how little risk there was of *no* places being accessible, and explained as to several of the boroughs being sure to be in whole or part in the hands of powerful proprietors. I said I was persuaded the evils of the London districts were greatly exaggerated, and that good members were sure to be returned by most of them.

He very distinctly said that *he* was quite clear the shock of the change was much overrated, and that when once the bill was passed, things would slide into any easy and quiet posture as before, but that there was no quieting the alarm of the Tories as to this, and that the great matter was to prevent the certain shock which would result from the bill being thrown out again. He dwelt on this, and I stated all that occurred to me of its mischiefs. (I think this introduced the last head of conversation, which I have again transposed.)

I more than once referred to the loss of the bill as synonymous with the breaking up of the Government, and the signal for every kind of evil—but not in this part of the conversation. One of the occasions I took for this allusion was while talking of the possible consequences of going into committee last time, instead of throwing it out on the second reading. I said that, if he had been defeated upon a matter not affecting the principle of the bill (though of such moment as to injure it greatly in our estimation), the question would have arisen, Shall we, because of this injury done to the measure, give it up, and break up the Government, and leave the king and country in the state that must necessarily follow, or shall we take all the good that the measure can still give?—and that there was always a chance of the latter alternative being adopted; but that any such thing was utterly out of the question before the committee.

Peel's name being mentioned, he said he could not comprehend him at all, and that, except the Duke of Wellington, every one of the last Government, when he saw them on their resigning, had stated their belief of some reform being necessary. On my saying I had always given them credit for rather going out on the Civil List division than on my Reform motion, he asked if I thought that would have been carried. I said I knew it as certainly as one could know any thing of the kind, and by twenty-seven majority, according to my calculation.

A good deal of conversation ensued as to the plans, and what they could be, of the Duke of Wellington and Peel. I said, after a good many observations both from his majesty and myself, that I really thought it a plain case enough; that though some, even a considerable number, of the anti-reformers were otherwise, yet they (the Tory leaders) were *politicians;* and that the Duke of Wellington and Peel no doubt wanted to throw out the Ministry, that they might come in and propose the bill themselves, which, after what we had seen, was quite on the cards. He almost anticipated this topic (of the Catholic question), and had it out before I named it; but said, even supposing that to be their object, it was to be so considered that they might have tried it in a safe way, by letting the bill pass, resisting it all the while, and then endeavoring to get into power and carry on the Government upon the ground of the Reform when carried. This began to be a somewhat delicate and difficult speculation (viz., what was to happen after I was myself officially defunct), so I only observed, that I supposed they thought that plan would have many fewer facilities.

He conversed a good deal about Peel, and his conduct on the Catholic question. I gave Peel all manner of credit for it, and said he had really made a very great sacrifice, but that he could not both be praised for that and expect to retain what he lost; and that it was quite clear he had entirely lost all influence in the country, both with Church and Tories.

He repeatedly expressed his surprise at the ultra Tories taking the line they did; and I showed him how they were actually joining the Hunt and rabble party as far as they could, in order to spite the Government and oppose the bill.

I dwelt on many other topics connected with the subject, and among others on the importance of his majesty using his influence with those about him, such as Lord M.; and stating that the Tories were still as busy as ever representing him (the king) as unfriendly to the bill.

He seemed aware of this, and only spoke of Lord M. as under the Duke of Cumberland's influence, from old anti-Catholic connection.

There was a good deal said by his majesty about the late king changing his opinion on the Catholic question, on which subject he (present king) and Lord Donoughmore, in 1806, used to be quite anxious about his committing himself so far and so indiscriminately. He said the late king had quite forgotten it before he died.

I saw Sir Herbert Taylor for about half an hour, and dwelt with him on the chief of the above topics, such as the impossibility of any change of the franchise. I also saw some of the females of the family of both sides, and intimated the risk they were in of having the public feeling directed towards them, were they to persist against the bill.

Of course abundance of denial here, as far as overt acts went, but candid avowals of direct enmity to the bill.

I forgot to mention that the king, on my speaking of the Archbishop of York's strong opinion that, *as a bishop*, he was bound to look with dismay at another rejection, he dwelt much on this and on the duty of bishops to prevent such horrors as might ensue. I repeated much of what I had represented the last audience I had, on the state of the country, about the universality of the feeling for the bill; that its enemies were either a few of Hunt's mob, or people small in number, though important in point of property. He said the only person he could find who was against *all* change was Lord Mansfield; and *he* had held a different language to him in April, saying he was not against Reform, but the bill. He said the Duke of Wellington himself had changed. I observed that he certainly had, late in the day, made a most surprising declaration on the subject.

He desired me (when I said I would send him a corrected copy of my speech, which he received very kindly) to send him Lord Harrowby's, and any others that had been *corrected.*

I don't distinctly recollect if it was to his majesty or to Sir

Herbert Taylor, or both, that I explained the degree in which newspapers *influence*, and the degree in which they only *indicate* the public opinion; and the difference between the London and provincial papers in this respect (the latter being found to follow the opinions of their readers much more closely).

One of the females (hostile) came upon this part of the subject, and said the "Times" was well known to change about, if ten less were sold. I said that might be an exaggeration, but that undoubtedly they generally followed the *city* opinion — and gave the remarkable instance of the Princess of Wales's case, in May, 1813.

I omitted to mention that the conversation on the bill began with his majesty asking what we had done yesterday at the Cabinet. I told him we had gone through a great many important points, and cleared the way for deciding them, which would be done to-day or on Wednesday.

I also omitted what he said of an idea having got abroad of divisions among us, to which I gave the most positive contradiction, and expressed my surprise how those stories could have originated. He said that Lord Durham was thought to keep himself aloof, but he did not seem himself at all to think this owing to any difference; and when I spoke of the state of his family in the distress his loss had occasioned to them, he spoke with the greatest feeling and kindness, and inquired about his regaining his spirits by the excursion to Brussels.*

This, however, and the knowledge of the reports industriously spread of differences of opinion between myself and Lord Grey, made me very explicitly restate my own opinion as to the bill, both to his majesty and afterwards to Sir Herbert Taylor, to whom I most distinctly said that I was just as firm a friend of the measure, and as determined to go all lengths for it, as Lord Grey or any one else could be, whatever might have been my opinion before it was first brought in, as to a smaller measure being sufficient; and I added that I did not feel thus now merely as being bound in honor to my colleagues, but that my opinion fully and heartily went along with my duty.

---

* Lord Durham's elder son had died on 24th September.

To resume the correspondence on the peerage question.

[*Private.*] TO LORD GREY.

"Brougham, December 29, 1831.

"MY DEAR LORD GREY,—I received your letter yesterday, and though it did not set me upon considering a subject which I have almost exclusively been thinking of since I saw you, it makes me give you the result of my deliberations.

"Every thing I have either seen, heard, or considered since the last Cabinet I attended, convinces me more and more of the course we ought to take—namely, to begin with a partial creation, say of ten or twelve—some to be made; others, the greater part, called up—as, for example, say four creations and eight calls. But these are details, and whatever way you arrange them signifies little compared with the measure itself. As for the numbers—if only three or four are new peer ages, I should not quarrel with fifteen in all.

"From this I expect a confident belief to get abroad, first at Court, then in the Lords, that you can make as many as you please, and this *may* prevent the necessity of making many, perhaps any, more. But I think we must go farther, and contemplate the *possibility* of that necessity as not a very remote possibility, and we ought, I clearly think, to be prepared for it. We may, after all, find that if not on the second reading, yet in the committee, a factious vote may in substance and effect destroy the bill. If this is done on the second reading, we are remediless; if in the committee, we can only recover the loss by means of fresh creations. It is also very likely that we may, on the eve of the second reading, discover that our force is short, and that more peers are wanted. Now, as I assume the absolute necessity of our not allowing the bill to be lost in any way, and that when the time comes (if it should come) for a second creation, we must be prepared to press it, I think it follows that an understanding should be come to with the king before that time arrives, and that we should not delay until we find it necessary to press the immediate creation.

"*First*, as to what this understanding should be.

"It appears to me that you should signify to the king the absolute necessity of the bill being carried, and that this is the only means of preventing confusion; that bad as carrying a measure by force of creations may be, the necessity of the case justifies it, and the expectations of the anti-reformers themselves are everywhere, in-doors as well as out, prepared for it—as a measure, indeed, which they would assuredly resort to themselves; that his servants think it quite necessary to submit to him this their conviction, and hope he will allow them to say that, with these views, they rely upon his sanctioning such a creation as may be found sufficient to insure the passing; that the necessity of making any more, and if any, the number required, can only be known when the second reading approaches, but that it would be extremely unfair to him not to explain ourselves thus early, and to express a hope that he feels with us the necessity of doing whatever may be requisite.

"In conversation you may throw in a good deal more, and the king is sure to write about it afterwards, so that you may make the statement more precise, as you find occasion, the object being plain (which you have in view)—viz., to be assured of such an agreement with you upon the peerage question as shall prevent the possibility of your being left in the distressing predicament, so dangerous to the public peace, of having made a few peers, and then being unable to make all that prove necessary for carrying the bill.

"*Secondly*, as to the time when you should come to this understanding. It can only be, either now, when you propose the partial creation, or afterwards, when the bill comes up.

"I strongly incline to the former. It is far better to do it all at once, infinitely more comfortable for yourself, and far more fair towards the king, to whom, I must say, we owe, both personally and politically, as much as ministers can owe, to a king, or indeed as any set of men can owe to any individual. But I also think the earlier time very important for the success of the whole measure. If it *can* be carried without a fresh creation (I mean beyond the first, which I don't regard at all as making peers to force the bill), every one must allow it will be a great advantage; and I feel quite persuaded that no sooner is such an understanding come to than the courtiers will smell it out, and then let it out—and so the necessity of acting on it may in all probability never arise.

"I own I feel so strongly the propriety of the two things being broached to the king at the same time, that, supposing the Cabinet now to feel assured that, if necessary, they will recommend the additional creation, I hardly think they could suppress this and recommend the first creation alone.

"It may be said on this subject (of the understanding) that you are doing to the king what his father did for you in 1807. The difference is plain: you don't say, 'Give us a pledge, much less a pledge in writing, as to what your majesty will do at a future time;' you only say, 'We hold certain opinions very strongly and very clearly on the most important of all matters, already in course of being considered practically, and we think it essential that your majesty should know this opinion, and that we shall counsel you accordingly, if the occasion should arise. We also think it quite useless to continue in your service if there is such a difference of opinion between us as makes it clear our advice will be rejected.'

"It is rather, in fact, giving a fair and timely notice than asking for a pledge. But even if we asked for something like a pledge, an assurance of his agreeing with us, and being prepared to act accordingly if need should be—the case is widely different from 1807. For then the king required a *general* pledge, applicable to all times, and to remote and unknown circumstances. We only now ask an assurance of agreement in opinion upon our specific line of conduct, to be pursued on an emergency fast approaching, and of a known and defined nature. Believe me ever yours,

"H. Brougham.

"I assure you I feel extremely annoyed at not being in town upon this occasion, but I can not travel fast enough to arrive in time, having been unwell."

[*Private.*] TO LORD GREY.

"Brougham, December 31, 1831.

"My dear Lord Grey,—Notwithstanding the unconscionable length of my last letter, I omitted some things which I must now add. Indeed they signify less, because they are more reasons than opinions or suggestions.

"The state of trade and of the country generally is, in my

firm belief, *very alarming*—I mean if the bill be delayed. All I have seen and heard since we parted convinces me that the question is not whether this Ministry shall be broken up or not—nor whether we who form it shall be collectively or individually undone (I mean in public character); but whether the whole country shall not be undone also, and apparently at least—perhaps really—through our means. This makes one naturally embrace means of preventing such a catastrophe very different from any we could desire to see. I don't much rely on the arguments of those who are for *infusing* fresh vigor, as they term it, into the House of Lords. But yet, as a creation may be necessary to save the country, and if necessary must be resorted to, I own this consideration (of improving the House of Lords) is in my mind, at least, a very feeble set-off against the admitted evil, which no one feels more than I do, of a *coup d'état.* You thus are lowering the House of Lords far less than at first sight appears. Of course I am now speaking not of the first or partial creation, but the unlimited one to be made 'if need be,' and to be, in my judgment, announced *now* to the king.

"There is one very remarkable circumstance which I hear from all quarters: the Tories, both in town and country (I mean not the highest of them, as peers, but the middle and even upper classes of Tories), are desirous of the creation to secure the bill. I had heard long ago that some even of our House of Lords adversaries were sneering at us for not making a batch, which they laid their account with; but I am now speaking not of these, but of persons out of Parliament.

"I have also heard a good deal of the state of Scotland, and it is truly more frightful than I had believed. I assure you, Abercromby does not confine himself on this subject to general statements. I had a long talk with him about the Scotch t'other day; and I should say there never was a people so determined not to be baffled. My opinion is that the mischief will begin there, and in such force as will reduce the Government, in whose hands soever it may be, to terms in forty-eight hours.

"There is one, and but one, way out of all this which I have been able to discover—I mean if we don't carry the bill. The king may be so averse to a creation, that he may say he would rather run some risk, and Wellington and Co. may undertake to carry the bill without peer-making, which he possibly might be able to do through our support.

"But, first, I don't feel that making peers is by any means so dreadful a thing as to induce me either to sacrifice myself, or advise you to sacrifice yourself, rather than do it; and I do assure you I should almost as lief see the former sacrifice as the latter. I say this without any compunction, because I really feel it.

"Next, I see extreme difficulties in the way of such a plan, supposing we agreed to the self-sacrifice. And, lastly, I think it is far more likely to fail than succeed. Suppose Wellington in force, Peel up to the mark, and all other obstacles removed, the country would never believe it was not destroyed — it would get enraged, and at all events would require a far larger measure than the bill. I believe the convulsion would be not, perhaps, quite so certain as by a rejection, but more probable than not; and for the mere *chance* of escaping it, what sense is there in incurring the certain evils of the sacrifice above mentioned? I mean the sacrifice of the whole influence of the Liberal and constitutional party. Yours ever most sincerely, H. BROUGHAM.

"I am better, but very weak, and shall have to take four or five days for the journey. Was the presentation of Moreton a lapse? for I see the bishop has presented to his living."

Lord Grey, always averse to the creation, had so expressed his opinion before the loss of the bill.

The following paper, written by Lord Durham, was read in Cabinet on the 2d January:

FROM LORD DURHAM.

"Sudbrook Park, December 29, 1831.

"MY DEAR LORD GREY,—I feel it incumbent on me no longer to delay declaring to you my decided opinion that the Government ought to advise the king to create a sufficient number of peers to insure the passing of the Reform Bill.

"I conceive that not only were we pledged to the country to propose a measure of Reform as extensive as the last, but, as a necessary consequence, are bound to take every means in our power to further the passing of that measure in the same form as that in which we introduced it, as to extent and efficiency.

"To consent to or connive at any other course of proceeding, would not only be a breach of our pledges, but a gross act of duplicity. It would be a mockery to carry the bill through all its stages in the Commons by large and increasing majorities — resisting their every attempt to impair its efficiency or modify its provisions—and then propose it for a second reading in the Lords with a probability of being again defeated, but at any rate with the certainty that we shall be so weak in the committee as to be unable to resist not only those alterations which we had successfully defeated in the Commons, but also additional encroachments on the efficiency of the bill, which would no longer enable us to assert that the principle of the measure had been maintained.

"Then also would come the great responsibility of deciding whether we should propose to the Commons an acquiescence in the mutilated bill, or its total rejection, in consequence of its being no longer the same measure which we had recommended to the king and proposed to Parliament.

"I say, therefore, that the adoption of those means which are necessary to insure to us a majority in the committee, as well as on the second reading, is absolutely essential to the honest redemption of our pledges to the country — pledges which, I repeat, are not merely limited to the introduction of the bill, but must extend to and affect every stage of it until it has received the royal assent.

"To insure that successful issue we have already the king's approbation, and a declared and overwhelming majority in the Commons. Our weakness lies in the other branch of the legislature. There we were defeated before, and there again consists the danger. It is now, I believe, admitted that all hopes of conversion sufficient to enable us to carry even the second reading are abandoned; and even the few conversions which are expected, no one asserts will be of the slightest advantage to us in the committee. We may, therefore, fairly anticipate that we shall find a majority of twenty against the bill on the second reading, unless it is suffered to go into the committee without a division, for the purpose of more quietly destroying it there; in which case we should then, as before, be met by the original majority of forty, if not more, on all questions affecting the vital parts of the measure.

"Are we then prepared to carry the bill into the House of Lords in these circumstances, knowing, as we must do, that its rejection or mutilation is thus inevitable? Ignorance of these facts, and their consequences, we can not plead; and, indeed, they are not only notorious to ourselves, but are the subject of general remark and discussion.

"If we are not prepared to pursue this line of conduct, as I trust we are not, there is but one other to adopt, namely, a large creation of peers.

"To this proceeding several objections have been stated, to which I shall now call your attention.

"1st. It is asserted that the carrying the measure by such means is unconstitutional. This I deny. I believe it to be in accordance with the best principles of the constitution.

"The king's power of creating peers is unlimited and undeniable. In the exercise of that privilege, he is absolute and uncontrolled by the forms of the constitution. It can then only be the motives which are supposed to influence that exercise, and the effects which follow it, which can be impugned as unconstitutional. Prerogative is defined to consist in the discretionary power of acting for the public good, when the positive laws are silent. If that discretionary power be abused to the public detriment, the prerogative is exerted in an unconstitutional manner.

"If, on the other hand, it is called forth for the public advantage, and the safety of the state, it is as wise and just as it is constitutional.

"How, then, tried by this test, does the present case stand?

"The king has recommended, the House of Commons has adopted, and the country sanctioned, a measure which the House of Lords alone seems determined to reject.

"That harmony which, therefore, ought to exist between the three branches of the legislature is interrupted, and the confidence and attachment of the people is shaken. This can not be remedied by an acquiescence in the objections of the one opposing branch; the utmost that could be attained thereby would be delay, attended necessarily by incessant irritation. The other alternative, therefore, remains, to which I have before adverted, and the adoption of which, in order to produce that harmony in the three powers of the state, by the exercise of a recognized, admitted prerogative, can be no violation of the constitution, but is in strict accordance with its fundamental principles.

"If, indeed, the case was different, and the king were advised to create peers for the purpose of defeating the declared wishes of the Commons and the country, and the ascertained intentions of the Lords, not only an unconstitutional, but an unnecessary act would be counselled — unconstitutional, because perpetuating dissensions between the two Houses, but unnecessary, because the same object could be attained by a refusal of the royal assent.

"2dly. It is said that the House of Lords would be destroyed by such an increase of its numbers.

"To that I answer, that, by calling up the eldest sons of peers, we shall not eventually increase its numbers to any great amount; but even if we did, I apprehend no danger from the House consisting of 450, or even 500, instead of 418 members. Neither its votes nor its deliberations would be deteriorated by the accession of talent, property, and liberality of opinions. On the contrary, the creations made under the Pitt system render such an adjustment of the balance absolutely necessary, not only for the carrying this particular measure, but for the support of those principles of freedom and constitutional government, without a strict adherence to which no Administration can now pretend to acquire or retain the confidence of the king or the people. As at present constituted, it is evident that the House of Lords is not in unison with the spirit of the age; it is opposed to the king and the people. Hence arise, on the part of the latter, complaints, discontent, and doubts, openly expressed, whether its existence is not incompatible with the happiness and welfare of the country. To check at once these opinions, and to remove these doubts by enabling the House to assume an attitude more in consonance with the general feeling, would be surely an act tending not to its destruction, but to its preservation.

"3dly. It is feared that a creation would not answer the purpose we have in view, because so many peers would be so disgusted at the addition to their numbers that they would be impelled to oppose the bill. I can not believe that such will be the case, because, until I witness the fact, I can not imagine that any peer, having voted for the last Reform Bill on the ground of its being a measure essential to the prosperity of the country and safety of the state, would vote against a similar bill now solely because to him had been added a sufficient number of colleagues to prevent his vote from being a second time rendered useless and inefficient.

"Besides, he would be aware that no vote of his against the bill would remedy the evil of which he complained; his change would therefore be useless as far as regarded the creation of peers, and most mischievous in respect to the consequences which he must be conscious would follow a second rejection of the Reform Bill. Any desertion, therefore, of the bill by reformers on account of a creation would be so notorious a violation of principle, without the slightest consequent advantage, that I can not believe it possible.

"For these reasons, and on these grounds, I have formed the opinion which I announced to you at the commencement of this communication; and I can not conclude without declaring my conviction that on the adoption of this measure depends not only the character of the Administration, but the preservation of the country from civil commotions of the most alarming and dangerous nature, etc., etc., etc.

"DURHAM."

FROM LORD GREY.

"East Sheen, January 1, 1832.

"MY DEAR CHANCELLOR,—I wish you a happy new-year. A person dined here yesterday, who unfortunately has no such prospect—poor Czartoryski.* It is really heart-breaking to see him; and now these d—d Russians are doing all they can to throw the whole Belgian affair into confusion. It is to be regretted that we had no power of sending a fleet into the Baltic last summer to settle the matter in Poland.

* Prince Adam Czartoryski, born 1770, died 1861.

"I have come nearer to your view of the matter of the peerage than I thought I ever could have done; and am much inclined to new creations at present, or before the meeting of Parliament, to the amount and in the manner you propose. But there will be a great difference of opinion in the Cabinet upon it. A letter from Lansdowne shows that his objections are not at all diminished. He comes to the Cabinet tomorrow. Palmerston and Melbourne are equally opposed to it. The Duke of Richmond also is against it, but I do not think his objections so insurmountable as they appeared to be some time ago. If this difference of opinion should go the length of producing resignations, you will perceive that it would be quite fatal.

"But there is another and a greater difficulty on the part of the king. You know how strong his objections were. Finding them supported by so many members of the Cabinet, he is less likely to give way. He expresses great confidence, too, in our being able to carry the bill on the second reading, and—without any alterations that could be considered as affecting principle or real efficiency—through the committee. This belief, proceeding, as I conjecture, from the general language that has been held to him by some of the anti-reformers, will encourage him at least in postponing any determination till we shall have better means of judging of the disposition of the House of Lords. In short, this question assumes a very embarrassing shape, and I hope it will not be long before we have you here to assist us with your counsel; for though your opinion is very fully and very clearly stated in your letter, there is nothing like personal discussion.

"They say the Duke of Wellington is recovering, but from all I hear of his case, taking the best view of it, there is not much chance of his being soon equal to much exertion. But the Tories do not seem to lose heart. I hear their language, founded on the assumption that the king will not make peers, is as violent and as confident as ever; and Lyndhurst is becoming more and more an avowed and prominent supporter of their views. Ever yours, GREY.

"I go to Brighton on Tuesday, and will let you know the result; though I hope to hear before my return that you are on your way to town."

FROM LORD GREY.

"January 4, 1832.

"DEAR CHANCELLOR,—I hope this will not find you at Brougham, but I take the chance of your being there to say that my conversation with the king has been very satisfactory, and that I have no doubt he will do what the Cabinet may advise; but he desires to have it in writing. He is, however, extremely anxious, and even nervous, as to this matter; but straightforward, confiding, and cordial as usual. I hope you will be with us as soon as you can, for really things are becoming very critical.

"Ever yours, GREY.

"I return to town on Friday."

The constant wish of the king, and his only plan for relieving the ministers, was a coalition—what he termed "an extended Administration;" and this he used both before the bill passed and to remove the difficulties in the House of Lords afterwards. I thus answered Lord Grey's letter:

[*Private.*] TO LORD GREY.

"Brougham, January 5, 1832.

"MY DEAR LORD GREY,—I am extremely vexed at being detained, and therefore I must trouble you with another letter. I may begin with mentioning one or two facts which have accidentally come to my knowledge, and—as particular facts are little to be trusted, either to believe or to reason upon, unless they agree with a general course of appearances, and with the probabilities of the case—I assure you I should not mention these, did they not seem to me plainly to fall within this description. But I have them from quarters, one of them especially, where there was no reasoning or speculating at all.

"The Opposition in Scotland are extremely sanguine, and the Duke of Buccleuch, I *know*, is going about in all directions bragging in a confident way. This signifies little, perhaps; but he says, as I hear, less publicly, that they rely on throwing out the bill as a certainty—that they have lost no lay peers, but gained a few come of age—and that their great object is to prevent new peers being made, by making the Government believe they won't oppose the bill on the second reading, and then throwing it out when we shall have fallen into the snare. Now I do not so positively vouch for this latter part of it, but I believe something very like it has been said by the duke and his set. A man who could talk in this way of such a plot is not, perhaps, very likely to have invented it. He openly says, as I am told, that the king will not make peers, and he patronizes addresses which thank him (the king) for resisting the solicitations of his ministers to make peers. You will be able to judge if this part of my information is incorrect, by inquiring whether any such have been presented, though it is just possible they may be only now getting up.

"Again, I find from Mulgrave that the language of the Opposition, with whom he is connected (I suppose by both blood and marriage*), is very much the same in substance, though somewhat more discreet. He says, 'They are just as determined as ever to throw out the bill, and do not anticipate any desertions to an extent which would take from them that power. This,' he adds, 'I heard in a way I think I can rely on,' and he mentions some other things of the same kind.

"Now, to resume a speculation I once before threw out, and have thought of a good deal since: Suppose they, full of alarm at the chance of our making peers (which haunts them beyond all other fears), were, as the time draws near, to have misgivings about the king, and to carry a resolution in the Lords? If the king were then wavering, that would decide him. If I were speaking of almost any other thing, I should say that would furnish him a pretext, did he want one; but I sincerely think he is not the kind of man to go this way to work. But even if he were not wavering, it is one thing to advise a creation before, and another to advise it in the face of such a vote. Then consider the fatal consequences. I don't mean fatal merely to ourselves individually, and as a body agreeing on the most important questions of policy, but fatal to the country, which would thus be delivered over

* He married the eldest daughter of Sir Thomas Liddell, the first Lord Ravensworth. Lord Mulgrave was created Marquess of Normanby in 1838, and died in 1863.

to a contest between the Wellington people and the Radicals—possibly to a union of the two classes; for it *must* happen that we should be utterly ruined in public estimation for having delayed to take the necessary steps till the moment was past. We never should get credit for not intending to create peers; but we should be charged, and justly, with having meant it, but delayed it till we could not. Now, the bill being thrown out is the same thing as general convulsion; but I think that mischief would be much increased, and the recovery from it greatly postponed, by the total destruction of all confidence in the leaders of the Liberal party.

"Notwithstanding the language held by the Opposition (and their resolution, I verily believe, to act up to it, *if they can* with any effect), I am quite persuaded that their leaders, and even many others, in their hearts believe we shall make peers, and at any rate that we shall try it. This comes round to one in various ways; and there is no doubt they would, were they in our position. As for the talk one hears that Wellington carried the Catholic question without it—to be sure he did, and by a large majority, and so he had no occasion for a creation.

"Of one thing we may be quite sure—the nearer the time comes, the more likely are they to perceive the difficulties they will get into by letting the bill get into the committee, and this is most likely to make them try the same game they before were driven to by something of the same difficulties. The fears they were at one time in are a good deal lessened, first by mere time, and next and chiefly by finding the mob (who alone, they think, break windows and burn houses) taking part against the bill.

"I therefore reckon on their venturing to oppose the second reading a good deal more than I once did. If I have a practical doubt remaining, it is not about the necessity of an indication being now given by partial creation, but whether that is enough. Ever yours, H. BROUGHAM.

"In favor of acting now, Wellington's state of health is not to be lost sight of. They will, in this and other respects, be far better prepared if they have longer notice."

I had written very fully to Lord Grey, explaining my plans

of a partial creation without delay, to show we had the power from the king, and should be prepared to go farther if we found it necessary; in short, it was the very plan which ultimately succeeded in enabling us to pass the bill without any creations at all:

[*Private.*] "House of Lords.

"MY DEAR LORD GREY,—I have so strong, and even *serious*, an opinion on the peerage question, that I have written all that occurs to me, and wish you calmly and fully to read it. I wish it, of course, to be considered as matter of full discussion, and not, *à la* Grant, as any thing like an ultimatum.

"Pray, when you have read it, return it to me, as of course I have no copy. I wish you could send it by a messenger across to Sefton's to-night or to-morrow morning. It is a convenient paper for discussion, because it puts the subject in various lights. As for your *little coronation* batch, one thing is lucky, Berkeley being one, we get *two* votes; for his brother Moreton* will, *I hope* and *trust*, take his seat at length.

"But *pray, pray* don't forget Hughes, one of our richest and most steady, and, in all money occasions, our most generous supporter. Yours ever, H. BROUGHAM."

[*Private.*] "Thursday,

"MY DEAR LORD GREY,—I found you had left town, which prevented me from calling in Downing Street.

"This flirtation of Wharncliffe with Lyndhurst and Ellenborough is only one of the many effects which the king's way of talking is sure to produce. I don't think Wharncliffe himself would fly back on being assured that one of his two fears (new peers) was at an end; for he really feels the other (the

* Thomas Moreton Fitzhardinge, fifth son of Frederick, fifth Earl of Berkeley. His eldest brother William claimed to be Earl of Berkeley; but his claim was disallowed by the House of Lords, it being proved that his father had not married until the 16th of May, 1796. Thomas was born in October, 1796, and was therefore, *de jure*, Earl of Berkeley; but, from regard to his mother's character, never would take the title. In 1831, William, the first-born, was created Baron Segrave, and in 1841 Earl Fitzhardinge. He died, *s. p.* in 1857, when that earldom became extinct.

country) to be what it is, most pressing. But I am sure Harrowby and others will go off at once when they are persuaded peers can not be made, which the king's whole language is setting about—for instance, to Keat, the surgeon, which I only mention to show how habitual it must be with him. Is there no way of suggesting to him that this is sure to destroy the bill—that is, to make a majority vote against Schedule A—and that he will thus be driven to the very thing he hates most—namely, peers? As for *our* position, I quite agree with you in thinking he had much better turn us out than cut our throats in this way, for it has all the effect of doing so. The difficulty is in knowing how to give him the suggestion, and I only want you to consider of it.

"Is it too late to have some communication with Lyndhurst and Wharncliffe as to what they mean to do? I asked Dover to see Wharncliffe and converse with him; but your communicating directly would, if it be possible, be on every account far better. Yours ever, H. BROUGHAM.

"I am going to Stoke till Tuesday. If the king goes on in this way, would it not be well to ask him to make one peer of each kind—as Lord Francis Osborne, some Irish peer, and some eldest son—in order to contradict the reports with effect? I mean before the meeting."

After Christmas, when we had nearly carried the new bill through the Commons, our greater difficulties came upon us thick and threefold with the peers. In February I had the following letter from Parnell on the difficult subject of Ireland:

[*Private.*] FROM SIR HENRY PARNELL.

"89 Jermyn Street, February 18, 1832.

"MY DEAR LORD BROUGHAM,—Doctor Doyle is in London, at No. 23 Bury Street, and I hope you will take an opportunity of seeing him.* You will be able to judge, from what he tells you, how far my communications about Ireland were accurate.

"I discontinued writing to you in consequence of a communication I had with Lord Althorp early in December. This

* James Doyle, Roman Catholic Bishop of Kildare, celebrated for his pamphlets and speeches during the Emancipation struggle, born 1787, died 1834.

made me come to the conclusion that there was not any chance of having O'Connell and other Catholics appointed to office so long as the Cabinet existed in its present form.

"I now again call your attention to Ireland, because I am still more convinced than ever that, if measures are not soon taken to stop the progress of the conspiracy of the lower orders against the laws, their success with regard to tithes will lead to a greater effort to have the union repealed, and to a still greater subsequent effort to separate the two countries.

"There is but one remedy for this, and that is to secure the support of all those persons in Ireland who possess influence over the people—namely, O'Connell, the leading Catholic members, and the Catholic clergy. Good public measures of concession now produce no effect in pacifying the people, from their minds being indisposed to see any thing in its true character, and therefore the first thing to be done is to cure this mental disease.

"But as no such remedy will be applied by the present Cabinet, and as the inevitable result of this will be those disasters which I have just mentioned, it has become essentially necessary that such a change should be made in the Cabinet, on the earliest opportunity, as will secure a fit system of government for Ireland.

"A change in the Cabinet is required on other considerations, for there has been so much mismanagement, that an opinion universally prevails that the present Administration can not long survive even the successful carrying of the Reform Bill.

"There are several questions which must come before the House of Commons, on which the Government is by no means secure of majorities.

"Recurring to Ireland, I must again press on you the urgency of your taking an active and decided part in its affairs.

"You are the only member of the Cabinet who at all comprehends the case. Most of your colleagues are not only ignorant of it, but, as it seems, incapable of understanding it. I assure you that open war will have to be carried on in Ireland to maintain the dominion of England, unless the management of its affairs be placed in other hands. Believe me yours faithfully, H. PARNELL."

Holland had the most sound opinions and right feelings on the necessity of putting down the disturbances in both parts of the kingdom, Ireland as well as England.

FROM LORD HOLLAND.

[*Private and confidential.*]

"Thursday, March 7, 1832.

"DEAR BROUGHAM,—For God's sake take good care that our winning the plate in one course does not slacken our pace or shorten our distance in the other. Believe me, the only friends in the majority who really prefer us to other men, do so from a persuasion that we are as earnest, as determined, and will be as prompt in promoting measures of the opposite tendency, as we have been in this; for this reason, I do not like our English Church measure — milk-and-water as it may be—being postponed. A measure short of men's wishes may disappoint; but even that defect does not breed suspicion and distrust so much as delay and hesitation. I still more disapprove and deprecate all squeamishness about the Jury Bill, which we passed through the House of Commons last session. Modify and alter it, if you think such modification and alteration necessary, though the less you think so the better; but do not start and stumble at such scarecrows and blocks as the amendments in Lords Select Committee, and the opinion of the Irish judges. What can be worse than taking the full odium of severe and repressive laws on yourselves, dragging your reluctant friends to vote for them, and then having the appearance of shrinking from the acts of grace you have announced, and even in part have passed—tapering them down either in number or efficacy—postponing them or leaving them to O'Connell, Hume, and the rest to adopt or to force upon you? I own I feel in some degree in the same way about the prosecution. It is not from any mercy or tenderness to the villains or fools who indulge in such disgusting and brutal language; but it is from an apprehension that such outrages, *while confined to words*, are made *more* and not *less* formidable by prosecutions and even by convictions; and more than all from a feeling that the moment of strength—derived from the confidence placed in us by a party *really* and *substantially popular*—is not, in point of prudence, that which I would select for assuming a forbidding aspect and upholding the rigor of the law. On these subjects I am so satisfied that you agree with me, that I always conclude your remarks on the details, even where I do not concur with them, will lead to the same conclusion; and you are certainly, from numberless reasons as well as station, the best mouth-piece to enforce moderation, caution, and conciliation on such matters in council, where it is much better to avoid than invite much debate or discussion. These things are better talked over *tête-à-tête*, or with two or three; but my opportunities are few, and I therefore write: I require no answer. I only exhort you to use the spur on Irish and English legislative measures of improvement, and the curb on prosecutions for foolish and wicked words written or spoken. I can assure you some among us, and hundreds of our best friends not among us, think as I do on this subject.

"Yours, VASSALL HOLLAND."

After constantly-recurring doubts and misgivings, Grey had at last become quite satisfied that what he had always regarded as an unqualified evil had become an absolute necessity; and he brought his mind up to the point that symptoms of any serious mutilation of the Bill in the Committee would justify a creation large enough to prevent the mischief, provided always that we could get the king to consent.

The waverers had accepted Schedule A—had agreed to the enfranchisement of the large towns, and almost entirely to the £10 qualification; and the final result of Grey's opinion was, that the wise course was to have no creation *before* the second reading—to obtain from the king the permission, but resolving not to exercise the power so given while any hope or chance remained of carrying the bill without it. I must add, that he never entirely lost his feeling of *extreme repugnance* to what he looked upon as a measure of unexampled violence; and as he used to tell me, nothing could prove this so completely as his having held out so long against Althorp, Holland, and myself. At this time (February, 1832), a very general opinion prevailed that Grey was not sincere in his intention to create peers. It was said he was becoming lukewarm and wavering: there never was a charge so utterly unfounded. From the close intercourse I had with him, I can testify that from the moment he made up his mind to the inevitable necessity, he never doubted or hesitated, except as to the *time* for acting. Disregarding all the clamors raised against him, he adhered to his own course, and to his determination to create no peers before the second reading, even if he had had the power, which at this time he had not—for the king had given no consent to the proposal sent to him from the Cabinet in the middle of January, and had subsequently peremptorily refused his consent. I most sincerely pitied Grey's sufferings, and I often wondered how a quick and sensitive temper like his could stand the unceasing worry he was subjected to. Occasionally something ludicrous would occur — such as Hobhouse, who had very recently been appointed Secretary at War, actually threatening to resign unless peers were *at once* created, or a pledge given him by Lord Grey that the bill should be carried. Think of Grey's political existence depending upon Hobhouse! However, Grey steadily pursued his own course, determined against any creation before the second reading—and in any after-stage, only should circumstances render it unavoidable. My own deliberate opinion had been for this course; and I am persuaded, had Grey acted otherwise upon the ill-considered advice or pressure of others, he would have caused the destruction of the bill, and incredible evils to the country.

The second reading was carried by a majority of nine.* The events which succeeded will appear from the following correspondence and narrative:

TO LORD GREY.

"April 19, 1832.

"MY DEAR GREY,—The enthusiasm is at its height everywhere *for* the bill, and rejoicing in the second reading and *for you* (which is delightful), in the most extreme degree, but just as much against the Lords; and in Yorkshire they are going to petition for making peers, and to show in every way

* Since the vote of the Lords against the second reading (p. 94), the bill was brought into the Commons in the ensuing session, when it passed on the 14th of March, 1832, by 355 to 239.

their distrust of the Lords. Nor, according to Morpeth, can any thing stop them in this folly.

"Ever yours, H. BROUGHAM."

[*Private.*] FROM LORD GREY.

"Downing Street, April 20, 1832.

"MY DEAR BROUGHAM,—I am here for a few hours. I got your letter yesterday. What you say of the effect of the king's conversations is most true. But how is it to be prevented? The only step that occurred to me was to write to Taylor, stating the expressions quoted, and inclosing two accounts from the 'Standard,' the last (that of which you had an extract) evidently Londonderry's. He showed the letter to the king, who expressed his indignation against the newspaper press as the vehicle of every thing that is false and capricious —stated the impossibility of his preventing such misrepresentations, and admitted at the same time the probability of their proceeding from persons who had access to his society, and even from members of his own family. All this is very well, but, as you see, does not remedy the evil; nor do I know what more is to be done. I think your going to Windsor might be of use; being so near Windsor, it is natural, perhaps right, as an attention, that you should do so: you might then see both the king and Taylor, and impress on both, and more freely on the latter, all the embarrassment the king will bring upon himself if something is not done to counteract the mischief done in his name; or, if you don't like to go, you might write to Taylor, enforcing what I have already said to him. Holland urges the necessity of the king been seen frequently by Palmerston and me; but how can we go, having no particular business to take us to Windsor, without being invited? and what I have stated will show that every thing else that was in my power has been done.

"I desired Palmerston to open a communication with Wharncliffe, but have not heard the result.

"If you see the king or write, make him aware of the feeling that exists with respect to Holland. The way, too, in which Russia has acted on the Belgian question, and in which she is extending her power on all sides, would not be bad topics.

"I still think it would be a good thing to get petitions and addresses during the recess, if they can be prevented asking for peers. Ever yours, GREY."

[*Private.*] FROM EARL GREY.

"East Sheen, April 21, 1832.

"MY DEAR CHANCELLOR,—I saw Palmerston after I wrote to you yesterday. He had had a communication with Wharncliffe, who expressed his willingness to meet me, and it is settled that we shall meet after his return from Newmarket. But I do not foresee much good from the interview. He told Palmerston that he, Harrowby, and Haddington had been in communication with Lyndhurst and Ellenborough—that the latter went farther than himself in reform—that Lyndhurst and Ellenborough had communicated with the Duke of Wellington after their conversations with Wharncliffe and Harrowby, and that the result was more favorable than he expected. A negotiation with a prospect of success, through Ellenborough and Lyndhurst, with the Duke of Wellington & Co., as this seems to imply, does not appear to me to leave much hope of an arrangement to which it would be possible for us to accede. I shall see my way better after I have seen Wharncliffe; but in the mean time we should consider the best means of defeating this intrigue; for in this light I must consider it. Ever yours, GREY."

[*Private.*] TO EARL GREY.

"April 21, 1832.

"MY DEAR LORD GREY,—I have received both your letters, one yesterday, and the other to-day. I had intended to go to Windsor, but your letter would have decided me if I had any doubt, and perhaps, but for it, I might have been indolent and not put my intentions in execution.

"I saw Taylor for a few minutes, barely long enough to come upon the subject of the rumors, and show how material I thought them, and to advert to the old story of the Duke of Kent's correspondence. For the king sent for me almost as soon as I let him know I was there, and I was with him above three-quarters of an hour, by which time I had to come away, having kept the Seftons waiting for me an hour at least.

"With the king I came upon all the subjects you suggested, and indeed upon almost every subject. The result is that he is quite firm and decided as to Schedule A, but as to that alone; that many unpleasant indications, both of a greater and a lesser kind, appeared; that he spoke of persons as well as things somewhat differently from what he had been in the way of doing; that upon some subjects, as Ireland, O'Connell's silk gown, etc., I was obliged to enter into discussion, and distinctly protested, were it for no other purpose than to prevent him from supposing I did not widely differ with him; that on the subject of France and Russia (where I took the line your letter draws) he was a good deal excited, and even irritable, but not so upon what I dwelt upon most—viz., the effects of those rumors as to his declarations, and their inevitable tendency to make the supporters of the bill leave us. Generally speaking, he was much less excited than when I last saw him, and very good-humored and personally civil and frank—also no reluctance to come upon subjects except that of the above rumors; none whatever to come upon the bill, and the division of parties respecting it.

"It would be endless to go into more detail till I see you, but I came away with the confirmed belief that he is stout with us for Schedule A, and no more.

"This much I should have said, and no more would have been necessary had I written before receiving your letter this morning, in which you show the intrigue going on (for such I certainly think it). I *now* look back to about a dozen of things which passed yesterday as proving strongly that at least *they* (the plotters) have contrived to let the king know what they are ready to do, though I am quite confident he has in no way committed himself with them. Among other things, he said no man in his senses could think of governing this country without a Schedule A; and if there were a new Ministry to-morrow, whoever was minister must lay his account with giving it. He asked particularly as to Lyndhurst's speech, and whether he was against all reform. Also, whether the Duke of Wellington himself could be considered as now against all reform, and denied that he was an ultra Tory. Indeed he was desirous of representing the ultra Tories as a mere handful, and would hardly allow any but Eldon and Wynford to be such — with difficulty Lonsdale. Hertford might be, but he was abroad; and of the Duke of Newcastle he said nothing; and as for the Duke of Buccleuch, he has persuaded him (the king) that he only opposes the Government in the Reform Bill, or at least till the Reform Bill is disposed of!!! My belief is, that if they can only agree to a very little beyond Schedule A, and either be defeated on Schedule A, or damage it enough to injure us without much lessening it, they will find no difficulties at Windsor when we make our stand. Some things I am certain of, and from others I may have formed an erroneous conclusion since receiving your letter to-day, for I *may* have fancied coincidences which don't exist; but there were so many things of this sort that I can not get them out of my mind.

"I go to town on Tuesday, unless I should be obliged to go to-morrow—which is very unlikely—as I must be in court all Wednesday morning. If I knew at what time you were sure to be at Sheen on Tuesday, I could call on my way to town, where I need not be till past six. Therefore, if this reaches you to-morrow in time to let me know your motions, I'll thank you to do so—reckoning, as you may, that any messenger you may send will find me till two on Tuesday.

"Lord Anglesey was to be with the king to-day about two.

"I have only run over the heads, or rather results, of my conversation.

"Yours ever, H. BROUGHAM."

It is singular how great an alarm was felt, and by some of our friends (and these, as Sefton, the least apt to take fright about any thing), when they heard from all quarters the cry about our having the means of passing the bill and not being disposed to use them. People took for granted that, because it was known how adverse the king had been to dissolve in spring, and had yielded, therefore, if we chose, we could get him to secure the passing of the bill. We were thus held to be playing false by the measure; and many of our firmest supporters really believed that the next act of violence, the next outrage, would be upon us individually. I never for an instant partook of any such fears; but I was quite aware of the violent excitement which had spread over many parts of the country, for it was in a great degree local. There had been enormous assemblies at various places, without any actual riot. At Birmingham was perhaps the greatest of these; but in other places there had been not occasional but regular mob-meetings on certain days; and though wholly unarmed, yet practising movements of a military kind. It was evident that, should this be permitted, after a little while there would be a great force collected and disciplined, and only one step more would be required, the obtaining some easily-made arms, such as pikes, to make them an overpowering body of troops. I considered it absolutely necessary to stop this, and advised the issuing of a proclamation, in which Denman entirely agreed, warning the people that if those meetings were continued they would be put down by force. This was effectual, and the meetings gradually ceased. Another very bad expression of public indignation was, the threat, pretty generally used at meetings, of refusing to pay taxes until the bill should be passed. This, though under cover of law—because only, it was said, that the law might be enforced by the usual process—appeared to me so near a conspiracy, that I declared in the House the illegality of such conduct; but if there were any grave doubts of it, that the Government would take steps to remove them by a legislative measure. It was, in my opinion, quite necessary that our whole course should be strictly in accordance with law, and that all demonstrations in favor of the measure, which were even of an equivocal character as to legality, should be repressed. They only tended to increase the obstruction in our way, and were used as the most powerful means of opposing us both at Court and in the Lords. Besides, we were engaged in great amendments of the law, and my maxim was, Let us strictly execute the laws, that they may be obeyed; let us diligently improve them, that they may be loved.

But having clearly showed that we were determined to preserve the peace, and to take no advantage of our adversaries by intimidation or threats, we waited quietly the passing of the bill in the Commons; and both there and in the country we had ample proofs of its increased favor with the community. The majority on the second reading, which had been only as seven to five, was now as two to one;* and our measures to put down all kinds of riot or disorder had been in general well received, the meetings everywhere in favor of the measure being more numerously attended and more orderly than during the first session of the new Parliament. We were nevertheless satisfied that the Lords stood firmly against the bill, but in different degrees. The majority were wholly adverse; but a certain number were disposed to accept it with alterations and omissions, and these were called the *waverers*, very incorrectly, for they stood firmly by their own view of the whole measure. We had a negotiation with them to see if a compromise could be effected. Harrowby and Wharncliffe represented them, and the former had certainly made the most powerful speech the year before against the second reading of the former bill. They now made important concessions; but they required so great a change in the bill, that not only the country would never have borne it, but the Commons were sure to reject the amendments. We therefore had no choice but to go on, whatever our own disposition might be, though the greater number of us were decidedly against their terms. Nothing, however, could be more fair than their conduct throughout; and they gave their support to the second reading, announcing their intention of resisting several of the provisions in Committee. We were therefore quite certain that the bill would, by a considerable majority, be so altered as to be substantially destroyed.

Our difficulty was now extreme. It was, perhaps, possible to tell upon what provisions we should be defeated, because our conversation with the waverers indicated where our scanty majority of nine on the second reading would fail us, though this was by no means certain. But one thing it was quite impossible to tell—namely, upon what defeat, or number of defeats, we must regard the measure as lost, and make our stand with the king. The enemies of the bill must have perceived that it was our determination to make a stand at some point; and I was always clear that they would avoid giving us the advantage of defeating any essential part as long

* On 6th July, 1831, the division in the Commons was 367 to 231; on the 17th December it was 324 to 162.

as they could, but would throw out or alter one after the other of the lesser provisions, so that we should be left in the greatest possible difficulty—indeed, under positive disadvantage. For, suppose we bore several defeats and went on, the friends of the bill in the Commons, and still more in the country, would be daily more dissatisfied, indeed even exasperated, and withdraw their confidence and support from the Government, as betraying the measure. On the other hand, at almost any one defeat it might be said, there remains so much, that you have no right to give up the measure though thus curtailed. I was therefore apprehensive that our adversaries would go on so long as to make the bill and its authors lose that support in the Commons and in the country upon which must depend our only chance of the king's compliance with measures necessary for carrying it through the stage which, though delayed, must come at last; either the change of some most essential provision in the committee, or the third reading.

While under this apprehension I was at my dear friend Dover's, then confined by illness, when Normanby came in, and stated that he had ascertained at Lyndhurst's his intention of moving to postpone the first clause (Schedule A) till after the disfranchisement clauses were considered. I pronounced so great a blunder quite impossible. I hastened to the Lords, and had not been half an hour on the wool-sack when Grey came to me with the same report. This was the greatest relief; it was, in fact, all we could desire, for at least it showed that they did not mean to pursue the course we so much dreaded, though it by no means followed that this motion would furnish the opportunity we so greatly desired. The debate in Committee began, and then came Lyndhurst's motion, as had been announced. We at once took our ground, and treated it as throwing out the bill. It was vain for the Tories to protest they meant no such thing; we would not hear it denied. We fought a fight, stout but short, and to the country quite intelligible. Grey, again and again urged by me to declare he should regard the bill as gone were we defeated on this point, again and again made that assertion, and, turning round to me, who sat next to him, it being in Committee, asked, "Have I said enough?" and I made him repeat and enforce what he had said. I then myself declared in more plain terms that it would be the whole bill gone as much as if we had lost it on the second reading; and I intimated that the Committee would be at an end. We divided, were beaten, and instantly adjourned the farther proceeding; and then came our crowning piece of good luck, Lord Ellenborough announcing that, if they took the Government, the Tories would carry all the provisions of the bill, with some trifling exceptions.

Next day (8th of May) we had a Cabinet, and resolved that, although instant resignation was our plain course, yet that we felt bound first to submit to the king the necessity of creating a sufficient number of peers to insure the success of the bill. On the afternoon of that day Grey and I carried to the king, at Windsor, the minute of the Cabinet to the effect above stated.

We went to Windsor together, as the king had always required we should on any great emergency, and with the intention of asking for an unlimited creation of peers as the only means of carrying the bill. We discussed on the way the names of those whom I had set down in my list, formed upon the principle of making the smallest possible permanent addition to the peerage; as by calling up eldest sons, by taking persons who had none, by selecting Scotch and Irish peers for British peerage, but also those not likely to have successors, to the number of eighty, which we considered might be required. He said, "This is a strong measure to propose, reduce it how you will, and you must state it." I said, "I had no objection to state the particulars, provided he would make the request and proposal." "No," he said, "it is your province officially, and you know the king required you to attend him on all such occasions." I said, "If it must be so, it must." "Of course," he said, "you speak in my name, as well as your own." I said, "And in that of the whole Ministry." He said, "Certainly, that is quite clear." We laid our account with a refusal, though it did not seem quite certain. We expected, however, a very great reluctance and some delay. As soon as Grey had stated that we came humbly to advise his majesty that he should accede to our prayer of having the means of carrying the bill, the king said, "What means?" I said, "Sir, the only means—an addition to the House of Lords."

He said, "That is a very serious matter;" and we both admitted that it was, and that unless quite convinced of its necessity, we never should think of recommending it. He then asked, "What number would be required?" and I said, "Sixty, or perhaps even eighty, for it must be done effectually, if at all." He said, "That was a very large number indeed; was there ever such a thing done before?" I said, "Never to that extent, or near it; Pitt had at different times made creations and promotions of much above one hundred; and Lord Oxford, in Queen Anne's time, had created twelve in order to pass one bill." But I admitted these cases did not afford a precedent which went so far as this proposed creation. He said, "Certainly nothing like it." We continued to dwell on the necessity of the case, and our great reluctance to make such a request, and tender such advice to his majesty. He said he must take time to consider well what we had laid before him; and when we saw Sir Herbert Taylor in the anteroom, while waiting for the carriage, and had some conversation with him, he said we were sure to have the king's answer to-morrow. Grey and I then set out, and on our way home had a wretched dinner at Hounslow, where he ate mutton-chops, and I insisted upon a broiled kidney being added to the poor repast. He laughed at me for being so easy and indifferent, and said "he cared not for kidneys." Nevertheless, he ate them when they came. And we were in all the print-shops in a few days.

Next day the king sent an answer, accepting our resignation, and refusing to consent to the large addition to the peerage which Grey and I had proposed to him.

Lord Grey in the Lords, and Althorp in the Commons, that evening (9th of May) announced that ministers had resigned.

Lord Ebrington immediately gave notice that he should next day move an address, the effect of which was to pray the king to appoint no ministers hostile to Reform. So far was Lord Grey from wishing to throw any difficulties in the way of a new Administration, that he got Althorp to appeal to Ebrington to withdraw his notice. It was found, however, that others would have taken it up in a more violent manner, and it was considered better that Ebrington should go on. It was carried by a large majority.

I had one or two audiences besides the formal one of tendering my resignation, which he did not accept. At one of these interviews he entered again into all the reasons against the proposition which had been given at Windsor, and asked if such a measure as Ellenborough had spoken of might not be sufficient. I explained to him why it could not. He then urged upon me to accept the Government, and said I was sure to have the cordial support of "my friend Richmond" (as he termed him), besides others of the Government, and I might carry a bill on the plan proposed by Ellenborough. He was very much agitated, and spoke of the desperate situation in which we placed him. When I answered that this was most distressing for me to hear, but that it was wholly out of the question, he was affected to tears, and asked if I too abandoned him. I said that most certainly, had I even a desire to accept his gracious offer, I should be wholly unable to render him the least service, or to assist him in his difficulties, for that I should only injure myself irretrievably without being able to form a Government which could carry the bill. He argued to show what materials there were in the present Government and in some parts of the Opposition, and I showed him how hopeless such an attempt would be, even if I had not the most insuperable objection to making it. I saw Sir H. Taylor, and told him what had passed. He did not quite agree with me, but felt and admitted how difficult it was to answer my objections. He begged me to reconsider the subject, and to write after I had spoken to my colleagues. He let me know that he had recommended an agreement with our proposal the day we were at Windsor (the 8th), from his sense of the great dangers occasioned by frequent changes of Government, as I had often heard him say, but not that he at all approved of the bill. Both on this occasion and when I afterwards saw him and repeated my peremptory refusal, he urged, as indeed the king had done, that Lord Grey would be sure to support the Government I should form, because he desired sincerely to carry a reform, though he was so pledged to the larger measure that he must stand by it, and refuse to carry a lesser one himself; and so it was a point of honor with him, which it needed not be with me, or those of my present colleagues who would join with others; but I said I considered myself as much pledged as Grey to the present measure, and besides, he never would submit to what would be deemed a juggle, like Pitt putting Addington in, for the sake of making peace; and that, even if he had no objection to play the part of Pitt, I had the greatest to play that of Addington. There was thus in every view an impossibility of the course suggested, and the king had nothing for it but to send for the Opposition. This he did. The duke obeyed the summons, and tried to form a Government. But he could not; and though various accounts were given of the obstacles—among others, that Baring declared against the attempt, and that the speaker refused to have any hand in it—the real obstacle was Peel, who would not undertake the House of Commons, where the duke's difficulty lay. That it would have been a very difficult task, can not be doubted; but I have always considered that it would have had a fair chance of success, and have often discussed the matter with the duke himself, who was of that opinion. The rally of the Tory party all over the country would have been most zealous and powerful; the demand of eighty peerages certainly would, after a little reflection, have been a fair ground of attack upon us; there would have been no small number of men in the House of Commons disposed to join a strong Government from various motives; and, above all, as time was no object, so firm a chief as the duke keeping the peace everywhere unbroken, by degrees the Reform fever, as it was called, would have been allayed, the more respectable of even our stoutest supporters giving no kind of encouragement to violent courses. The duke cared nothing for the taunts which would have been thrown out, of his declaration, November, 1830, contrasting with the reform he was now proposing to give; and his great object being to maintain the constitution, by supporting the king and the House of Lords, and, as he thought, saving the House of Commons from the mob-power, he conceived that a great opportunity had been lost by Peel's refusal—an opportunity he never expected again to have.

On the 14th, Baring announced in the House of Commons the failure of the attempt to make a Government. The consequence of the failure was of course that, our resignations never having been finally accepted, we were continued in office. The king then wrote to Lord Grey recapitulating his objections, and trusting that the measure might be carried without the necessity of calling upon him for a creation of peers; and adding, that if a creation should be required to give additional strength to the Government, his sanction, to a reasonable extent, would not be wanting.

Thereupon Lord Grey wrote to me as follows:

FROM EARL GREY.

"May 16, 1832.

"DEAR CHANCELLOR,—I got an answer from the king late last night. It amounts to an acceptance, but is not pleasant, and will require an answer from the Cabinet. I am to be with the king at one, and afterwards, I suppose, I must appear at the levee; so that I shall not have time to prepare the answer before the Cabinet meets. If you come here before I go, I shall be glad to show you the letter, and consult you upon the answer. Ever yours, GREY."

We had a Cabinet on the same day, when we agreed that, unless the opposition to the bill was withdrawn, such a creation of peers as would enable us to carry it was indispensable, and that the king must be urged to give his consent to this.

The king, on the 17th, sent a letter to the Duke of Wellington, stating that all difficulties would be removed by a declaration from a sufficient number of peers that they had withdrawn their opposition to the bill. A copy of this was sent, by the king's desire, to Lord Grey. In his answer to the king, Lord Grey referred to the extremely violent speeches made by the Duke of Wellington, Lord Lyndhurst, and other Opposition peers in the House of Lords on the 17th of May, and stated that a Cabinet would be held immediately, to consider the communication which he had received from the king.

The somewhat unusual step of writing to the Duke of Wellington proves how intensely the king disliked the proposal of an unlimited creation of peers, and his anxiety to try any scheme to escape from it. Well meant as it was, the attempt was not successful; because the duke, in replying to it, simply stated his determination to absent himself from any further discussion on the bill, but refused to commit himself further; so that, as Grey truly said, nothing could be more embarrassing than the position which the king's act had placed him in. My answer to all this was, that we must now insist more strongly than ever upon having full permission to create as many peers as we should find to be necessary, and that we must have this in such a way as to leave no doubt whatever on the subject.

Next day, the 18th, we had a Cabinet, in which it was decided that we could not continue in his majesty's service without a full security for insuring the passing of the bill.

On the same afternoon Lord Grey and I went to the king. It was one of the most painful hours I ever passed in my life, because the king evidently suffered much, and yet behaved with the greatest courtesy to us. It is, however, the only audience I ever had in which he kept his seat, and did not desire us to sit down. After we had urged the matter in the strongest language it was possible to employ, he said, "Well, now it must be so, and I consent." I think he added that he retained the same objections to the creation which he was then agreeing to. We stated that it might be necessary to make the creation at any part of the proceedings, and I added, "Even on the bill coming back from the Commons, as there might be amendments upon what had been added in the Lords." There was a good deal of conversation upon the probability of the creation being required. But he again said he gave his promise to make such peers as *both* of us (and he dwelt upon this) should advise. We were then about to take our leave, when I said that I hoped his majesty would not be offended if I ventured to make an additional request. "What!" he said, "are you not satisfied? Have I not done enough?" I said, quite the reverse of being dissatisfied, and we must ever feel deeply grateful for his great kindness in agreeing to follow our advice. "Then what is it," he said, "that I am to do more than I have done?" I said, "Your majesty must consider that this is a most delicate position in which we your servants are placed, and it would be most satisfactory to us, and greatly relieve our minds, if you would graciously consent to give us your promise in writing." He was a little, and but a little, angry at this, and said, "Do you doubt my word?" We both said, certainly nothing of the kind; but it would be more satisfactory for both his majesty and us if he would add this to his other great kindness. I said I was sure Lord Grey would agree with me—which, on the king looking as if for an answer, he signified that he did. The king then said he should comply with the request, and send me a few lines to-morrow morning. When we came away, Lord Grey said he was perfectly shocked with what I had done, and he wondered how I could be so unfeeling after all that had just passed, and seeing the state of vexation in which the poor king was. I said you may rest assured that, before twenty-four hours pass, you will be fully convinced not only that I was in the right, but will in all probability find that this written promise may render the measure of creation unnecessary, which both of us think an extremity on all accounts to be avoided. He said, "God grant it may."

The same evening the king wrote, in reply to the minute left with him by Lord Grey and myself, that he authorized a creation of peers to such an extent as would enable Lord Grey to carry the bill, avoiding as far as possible any permanent increase to the peerage, by "comprehending as large a proportion of the eldest sons of peers and heirs of childless peers as can be made available; and, in the words of the chancellor, to exhaust the list of eldest sons and collaterals, before resorting to any which should entail permanent addition to the peerage."

Sir Herbert Taylor took upon himself, without any authority from the king, or any communication with us, to let some of the peers, the most active adversaries of the bill, know that the king's authority had been given, and was in hands which he was certain would use it. This led to the secession of such a number from all share in the subsequent debates, at least in the divisions, that we carried all the clauses in Committee, and the bill passed.

It is to be remembered, however, that the duke, in explaining what he had done to advise the king, strongly declared that whoever seceded made himself an accomplice in the offense of calling for a creation of peers, because he enabled us to carry the bill, the alleged necessity of which was the very ground of that call. This declaration did not prevent the secession which Sir Herbert Taylor's letter occasioned.

Great complaints were made of him (Sir Herbert Taylor) for having used the king's name to intimidate the House of Lords. In truth, he only gave them fair notice of the risk they ran, that what every one must believe to be a serious, perhaps an irreparable mischief to the constitution, might be avoided. It is needless to say that Lord Grey and I avowed our responsibility for his act, though entirely ignorant of it, and would not listen to certain of our friends — indeed colleagues—who were disposed meanly to throw the blame upon Taylor. The same persons being strongly prejudiced against him from his long-continued connection with one king after another, had foretold, when we came into office, that we should find him faithful and even friendly on all occasions, possibly on important ones; but that when any great crisis happened, he then would make an exception. They little knew the man; and the most important crisis of all—the most unexpected—showed it more strongly than any other.

We had no further difference with the king connected with the Reform Bill, except on the unimportant part of his giving the royal assent in person, which he refused, probably because he was unwilling to show more favor towards the measure than was necessary; perhaps, also, because he felt that the Lords would regard it as a mark of disrespect to them after what had happened. But we had a difference, of which we did not perceive the full extent till some time after, upon a much more important matter, arising out of the bill—the dissolution of Parliament—which was manifestly a necessary consequence of it. He had shown, in conversation on the subject, that he was averse to this step, but he did not positively object either to Lord Grey or myself. But I found, on an audience which I had upon law appointments, on the day when the order for the dissolution was to be made, that he still did not regard it as settled, and renewed his expressions of dislike to it. He asked me why it was considered necessary, and I explained how impossible it was to have the House of Commons sitting for another session, when it had been declared incompetent by its construction to perform its duties, and when so many great towns, now entitled to send representatives, were still unrepresented. He said he must see Lord Grey upon the matter, who came accordingly, and, after an audience, told me it was quite necessary to enforce this necessity further, and that I must have another audience, which was only a repetition of the former. We afterwards found from Errol, the queen's equerry, the cause of this reluctance, and, indeed, this attempt to avoid the dissolution. The queen, who generally took the Tory view of subjects, had been urgent with him to refuse at the last moment, and he had come to town after promising that he would refuse, be the consequences what they might. The advice was extremely foolish, whoever had given it; for, though the Reform excitement had very much subsided, on the success to which it had led being gained, yet it would have been renewed in great force by so violent a proceeding as keeping those on whom the franchise had been conferred out of its exercise. He was extremely alarmed at the tendency of the new experiment, as he called it, to fill the House with Radicals; and I had to send constant accounts during the election of the kind of men who were returned. He was greatly relieved at finding that so many moderate men were elected at popular places, and generally that the Parliament was very much of the same composition as in former elections.

It might have been supposed that the Reform party, and especially the supporters of the Government, would be satisfied with our conduct of the bill to its final success; but there were many and remarkable exceptions. They were of those who were still more anxious to obtain a general power of thwarting the Lords than to carry any specific measures, and who greatly lamented the creation of peers in large numbers not having become necessary. They complained that we had not made that creation, even when the patriotic and wise conduct of the duke, in withdrawing, upon farther reflection, his original opposition to the secession, had rendered the creation unnecessary—indeed, had taken away all pretense for it; and they charged us with having, in order to carry one measure, foregone the power we might have had to carry every measure. I reasoned with these unreflecting persons sometimes in vain; but most were convinced of the folly of this notion; and many others, as Joseph Hume, though generally not easy to make any impression upon, could not resist our plain defense. My reasoning was to this effect:

The Crown is the fountain of honor, and can alone confer rank or precedence. The unlimited power belongs to it of creating peers—a prerogative which has on several occasions been exercised to influence the proceedings in Parliament. Lord Oxford carried an important question in the Lords by a sudden creation of twelve peers in the reign of Queen Anne. Mr. Pitt, too, extended the influence of the Crown in the Commons, and diminished the importance of that body, by transferring many of his adherents among the landed gentry to the Upper House. In recent times, the Government of Lord Grey, backed by a large majority of the Commons and of the people out of doors, carried the Reform Bill through a hostile House of Lords by the power granted by King William IV., of an unlimited creation of peers at any stage of that measure. Most fortunately, the patriotism of the Peers saved the constitution from so perilous a measure. I have always regarded this as the greatest escape I ever made in the whole course of my public life. Yet there never was any measure on which a powerful party, supported by nearly the whole people, were more unanimously bent, than that of a large creation of peers in 1832. But nothing could be more thoughtless than the view then taken of this important question. The advocates for such a wholesale measure never considered what must happen if the Peers, our partisans, should ever be found at variance with king, Commons, and people; they never foresaw that, in order to defeat such an oligarchy, a new and still larger creation must be required; they never reflected upon the inevitable ruin of the constitution, by the necessity thus imposed of adding perhaps a hundred to the Lords each time a Ministry was changed. Among all who were the loudest clamorers for a large creation, I have seldom found one who did not admit how wrong he had been, when these objections were plainly stated to him, and these fatal consequences set before his eyes. Since 1832, I have often asked myself the question, whether, if no secession had taken place, and the Peers had persisted in opposing the bill, we should have had recourse to the perilous creation?

Above thirty years have rolled over my head since the crisis of 1832. I speak as calmly on this as I now do upon any political matter whatsoever, and *I can not answer the question in the affirmative.* The list I had prepared of eighty new creations, when I went with Lord Grey to Windsor in May, 1832, was framed upon the principle of making the least possible *permanent* addition to the House. When I supported Grey, in pressing the measure upon the king, I felt strongly the necessity of the case, circumstanced as we then were; but so greatly did I fear the dreadful consequences of the act, that I am persuaded I should, when it came to the point, have preferred running the risk of the confusion which would have attended the loss of the bill. I *know* that Grey would have more than met me half-way in resolving to face that or any risk, rather than expose the constitution to the imminent hazard of subversion; and I feel assured that the patriotism of our most distinguished political opponents would have helped us to carry a sufficiently large measure of reform; not enough to have satisfied those reckless men who were more bent upon the *mode* of obtaining reform than upon reform itself, but ample for the requirements and real interests of the country.

I more than twenty years ago published in a book, which I dedicated to Lord Grey, the substance of what I have now written; and I have only to add that, when he read the proof-sheet of that part of my work, he expressed to me his entire concurrence with what I have here stated.* And he distinctly told me that I had very much understated his repugnance; and that when the time came he never would have consented to take the step.

When the Duke of Wellington read my statement to the above effect, two or three years before his death at Walmer, where I always passed a day or two before going to Cannes, he said: "Oh! then you confess you were playing a game of brag with me; indeed I always was certain it was a threat, and that you never would have created peers." To this all I could say was, that we were thoroughly convinced *at the time* of the necessity, and that he himself must have been so satis-

* Political Philosophy, part iii., of Democracy and Mixed Monarchy (London, 1843).

fied of our resolution to take the step that he would not run the risk of it; and that if he had not caused, he had at least acquiesced in the secession.

In the course of the summer the king was so incensed at the abuse of himself and his family which had filled the papers, that he became quite disinclined to do any thing but prosecute the press, which we never could advise, either with a view to his interest or our own, or that of the public; for the abuse was quite universal, and all the papers in town and country, except two or three, must have been prosecuted, with the public mind in a state to insure in every case an acquittal. The following letter shows how the king submitted, though with some reluctance, to our advice:

[*Copy.*] "St. James, May 26, 1832.

"The king acknowledges the receipt of Lord Althorp's letter of yesterday, including one from the attorney-general, containing the explanation or statement of his sentiments on the subject of prosecutions for libel, which his majesty has read with great attention. The king assures Lord Althorp, and desires he will assure the attorney-general, that the desire which he expressed for a statement of his real sentiments upon this occasion did not result from any doubt his majesty entertained of his zeal and devotion to his service, but from feeling it right that the attorney-general should have the opportunity of doing justice to himself, in a matter in which his sentiments might have been misrepresented. His majesty is satisfied, from the observations which his letter contains, that he takes a sound and reasonable view of the subject; and much as he laments the existence of such a curse to this country as a licentious and uncontrolled press, and of a state of things which renders the law with respect to libellers and agitators a dead letter, his majesty admits that it would not be advisable to resort to proceedings which would increase rather than diminish the effects of so deplorable a condition of the country. WILLIAM, R."

The following letters relate to the difference we had with the king on the subject of his giving the royal assent to the Reform Bill in person:

[*Private.*] TO SIR HERBERT TAYLOR.

"1832.

"MY DEAR SIR HERBERT,—There is a subject upon which I feel so strongly that I really can not refrain from writing a few lines to you, wishing you either to bring it before the king or not, as you yourself think best; for I am anxious not to harass his majesty with it, if you consider that he has made up his mind.

"The more I reflect on the matter, the more I am impressed with the importance of his majesty's going to Parliament to give the assent to the Reform Bill. I am quite certain that it is a step which would contribute incalculably to his majesty's own comfort in a thousand ways, and that he would experience the salutary effects of it beyond what I can describe. This consideration is of itself sufficient to make me feel very sincerely desirous that his majesty should go. But I am also solicitous on another and more extensive ground. In these times I really regard it as of great use to the established constitution—I mean particularly to the kingly portion of it. Nothing can tend more to give the people, not of London merely, but all over the country, a favorable leaning towards the Crown, and all that is connected with it, than his majesty's appearing at the bill passing. The affection of his subjects towards him, I am morally certain, will be preserved undiminished—nay, I will say augmented, if possible—by this proceeding; while his not going will be regarded as separating himself from them and the measure. The going, I am sure, will amply repay the trouble it may give. I write this to you personally, that you may use as much of it as you think fit. I don't write to his majesty direct, because it might plague him to answer me; but I assure you I don't feel the less anxious about it. Yours sincerely,

"H. BROUGHAM."

[*Private.*] FROM SIR HERBERT TAYLOR.

"Windsor Castle, June 5, 1832.

"MY DEAR LORD,—I regret that I was not favored with your lordship's letter in sufficient time to reply to it by this evening's post, but I hope you will receive this before you attend the king's levee, as I am anxious that you should not speak to him upon a subject which has more than once been brought under his consideration by Lord Grey or by his desire, and upon which I am convinced that his decision had been formed and can not be shaken.

"I have more than once had occasion to hear the king express his sentiments with respect to his going to Parliament to give the royal assent to the Reform Bill, and no later than this morning, in consequence of a question put by one of his majesty's household in a letter which I submitted.

"His majesty observed that, in ordinary times, he should have doubted the propriety and necessity of a step for which the precedents are few, if any, but that nothing on earth should induce him to take it in deference to what is called the sense of the people, or in deference to the dictates of the press, its ruler, after the treatment he has experienced from both; that he had endeavored to discharge his duty to the best of his judgment, and according to the dictates of his conscience; that he had been misrepresented, calumniated, and insulted; that the insults had not been confined to him—they had been heaped upon his queen, on all belonging to him; and that the law had been declared not to be strong enough to protect him and them against such insults. Was he to cringe and bow? Was he to kiss the rod held out *in terrorem* by the mob?

"He had never attached any value to that popularity which results from the effervescence of the moment—that which is not felt to be due to, and to arise from, a sense of the correct and honorable discharge of duty. But if it had been in his nature and disposition to be misled by applause and acclamations given to his supposed *unqualified* sanction of popular measures, what has recently passed would have undeceived him, and would have discovered to him how valueless is popular favor; how little deserving of the solicitude of those who are responsible to God and to their conscience for their acts. He is told that his giving the royal assent in person to the Reform Bill would be agreeable to the people—to those who, within the last fortnight, had so grossly insulted him; and that, by this step, he would regain the popularity which he is assured he had enjoyed — that he would set himself right again. But he observed, upon this, that he would greatly prefer their continued abuse, to the conviction that he had merited it by degrading himself in courting applause which he has learnt to despise.

"I believe that I have correctly stated to your lordship the king's sentiments expressed to me at various periods, certainly during periods of excitement, and occasionally uttered under irritation of feeling, but nevertheless unchanged; and I freely own that I believe them to have taken such firm possession of his mind, that I should not like to be the man to propose to him to gratify the popular feeling by going to Parliament at this juncture.

"Under such circumstances I am certain that you will think that I have correctly availed myself of the discretion which your letter allows me to use in not submitting it to the king. I have the honor to be, with great regard, my dear lord, your lordship's most obedient and faithful servant,

"H. TAYLOR.

"Upon reading over your lordship's letter, I almost doubt whether I am warranted in withholding it from his majesty; but as he had left Windsor before I received it, and I shall not see him before to-morrow, I think the safest course will be to leave the question to your option, after reading this."

FROM SIR HERBERT TAYLOR.

[*Private.*]

"Windsor Castle, June 7, 1832.

"MY DEAR LORD,—I have been honored with the king's command to return to your lordship the commission for giving the royal assent this day to the 'Act to Amend the Representation of the People in England and Wales,' which his majesty has signed.

"Upon this occasion I felt it to be my duty, and (I am willing to hope) to be consistent with your lordship's intentions, to submit to his majesty the private letter to me which accompanied the bill, as well as the correspondence which has passed, and to which it referred; and, as you observe, it was this morning open to his majesty, 'if any change should have occurred in his view of the subject, to take the other mode of passing the bill.'

"His majesty orders me to assure your lordship that he

gives you full credit for the feeling of devotion and attachment which influences you in urging him to adopt a course to which his own feeling is so repugnant, but that his sentiment and his determination continue unchanged. But this is a question of feeling—that which ought to actuate his conduct as a sovereign and a gentleman, not one of duty nor of ordinary usage or precedent—and he can not bring himself to truckle to that mob which has grossly insulted him, instead of giving him the credit which he feels he deserved for having endeavored to discharge his duty to the best of his judgment, and according to the dictates of his conscience. I have the honor to be, with great regard, my dear lord, your lordship's most obedient and faithful servant,

"H. TAYLOR."

The royal assent was accordingly given by commission, Lord Grey acting as one of the commissoners. He told me he was not much surprised at the king's refusal of the request I had urged, but was very sorry the king had not consented. He had received a letter from Taylor informing him of what had taken place.*

* See Appendix A.

CHAPTER XXIII.

The King, the Duke of Sussex, and Sir Augustus D'Este.—The Vacation.—Death of Lord Tenterden.—Difficulties in getting Denman made his Successor.—Sir John Campbell Solicitor-general.—His Applications: Sydney Smith's.—Sir John Williams.—First Parliament under the Reform Act.—The Speakership.—Ireland and O'Connell.—Project of removing Stanley from Irish Secretaryship to another Office.—Difficulties with Lord Grey on the Proposal.—Controversy.—Threatens to break up the Ministry.—Settlement of the Question.—Position of Lord Grey and Lord Althorp.—Character of Lord Althorp.

DURING great part of this year (1832) the king had been, in addition to his Reform troubles, much harassed by D'Esté.* I had many letters from him upon the subject of what he called the "Pretender's" preposterous pretensions. In this matter the Duke of Sussex had been necessarily implicated, and this led to a coolness between him and the king. The circumstances are of much too private a nature to admit of publication, but I may, without impropriety, refer to a part of the subject on which the following letters passed between Lord Grey and me:

TO EARL GREY.

[*Private.*]

"Brougham, August 19, 1832.

"MY DEAR LORD GREY,—I inclose a copy I have to-day received of a letter from the king to the Duke of Sussex. It is, I believe, owing to what I told you had passed about D'Esté's consulting O'Connell and doing other fooleries, and to the Duke of Sussex behaving with great propriety on the occasion, and expressing to me how much annoyed he was with the attacks on the royal family which D'Esté's supporters were always making through the press, coupled with insidious distinctions by praising him (the Duke of Sussex), at

* Sir Augustus Frederick d'Esté, born 1794, son of the Duke of Sussex by his marriage with Lady Augusta Murray, daughter of the Earl of Dunmore.

the very time D'Esté was writing him privately the most cutting letters.

"I had represented to the king repeatedly those sentiments of the Duke of Sussex, as he evidently desired I should. I think this letter of the king's is the result.

"I really conceive that now the duke will put himself in the wrong if he does not immediately write a few lines expressing that 'he is sorry to think he should, through inadvertence, have allowed himself to be the channel of conveying an address (Bristol) which his majesty considered of so reprehensible a tendency.'

"Surely he may say this without doing any thing that lowers himself, or even insidiously inflames the people who sent him the address. I think if you were to recommend some such expression to him, it would be sure to produce the desired effect. I have no objection to back your advice, but it will be more likely to be taken coming from you. Let me know what you do.

"My letters from Windsor are as good as possible. I hope you took the same view I did of the *House* affair. The more I reflect on it, I am the more convinced that this is the moment, and that you turn to much account now what you will afterwards have to give for nothing. If my lungs will stand your climate, I shall cross the Alps and go over to your *transmontane* country one of these days, and we can then discuss several things.

"I left Lord Carlisle much better in general health, but still as weak as ever in the ankles. Yours ever truly,

"H. B."

FROM EARL GREY.

[*Private.*]

"East Sheen, August 21, 1832.

"DEAR BROUGHAM,—I had intended to speak to Taylor on the subject which you mention, but was prevented by his not being able to come to town. I have determined to postpone it till my return in October. But in consequence of your suggestion I wrote to him the day before yesterday, and have received an answer which shows that what I said had been most graciously received by the king, and affords the best hope, though no communication had yet been made to Lord H., that this matter may be settled.

"I took the same opportunity of opening an overture for reconciliation with the Duke of Sussex. The answer was gracious beyond my expectation, and it now rests with H.R.H. to be cordially received at Windsor, without a word being required from him that could hurt his feelings.

"I spoke to Goderich about Stuart, and inclose a letter which he wrote to me upon it afterwards. I really don't see what more can be said or done on this subject: at least, if any thing is to be done, it will be best for you to write to him yourself, in consequence of my having communicated to you his letter.

"I am in all the turmoil of preparing to set out to-morrow.

"Van der Weyer is come without powers or instructions. They are now unreasonable in their turn. I see nothing but for the conference at least to make up their minds to a fair and equitable proposal, and to enforce it. No more last words. Ever yours, GREY.

"Direct, if you write, to Howick."

FROM EARL GREY.

[*Private.*]

"Howick, August 28, 1832.

"MY DEAR CHANCELLOR,—We arrived here on Saturday, all well. I have since received your letter. You will also have received one from me, which crossed it, and which stated the prospect of a reconciliation between the king and the Duke of Sussex. Taylor, in his answer to my letter, stated what had passed on the subject of Sir Augustus d'Esté, and inclosed a copy of the king's letter to the duke—the same that you have sent me—adding that he considered it as an overture, if the duke would so understand it; that the king would not think it necessary to recur to the cause of their difference, if the duke proposed to go to Windsor; and that he might be sure of a cordial reception. This I lost no time in communicating to the duke, and the result has been, as you of course know, that he first saw the king before the levee on Friday, and is to be at Windsor to-day.

"Don Pedro's affairs look rather better. The return of Miguel's fleet to the Tagus, leaving that of Don Pedro master of the sea, is a great event for him. But they seem to have none of the qualities required for such an enterprise, and to be chiefly thinking of the best means of securing a retreat in a case in which retreat ought not to be thought of.

"The Belgian affair is still the subject of conferences, in which, if there could be one will and one decision, the matter might soon be settled. The point to which the negotiation should now be brought is the free navigation of the Scheldt. To this the King of Holland should be pinned, and if he can be brought to acknowledge it substantially, but unequivocally, Leopold must not expect to be supported in an unreasonable and pertinacious adherence to the letter of the treaty of November, which, by the way, if literally adhered to, would not be advantageous to him.

"I shall be delighted if you can come here, and should be very glad to have an opportunity of talking with you on many subjects which require consideration.

"Ever yours, GREY."

Nothing very material marked the remainder of the long vacation after the passing of the bill. The death of the Lord-chief-justice Tenterden came somewhat unexpectedly on us. At the Recorder's Report Council early in November, he was extremely ill, and I besought him to go home. A long levee, with many audiences, had prevented our going to business till nearly six o'clock, and we were then kept by one or two long cases till eight. Sitting near him, I said, "Go, chief-justice, you will kill yourself." "It is done already," was his answer. I was resolved that Denman should succeed him on every ground, political, party, public, and private: this was quite plain. Among my colleagues, some were averse secretly, some openly, and proposed others among the *Tory* puisne judges! I *roared* this down in a way to prevent repetition of what I felt to be an attack on me personally, as well as on the honor of the Government and of the party. On sounding the king in expectation of the vacancy, I found him very averse; I therefore resolved to lose no time; and when I received early on a Sunday morning a note from Tenterden's son announcing his death, I sent off a messenger to Windsor, and wrote to Lord Grey as follows:

[*Private.*] TO EARL GREY.

"Berkeley Square, November 3, 1832.

"MY DEAR LORD GREY,—Lord Tenterden died this morning at half-past eight, without pain. His mind had for a day or two been gone. He was all the time *in business*, and the last words he spoke were (addressing a jury)—'Gentlemen, you are all dismissed.'

"I send by your messenger a letter to the king announcing this, and, of course, saying nothing else; but you ought to go on to Windsor in the course of the day.

"I inclose a copy of the king's letter to Althorp, about what you mentioned t'other day. I can't lay my hand on his answer to my letter on the same subject, but it was fully stronger both in acquittal of Denman and condemnation of the press. Yours ever, H. BROUGHAM.

"P.S.—Denman's attack on Scarlett you may hear spoken of as ferocious, but *all* admit that it was deserved, and that it was purely in retaliation of a most wanton aggression on us all. I hear there never was any thing more savage, but nobody blames it. My throat is mending, I *think*, without suppuration."

[*Private.*] TO EARL GREY.

"November 5, 1832.

"MY DEAR LORD GREY,—I think with you that the proposed appointment of Denman should be communicated to our colleagues, and I have written to Althorp (who has some of them dining with him) to communicate it to them and the others this evening; but the appointment and swearing in can not be delayed. The Court were kept near an hour today consulting whether the vacancy did, or did not, prevent the sittings at *nisi prius* during term, and it ended by their resolving that there can be no sittings, and accordingly Littledale (the *nisi prius* judge) was obliged to adjourn. Besides, I quite agree with you that there ought not to be even a day given to the enemy to torment and even *work upon* the king.

"I shall fully write to Taylor in the sense you mention. But there is one thing I had far rather say (and that you said) than write — viz., that the only charge I ever made against Denman for his judicial conduct was his severe sentence on libellers, Carlists, etc., having been tried before him. I remember Lambton, Ferguson, and others of our friends in the House of Commons, were quite indignant, and said, 'All lawyers are alike—who could have expected this?' The fact is, judges *must* go by the law.

"I have sent for Denman, and shall communicate what you bade me say. The result of your audience is certainly a relief to my mind, for I should not have wondered at a stand being made.

"He should be sworn in at the Privy Council to-morrow.

"Yours ever, H. BROUGHAM.

"The urgency of the thing, and the accident of your being at Stoke, and my being confined, will account for our not having had a Cabinet to-day upon it."

[*Private.*] TO EARL GREY.

"November 6, 1832.

"DEAR LORD GREY,—I was quite aware of the necessity of dispatch, indeed from the beginning, and I have now, after some little anxiety at the delay, just received back the box (which I had sent at once) with the king's signature. So all is quite safe, indeed done, for the process is the shortest in the world—much shorter than that of making a puisne judge. Taylor's letter takes *not the least notice* of the only part of mine that was of the least importance.

"Yours ever, H. BROUGHAM.

"I firmly believe there would have been a push made at him and *at us* if the enemy had had a day or two to turn about in."

Lord Grey nad gone to the king at Windsor, and settled the matter after a short struggle. Grey's behavior on this, as on all great occasions, was absolutely perfect—manly, honorable, firm, and judicious. Immediately after, Denman was sworn in at my private residence. This made a vacancy in the office of attorney-general, and Campbell was made solicitor.

Nothing could exceed the gratitude which Campbell loudly *professed* for this appointment. From all I have known and observed of his character, I much doubt if he *felt* all he said and wrote to me on the subject. I really believe he kept a form of thanksgiving, that he might always be ready to express, in appropriate terms, his gratitude in the event of any of his everlasting applications for something for himself or his connections succeeding. It is incredible the number of engines he set to work to get me to support his desire to be solicitor-general, yet he was so obviously the right man for the place, that from the moment his name occurred to me I had never hesitated.

His applications to me began very soon—in fact, almost the day after I was in office, he pestered me to appoint a Mr. John Campbell, Deputy-Registrar of the Court of Bankruptcy. He pressed this so strongly, urging it as one of the greatest favors that could be conferred upon him, that I acceded, and he then wrote to me expressing his warmest thanks, and saying it was a kindness he never should forget.

When I helped, and that most willingly, to make him solicitor-general in November, 1832, his letter of thanks was almost a fac-simile of his letter in Mr. John Campbell's case.

As a specimen of the kind of applications I constantly received from him, I may give the following, as it followed close upon those of my early office days; but I shall have more to say about Campbell hereafter:

"New Street, November 24, 1831.

"MY DEAR LORD CHANCELLOR,—From your intimation that you wished Mr. John Campbell, when deputy-registrar, to be at the bar, I made an attempt to have him called this term, although his name had not been up the usual time in the Hall. Notwithstanding the display of a little political feeling arising out of the Bankrupt Bill, I believe I should have succeeded, had it not been for an unlucky notion of Mr. Solicitor-General that the situation of deputy-registrar is not fit to be held by a barrister, and therefore that it would not be proper to call to the bar a gentleman who has accepted such an appointment.

I should be glad if your lordship would take an opportunity of explaining to Mr. Solicitor that, far from considering the two characters incompatible, you intend that half the deputy-registrars shall be barristers. I must own the scruple seems to me wholly unfounded. The deputy-masters of the King's Bench are barristers, and were called after their appointment.

"I am afraid of trespassing upon your lordship's good-nature by again mentioning my brother's knighthood. But he and the future Lady C. have become very impatient to enjoy their honors, and seem to think that I am neglecting them. I am desired to say that, though the Guelphic would be very gratifying, if there be any difficulty about this, common knighthood conferred without personal attendance will be quite satisfactory. I ought to add that I really believe this mark of royal favor would give pleasure to the Reform party in the county of Fife. I remain, my dear lord chancellor, yours very faithfully, J. Campbell."

Apropos of applications, I had about this time the following letter from Sydney Smith asking for preferment:

"My dear Brougham,— . . . I want another living instead of this (Coombe Fleury), and as good—about £700 a year clear; and I want a prebend of about a thousand per annum: the latter I want to have from the minister; but I see little prospect of it. These are my objects in the Church. These points obtained, I give you and fortune a *receipt in full of all demands,* and I think I shall have obtained fully as much as I merit, and more than before this latter period I ever expected.

"Now nature, time, and chance have made you one of the greatest men in the country, and it will be very much in your power from time to time to forward my views.

"I appeal, therefore, to your justice, in consideration of the bold and honest part I have acted in the Church—and next, to your kindness, from a long acquaintance and friendship—to lend your assistance at convenient seasons, and to aid me with your voice and just authority. Yours ever very sincerely, Sydney Smith."

Nothing could be less objectionable than such an application. I answered him that he might rely on my doing all I could, and accordingly I gladly took an early opportunity of showing his letter to Grey, who thereupon soon afterwards gave him a stall at St. Paul's, which greatly pleased him, as it removed him from Bristol to London. Grey had always a high opinion of Smith, and considered he had been of infinite service to the party. Smith, in the next letter I had from him, warmly thanked me for what I had done.

To go back to the solicitor-generalship: I had wished to promote Williams, but Campbell was wanted in the House of Commons, where Williams had not a seat.* Moreover, Campbell had uniformly supported us, while Williams had very improperly (the only wrong thing, public or private, I have ever known him to do in a long and intimate acquaintance) left us when the Duke of Cleveland seceded in 1830. This desertion of Williams was partly owing to a grudge on account of silk, political economy, Huskisson and Canning; but it was very bad, for he took the worst form of desertion —viz., that of leaving us on his own Chancery reform question. It was as if I had left the party on slavery or education. I took an opportunity afterwards of giving him compensation for what I could not do in 1832, by making him a puisne judge. That was in my gift, the solicitor-general in that of the Government at large—of course with the preponderating voice of the Great Seal. But I had already incurred too much odium about Denman to make a second personal stand against my colleagues possible. In Denman's case I was clearly right; in Williams's I should have been as clearly wrong.

An event more affecting the interests of the Cabinet and of the party than any appointment of judges now approached. It was a matter of course to dissolve the old borough Parliament, lying under sentence of incapacity by the bill, and to elect a new one under the Reform Act. The dissolution was therefore resolved on by us in November, and submitted to the king. He appeared on that day, when he was to agree

* Sir John Williams, born 1777; called to the bar, 1804; appointed a baron of the exchequer, February, 1834, on the retirement of Sir John Bayley. Next term he was transferred to the Court of King's Bench, where he continued until his death, on the 15th September, 1846.

to the measure, very much out of humor. This first showed itself when I asked him to let me present the new solicitor-general (Campbell) for knighthood, which I had always followed the practice of having performed in the closet, to distinguish this kind of knighthood from that ordinary knighthood "despised of all men." "Let him wait," was the answer. I afterwards said he was anxious to go to Dudley for re-election, and not to have any extraordinary difficulty arising from the approaching general election. "What general election? Let him wait till after the levee." I saw there was something wrong. I hastened the council. He made no objection; looked sulky; asked me if it was quite necessary; received for answer, "Absolutely, sir;" and we dissolved and returned the great, liberal, and reformed Parliament—the last of the kind we are ever likely to see.

Some time after, we learned through Errol that the queen had that morning, at Brighton, made him promise on no account to dissolve, and that he would rather turn out the Government—as out, of course, we should all instantly have gone, had he refused. Any thing more silly than this plan I never heard. The House of Commons then in being was ours by a working majority of above 100, and the country was eager to have possession of the newly-acquired franchise, so that no Ministry could have then stood for a day on that ground of not dissolving. No man who looked to a popular re-election durst have supported such a Government, and the old borough members now abolished would alone have been left against a Tory Ministry and the people. Also, we had not then had any quarrel with the Commons or the country.

When the new Parliament met in January, our first quarrel was about the speakership; but that was only a personal one with Abercromby, and occasioned some coldness in Devonshire House, he being the duke's auditor some time before the other duke—Wellington—gave him a Scotch judicial sinecure. That sinecure I had—with infinite difficulty, and no support from Lansdowne, Althorp, or Abercromby's other friends in the Government—contrived to commute for a pension of £2000 a year for life, after a year's service by Abercromby of about twenty working days. He has since behaved with infinite ingratitude, being altogether, as Althorp once said, "about the most selfish man in the world." The speakership was the thing he had set his heart on. But to work the first Reform Parliament with an inexperienced speaker seemed to us all too hazardous a thing to be thought of, and we chose Manners Sutton. The very first thing the would-be speaker did was to pick a quarrel with us on the Irish Bill, and take his stand on the court-martial clauses. He gained little credit by this move, the motive of which no one could doubt. Next year we offered him the Irish secretaryship, when Stanley went to the Colonies. He refused it, standing out for the Cabinet, which all felt to be a thing that should never again be joined with the Irish secretaryship, which had been submitted to only in the very peculiar circumstances of Stanley's position. After Grey retired, Abercromby was put in the Cabinet; but as his salary at the Mint only equalled his pension, he never liked his place, seemed always desirous of any change to better his condition, and not unwilling, failing that hope, to see the Government turned out, and fish in troubled waters for something better. He was lucky enough to catch the speakership; and not long after, quarrelling with the Commons, disliked by all parties, backed and defended by none, he retired to his pension and his peerage, and will probably be never much more heard of, but bear about his discontented figure and habitual grumbling to whoever will now, joining in his feelings from their own disappointments, allow him to pour his refinements and his nostrums into their ears.

From Parnell and others I had received many warnings of the state of Ireland. Parnell, convinced that O'Connell would commence, as he had threatened, a system of agitation either for Repeal or upon any other grievances, real or imaginary, strongly urged us to make him our friend, and suggested that appointing him attorney-general would be the most effectual way of neutralizing him. Grey never would listen to any proposal to treat with O'Connell, and so nothing was done.

As time went on, things got worse and worse. A bitter feeling against the Church had been excited by O'Connell and other demagogues. Resistance to the payment of tithes was counselled. The excitable people of that most unhappy country soon acted upon this advice. All who paid tithes were denounced as traitors to their country. Tithe-owners who attempted to enforce their dues were murdered. Tithe-proctors acting in the discharge of their duty were shot. In almost every part of the country there was a systematic disregard of law. An association of the most dangerous character had been formed. The objects it had in view threatened the peace of the country and the integrity of the empire, for it was no secret that *Repeal* was its ultimate aim. Combinations were formed which defied all law; armed bodies were organized, and perpetrated the most atrocious outrages; juries were intimidated, and did not dare to convict; witnesses refused to give evidence. No kind of property was secure; no man's life was safe. The whole country was in a state of disturbance quite unexampled. The magistrates, finding themselves incapable of acting effectually, applied to the Irish Government for help, urged strong measures, called for Insurrection Acts, and even proposed that military law should be proclaimed; but the Government did nothing.

Aware of what was going on, so deeply did I feel the danger, that I considered nothing but an important change in our proceedings could stop the mischief and avert the evil which I saw was imminent. After much reflection I deemed a change in a high office absolutely necessary, and urged this upon my colleagues very earnestly. This change involved the substituting Melbourne or Goderich for Anglesey, as lord-lieutenant, and giving the place of secretary of state thus made vacant to Stanley (Derby).

I made a point of this in December, 1832, just before the dissolution. Grey, Althorp, and I had a long discussion of the subject, and Althorp agreed with me, Grey very strongly differing. I intimated the impossibility of my remaining in office unless some such change were made, though aware that my withdrawing might be inconvenient, but quite clear that they could go on without me, as neither Althorp nor any one else would, in all likelihood, retire with me. This subject occupied my whole thoughts, and I wrote thus to Grey:

[*Private.*] "December, 1832.

"MY DEAR LORD GREY,—I *hope* we shall be able to keep together till Parliament meets; but I don't think it easy, and don't expect it. The difficulty is extreme, and I never saw much good come of putting off the evil day, without the most remote chance of circumstances changing during the delay.

"I see the bishops are going to meet, and I beg that the Church reform papers may not be shown to any of our colleagues. There is no other way of preventing the whole plan from being destroyed almost before it is prepared. If it is kept equally from all, no *one* can have any right to complain. You and Althorp, and no one else, has seen them.

"Yours ever, H. BROUGHAM."

We met and had a long discussion. I next day wrote to Lord Grey, stating what I had omitted at our interview.

[*Private.*] "Tuesday morning.

"MY DEAR LORD GREY,—I ought to have added to what I told you yesterday, that if *you* think it necessary to state my resolution to any one, you are, of course, at liberty—only take care it does not get wind till the elections are over, as it might do harm. *I* shall, of course, not mention it to a human being except Althorp (who, indeed, knows it), and I think it must be fully explained, and immediately, to Stanley, because, unless this is done, it is extremely liable to be misconstrued as regards him. Nothing is or can be farther from my intention than any thing in the slightest degree offensive to him, as you well know, and I hope he will easily believe. Indeed, I consider him to have a much greater interest than any other individual in the arrangement being made. Yours ever most truly, H. B.

"Stanley being now in Lancashire will make this much more easy."

"6 o'clock.

"I'll thank you to send *my Church papers* by return of the messenger. I agree that it is much better you, Althorp, Melbourne, and I should meet than have a Cabinet; but I really shall be much obliged to you to come to-morrow. I shall be in Downing Street at *half-past one.*

"Yours ever, H. B."

I received the following letters from Grey:

[*Private.*]

"East Sheen, December 4, 1832.

"My dear Chancellor,—I was just sending off the inclosed letter when the messenger arrived with your box. I need not say that it has added to my distress and disappointment. Though you had pressed this matter very urgently, I had no idea till yesterday evening that you looked to the alternative of resigning. Had I known it before, I certainly should have advised the king to postpone the dissolution.

"I trust and hope—I will add I earnestly entreat, that you will reconsider this determination; till then, I will not mention it to any body. If you persevere in it, you must consider the Administration as broken up, for at the same time that I communicate your resignation to the king, I must desire him to accept my own; as no earthly consideration can, in that case, induce me to go on with the Government, to which I already feel my strength altogether unequal. Added to all the other difficulties which I have stated, there is that of appointing a new secretary. We have no one ready to recommend; and if we had, we should be under the necessity of explaining and discussing with him the measure in progress, from which, if Stanley is to continue a member of the Government, we can not materially depart.

"Ever yours, Grey."

"East Sheen, December 4, 1832.

"My dear Chancellor,—The last words you spoke to me last night have dwelt on my mind ever since. It can not be necessary for me to say, if my whole conduct has not convinced you of it, that nothing can be more painful to me than any difference of opinion with you, and that I am by no means pertinacious of my own where it is possible to find the means of preventing such a difference.

"If in the present case I have not done, or can not immediately do, what you desire, you can not attribute it, therefore, to any unreasonable obstinacy on my part, still less to any personal interest, or, to my not giving all the weight which is due to them, to opinions which you so strongly press.

"I am far from contending that I may not have shown weakness in not acting more decidedly while it was possible to effect changes in the Irish Government which I admit to have been desirable. But you know the feelings which have restrained me. I really can not bear to give just cause to any one who has acted kindly and honorably towards me to say that I have not used him well. To all my colleagues I am indebted for the most cordial support. They took office when the prospect was not encouraging. I have never had a difference with any one of those whose situations are connected with this discussion; and I really felt that it was impossible for me to say to them—a more convenient arrangement might be formed by your retiring from the office which you now hold, and therefore having served as long as I wanted you, pray give it up, though I have nothing to offer you that you might be willing, or perhaps think it consistent with your station and character, to accept. Whether means might not have been found at an earlier period to have obviated this difficulty it is now too late to inquire. I did, however, with respect to Lord Anglesey, endeavor to open the way for his retirement from the government of Ireland in the only way in which I could do so without being wanting to all the claims he has upon me—*i. e.*, by making an arrangement which might be both honorable to and agreeable to himself.

"I am therefore, I repeat, not unconscious of my own failings, and that I may have suffered feelings of delicacy to prevail too far. It is a defect, however, which I am afraid it is too late for me to correct, which renders me perhaps unfit for the situation which I fill, and which could have been best remedied in the way which I suggested in the last consultation between you, Althorp, and me on this subject.

"But in going into this retrospect I have rather indulged my personal feelings than made any advance as to the practical difficulties of the moment. Whatever might have been desirable, or even necessary, it is at this moment impossible to retrieve the omission of which I may have been guilty. There is no longer time. There is not one of the arrangements which you have suggested which could be made within the short period that is left to us. You have yourself admitted that if not done to-day it is too late. To begin, then, with the first. It would be impossible for me, without feeling that I used them extremely ill, to propose to any one to fill Anglesey's place without having previously proposed to him some mode of retiring from it with honor. Had I such an offer to make, I must have his answer to it before I could take a step. There then would be the other arrangements consequent upon his retirement to be made, which would again require communication with the persons whose situations would be affected by them, and to all of whom I owe equal consideration; for I really feel, as I have already stated, that it is quite impossible for me to say to them, This is an arrangement which I require for the Government, and therefore you must submit to it, whether you like it or not. There is, then, as I see the thing, under all the circumstances of the moment, nothing for me but to leave for the present the general constitution of the Government as it is.

"But is this really, taking all the interests involved into our consideration, so intolerable as to justify the resolution which you announced to me last night? There may be advantages in a change of the Irish Government; but it would also be exposed to many and not trivial difficulties. Any change in a moment of so much irritation, when the elections are likely to increase that irritation, and the vigorous exertion of all the power of the Government will be required, is in itself an evil which ought, if possible, to be avoided; and how much would that evil be increased by an apparent acknowledgment of weakness, in removing the head of the Government, for no reason but that he had, by a faithful discharge of his duty, become obnoxious to those who are not opposed to him so much as to the authority of the British Government, and who, having gained this advantage, would attack his successor with increased violence, and perhaps with increased means? To Stanley there is also no other objection than that of his being unpopular. His ability and diligence in the execution of his office are undisputed. He possesses a more accurate and extensive knowledge than any other person of the very difficult question which we have to settle. He has means of gaining for the settlement of that question a concurrence, if not a support, which nobody else would be likely, in the same degree at least, to obtain. He may perhaps not be inclined to go all the lengths which many desire. But it is a large and effective measure which he is preparing, one which I believe will satisfy all those who are to be satisfied at all. Sure I am that it is as much as could, with every facility that could be hoped for, be carried at the present moment, and more, much more, than we could hope to carry against a strong exertion of the Protestant influence, both in Ireland and here. Besides the doubt that a new secretary might have the same power of obviating formidable opposition, a necessity would arise of opening the question again, to discuss it with him before the arrangement could proceed.

"I therefore think, upon a comparison of difficulties, that being brought, by my fault if you will, to the situation in which we are placed, the best thing is to stand as we are, even if we had the choice of a different course. Nor does this determination prevent a new arrangement when circumstances may be more favorable. I see no reason why a change might not be made at another period of the session, provided the affairs of the Administration go on prosperously in the mean time. It would then come naturally, and be attended with much greater facilities. It would now have all the disadvantage which any change, made at a moment when the appearance of union and strength is most required, must have, in diffusing a suspicion, and too probably producing the reality, of divisions among ourselves, and consequent weakness.

"I have written in a great perturbation of spirit, and therefore still less clearly and satisfactorily than usual. I will therefore add nothing but on the single point with which you concluded our conversation yesterday, your determination to retire. It would cause me a degree of pain, if I thought you really could carry that determination into effect, which it would be impossible for me to express. I will not put before you all the consequences of such a step, with respect to the country, the duty we owe the king, and the character of the Administration itself. It would inevitably have the effect of breaking it up. All the consequences at which I hint must at once present themselves to you. For it is impossible that you could retire without the Administration being dissolved. Upon this my determination would be as firm as yours. There is little chance of my being able to go on as it is, certainly none that I can do so for any long period; but on such an event I must abandon public life at once and forever. And, for God's sake, ask yourself what would be our condition with regard to public opinion if, after having dissolved Parliament, and, added to the difficulty of forming a new Administration, we were to abandon the Government, not because we differed as to any public principle, or because we had lost the support of the king and of the people, but on account of internal disagreements of office, and of divisions among ourselves. I will not believe such a thing to be possible. Ever yours, GREY."

As it was absolutely necessary that this matter should be disposed of without the least delay, in consequence of the approaching general election, an early Cabinet was held, at which I could not be present till late, owing to pressing business in the Court of Chancery; I therefore sent the following letter to Grey:

[*Private.*] "Berkeley Square, December 5, 1832, Friday.

"MY DEAR LORD GREY,—As I may be kept in court till too late for the Cabinet, and certainly shall not be there till long after it is begun, I write to entreat your immediate attention to what I really think by far the most pressing subject of all at this moment, because from the elections coming on something must be settled in a very few days—I mean, of course, *Ireland.*

"To think of going on with Stanley (and indeed Lord Anglesey) there is evidently quite impossible; and Stanley, though willing, if absolutely necessary, to remain for a little while, is naturally as anxious as can be to get out of it. Lord Anglesey is less disinclined to remain, and the reasons are not by any means so strong for his leaving it. But, unhappily, without that vacancy there is no possibility of obtaining a secretaryship of state for Stanley. That either by taking India or the Ordnance (and Cabinet), Lord Anglesey will be removable, and in a way to make him feel no kind of annoyance, seems almost quite clear. It may not be for a few weeks, if India is the manner of doing it. But if the Ordnance, that may be done any day. Suppose, however, you prefer (as I should do in your situation) giving him his choice, this would only delay the actual vacancy a very few weeks; and I can not see any difficulty in the plan suggested by Althorp (who, I think I may venture to say, sees the necessity of the case as strongly as I do), namely, that Goderich should give up his place to Stanley, and remain in the Cabinet till Melbourne or himself take the lord lieutenancy.

"The necessity of the Irish secretaryship being settled before the end of next week is really obvious. You can not have a second election for Lancashire in the spring with a single vacancy; it will not be safe. But that is not all; you can still less have an election, with a single vacancy for Westminster or for Edinburgh, after such contests as are now going on in both places; and where you are to look for an Irish secretary, except to Abercromby or to Hobhouse, I really don't know. The other appointments of Howick, Ellice, etc., all very important, come within the same description; they must be made before the general election. If, then, Stanley is not removed now, he will not be for an indefinite time—not till next autumn at the soonest. Indeed, who would come into such an office, even if re-election was out of the question, at a moment's notice, without time to learn his business, in the middle of a session, and while Stanley was going on with Irish measures? The thing is out of the question. Are we prepared to say, deliberately, and with our eyes open, that Stanley shall remain there the whole of such a session as the next?

"I put all elections now out of the question. If there were no dissolution impending, I should say as clearly as I now do that there is not a day to lose; for whoever is to succeed him must be allowed six or eight weeks to turn about in his office before he is called upon to bring forward such measures and in *such* a Parliament.

"The more I reflect upon the state of Irish questions, and the prospect of the elections there, the more heartily I agree with Stanley himself in desiring anxiously this change. If ever there was a question which, though nominally of a person, is really of a great measure, this is that question. His leaving Ireland, provided it be for great and visible promotion, is essential to the settlement of the Irish question. The effects of it upon the reception of the measures respecting the Church will be great beyond calculation; and upon the elections, I have no doubt whatever, they will be as apparent. I also think it very unfair towards Stanley himself that we should keep him in the position he now stands in—not only full of discomfort and annoyance, but lessening his popularity and his weight every day; while it is so much for the interest of the Government to preserve and increase them. From some accidental circumstances, too, without the least blame on his part, it so happens that there is no man in or out of Government whose bringing forward Church reform (in Ireland) will create so many opponents, and gain so few supporters, among those the most likely to be dissatisfied with our plan.

"I am sure, when any thing relating to Ireland, as well as Irish members in the House of Commons, is considered, no one can possibly think that things can go on as they did last session. Nobody dreamed of Stanley meeting Parliament again in that capacity: he as good as announced it on all occasions in private—almost in public. We all felt it quite out of the question. Surely whatever has since occurred strengthens the reason for the change; *and there is not a single argument against it.* I can not allow for an instant that any feelings of delicacy towards individuals amount to an argument or any thing like it. *We are governing the country*, and it is our bounden duty to do all we can to protect it from injury; and, of course, we have no right to think of such scruples. But in reality there are no feelings of personal delicacy to overcome. The arrangements you would have to propose are all of the most honorable and even flattering nature to every party concerned.

"I can not easily express to you how this hangs upon my mind. To go through even a month of such a session as the last was in the House of Commons, is what no one could bear to think of who had not forgotten all about the last session, after the Reform Bill was over. But that is the least of it. Who shall say that he can calmly contemplate what may fall out in Ireland, and feel that he has left any thing undone to lessen the dangers which threaten us there? I am far from saying that any thing we *can* do will give us security; but I do really say, and with the greatest anxiety press it upon you, that we are not excusable if we *even hesitate* about taking every precaution possible against mischief in that quarter. I am sure that there is nothing in the way of individual vexation and party discomfiture which we do not richly deserve if we leave any thing of importance unattempted. But that is little; for the public mischiefs that may arise will throw the heaviest responsibility upon us — a responsibility which any one may well shrink from. These are matters which can not, of course, be discussed in Cabinets. But I will venture to say that there is scarcely one of our colleagues who is not alive to the necessity of the changes I am urging.

"I have written you a long letter, but I assure you I have not expressed half what I feel upon the subject. If you think it right that Althorp and you and I should meet upon it, I could come at the breaking-up of the Cabinet to-day, or to-morrow at three; but really I don't think one day is to be lost. Ever most truly yours, H. B."

The Cabinet generally agreed with Grey; at least they saw insurmountable difficulties in respect of the time; and, fortified by their concurrence, he wrote again entreating me to remain, and repeating the expression of his great uneasiness at our difference. I answered him as follows:

"Tuesday evening.

"My dear Lord Grey,—I assure you I can not describe to you how much pain it gives me to think I have been the cause of any uneasiness to you. There is nothing I am not ready to undergo myself to relieve you from any discomfort. In short, I at this moment feel exactly towards you as I blamed you t'other day for feeling about others, with this great difference, that I really think I have a right to consult *your* feelings, and to go a very great way in abandoning my ground, in order to keep *you* easy; whereas I don't conceive you ought to have the least scruple about those you refer to. In fact, not one of them would have any right to complain at your calling upon them to make the arrangements in question.

"Don't think me obstinate and pertinacious if I say that I am quite sure all might still be arranged. I could myself go with your message to Brighton to-morrow morning, and be back before the post goes. Melbourne is as certain to agree as your name is Grey; and I am clear that Lord Anglesey will come into it the moment you mention it. But if you prefer it, I will go over myself to Dublin and explain it—or, if you please, I will take it all upon myself. All that is wanting, in truth, is a few words to Melbourne, and as many to Kemp. If you prefer it, I will speak to Melbourne. I am sure Althorp will to Kemp, whom he knows better than I do.

"I wish, above all things, to impress upon you that my notice of resigning is *very, very* much the reverse of such notices in general. *They* are in the nature of threats. I need not say how very distant from my nature any such thing is; but above all men in the world, with you. It is only that I feel the *consequence* of our going on in this way (letting measures and great interests bend to personal feelings) *must* drive me from the Government; that I am sure I shall not be able to stand it; that I foresee, struggle as I may (and, God knows, any struggle that man can make I must at all times and in all circumstances be ever anxious to make, in order to keep by you to the end of my days); yet I shall be unable to do so if great things are to give way to personal considerations.

"I don't feel the force of what you say about the Government being broken up if I am compelled to quit it, because there is no occasion whatever for either you or Althorp moving. But never fear my being ready to go so long as I *can* stay.

"I won't write upon any other matters now, because I think this is enough at once. But I should be deceiving you if I left you to suppose that our only difficulty would be got over if I made up my mind to the present Irish arrangement. It may be that to stick by you I should do so; but I see other things sure to raise difficulties, and of a personal nature even greater than this. However, 'Sufficient for the day is the evil thereof.' But I must again say how exceedingly painful to me all this is—much more so than it can be to you. I don't like to make phrases; and if I did, I am sure I could not express half the devotion I feel towards you, and which many others have seen much more of than you. Ever most sincerely yours, H. B."

To this he answered the morning after, having received my letter very late:

"East Sheen, Dec. 5, 1832.

"DEAR CHANCELLOR,—Your letter came so late last night, that it was impossible for me to answer it till this morning. Its kindness has deeply affected me; and I can with truth say that there is no personal sacrifice that I would not make in my turn for the purpose of removing any difficulty that you may feel.

"But a night's reflection has convinced me that an extensive arrangement could not be made in this manner—that the very attempt, if it failed, would be fatal to the Government—and that even its success at this moment would not give us the strength which you suppose; the unusual and extraordinary character of the proceeding, and the person employed in it, would give rise to conjectures and discussions, which would have the very worst effect at home during the elections, and abroad upon the interests involved in the questions which are now at issue.

"If I could believe that our continuing as we are would have the effect of making measures of the greatest public importance bend to personal feelings, I should be willing to risk almost any thing.

"But I can not view the matter in this light. My real belief is, that all these measures will be best promoted by our avoiding the interruption which such a change so effected, and at such a moment, would give them; and that if we can only arrive at the settlement of the two important foreign questions now depending, we shall have a degree of strength which we never before had, both to introduce and to prosecute the measures of reform which the times require, and to make such arrangements among ourselves as may be necessary for conducting comfortably the affairs of the Administration.

"But really, if you will only calculate upon the time that is left us you must perceive that if not a minute was lost either by objection or discussion in any one of the quarters where consent must be obtained before the thing can proceed one inch, yet it would be impossible to complete it before the elections.

"Besides, though the previous arrangements may, in such

cases, be contrived and agreed upon, could we make such a change in the composition of the Administration without having brought the matter before our colleagues? Would not any or all of them have a right to complain if they heard for the first time, in the midst of the elections, that such a change had been made?

"It is most painful to me not to be able to come into a proposal on a subject on which you feel so strongly, and which you press at once so urgently and so kindly. But my judgment is convinced that in our present circumstances there is nothing left but to go on as we are; that by doing so we shall endanger no great measure; that, on the contrary, much danger would more certainly result from any precipitate attempt; and that we shall stand better in all respects for promoting the interests with which we are charged, or for making new arrangements, by making up our minds to meet the present difficulties, whatever they may be, as we are. There is nothing in point of principle which requires us to do otherwise. It is a question whether the principles and objects to which we are pledged will be best promoted by the one course or the other. My opinion is quite clear as to which, all things considered, would now be the best; and all that I entreat of you, therefore, is, that we may go on together as long as we can, and when the moment comes when any decisive measure must be taken, I feel confident that there will be no separation between you and me. Such an event, indeed, would be personally so painful to me, and so decisive as to my public utility, that from that moment I should consider myself as politically dead. If such a break, therefore, should now take place, which your letter gives me the comfort of thinking that I need no longer fear, I must repeat, as my solemn and unalterable resolution, that I could not continue in the Administration a single hour.

"Let me once more thank you for all the kindness of your letter. I beg you to believe that I feel it as I ought to do, and share in it to the fullest extent.

"Ever most sincerely yours, GREY."

The offer which, in the letter immediately preceding the last, I had made to remove the personal difficulties, did not get rid of the objections made, and Grey continuing as firm as I was, it became necessary to acquiesce. I must add that not the slightest unpleasantness was occasioned by this difference between us, although I was grievously vexed at the result, both on public grounds and, it must be confessed, at my being obliged to remain in office on account of what I deemed a necessary change not having been made, and, as I had often stated to my colleagues, on account of the Government being in a position which gave them no security of being able to carry measures of importance. But I also personally felt the annoyance, after my incessant labors, of having lost the chance of release to which I was entitled, and which my health required.

I used always to say that Grey was as anxious to resign as I was, but only at the beginning of the session. At the latter end, and in view of the long vacation, he did not so much object to remain. His answer always was, that I wished to get out at *all* times, as well as in view of the end of the session; but he admitted that I always did my best to keep the Government together, and readily gave up my individual wishes to that consideration.

In the discussion of the question of my resigning, I had both said and written to Grey that, even if I left the Government, there could not be the smallest occasion either for himself or Althorp retiring; but, on reflection, I am rather disposed to doubt this as to Althorp, because I well know that nobody ever hated office as he did. Others I have known hate it occasionally, but he detested it at all times. He often said, when he got up in the morning, he wished he might be dead before night, but he always went through his duty manfully.

There never was a man of real merit who had an opinion of himself so unaffectedly modest. Without a particle of cant, he was most deeply imbued with religion, and this, perhaps, as well as any other part of his nature, indisposed him to exert himself to attain the usual objects of earthly ambition. Always undervaluing himself, he never could comprehend why he had attained to so high a position in public life, and frequently expressed his astonishment at the great power he was conscious of exercising over men of all kinds and natures—a power which proceeded from the complete conviction which all men felt in his thorough honesty and simple love of truth.

His extreme modesty was ludicrous, and even painful—always ready to admit his faults, from his perfect candor; but his powers were great. His ability was never so remarkably shown as in the Reform Bill, both in 1831 and 1832. He had a knowledge of all its details, and of all the numberless matters connected with it, that was almost supernatural. The others knew it so ill, and got into such scrapes when opposed to formidable adversaries, such as Croker, who had attained something of Althorp's mastery of the subject, that it became necessary to prevent them from speaking, or, as it was then called, "to put on the muzzle," and Althorp really did the whole. His temper was admirable, and invariably equal. Sugden said he had learned a lesson from it, or, at least, that it was his own fault if he had not—which was not ill said.

He had a very bad opinion of the newspapers and of all connected with them, whom he looked upon as persons of no faith, and whose opinions, if they ever had any, were merely framed to suit their readers. Yet his calmness of judgment and constant sense of justice made him waive any objection arising from this prejudice, if prejudice it be. When Mr. Coulson was proposed for the Poor Law Inquiry, his having been the conductor of a newspaper was stated as a ground for objecting to him; but Althorp said it rather was an argument in his favor, he having raised himself to be a conveyancer.

CHAPTER XXIV.

Holland, Belgium, and the Siege of Antwerp. — Politics at Court. — Lord Lieutenants and the Nomination of Justices.—Irish Coercion Bill.—Divisions on the Malt-tax.—Condition of the Ministerial Force in the House of Commons.—Whittle Harvey.—Cobbett.—Anticipation of Political Reaction.—Measures that must be pushed.—Corporation Reform.—The Irish Church.—The Appropriation Clause.—Estimate of the Duke of Cumberland as an Opponent.—The Duke's Projects.—The King's Letter to the Archbishop of Canterbury.—Question of the Creation of Peers revived.—Sir Herbert Taylor.—Miss Martineau's Pension.

THE following letters from Lord Grey relate to the objections which Holland had made to the treaty of October, 1831, to which Belgium had acceded. The conferences and discussions which lasted throughout the summer of 1832 ended in a treaty proposed by Prussia and accepted by Holland, but rejected by England and France. In November the French army entered Belgium, and then came the siege of Antwerp.

[*Private.*] "East Sheen, December 7, 1832.

"MY DEAR CHANCELLOR,—I have just received your letter, and have sent Tooke's, as you desired, to Althorp.

"Immediately on Wellesley's saying that he could not go for a fortnight, I stated that we could not wait so long, but proposed to him that Stratford Canning should go immediately, and if any thing came of the opening which caused his being sent, then Wellesley should follow to take up the work which he had begun. This Wellesley liked exceedingly, and I immediately settled this arrangement with Palmerston, and it only waits now for Palmerston's instructions, which I had hoped would have been prepared before this. In the mean time, however, Lord William Russell is instructed how to act, and though there has been more delay than was convenient, I am sanguine in my hopes that good may come of this.

"I am sanguine, too, as to the result of Antwerp. It seems to me impossible that the thing should last long, unless the

Prince of Orange should be able to relieve the place, to do which it would be necessary previously to beat both the French and Belgian armies. These two affairs settled, our prospects would be much improved; and if we do not break up amongst ourselves, I think every thing may be satisfactorily arranged before the meeting of Parliament.

"I have a letter from Stanley, most kind to me personally, and agreeing to put off the matter with respect to Lambton for the present. This is a great relief to me, though I feel the necessity of a clear understanding before Parliament meets. Stanley gives a dreadful account of the state of Ireland. The elections likely to be swayed by the system of intimidation which has been organized by O'Connell and his priests on the one side, and by the Conservatives with their money, of which we have none, on the other. Not only have Duncannon and Leader been driven from Kilkenny, but Lord Killeen, it is said, has been obliged to relinquish the county of Meath!!! Ever yours, GREY."

"East Sheen, December 28, 1832.

"DEAR CHANCELLOR,—The surrender of the citadel is a good job well done, and I have no doubt that the French will act with perfect good faith. We are now preparing an offer to be made immediately to prevent further hostilities. To prevent the delays which would attend the reassembling the conference, and the embarrassments which are always met with there, we think it best, in the first instance, to make the proposal for a settlement of the territorial division, and the points immediately arising out of it, which would establish a mere *status quo* till the other matters could be settled by a definitive treaty. Palmerston is gone to-day to Brighton to present the note, and will lay this view before the king, who is very desirous, as you saw in a letter which I showed you, of having Austria and Prussia with us in any thing we may do. He works hard at the Unions. I have had two or three more letters of four and five sheets each on that subject. * * * *

"Ever yours, GREY."

[*Private.*] "Brougham, December 30, 1832.

"MY DEAR LORD GREY,—Antwerp is, as you say, well over

and well done. I am extremely glad the line you mention is to be taken. It is plainly the right one in every way.

"My accounts of Brighton are worse and worse. 'Such an one is a Tory.' 'Nothing the worse for that,' was the answer at table. But the queen and D'Esté are quite outrageous. I really begin to think they have direct communications with Holland.

"The elections, as you say, in Scotland are admirable. But be on your guard against the inveterate habit of *Alexander* to praise himself; he is the easiest satisfied with his own doings of any animal—though not so easily with his own lot, as we all know. You will find, after all, that the proportion of out-and-out Tories from Scotland is quite as great as from England. Yours truly, H. BROUGHAM.

"P.S.—Since writing the inclosed, I have received a letter from Lord Maynard, Lord Lieutenant of Essex, desiring five names to be inserted in the commission of the peace (A. Baring is one). This looks so very suspicious (as if for election services), that I have suspended the proceedings, and inquired of Western, first, whether these persons had been distinguished for electioneering; and secondly, whether any others are fit to be put in. My intention being, not perhaps to refuse the lord lieutenant's names, but to call upon him to show cause why the others should not also be inserted. I think of doing the same in Norfolk and Cumberland, and also in Northumberland. *Pray consider this*, and say if you do not think it a right way of making a transition from the present strict and absurd rule which really subjects the Government to its own deputies — the lieutenants. I think this is the proper moment to strike that blow. As for Essex, that and William Ord are the only blows which I have at all felt; and my opinion is, and I am sure so is yours, that in the former case at least we have the plaster in our hands, namely, peerages to Western and Francis Baring."*

[*Private.*] "East Sheen, January 1, 1833.

"DEAR CHANCELLOR,—Many happy new-years. I am just

* Son of Sir Thomas Baring. He had been Chancellor of the Exchequer and First Lord of the Admiralty. He married Lord Grey's niece, Jane, daughter of Sir George Grey, and was created Baron Northbrook.

setting out for Goodwood, where I stay to-morrow, and go on Thursday to Brighton; return to this place on Saturday, and settle in town on Monday.

"You have not made the necessary allowance for idle and negligent men like the Duke of Argyll. He is one who has not qualified, and there are others.

"Who is the Alexander whose inveterate habit is to praise himself?

"I take very much the same view that you do of the returns and of their consequences.

"A very unnecessary, not to say a very unjust, cry has been raised against Stanley's speech. There is not a word in it to which I would not subscribe. But this is always the way with our friends—always full of complaints and objections, with or without cause, as if we had not difficulties enough to contend with from without. But there are in this case the secret workings of a jealousy of Stanley's superiority.

"Althorp will probably have written to you about the Speakership. Sutton would certainly have been proposed. He told Ellice that he would accept the chair either if offered to him by the Government, or if he was called upon by the House to take it. There was therefore no choice.

"I will try the ground about Western at Brighton, and hope to succeed, but I must stop there for the present. The king is just now in good-humor with us, and our correspondence about the Unions has closed by his ceasing to urge any preventive measure. Ever yours, GREY."

[*Private.*] "Brougham, Monday.

"MY DEAR LORD GREY,—I agree in expecting the Dutch trade to refuse, but it is quite necessary the proposition should be made. The retirement of the French army is very excellent.

"Alexander, about whom you ask, is the same with *Sandy* or *Sawney*, and means not one man, but a million or thereabouts — namely, all men in Scotland, whose characteristic I think is to be mighty easily satisfied with themselves, but not with their condition, which you have daily proofs of.

"Alexander, therefore, differs very widely from Charles Grey in both respects. Ever yours, H. BROUGHAM.

"I hope to God the report I heard of *Fanny* Lambton being ill too is not true."

On my return to London I had the following from Lord Grey:

[*Private.*] "Downing Street, March 13, 1833.

"MY DEAR BROUGHAM,—I return the Duke of Wellington's notes. His objections appear to be entirely technical, and should be looked into by those who understand the matter, and obviated where necessary in the Committee in the House of Commons. The time of sending them is rather extraordinary (the 10th of March), the receipt of them by you being on the eve of the Committee, when it was almost too late to make the alterations which might be necessary, the bill having now been out of the House of Lords about a fortnight.

"You do not know how ill Lambton really is. Hammick tells me that nobody can imagine how much he suffers. I really believe the anxiety and irritation arising from the delay of another fortnight would have added not only to his present suffering in an incalculable degree, but to the difficulty of his recovery. His coming to the House of Lords is quite out of the question; but if any thing should be said to make it necessary, there could be no difficulty in stating that his resignation was not occasioned by any difference of opinion, but solely by the state of his health. Indeed, I do not believe any misrepresentation, if any should be attempted, will have the least effect. His brother, and every person who is most connected with him, votes with us; and his having the earldom—which, by-the-way, was entirely my doing, and without any communication of my intention to him—is of itself a proof that he goes out in perfect good-humor.

"Ever yours, GREY."

[*Private.*] "April 5, 1833.

"MY DEAR LORD GREY,—I was with the king for an hour and a half, and nothing can be more satisfactory than the conversation on all subjects. I saw Sir Herbert Taylor also afterwards, and the queen, who was extremely gracious and kind. On hearing that Talleyrand and M. de Dino were to be here this evening, she asked with some eagerness if the Duke of Orleans was coming to-night, or when; and I told her majesty Tuesday, as I understood. There was nothing at all unkind in the manner of mentioning him, and indeed I should rather think she would have avoided the subject had she intended to show any such feeling. However, on this head I can not be quite so sure. Yours ever,

"H. BROUGHAM."

The state of Ireland rendered some coercive measure absolutely necessary, and accordingly Lord Grey, soon after Parliament met in February, brought in a bill for the suppression of disturbances and dangerous associations in that country. This bill was not opposed in the Lords, and, with some trifling amendments suggested by the Duke of Wellington, was speedily passed and sent to the Commons, where, as might be expected, it was opposed by O'Connell, who, as a matter of course, denounced it as having been engendered by "malignant hatred of Ireland." Stanley, in replying to an observation of O'Connell that the progress of the Coercion Bill would cause a delay fatal to the expected remedial measures, distinctly stated that if ministers were unable to carry both measures (meaning the Coercion and the Irish Church Bills) they would resign. This determination of the Government was perfectly understood in both Houses to be fixed and irrevocable. It greatly annoyed the king; he now disliked frequent changes of the Ministry. He felt that if we resigned there was no certainty that a Tory Government would be permanent, and then would follow a third change. He wished us to withdraw from our pledge to resign if the Church Bill was thrown out; but this was, we all agreed, impossible.

[*Private.*] FROM EARL GREY.

"April 14, 1833.

"MY DEAR CHANCELLOR,—I did not get your note till late to-night on my return from a dinner at Lord Clanricarde's. I am quite knocked up, and not the better for having dined out, which was a great folly.

"The king seemed pleased with the result, but I am not quite easy about him. I suspect he is tormented to death by all the people about him. He told me that the Duke of Cumberland was loud in his praises of you. This must please you. 'Laudari a laudato viro.' Ever yours, G."

[*Private.*] "Downing Street, April 27, 1833.

"DEAR CHANCELLOR,—The consequences of the vote of last night* are so infinitely serious, that I hope you will be punctually at the Cabinet which is summoned for two to-day. I can see but one course to be taken, at least for myself. But nothing can be determined upon without the most careful consideration. Ever yours, GREY."

[*Private and Confidential.*] "Whitsunday, 1833.

"MY DEAR LORD GREY,—'The day of Pentecost being come,' I must trouble you with some observations suited to the feast, upon a subject of great, and, in my opinion, pressing importance. I have once or twice of late had the intention of formally inculcating among our colleagues the substance of what follows, and, if you wish it, I still will do so. But, at all events, you must first approve—and indeed it will most properly come from yourself, officially, whereas from me it could only proceed from an individual. However, if you, as head of the Government, take any step, you have my full authority to say I entirely concur; and I am the better able to form an opinion, because, having been very recently mixed up with the House of Commons, and even since I left it having most closely observed all the proceedings, I may be said to know very exactly the turn of matters there.

"It is quite vain to conceal from ourselves that the Government is seriously damaged, both in the eyes of the country and even of the House of Commons itself. This is in part unavoidable, because it had been extravagantly popular—because absurd expectations, impossible to be realized, had been formed—and because all Governments, after being a little while in office, have to contend with the selfishness of disappointed

* On Sir William Ingilby's motion, "That the duty on malt be reduced from twenty shillings and eightpence to ten shillings the quarter." This was carried against Government by a majority of ten.

This vote was afterwards, on the 30th of April, rescinded by a large majority—198.

individuals, and the fickleness of an unreasonable public—and all this we should long ago have felt (indeed were beginning to feel three months after we came in), but for the excitement of the Reform question. But a great part, I firmly believe the greater part, of our unpopularity is owing to ourselves, and, to come at once to the point, the Cabinet ministers in the House of Commons either despise their adversaries or fear them; I should rather say they despise some and fear others—and the error is equally great, and will soon be equally fatal, in both cases. Grant and Graham sit as if they had not the gift of one tongue apiece (I speak on Whitsunday). Palmerston I pass: it would be most unjust to expect any thing from him, worked and worn to death as he has been; but Grant and Graham are wholly without excuse. Robert Grant is as loquacious as his brother, to the full, but he is not in the Cabinet. I speak now of Cabinet ministers. How can men in the back rows get up and take part in debate, when the Government itself abandons its case? Althorp is admirable and invaluable, but he is also quite indifferent, and cares not how much either himself or any one else is attacked. What with his indifference, Grant's indolence, and Graham's alarms, we are left entirely to Stanley and Spring Rice. The former is a host in himself; the latter is, next to him, by far our best man for debating. Lord John, too, is invaluable, and shows a spirit, and debates with an effect, which are admirable. And in former times that force would have been quite enough, when there was but one debate in a week, and two or three speeches only were attended to. But now things are mightily changed. The debate ranges from Monday to Saturday, and twenty speeches are made in a night, most of which are much attended to in the country, and some of them in the House. Now, to see two Cabinet ministers, *who can speak*, sitting silent under an attack upon the Government, is enough to discredit any majority in the House, and I *know* it has that effect nightly at the present moment. Some of the assailants are left unanswered, as is said, because they are despised. This is quite wrong, even as to the House, but in the country it is fatal. Who knows that Whittle Harvey is a man of abandoned character, and who cares—I mean among the people? What they read is that a clever speech has been made, and that no one has answered it. Cobbett was left unanswered, and our wiseacres said, 'What signifies Cobbett?' Meanwhile he was making great way in the country, owing to his unanswered nonsense, when Spring Rice, at one blow, overturned him, and Peel (with Cobbett's own lawful help) finished him. Depend upon it, that is a far better way of treating an enemy than to smile and say, 'What does it signify?'

"It really won't do for men in public life to speak or not as they happen to feel inclined. How often have you and I spoken, both in and particularly out of office, when we had as lief been hanged? But it is a *duty;* and for a CABINET MINISTER to sit silent because he don't feel an inclination to speak, is really childish and laughable, if it were not also shameful, and I must say, scandalously so. His own particular department not being attacked is just nothing to the purpose. His department *is* attacked, and *he* is *himself* attacked, if the Government he belongs to is; and his speech may have twice the weight for the very reason that it is made not in defense of his own department.

"The necessary consequence of those ministers speaking will be to open the mouth of other official men. At present, the general party feeling is, 'Oh, leave it to Lord Althorp, or Stanley, or Lord John.' In fact, Althorp is quite careless, reckoning upon his majority, and this feeling spreads among other official men. But the friends of the Government are humbled night after night in the House, and fall off day after day in the country, because they see a Ministry which does nothing for itself. How differently we should have stood had the rule been that every speech of importance should get an answer from a minister! The second-rank men would then have been also on the alert, and all our proceedings would have stood upon a vantage-ground, and all have been thoroughly defended and comprehended. The unfortunate affair of the malt-tax was not only, in fact, owing to the bad whip; it was much more owing to the silence of the ministers. Who had any right to suppose the Government was pressed, when they threw out no signals for distress? Had Grant and Graham both spoken that night, there is not a doubt we should have had a majority; and, as you know, they would not even speak the following Tuesday!

"If this Government were to break up at the end of the present session it would go out with far less credit than the feeblest Government that ever ruled—at least for a while—and yet it would have reformed the Parliament, abolished slavery, opened the East Indian monopoly, settled the bank question, and reformed the whole administration of the law. After a year or two, people would begin to discuss what had been done; but for some time we should pass for imbeciles, who could not defend our own measures or keep hold of power; and nine-tenths of this delusion would be owing to the conduct of our affairs in the House of Commons.

"But the worst of it is that by these blunders we have a great chance of not carrying some other great things now on the anvil, and possibly of being upset before we finish even those I have referred to. The feeling in the House of Commons, and especially in the country, is daily encouraging the Tories. I don't mean, merely, to take office and try a game which no longer seems desperate, but *to vote in the House of Lords.* You will soon perceive how much that House has recovered its courage, and how ready it is for mischief. If the country don't recover also some respect for us, there is nothing the Lords won't be prepared to attempt.

"That a good deal of the evil brought on us by the conduct I have been describing, is, for a while at least, remediless, I admit. But something may be done, even now, by our colleagues and those below them turning over a new leaf; by Althorp no longer acting the wet blanket, but rather blowing the bellows; and by the rule being laid down, 'Every speech of an adversary to be answered by a man in office.' This, however, is not enough. The Irish Tithe question *must* be settled, and by a land-tax; and the new Corporation Bill must be brought in and explained in an *audible voice,* though it can't be passed this year. The commissions for examining the old corporations must be prepared and issued, and the grant of what can be spared (£100,000 in two years) for providing schools in the great towns must be announced. And, moreover, these things must be announced with some effect, and not as if we were ashamed of what we were about. Rely on it that you can not govern by a House of Commons, and neglect all that gains both the people and public assemblies. Yours ever, H. BROUGHAM."

[*Private.*] TO EARL GREY.

"Sunday, June 1, 1833.

"MY DEAR LORD GREY,—The more I reflect on it, I feel the more absolutely persuaded that as all this outcry is confined to the single point of Auckland, so Radnor's appointment *will* at once set all right, and give you the entire command of every thing for the session, or as long as you please.

"The entire alteration in men's feelings is since that was announced. It is materially lessened, and wears away; but before to-morrow at Althorp's it will not have entirely subsided. If Radnor's appointment be announced there, all is at once decided, and most favorably. Why you could not see the king at twelve and Radnor at one, I can't see. The scrape (of Auckland) is certainly none of my making; but I want to do all I can to help us out of it, and surely this is of all ways the most easy as well as the most desirable. But you will say that, as you are of that mind yourself, I need not argue it. True, if that were all; but I fear that you will do it *after the meeting is over*, and thus lose the benefit of it at the right and critical moment. As long as men are men, and this Government is to be carried on in Parliament, and by the confidence of 200 or 300 people all independent of us, there is no such thing as getting a blind confidence, and keeping people from exercising a will of their own. They must and ought to think for themselves; and if they did not, or if all were to be done by power, neither you nor I ever would have been in office.

"They are bent on having some one popular and respected name added; and they feel this, as on our account and *out of regard for us*, far more than for any reason else.

"Yours ever, H. BROUGHAM.

"P.S.—I hope and trust your note don't mean that any other name has been suggested from Lansdowne House, Althorp,* or elsewhere—or at least that, if it has, I may know of it this time before the decision is taken. Indeed I can not doubt it."

While the House of Lords were passing the Coercion Bill

* Lord Spencer's country seat in Northamptonshire.

in February, Althorp stated in the House of Commons the measures the Government intended to introduce relating to the Irish Church. He made a full statement of the plan, entering into great details.

The first effect of his announcement was indications of hostility from the Repealers and Radical members, who said the plan would be productive of no good; while the Tories described the proposed measure not as a reform but a destruction of the Church, and a wanton attack upon the Protestant religion. The Irish members rather approved, although they did not think the measure went far enough. The bill was read a first time in March; and after sharp debating and opposition from Peel and the Tory members, the bill passed, although many of those who had supported it in the early stages voted against it when the Government gave up the clause for appropriating the funds to state purposes. The time was now approaching when the contest on which depended the fate of the bill and of the Ministry would be decided. It was a period of great anxiety, and was so felt by none of us more than by the king himself, who perfectly well understood how critical was the position of affairs.

Every day proved more and more clearly that the defeat of the attempt in May, 1832, to change the Ministry had not altered the resolution of the Opposition peers. They now firmly believed that they could throw out the Irish Church Bill, unless a considerable number of their usual supporters became alarmed and seceded. The king was aware of these things, for I took care to keep him well informed. I had an opportunity of stating through Sir Herbert Taylor many of the alarming symptoms. I referred in particular to one man, whom recent circumstances had made particularly conspicuous: I mean the Duke of Cumberland, against whom personally I had not a word to say. I respected the courage with which he had faced the odious charges made on his reputation, the effect of which courage had been to clear him; I also held him to be a fair open enemy, and not one who pretended to more liberality than he possessed, but was content to appear what he really was—a rank, violent, ultra Tory of the strongest Orange breed, and whose principles and propensities were purely arbitrary.

He had for many years lived abroad, and there formed his habits of thinking and his political opinions. He kept himself for some time after his return in the background, knowing how unpopular he was all over England, with the single exception of the universities of Oxford and Dublin; but he had now broken through this discreet resolution, and was putting himself more and more in the public eye. At the time I speak of he had assumed the position and attitude of a leader, as the chief of the ultra party; and with Kenyon and Falmouth for his supporters, and Wynford to back him, he claimed as distinguished a place as the Duke of Wellington on the Opposition side of the House of Peers. He no longer confined himself to asking a question upon the order of business, or on a point of form; he spoke upon the gravest and largest subjects; and in one evening he spoke two or three times, one of these being on the Poor-Law Bill!

It became, therefore, manifest that his royal highness now thought himself destined to play a great part, and he was flying at high game.

Now I was entirely persuaded that the people of England never would endure any government or any party in which the Duke of Cumberland bore any thing like a prominent share.

But, then, at this time the whole Tory party had chosen to coalesce with the illustrious duke. He sat always side by side with the Duke of Wellington. They appeared to agree upon every one subject; they associated together in private; they went together to Oxford festivals; they met at assemblages of the party; in short, it was quite impossible to say that he was less a member of the Tory party than any one other individual of its body.

It became, therefore, a question between a Liberal Government and one of which the Duke of Cumberland would be an influential member. A correct view of this state of things ought to have made the hopes of the Tory party desperate, and I have no doubt that the result *was* much influenced by their apprehension of being linked to such a colleague.

All these things made so deep an impression upon the king, and so anxious was he to prevent mischief, that, without consulting any body, he conceived the idea of writing to the

Archbishop of Canterbury to use his influence with the Episcopal Bench that they should support, or at all events not oppose, the Government. This singular proceeding was somewhat analogous to the letter he wrote in May, 1832, to the Duke of Wellington. The letter, a copy of which he sent to me, was as follows:

"Windsor Castle, June 6, 1833.

"Thoroughly convinced as is the king that not one of his subjects can share more sincerely than does the Archbishop of Canterbury his majesty's anxious desire to maintain the peace, the happiness, and the security of this country, and to promote whatever may seem calculated to insure this important object, his majesty does not hesitate to address him upon a subject of some delicacy, and to appeal to him for such exertion of his influence with the bishops as he shall consider himself at liberty or shall feel disposed to afford, if the circumstances which appear to his majesty to call for it should strike him in the same light.

"The Archbishop of Canterbury must be impressed with the difficulties and the embarrassments which have arisen in this and other countries from the disposition shown to resist the exercise of lawful and legitimate authority; and his majesty is persuaded that he will concur with him in considering that the ministers of the Church and, above all, its dignitaries, are especially called upon to use their utmost efforts towards promoting a cordial union of the means which shall strengthen the Government of the country, and enable it to maintain its laws and institutions, and the stability of its monarchical constitution.

"He will therefore not be surprised that his majesty should express to him the concern with which he has noticed the appearance of so large a portion, or indeed of any, of the bishops in the ranks of those who are opposed to his majesty's government, upon a recent occasion when the question was one of general foreign policy, agitated and brought forward with a view to embarrass the Government and to affect its existence—to be considered therefore as a party question.

"His majesty apprehends that it has at no time been desirable that the bishops, having seats as such in the House of Lords, should put themselves forward in party questions; and he can not but feel that it would be more advisable and consistent with the peculiar duties assigned to them in the State, and with their own interests and those of the Church, that they should pursue a course which may not have the effect of bringing them into notice as the advocates and the champions of designs levelled at the stability of his majesty's Government.

"The king conceives that he does not exceed the bounds of reason or discretion in making these remarks, or in suggesting a more prudent course to those so situated, while he appeals to their good sense and to their calm view of the embarrassment and the mischief which in such times as the present would inevitably ensue from frequent changes of Government, and from the difficulty, not to say the impracticability, not long since demonstrated, of forming another sufficiently strong, if circumstances should cause the dissolution of that in actual existence.

"The king may with full sincerity declare to the Archbishop of Canterbury, that his own sentiments are entirely free from party feeling and prejudice, or personal predilections, and that he would cordially rejoice if it were possible to remove any obstacle to the union of all that is respectable in the country, of those who have a common interest in its welfare and preservation, and to oppose that union to the designs and combinations of those who aim at the destruction of established institutions, lawful authority, and social order. But so long as this desirable object can not be attained, it becomes his majesty to endeavor to avoid, by all legitimate means, the risk and the evils to which the people which Providence has committed to his rule may be exposed from the prevalence of party feeling and a continued struggle for power, of which the effects, by conveying the executive authority of the State into the hands of successive short-lived administrations, must gradually destroy its energies, and finally endanger its existence. WILLIAM, R."

Watching events, and carefully scanning the signs of the times, I firmly believed that the leaders had made up their minds to all consequences, and that some of their followers were convinced that things would go smoothly the moment the blow was struck. The more prevailing language was, that the time was come for a struggle, and that the battle must now be fought out.

Those who used such pernicious language were not aware of the mischiefs to which they were hurrying on the country. They were blinded by their hatred to the ministers, and their revengeful feelings against the Reform Bill, to gratify which they were ready to run any risks. They had openly avowed that their great object was a dissolution—"any thing to get rid of the present House of Commons;" quite overlooking the fact that a new one, even if chosen within a few months, would give them nothing like such a number of supporters as would enable them to carry on the Government. Their calculation, therefore, was, that a new Parliament would probably be too equally balanced for those who succeeded them to govern with; and thus a *second* dissolution would be unavoidable, and that under the influence of the greatest popular excitement and agitation, so that the Government then to be formed would be entirely in the power of the most violent parties. Under such circumstances, I was fully persuaded that not one of the institutions of the country would have been safe. I was equally convinced that our opponents were solely intent on their immediate object, and were regardless of consequences. They were willing to jeopardize the very existence of the House of Lords, provided only they got rid of the Ministry and the present House of Commons. I wrote fully on this subject to Sir Herbert Taylor, and I added that much of the success of our opponents in persuading more timid or more reflecting men to go along with them was owing to the pains industriously taken by certain persons to misrepresent what was going on at Court, sometimes by suppressing facts, at other times by direct misrepresentation. As an instance of suppression, I mentioned the care with which his majesty's letter to the archbishop was confined to the six or seven bishops who voted against the Government, no knowledge whatever of it having been communicated to any other. Even the Bishop of Chichester (who voted with Government) had no intimation whatever of such a letter having been written.

There was one thing which I considered that the parties in

question had *wholly* overlooked, and yet it is a most indisputable truth. Men, but especially great bodies of men, are found to act far more strenuously, and when bad times come, far more violently, from antipathy and enmity than from opposite feelings. Accordingly, already there were the plainest indications that in some quarters where the present ministers had been attacked (as in the metropolitan districts and midland counties), the late proceedings in the Lords had produced a reaction, and all were waiting with anxiety to attack the Tories. When the struggle came, the animosity against *them* would be certain to carry men much farther than any popularity of the present or any other ministers ever would do; for, indeed, that animosity would be quite consistent with a dislike of both, and the common enemies of all respectable parties in the State would join in the attack, and obtain far more than their share of influence.

To avert the inevitable consequences, I could see no other course than that which the king so successfully pursued the previous summer, and by which I am convinced he saved the monarchy. The House of Lords were very much discontented with it at the time. But I am quite confident, I may say I know, that many who felt greatly vexed at the moment had since become persuaded that the House of Lords itself owed its safety, I may say its *existence*, to the course pursued. The king firmly took and kept his ground; and the Lords, knowing that he was determined to prevent the dreadful consequences of a collision, took care that no collision should happen, and therefore that there should be no necessity for having recourse to the only effectual expedient for preventing it. My belief was that the creation at once of four or five peers, with a plain intimation that more would be created, if necessary, would effectually discomfit the scheme now brought to the very point of execution.

I urged all this in my letters to Taylor, in order that he might submit it to the king. The effect of all this will appear from the following correspondence:

FROM SIR HERBERT TAYLOR.

"Windsor Castle, June 16, 1833.

"MY DEAR LORD,—The king did not return until late yesterday evening, and I therefore deferred submitting the letter I had the honor of receiving from your lordship by messenger until this morning, when I also read to him that which came by the post.

"His majesty orders me to assure you that he enters with anxious solicitude into all that you state with regard to the present critical posture of affairs, and that it is impossible for you or Lord Grey, or any other of his confidential servants, or of his other subjects, to take a more serious view of it than he does. His majesty has contemplated the growing evil with apprehension, and, without endeavoring to scrutinize too closely the causes which may have produced such effects and such a crisis, he has earnestly endeavored to give his best consideration to, and to promote, all that may lessen the embarrassment, and relieve the monarchy and the country from the pressure of the mischief.

"But he can not conceal from himself that every day, every hour almost, throws fresh difficulty and obstacle in the way of any attempt to effect that union of desirable and respectable influence which appears to him so necessary for the prosperity and security of the country, and the maintenance of its institutions; and his majesty laments this the more, as it must strengthen an impression, very frequently admitted, that the danger arises more from the violence and hostility of parties which have a stake in the existence of these institutions, and whose feelings and purposes ought to be, and he firmly believes are, strictly Conservative, than from the revolutionary and demoralizing designs and proceedings of those who would seek to raise themselves by introducing anarchy and confusion in the State.

"His majesty sincerely laments the continued prevalence of the hatred to the present Administration, and of revengeful feeling against the Parliamentary Reform Bill, to which your lordship ascribes the opposition of the Tories to the Irish Church Reform Bill, and to other measures of the Government; and although he thinks that the estimate of the first may be overrated, he does not doubt that the feelings of many may be excited to continued bitterness and soreness by the effects of Schedule A, which they view as having deprived them of property and influence. Rooted prejudices, principles, and opinions may weigh with others, and the desire of coming into office with some; but whatever may be the combination of causes, it has the effect of producing a combination of purpose which is seriously to be regretted and deprecated by those who contemplate, as does your lordship, and as does the king, all the evils and the risk which may arise out of it from a collision between the two Houses, and the continuance of a struggle which may defeat every attempt to maintain or form a strong and Conservative Government, and may eventually throw the affairs of the country into the destroying hands of those who are anxiously watching the occurrence of so fatal a result.

"All this the king feels; and he is surprised, as you are, that it should escape the observation of those who are so deeply interested, as they have always professed to be, in averting such a state of things; who, after the failure of the attempt to form an Administration when called upon by the king to do so, ought to be very cautious of placing themselves, his majesty, and the country under the serious embarrassment which must result from a second failure, or from the uncertainty which, as you justly observe, and as his majesty feels, may attend the returns of another general election in the present temper of the country, or the attempt to improve them by successive dissolutions. There are some, indeed, whose violence might lead them to go all lengths, and to feel callous as to the consequences, as they showed when they supported Sir Henry Parnell's motion, which assailed the prerogative of the Crown; but his majesty can not, under any circumstances, or with reference to the influence of any feeling, believe that such would be the acts of those who opposed that motion.

"The king does not doubt that some effect is produced by misrepresentation of what passes here, and of his sentiments, as well as by the suppression of what may be known to those who exercise an influence over the more timid or more ignorant; but it is impossible that these should wholly shut their eyes and ears, and his majesty has not been sparing of the means and endeavors to undeceive. His sanction to the answer to the address of the House of Lords, which has been generally allowed to carry a sharp rebuke, was given, as you know, without the slightest hesitation; and I am warranted in saying that it would have been given as freely if it had been simply sent to him as on other occasions, and had not been obtained in a manner which might have had the effect of betraying a doubt to the public and to the opposite party of his majesty's inclination to support the Government.*

"His letter to the Archbishop of Canterbury, perhaps one of the strongest steps ever taken towards placing beyond the possibility of doubt the sentiments he entertained, and towards influencing the course of others, originated with his majesty, and was not communicated to any of his servants until it had been sent to the archbishop. One of his objects in writing it was, that his sentiments should become generally known to the Opposition; but this has failed, from the reserve adopted by the person to whom it was addressed; and it is therefore his majesty's intention to give a copy of it to the Archbishop of York on Wednesday next, when he will see him, and urge strongly the embarrassment he apprehends from the opposition made to the measures of his Government.

"Your lordship has, in your last letter, stated that the Opposition in the House of Lords are making an effort to throw out the Local Courts Bill; and although it confirms and affords a strong indication of their hostility, his majesty considers it to be ill-judged, and by no means calculated to serve their purpose, as their opposition to a popular measure must diminish their hopes (if, indeed, they can entertain such at present) of establishing a popular ascendency; and as it can not otherwise answer their purpose, inasmuch as the defeat of the Government on this question, however otherwise unpleasant, would not place them under the necessity of resigning, nor, indeed, need, in his majesty's opinion, the loss of any other question in the House of Lords; while his majesty shall decline to admit such tender of their resignation, and shall continue in the persuasion that nothing could be more inconsistent with the interests of the country, and therefore with the correct discharge of his own duty, than to risk the frequent change of Government.

* This refers to my going with Lord Grey to Windsor, which we considered it our duty to do, as explanations might have been required which were better given personally than by correspondence.

"This, unfortunately, does not apply to the Irish Church Reform Bill, and this has consequently become a source of uneasiness and embarrassment, from which, as threatening in its result the dissolution of the Government, his majesty might have been relieved, if the existence of the Government had not been staked upon it. Allowing that this was rendered unavoidable by the circumstances under which that pledge was given, his majesty must lament it, as it has deprived him of the option which he was prepared to exercise, and has forced upon him the consideration of an alternative to which he had on a former occasion shown a repugnance which continues undiminished.

"His majesty believes that the Opposition would not drive matters to an extremity if they had felt that the collision would be produced without enabling them to carry their point; and it must be obvious that they connect the defeat of the Government on the Irish Church Reform Bill with their pledge that they will stand and fall by its result, and are sensible that his majesty's determination to retain them, in spite of the efforts of their continued opposition, can not avail whenever *this* question shall be decided against them.

"To obviate this difficulty it is proposed again to his majesty to resort to the obnoxious alternative of making an addition to the peerage; and your lordship states that this is consistent with the course which his majesty so successfully pursued last summer, and to which the House of Lords owes its existence, and which prevented the collision and its dreadful consequences. But his majesty orders me to remind you that he had declined to make peers to the extent required, that his refusal produced the resignation of the Government, and the failure of an attempt to form another; and it was owing to that failure, and the apprehension of a collision which, objectionable as it was, at any rate could not have realized any object of ambition or party, that the creation of additional peers was abandoned and the House of Lords saved.

"No person can view the effects of a collision with greater apprehension than his majesty, but he dreads also, in a yet greater degree, the effect of any measure which may degrade the House of Peers and the aristocracy of the country. The former evil must be temporary, and may yield to measures of prevention before its prejudice can be seriously felt, but the latter would be lasting; and the unfavorable impression which must be made by resorting to the *nomination* of peers in order to control the independent vote of the House of Lords must be yet more striking, as it would follow a reform of the other branch of the Legislature, a chief feature of which was the abolition of *nomination* boroughs.

"But the king feels also that his character and his credit are deeply implicated in this question, and that, after all that has passed, he could not resort to this expedient without something like degradation, such as would take greatly from the value of the support he does give, and is disposed to continue to give, to his Government.

"Your lordship proposes the creation of four or five peers, with a plain intimation that more will be created if necessary, and you think this would effectually discomfit the scheme now brought to the very point of being executed. But his majesty conceives there can be very little security for so restricted an exercise of the prerogative, or for its effect.

"The selection of four or five could not be made without giving umbrage to other candidates, and without possibly producing the secession of an equal number of those who may be disappointed. Others must then be created to supply the consequent vacancies in the ranks.

"The experiment and the *intimation* may fail of producing the desired effect, but the principle having been admitted, it would be submitted that there could be no objection to *carry it farther*, and that the intimation is a pledge which must be redeemed; and it is natural to suppose that the proposal would not be made without looking forward to its proving effectual, and that, if the engine prove too weak, his majesty might, having conceded its use, agree to its being strengthened.

"Thus his majesty would be led on from step to step, and engaged in a measure which he dislikes beyond expression; and those who urge him to it, and who probably would not do so if they apprehended such a result, would have in their favor the strong argument that it is unwise, weak, and impolitic to have undertaken that which you have not made up your mind to complete after having abandoned the chief objection, which is to the principle.

"The king believes Lord Grey to be himself extremely averse to any other than a very limited addition of peers—namely, of four or five; and his majesty has been assured by him that he would never propose any other. Lord Grey must, therefore, enter into his feelings as to the inconvenience of resorting to this expedient in order to escape from the embarrassment which arises from the pledge given on the Irish Church Reform Bill.

"Upon the whole, the question is full of difficulty; and this and other considerations connected with the state of the country and the signs of the times engage his majesty's solicitude, and render him daily more anxious for the possibility of finding a solution of the difficulty, and a remedy for present and impending evils in the union of men of talent, influence, and property, who have a common stake in the country, and a common interest in its happiness and safety, and in the maintenance of its monarchical institutions. His majesty is very sensible of all the impediments to the realization of so desirable and so essential an object, and of the wishes which he is bound to form, as well as of the difficulty of setting it on foot; but he would readily agree to any suggestions which might be offered to him for the promotion of such an object, and the day of its success would be the happiest of his life.

"In the contemplation of the possible though dreaded result of the present struggle, it is natural that the king should consider what may be the situation of the Administration by which the present should be replaced, and the unavoidable effect of difference of political opinions and principles which must lead to the establishment of a formidable and embarrassing Opposition, consisting in great measure of those who are so ably conducting the business of the country at this period. It is not extraordinary that, in addressing your lordship on this occasion and this subject, his majesty should contemplate with apprehension the possibility of your transcendent talents and formidable energies being again arrayed against the Government of the country, and this must strengthen the anxious desire he has ordered me to express.

"I have read this letter to the king, and his majesty authorizes me to add that it expresses correctly the sentiments and the feelings he had commanded me to convey to you. I have the honor to be, with great regard, my dear lord, your lordship's most obedient and faithful servant,

"H. Taylor.

"The Lord High Chancellor."

TO SIR HERBERT TAYLOR.

"Berkeley Square, June 18, 1833.

"My dear Sir Herbert,—I received your letter of the 16th late on Sunday night, and as I wished to see Lord Grey before I answered it, this has caused the delay.

"Every thing that has happened must tend to show his majesty's firm and gracious intention to support his Government; and, above all, his letter to the archbishop, which was in the archbishop's hands before any one of the ministers had seen it. His majesty's communication of this, in the quarter you mention, can not fail to have a very salutary effect.

"His majesty's solicitude on the present occasion is most natural, and does the highest honor to his principles and his feelings. The repugnance his majesty feels to the course alluded to in my letter of Saturday is really not greater than I feel myself; and I beg you to assure his majesty that, in throwing out the suggestion, I by no means intended to give a final and conclusive opinion, still less to speak on the part of any one else; but having stated what I most deeply felt impressed with, upon the approaching crisis, and described the dangers towards which the proceedings of the Opposition were plainly driving the country, I naturally conceived that his majesty would say, 'There is no need of dwelling so much on the evil, if you have no plan for a remedy.' I therefore stated *one* remedy which appeared to me sure and effectual, though certainly attended with many objectionable consequences; and I only stated it as fit to be considered and kept in view, and, as it were, in reserve, should the necessity become as pressing as I feared it would.

"If there be any other, I shall most sincerely rejoice, but I am sure I do not see it. Those combinations to which you allude appear wholly impracticable, while men are in their present state of hostility; and if attempted at this time, would inevitably produce the most disastrous consequences, utterly destroying the character of all public men, and placing the country in the hands of the enemies of all good government.

"The conduct of the House of Lords renders this the more unquestionable. Those men are bent upon dictating to the Crown, the Commons, and the country. They think that they have in their hands the absolute power of ruling all, and I much fear they will injure all, without exercising that power. But they themselves will be the first to suffer; and I assure you that the feeling towards them has already risen to a very alarming height.

"What you say respecting the pledge (on the Irish Church Bill) must be very materially qualified, by considering that such a measure as the Coercion Bill could never have been otherwise carried, or indeed even proposed, by the present ministers; but I really think that this very circumstance of the pledge given affords almost the only chance of the Opposition failing in their meditated attempt; for it may make some of their followers hesitate to join them in an attack which they know must produce such a result. Certain it is that at this time the only parties who are in great spirits are those strong adherents of the Opposition, and the Radicals; others are very generally thoughtful, and even desponding.

"Believe me ever, my dear Sir Herbert, most faithfully yours, H. B."

[*Private.*] FROM SIR HERBERT TAYLOR.

"Windsor Castle, June 19, 1833.

"MY DEAR LORD,—I do not delay acknowledging the receipt of your lordship's letter of yesterday, and acquainting you that I have had the honor of submitting it to the king, who has ordered me to notice that part of it relative to which you communicated with Lord Grey. * * * *

"I have received his majesty's commands to say a few words also on the subject of the pledge which has been appended to the result of the Irish Church Reform Bill.

"The king had stated that, '*allowing the pledge to have been rendered unavoidable by the circumstances under which it was given*, he laments it as having deprived him of the option he was prepared to exercise;' and this he repeats. He does not mean to say that his Government could or could not have carried the Irish Coercion measure without entering into such a pledge with respect to further measures, nor does he enter into any consideration of the effect which it may or may not produce upon those who may not be disposed to go the lengths of the ultras in the ranks of either class of your opponents; but his majesty can not help feeling and saying that by such pledge on the result of any measure, whether the effect of necessity, of policy, or of the principle on which the Government consider it their duty to act, they deprive themselves of the advantage of his majesty's determination to support them against the successful opposition in the House of Lords, and therefore deprive his majesty of the option he was prepared to exercise with respect to this, as with respect to other measures, upon the principles stated in my letter of the 16th instant.

"His majesty has ordered me to add that he has had a very satisfactory conversation with the Archbishop of York, the particulars of which he will state to Lord Grey. I have the honor to be, with great regard, my dear lord, your lordship's most obedient and faithful servant,

"H. Taylor.

"The Lord High Chancellor."

FROM EARL GREY.

"Downing Street, June 19, 1833.

"My dear Chancellor,—All the material points in Taylor's letter seem to me to be satisfactorily answered in yours. In your first letter you certainly propose more directly than was consistent with what I had said to the king, the possibility of an eventual creation of peers to counterbalance the majority against us. This, you may remember, the Cabinet had agreed in considering as out of the question on the present occasion. This certainly was very strongly my own opinion; and I stated to the king, for the purpose of removing the apprehension by which he was considerably affected, that no such proposition would be made to him.

"I made a reserve, however, of five or six, as an indication, if necessary, of his continued confidence and support, but not as the proof of a determination to go farther.

"The manner, however, in which you explain this, as your individual suggestion of a remedy for the evil with which the country is threatened, if no other could be found, with all the repugnance you express to it, ought to satisfy the king, and I have no doubt will do so.

"We have done all we can. We have laid the whole case before his majesty—the danger which exists, and the means of averting it. We have, therefore, nothing now left but to wait the issue, our line of conduct being clearly marked, and being indeed without an alternative. Ever yours,

"GREY."

[*Private.*]

"Windsor Castle, July 14, 1833.

"MY DEAR LORD,—I beg to acknowledge the receipt of your lordship's letter of yesterday, which I had the honor of submitting to the king. His majesty also had learned conflicting reports respecting the plans of the Opposition on Wednesday, and the probable result. But he still clings to the belief that they will not throw out the Irish Church Reform Bill, at least to the belief that the Duke of Wellington will not be a party to that proceeding, although he admits that Sir Robert Peel's vote upon its last stage in the House of Commons is calculated to shake it. On the other hand, after the communications made to your Lordship on Tuesday as to the expected result of the debate, which were so decidedly contradicted by that result, it is not very safe to trust any reports or communications from the Opposition on these occasions.

"His majesty has heard also that some of the party are busily engaged in arranging a new government—and, on the other hand, that this has been given up as a hopeless business. In short, rumors and reports reach him as they do others, but he very much doubts whether those who would carry weight have any plans, and he doubts yet more the practicability of their forming a government upon the strength and stability of which any reliance could be placed.

"You are perfectly aware of his majesty's feeling with regard to a change under such circumstances, and he concludes that you will have seen the communication to Lord Grey of his determination not to accept the resignation of his present ministers, unless satisfied that there exists satisfactory means of forming another government which can carry on the business of the country and *hold on.*

"The king is not surprised that you should be tired and disgusted with the present course of things, and with holding office in such times, and with the annoyance of encountering almost daily the bitter hostility of the House of Lords; and he can easily conceive that you often heartily wish yourself out of so unpleasant and unprofitable a concern; but I need not say how strongly his majesty feels that you can on no account be spared. Times may mend, and the best chance of their mending is afforded by the continual services of such men as yourself. If these should cease to put their shoulder to the wheel, the machine will stop. The result of Tuesday's debate, and of the previous progress on the Local Courts Bill, was certainly very mortifying and discouraging, and I am not surprised that your lordship should have felt it so acutely; but it would not have justified resignation; and I question whether *in these* times, and with such uncertain and hazardous prospects, the loss of the Irish Church Reform Bill would justify resignation if a pledge had not been attached.

"The conduct pursued by Lord Hill has annoyed the king extremely, and it is impossible that any one should attempt to justify it. To his friends especially it must be a subject of great concern.

"As to the difficulties of the present crisis, and the mischief which may arise out of them, no one can be less disposed than I am to underestimate them; but I have always felt that difficulties are made to be overcome, and with God's blessing I trust I shall live to congratulate you upon their being overcome, and upon the country being in full possession of benefits to which your labors will have so essentially contributed. I have the honor to be, with great regard, my dear lord, your lordship's most obedient and faithful servant,

"H. TAYLOR.

"THE LORD HIGH CHANCELLOR, etc., etc., etc."

[*Private.*] "Windsor Castle, July 23, 1833.

"MY DEAR LORD, — Your lordship's letter of yesterday did not reach me until past eight o'clock, upon the king's return from London; and although I took the earliest opportunity of submitting it to the king, I could not reply to it by post. You will forgive my saying that it appeared to me that you were disposed to take too gloomy a view of your prospects with regard to the ultimate fate of the Irish Church Reform Bill, and one not borne out by the conclusions which it is reasonable to draw from what has already passed, and from what you yourself state to be the present feeling; and these were also the remarks of the king on reading your lordship's letter.

"That the majority of the Opposition Lords would be glad to throw out the bill, no one can doubt, and as little that they would be glad to turn the Government out with it: that they might do the former, if they set about it in good earnest, appears equally indisputable; and that the second contingency must be the effect of such defeat, results necessarily from the pledge which has committed the existence of the Government with the fate of this bill. But although there may be some who are so mad, mischievous, or short-sighted as to prefer a serious collision between the two Houses, or a convulsion in the country to the abandonment of an opposition which may in their view produce such consequences, there appears to his majesty sufficient reason to believe and to hope that such are not the feelings or the views of others in sufficient number to prevent such results; and his majesty persists in giving credit to these for such good sense and policy, and also for a desire to preserve the peace of the country, as shall prevent them from driving or allowing things to be driven to extremities, while they are conscious that any attempt on their part to form an efficient Administration, in the event of the dissolution of the present Government, would be hopeless. They may continue to annoy you with meetings, reports, and demonstrations tending to keep you in a state of teasing and feverish suspense; but their hostility to you will not carry them to the length of cutting their own throats, which they must be sensible they would do if they were to force on the dissolution of the Government upon a question decidedly popular, and accompanied by a strong collision with the other branch of the Legislature, of which the influence in the country, and in the administration of its concerns, has unfortunately become gradually so preponderating as to be almost paramount.

"Nor can they be ignorant of the feelings and sentiments of the great majority of that House, or callous to the conviction that the moderation with which (with few exceptions) they are pursuing their course as respects the House of Lords, and the quiet manner in which they are observing its proceedings, arise from a sense of their power and of that paramount influence.

"All these considerations lead his majesty to believe and to hope that the blow which your lordship apprehends will not be struck. I have the honor to be, with great regard, my dear lord, your lordship's most obedient humble servant,

"H. Taylor.

"P.S.—The king has just received Lord Grey's very satisfactory report of the past evening's proceedings in the Committee."

[*Private.*] "St. James, July 24, 1833.

"My dear Lord,—I can not leave London without acknowledging the receipt of your lordship's letter of this day, and acquainting you that I have submitted it to the king.

"His majesty was by no means disposed to think that it was in your nature to take a gloomy view of things, but you certainly did appear to him to have done so in your last letter, with respect to the probable course and the results of the discussion on the Irish Church Reform Bill; and his majesty considered also that his Government in general were less sanguine than he was himself, and that they formed their opinions on reports raised and spread for the purpose of annoying them, rather than upon any reasonable view of general circumstances. Without repeating what I have said on this subject, I will only observe that up to this day the king's anticipations have been confirmed, and that the occurrences of last night are calculated to strengthen them. His majesty was well aware of the violence of those who are anxious and have endeavored to drive the Duke of Wellington to a course of opposition and measures which are repugnant to his own good sense, and to his probable conviction of and dread of the evils which would result from the dissolution of the Government at this period. But the violence on the one side, and the reluctance to yield to it on the other, were the very circumstances upon which his majesty felt justified in building his expectations of your success; and it appeared to him impossible that this diversity of feeling should not produce schism and divisions which must serve your purpose. His majesty sincerely hopes that his Government will very soon be satisfactorily relieved from suspense. I have the honor to be, with great regard, my dear lord, your lordship's most obedient and faithful servant, H. TAYLOR.

"THE RIGHT HON. THE LORD CHANCELLOR, etc., etc., etc."

[*Private.*] "Wansted, August 30, 1833.

"MY DEAR LORD GREY,—I forgot before leaving town to renew my urgent request about Miss Martineau's pension, of which we talked last winter. I am sure Lady Grey (if I wrote to her, which I have a great mind to do) will join warmly in this. You know what was her (Miss Martineau's) case. When her father failed in the panic, she refused an annuity from some of her relations, and supported herself and her mother *by her needle.* This I know to be the fact; she went on for two years in that way, then discovered that she had another gift and another vocation. She has since made a good income by her books. But she is driven to write *too much* and too constantly; and this is spoiling her, and indeed wearing her out. So that £100 a year might be the means of saving her from going down, and finally going out. Whether or not she might be romantic about it, as she was about her cousin's offer, I can't tell. But, at all events, your offering it to her would be a most creditable thing to you, and be most agreeable to all our people.

"Yours ever, H. BROUGHAM."

CHAPTER XXV.

Bishop Phillpotts.—Court Politics.—Affairs of Portugal: of Spain.—Policy of Non-intervention.—Duc de Broglie.—Trades-unions and Conspiracies. —Lord Sligo.—Dissensions in the Ministry.—Lord Grey's Resolution to resign.—Remonstrance against it.—The Effect of the Remonstrance.—The Crisis in Portugal.—Project of an Edinburgh Testimonial to Lord Grey.—Clearing off of Arrears of Chancery and other Business.—Judicial Arrangements.—Denman, Lyndhurst, Sir W. Horne, Pepys, Campbell.—The Retirement of Baron Bayley.—Sir John Campbell's Claims.

Some mischief-making person had carried to the Bishop of Exeter a tale that I had taken offense at some expressions he had used in a recent debate, as if they had been an attack upon me. This had no foundation whatever, but the story produced from the bishop the following excellent letter. I may here state that ever since I knew him in the House of Lords I had entertained the highest opinion of the great talents of that prelate. Sure I am that, had he taken to the Bar instead of the Church, as a profession, he would have risen to the very highest place. Lord Grey never could endure him.

FROM THE BISHOP OF EXETER.

[*Private.*]

"34 St. James's Place.

"My dear Lord,—I have been informed that it has been supposed, or that it has been affected to be supposed, that I alluded to your lordship the night before last, when I said something about the offices or officers of state who had been believed to communicate with the 'Times.' *I give your lordship my honor that I had no such purpose.* The party to whom I really alluded was Lord Durham, and the ground of my allusion was, what has been so much the subject of recent talk, the alleged estrangement between his lordship and Lord Grey, on the notion, whether true or not, that the 'Times' had been enabled to say what ought not to have been put within its power.

"I was much hurt when I was told that I had been supposed to have said any thing, by mere implication, adverse in any way to you; for although no private consideration would or ought to prevent my saying *openly* what it might appear to me that I had a right to say in defending a great public cause, yet I should certainly be restrained by the strongest feelings from saying any thing *covertly* against you. To you I feel indebted for disinterested and most judicious kindness, shown to me when I needed kindness; and I should blush for myself if I could ever act in a manner unworthy of that feeling.

"Do not think that I write this to deprecate your powerful attack on me for any thing I may have said. I only wish that you should know I am not so base as to *insinuate* any thing against you. Yours, my dear lord, most sincerely,

"H. Exeter."

In the autumn I had the following correspondence with Lord Grey:

FROM EARL GREY.

"Howick, September 14, 1833.

"My dear Chancellor,—I received your letter on my arrival here, where, I am sorry to say, I have not found the weather of which you boast in Westmorland.

"The king's speech on the investment of the Speaker was very generally known from the report of many who heard it, and I see is stated in the 'Globe,' though not correctly, as he did not use the phrase 'Reformed House of Commons.' I should not like to give my authority for its publication, not remembering accurately the precise expressions; but the substance was what I stated to you. I do not believe in any intrigues at Windsor. I never saw the king less in a disposition to say or do any thing which could afford hope or encouragement to those who might be willing to engage in them, though on certain subjects he is apt to run a little out of the course when he is in the vein of speaking. For instance, after the great military dinner, which he gave last week in St. George's Hall after a review, he launched out against France, and, raising his voice to its highest pitch, told his guests that he hoped, if ever they had to draw their swords, it would be against *the French, the natural enemies of England.* *Per contra,* he holds language equally strong with respect to Russia, though not in speeches. He has conducted himself, according to my last accounts, with perfect discretion in his reception of the young Queen of Portugal. * * * * I have heard nothing worth repeating since I arrived here; but the course things are taking in Portugal makes me fear, more than I did, that we shall not be able to abstain much longer from taking measures to put an end to a war which must ruin that country, and can not continue without producing injury and discredit to us. Ever yours, GREY.

"The pamphlet is quite excellent. The Tory papers, of course, will say many things that can annoy, whether true or false. I never read them."

[*Private.*] "Howick, September 21, 1833.

"DEAR CHANCELLOR,—I am quite as well satisfied as you are that we have not hitherto interposed in Portugal, but if Bourmont continues a war of devastation there, I think it will be impossible for us, consistently either with the interest or the honor of this country, to abstain from taking effectual measures to put an end to it. France is quite willing to join with us; and Leopold, if he is not a traitor, ought to be equally ready to do so. We three concurring, the thing would soon be settled. I am sure you will agree with me in thinking that the Holy Alliance must not be allowed to interfere.

"I am perhaps too indifferent to attacks in the newspapers, and had only seen a very unfair article upon the Westminster stall in the 'Morning Herald,' of which I had not intended to take notice; but, in consequence of what you say, I have sent the facts to Ellice, to deal with as he pleases. They are very strong.

"The Bishopric of Hereford, held by the late bishop with the Wardenship of Winchester, became vacant just as we were going out.

"The king desired that my brother should be appointed to it, as a mark of his regard to me, and signified his wish that he should keep the living of Bishopsgate with it *in commendam*, as the Bishop of London had done when he was Bishop of Chester. This I declined, but, our resignation [not] having then been accepted, asked a stall for him when an opportunity should offer.

"The first that became vacant, St. Paul's, ought therefore to have been his, but for reasons of which you are aware I preferred giving it to Tate.*

"I really could not in justice pass over him a second time.

"Every bishop with a small bishopric has some preferment with it. Hereford, with the Westminster stall, will not exceed what by the Irish Bill is stated as the income below which the Irish bishoprics ought not to be reduced. They live at less expense there, and come to London only *once* in four years. My brother, as junior bishop, has been obliged to reside constantly in London during the two longest sessions that ever occurred. Is not this a strong case?

"Ever yours, GREY."

FROM EARL GREY.

"Howick, October 17, 1833.

"MY DEAR CHANCELLOR,—I have received your letter, having heard previously an excellent account of you from Holland, on your passage through London.

"Melbourne had written to me about the prorogation. I suggested the 5th or the 12th December, and I understand that they have determined on the latter, and the council would be held for this purpose on Wednesday last.

"I am very glad to hear that the Municipal Commission is going on so well. This and other important questions, especially that most difficult one of tithes, should be, if possible, in such a state of preparation as to be introduced immediately after the meeting of Parliament.

"Wellesley writes me word that the Duke of Cumberland, as grand master, is giving great activity to the Orange lodges, and if his proceedings are not checked, that the Coercion Bill will be rendered nugatory in that part of the country. I have desired him to get an accurate account of all that has been done, to be laid before the Cabinet when it reassembles officially. In the mean time, to exert the powers of the Government to stop the processions on the 5th November.

"Ellice is now here, having been some time in Scotland.

---

* James Tate, many years the distinguished master of the Grammar School of Richmond, Yorkshire, editor of "Horatius Restitutus," 1832.

He has given me much useful information with respect to the state of that country, which will require serious consideration. He heard from Gillies* that two vacancies are likely soon to occur on the Bench. The filling them up will require great care and attention, and I trust nothing will be done till I have had an opportunity of considering it with you and Melbourne.

"I hear very good accounts of the king, and they are confirmed by my correspondence with him, which, on his part, is quite cordial, but strongly marked by a dislike of too close a connection with France. On the other hand, he is very much excited against Russia.

"The Peninsula does not promise much diminution of our difficulties. A contest for the crown in Spain seems nearly certain. Our conduct must be governed by circumstances of which we can not at present sufficiently judge; but I think there can be no doubt that our interest is on the side of the queen, and that while we risk nothing by sending credentials to Villiers,† with a discretion to withhold them if circumstances, at the time of his receiving them, should make him think it expedient to do so, a great moral effect in favor of that cause would be produced by this recognition.

"At Lisbon, Pedro is acting the part of Don Miguel, and I am convinced no good can ever be done while he remains there, unless his present ministers can be removed, and a wholesome constraint put upon him by the appointment of others whose principles and character would give confidence to the country.

"I have lately been very far from well, but am better. I shall be in town on the 10th of November. Ever yours,

"Grey."

[*Private.*]

"Howick, October 25, 1833.

"My dear Chancellor,—* * * * It is quite clear that all active interference, on the part both of England and France, in the Spanish affairs, should be avoided as much as possible. The best chance of obviating this necessity is to be found in giving to the queen all the moral support that

* Adam Gillies (see vol. i., p. 167).

† Sir George Villiers, at that time our ambassador at Madrid, afterwards Earl of Clarendon and Secretary of State for Foreign Affairs.

we can, without committing ourselves to any thing further. But there are two dangers—the one, of the intrigues which will be carried on by the ministers of our good allies in the North against us; the other, the real danger that may be created to France if Don Carlos should be able to make head so far even as to carry on a doubtful conflict in Spain, in combination with the French Carlists. Your advice to De Broglie is perfectly good, but you must consider the difficulties in which he may be placed in such a state of things as I have supposed, and how strongly he may be controlled by public opinion. The result of all is what I begun by stating, that we should do all we can, without interfering, to favor the cause, the success of which is closely connected with our own most important interests.

"It was therefore of the utmost consequence that [*illegible*] credentials should be received, and credentials sent to Villiers, and it is most fortunate that our royal master has been brought to consent to it. But this violent prejudice against every thing French, and principally against Louis Philippe, has been, and will be, productive of great embarrassments. I believe the best course will be to let this matter alone for the present, and trust to opportunities to convince him that the projects of Metternich, and not those of the French Government, are those which are likely to lead to a general war of the most fatal character.

"The truth is that it is Metternich who, as he was, in what was so falsely called the settlement of Europe after '14 and '15, the cause of all the mischief that now exists, is the chief promoter of all the measures which, urged with a view to suppress the revolutionary spirit, are the most likely to bring it into action. I think something effectual might be done to counteract this by the press—a series of good articles headed 'Metternich.' * * * *

"The question of secondary punishments is certainly one of very great importance. Howick has taken great pains upon it, understands it thoroughly, and I should like very much to see it placed in his hands, more especially if it were possible to make an arrangement for George Lamb, by which he might succeed him in the Home Department; but there are more pressing questions—that of tithes, which can not be delayed; the poor-laws; to say nothing of the corporations, and the financial arrangements which must be made in consequence of the opposition to the assessed taxes. These furnish of themselves work enough for a whole session. Besides, in politics as in war, I believe the wisdom of the maxim, to finish one thing before you begin another, to be incontrovertible.

"I shall, if alive, certainly be in town on the 10th, and I see no reason to think that I can be wanted sooner.

"Ever yours, GREY."

At this time I received the following letter from the Duc de Broglie:

"Paris, Octobre 25, 1833.

"DEAR BROUGHAM,—J'ai eu un très grand plaisir à revoir quelque peu de votre écriture. Ce n'est pas qu'elle soit belle, mais elle est rare.

"Je ne disputerai point avec vous sur le sujet de vos deux épitres; car nous sommes parfaitement d'accord. Il est clair que l'intervention dans les affaires intérieures des gouvernements n'est pas plus légitime au nom du principe constitutionel qu'au nom du principe absolutiste, et qu'il faut laisser les peuples de donner la forme d'administration, qui leur convient. Aussi n'avons nous pas la moindre idée de prendre les armes pour rétablir en Espagne la constitution du Cortès, ou pour y établir toute autre constitution quelconque. Il est clair, également, qu'il faut laisser chaque peuple de donner le souverain qui leur convient. Et quand à nous, nous aurions fort préféré que Don Carlos eut succédé naturellement à son frère, selon la loi de 1713; cela était infiniment plus dans l'intérêt de la France. La succession feminine qui nous menace de nous donner ce jour pour voisin, je ne sais qui, nous est au fond très défavorable. Nous ne nous engagerons donc à l'égard de la rein eIsabelle dans aucune entreprise chevaleresque; nous ne nous batterons pas uniquement pour les beaux yeux. Mais permettez-moi de vous le dire, vous êtes bien [mieux] placé à votre aise pour préférer le principe de non-intervention dans toute la pureté que nous: vous êtes des insulaires; *toto divisos orbe Britannos;* vous n'avez point de voisins, et quoiqu'il arrive sur le continent, vous vous croisez les bras, et vous n'en faites que rire. De plus, votre révolution est vieille de 150 ans; elle a de la barbe sur le menton, et le Roi de Sardaigne n'est pas pour vous un prétendant fort et redoutable. Nous, nous n'avons que trois ans de date, et nous avons des voisins. Cela change grandement la thèse. Don Carlos arrivant au trône par voix de succession ordinaire, nous était donc aussi indifférent que son frère; mais Don Carlos arrivant au trône en chef de partie, comme un héros de contre révolution, à la tête des moines et des volontaires royalistes, en criant 'Mort aux libéraux Français,' et 'Vive l'inquisition,' offrant asile à tous les Vendiens de France, accueillant selon toute apparence la Duchesse de Berri, le Duc de Bordeaux et toute sa séquelle, instituant une Vendée sur notre frontière du midi, est pour nous un voisin très incommode. C'est pour ce motif que nous avons jugé convenable de nous déclarer sur le champ en faveur de la reine, et de lui assurer en l'avouant hautement, tout l'appui que dépend de nous à lui donner. Si cela affermit le gouvernement de la reine, ainsi que j'espère, nous aurons bien fait. S'il succombe malgrè l'intérêt que nous avons témoigné pour lui, nous prendrons conseil des circonstances, et nous ferons de notre mieux pour nous défendre contre celui qui le remplacera. Voilà tout notre politique dans cette affaire. Nous n'avons jamais pensé à nous faire ni en Espagne, ni ailleurs, les Dons Quichottes de la constitution et des Cortès. C'est une entreprise assez difficile que d'établir la liberté chez soi, en la conciliant avec l'ordre public. Aucun gouvernement n'a pour mission de l'établir chez les autres. Nous nous bornons à cet égard à faire des vœux bien sincères, et à ne rien empêcher. Pardon de ce long griffonage. Donnez-moi de vos nouvelles, etc., etc.

"ID. DE BROGLIE."

[*Private.*]

"Brougham, November 4, 1833.

"MY DEAR LORD GREY,—I have really *no doubt at all* about the expediency, not to say the necessity, of your seeing the king, and at once settling it. The enemy are already at work, I doubt not. They are, I know, flying reports about the town in all directions of the king insisting on Lyndhurst, etc., etc.; and who knows what the Duke of Cumberland may put into certain people's heads? Moreover, the vacancy of the office is of extreme inconvenience.

"As for any other arrangements, there is not the least hurry. You will have two or three weeks at least (if necessary) to make up your mind upon these. A solicitor-general by law has *all* the attorney-general's power when that place is vacant. Yours ever, H. BROUGHAM.

"P.S.—I expect to see you on your way to town.

"If any delay is suggested, in order to speak to me on Monday, you may say I have not the chance of being able to go to St. James's. Indeed it may be quinsy, after all, having only gone over to the other side of the throat, though certainly the pain is considerably less.

"I think it as well to send the Irish part of the Reform, as it completes the whole, though very possibly the voters are taken too high; but I have transcribed the whole notes just as they were, and have not added some things that occurred since our discussions with Stanley. * * * *

"I delivered your challenge to Lord Thanet. He says, with such a climate as you have, there is nothing wonderful in *any* turnip crop. Even here one field yields £10 an acre by feeding off."

[*Private.*] "Lambton Castle, November 5, 1833.

"MY DEAR CHANCELLOR,—I return the copies of your letter to De Broglie and of Taylor's to you, and Lord Granville's, which I received with yours yesterday just as I was leaving Howick. I need not say that I concur in all you have said to De Broglie: you might have added that nothing would probably so much encourage and assist any designs hostile to France which the three Powers may entertain—and that they have such can not be doubted—as her Government's getting into a contest, which would occasion a great division of its force in Spain. I shall be glad to see De Broglie's answer at your convenience.

"The foolish scheme of the procession to Westminster Hall turned out as might have been expected. But this system of constantly agitating any subject on which any part of the community may feel itself aggrieved, is very annoying and very mischievous. How is any Government to go on under such a system, or what is the use of a reformed Parliament if we are to have a hundred mock Parliaments sitting in every part of the kingdom prescribing to the Legislature the course which it is to pursue?

"The trades-unions, too, afford another subject which calls for the most serious consideration.

"They had an excellent meeting yesterday at Newcastle for poor Losh. Lambton was in the chair, and every thing, I am told, went off most satisfactorily—no Radicals; £400 subscribed in the room.

"I proceed to-morrow on my journey, stop one night at Lord Howden's and two at Lord Dacre's, and hope to be in town on Monday to dinner.

"If you have any thing to send, direct to me on Thursday to the George Inn, Grantham; Friday, Cock Inn, Eaton; Saturday and Sunday, The Hoo, Welwyn.

"Ever yours, GREY."

[*Private.*] "December 23, 1833.

"MY DEAR CHANCELLOR,—I received your letter from Wansford this morning. I had already, on the morning you left London, desired Phillips to make an abstract of all the information received respecting the unions, which, as soon as it is completed, I will desire him to send to you. The laws against unlawful combination, secret oaths, etc., are already sufficiently strong; the question will be whether any thing can be done to enforce them in the way of exhortations to the masters and magistrates, and warning to offenders; and whether in the more aggravated form of the offense, when actual violence is offered to persons willing to work, the penalty should not be increased to transportation, for instance. I will endeavor to see Parkes, who knows, I believe, more upon this subject than any body. I think it better to say nothing to the king till we have made up our minds whether or not any thing can be done to strengthen the law. The great difficulty is in convicting, and the remedy for this is not easy.

"I have desired at the Foreign Office that bulletins may be sent to you. There is nothing new, since I saw you, from the Peninsula. I have had two long conversations with Lieven and Esterhazy. Upon the whole, I think we shall be able to avoid a collision in the East for the present, but how long is another question. * * * Ever yours, GREY."

[*Private.*] FROM EARL GREY.

"Woburn Abbey, December 28, 1833.

"MY DEAR CHANCELLOR,—I can no longer deny myself the melancholy satisfaction of expressing to you my sincere and affectionate sympathy in the affliction which you have suffered.* I should have done this sooner, but for the fear of adding to your distress in the first moments of your sorrow, and am not without a doubt as to the effect of writing now. But I have myself experienced pleasure from the kind attention of my friends when I have experienced similar losses; and I am not without hope, though comfort there is none to be given, that this assurance of the feeling in which I have participated with all your friends may not be unpleasing to you.

"I will not trouble you with any business at this moment, beyond expressing a hope that, when all your melancholy duties are performed, you will return to occupations for which you will be so much wanted, and which may assist in diverting your thoughts from the constant reflection on your irreparable loss.

"I came here yesterday, and return to town on Monday; the duchess is very unwell, having been poisoned by colchicum given imprudently and in too large doses for an attack of rheumatism. She has now a confirmed jaundice. Believe me, my dear chancellor, yours very sincerely, GREY.

"If you can write without distressing yourself, a single line to say that you are well would give me the greatest pleasure."

[*Private.*] "Brougham, December 31, 1833.

"MY DEAR LORD GREY,—I got your letter yesterday, and am very much obliged to you. If you see Lord Holland, tell him the same.

"This refusal of Miguel (which I learn by this day's abstract), and Sarmente's arrival, will require an immediate determination, for which reason I write to trouble you with one or two things that occur to me.

"I suppose we must now, in concert with Spain and with

* The death of his brother James, on 22d December.

the concurrence of France, if not with her help, put down the anarchy, which can not be supposed to last forever, when we have ministers both at Madrid and Lisbon, and there are queens in both countries, *de facto* as well as *de jure.* But two things must plainly be attended to: First, so to act as may give the least possible color to Russia and Austria for setting up our conduct in the Peninsula as a precedent when they desire to interfere in Germany, and perhaps elsewhere; and next, to take all the security we can for Don Pedro's better behavior. Of course he must agree to certain previous conditions, as a more respectable and popular Ministry (Palmela, etc.), and to certain measures of amnesty, and, above all, of conciliation towards the priests, as far as that can safely be attempted. His leaving Portugal altogether and allowing a *Council of Regency* would be the only real security; because what he agrees to *now*, either as to men or measures, he is sure, or nearly sure, to go from when he is or thinks himself safe. But that, I conclude, is impossible. The next best thing, and it seems essential in every way, is the immediate calling the Cortes. Nor can I see the least difficulty in this, unless the Spanish Government is alarmed at the *name* and the *nearness* of it. From this hasty statement you can judge what I should be likely to think and advise were I on the spot. I only give it to you as a provisional opinion, being at a distance, and knowing that other things may be known to you and our colleagues which have not yet reached me. You can tell what difference such things would make on my notions, and I trust my conscience to your keeping. Pray tell Palmerston, with my best regards, that I had occasion to write to the Duc de Broglie the other day, and I gave him a hint about *their law proceedings.* But as it was only a sentence or two in a letter quite private, I kept no copy.

"Yours ever truly, H. BROUGHAM."

[*Private.*] FROM EARL GREY.

"Downing Street, January 3, 1834.

"MY DEAR CHANCELLOR,—Many thanks for your letter, which gave me the greatest pleasure. There is little difference, if any, between your opinions and mine with respect to the Peninsular question. Before we give him any assistance, we must have some security that Pedro will improve his conduct. The best and perhaps the only one to be relied upon with any confidence, would be that he and Miguel should pair off. But I don't see how we could insist upon this; and if we could find a good husband for the young queen, with the restrictions which the Cortes might impose upon him during the short period of his regency, an arrangement upon the whole satisfactory may, I think, be made. I was in hopes you might have been here for the Cabinet dinner here on Tuesday, and should have much preferred your personal opinion to your proxy. Having been intrusted with it, however, I shall hope for your approbation of the use I shall make of it.

"I have all the papers respecting the trades-unions, but did not trouble you with them at a moment when I thought you could not attend to them. I don't know that they will be of any further use than recalling to your memory what you have already known. Yours ever, GREY."

Trades-unions, or the combinations of workmen against their employers, were by no means formed solely with a view to compel an advance or prevent a reduction of wages. Their influence as a social evil is far more extensive, for they exercise a permanent effect upon the freedom both of capital and labor.

No persons are more grievously oppressed by them than many classes of the workmen themselves.

In their construction, and in their enforced regulations, it is scarcely possible to conceive a more thorough despotism. One of their methods for preventing or punishing disobedience or infringement of their rules, is to place sentinels, pickets as they are called, near any suspected manufactory or workshop: these pickets were to prevent men working for a master the union had denounced; and this picketing system had led to acts even of violence.

I had much communication with Grey on the subject; agreeing as I did with him that these trades-unions were in the nature of *conspiracies* of the worst kind; their existence a blot upon a system such as no government ought to suffer; but how to deal with them was no small difficulty.

FROM EARL GREY.

"January 4, 1834.

"If the laws against conspiracy were not rendered in a great degree ineffectual by the difficulty of proof, nothing more would be required. The only alterations that appear to me to be wanted are: a summary power to the magistrates, where there appeared to be [people] stationed round a manufactory upon the system of what is called picketing, to order them away, and, upon their refusal, to commit them; and in cases of actual violence, as I suggested before, an increase of the punishment. I saw Parkes before I went to Woburn. He acknowledges that the system is extending itself, but is against any alteration of the law.

"I hope your return will not be delayed much longer. Tithes, both English and Irish, the general state of Ireland, Church reform—at least as far as regards Church rates, and the particular grievances of the Dissenters — and poor laws, all and each call for immediate consideration.

"Poor George Lamb!* I sincerely partake in all the regret which I know you, and indeed all who knew him, must feel for his loss. Another sad proof of the baneful effects of the constant use of colchicum in gout. Mrs. Lamb and Melbourne, I hear, are tolerably well.

"Ever yours, GREY."

FROM EARL GREY.

"Downing Street, January 7, 1834.

"MY DEAR CHANCELLOR,—I have received your letter this morning, and am very sorry that you should have felt any annoyance with respect to the appointment of Lord Sligo. If there has been any omission, and I am not prepared to say that there has not, I am quite as much to blame for it as Stanley.

"He consulted me about it, and the objection as a West Indian proprietor having been removed by the settlement of the slave question, and seeing no other, I gave my full consent to the appointment, which, I have no doubt, will turn out

* George Lamb, Lord Melbourne's brother, died January 2, 1834.

to be a very good one; and the state of things is so entirely changed, that I can not think you can have any reason to apprehend an attack either from Ellenborough or Calthorpe. In truth, I thought every body had known of the intention to appoint Sligo, before we left town.

"At all events, be assured that there was no intentional concealment.

"It is also my fault that the trades-union papers were not sent. I had them, and I kept them for the reason I gave you. There is not, however, much to be learned from them.

"Ever yours, GREY.

"Melbourne has offered the appointment of under-secretary to Howick, who is now at Sir Joseph Copley's, so that we have not yet been able to get his answer."

FROM EARL GREY.

"Downing Street, January 13, 1834.

"DEAR CHANCELLOR,—I am sorry you can not be at the Cabinet, as I find we are not all agreed as to the expediency of the course proposed by Palmerston and me with respect to the Peninsula.

"I have not seen any letter or dispatch from Granville since De Broglie's second speech. The first was imprudent. The second made matters worse. Talleyrand accounts for it by De Broglie's being ill, and not sufficiently accustomed to the bothering of the Chambers.

"Lord Grenville died yesterday evening at six o'clock. I have sent to the king to propose Auckland, subject to reductions and regulations. The thing can not wait, as not a shilling can be issued from the Exchequer till there is a new auditor. Ever yours, GREY."

FROM EARL GREY.

"January 15, 1834.

"DEAR CHANCELLOR,—I have little previous knowledge of Lord Howard,* but Palmerston speaks highly of him, and the

* Charles Augustus Ellis, Lord Howard de Walden, British Minister at Lisbon. His father was Charles Ellis, created Baron Seaford in 1826; his mother, the only daughter and heiress of John Augustus Lord Hervey, son of the fourth Earl of Bristol.

little intercourse I have had with him induces me to believe that he is both a sensible and a steady man—the qualities that are most wanted. Sending Villiers* to meet him might be of use, if things were in a state at Madrid to enable him to leave it with safety.

"As to a military man, there are many excellent in their profession, but hardly one that is who is not an enemy in politics. Kempt is the only one we have; but his health is bad, and I doubt his fitness for such a mission.

"We have no power of giving the place of auditor *ad interim*, or making any change in it, but by Act of Parliament. We can only, therefore, make the arrangement under an understanding, which, with a man of honor, will be quite sufficient. Our answer to any attack will be that there is nothing to bar any regulation or reduction which it may be necessary to make, and that this power is expressly reserved.

"Ever yours, GREY."

At the foot of this letter I wrote what follows:

"Of course I shall see you afterwards at the Cabinet; but, pray, don't let any thing pass with Auckland to prevent what clearly we can do without any Act of Parliament—viz., that till the office is regulated he shall do the duty on his present salary, and the equivalent which he has is the very great one of a large place for life when the Act passes. H. B."

[*Private.*]

TO EARL GREY.

"Court of Chancery, January 15, 1834.

"DEAR LORD GREY,—It strikes me as of extreme importance that if (as I hope and trust we shall) we *interfere*, the *preliminary* treating with Don Pedro should be in *very firm hands*. It is a thing of the very utmost magnitude, and on which every thing may turn. Howard is all very well for smooth water, but you want another and a stronger hand for a week or ten days at least. Now there are two obvious ways of supplying this plain and manifest deficiency—one is

* Our Minister at Madrid, afterwards Earl of Clarendon, and Secretary of State for Foreign Affairs.

by moving Villiers to meet him at Lisbon, and the other and best is for you immediately to choose your Commander of the Forces and to send *him* off. This is quite a regular proceeding, and was followed in 1806, as you must well remember, when Lord St. Vincent, General Simcoe, and Lord Rosslyn were to take the command of the expedition, *if it went*, but to negotiate previously.

"Pray do think of this in the course of the day, and be ready with your man when we meet, as we should lose no time. Yours ever, H. B."

FROM EARL GREY.

"DEAR CHANCELLOR,—I have got your letter, but would rather talk to you about it than answer it. Indeed I can not do so just now. I am to be with the king at three, and should wish to see you either before or after that hour. I almost doubt the possibility of my going on after all.

"Ever yours, G."

The last paragraph indicates "a resigning fit," which at this time attacked Grey with more than usual violence. From what passed at this time, it may easily be imagined how ready he was to retire a few weeks later, especially when he was assured by us that, should the necessity arise, we thought we could find the means of going on by another arrangement.

There had occurred at the very beginning of this year a difference of opinions on a very important question which divided us. It regarded the Portuguese affairs; and Grey was clearly of opinion that a course should be taken which he, and to a certain degree myself, thought necessary, but to which most of the others were decidedly opposed, as encountering a great risk of war. After the consequent discussion, he resolved to resign. I drew up a remonstrance, which the others joined me in signing. It was as follows:

"TO THE EARL GREY.

"January 14, 1834.

"Your colleagues most earnestly entreat you to suspend executing any resolution which you may have formed in consequence of the discussion that took place this morning.

"They consider the entire and immediate dissolution of the present Government as the inevitable consequence of your resignation, and they do most solemnly assure you that this representation is not made to you merely from the respect and affection which they all so entirely bear towards you, but from their anxious wish to continue to serve the king and the country with you. You require no proofs that such are their sentiments. But their present representation is made from their deep and settled conviction of the fatal consequences which must instantly ensue, from your resigning, to the best interests of the country.

"BROUGHAM.	VASSALL HOLLAND.
LANSDOWNE.	ALTHORP.
RIPON.	J. RUSSELL.
RICHMOND.	E. G. STANLEY.
MELBOURNE.	J. R. G. GRAHAM.
PALMERSTON.	C. GRANT."

With this remonstrance I sent him the following letter:

[*Private.*] TO EARL GREY.

"January 14, Tuesday evening, 1834.

"MY DEAR LORD GREY,—I have the less reluctance in signing and sending this most earnest and most affectionate representation, which faintly expresses the feelings of all your colleagues—except Lord Carlisle, who was absent—that I so entirely agreed in your views of the question. But I really can not in honesty and conscience towards the country and its whole interests, and, among others, towards *those very foreign concerns which are immediately in question*, contemplate, without dismay and without resisting to the uttermost, the fatal step on which our representation is made. Suppose England were out of the question, and all merely English interests, the breaking up of your Government is absolute and instant ruin to all the hopes of success in Portugal, Spain, and France, not to say the peace and independence of Europe at large. How can I feel that I am justified in putting all those great interests, as well as the safety and happiness of this country, which I am bound first of all to consider, in the utmost peril, because I have not found such concurrence among our colleagues as to enable the measures I thought right to be effectually executed? *This is the light in which I and others have felt the matter, independent of the universal feeling of the country*, and those in it whom we most esteem, to which we are exposing ourselves. Yours ever, H. B."

[*Private.*] TO EARL GREY.

"January 15, 1834.

"MY DEAR LORD GREY,—Before you go to Brighton (upon a much more serious expedition than even those you and I have had together at Windsor), I must write two lines in consequence of a word or two that fell from you to-night, and which I did not sufficiently attend to at the moment. I mean what you said about 'not being able to see why a Government should not be formed,' etc., etc.

"Set your mind quite at rest on that score. The thing is out of the question. I have long made up my resolution to give myself my discharge when you go; and I am not very likely to break through my intention on an occasion like this; and others, I know, are of the same determination. But that is nothing. If we would, I KNOW and can *demonstrate* to you that the thing is utterly impossible. The moral of my tale is this—That we must make a wry face and gulp it—which I feel to be bitter, but it can not be helped; and if ever there was an occasion in which it was more especially the bounden duty of us both (but I speak of *you*, and only of myself as your companion) to sacrifice every personal feeling, it is this very time and circumstance, when we look at inevitable consequences to *country*, *friends*, *principles*, and party.

"My perfect conviction is that Althorp, Melbourne, Stanley, and even Grant, and I should almost say Richmond, will go as far as we can take them *short of troops*, and that even on that their repugnance is for the present and in this stage merely; at least the first three, and the most important, I may say I know to be of this mind. Good-night, and believe me ever most sincerely and affectionately yours,

"H. BROUGHAM."

He answered the remonstrance and my letter from Brighton, where he had gone to lay his resignation before the king, but had not done so before our paper reached him.

[*Private.*] "Brighton, January 16, 1834.

"MY DEAR CHANCELLOR,—I could neither encounter the responsibility laid upon me by your paper, and the wishes expressed by all my colleagues, nor resist the earnest representations of the king. I have therefore, at a sacrifice of personal feeling, and I fear of what is more to be considered than personal feeling—greater than I can describe—agreed to remain. God grant it may end well, but I have little hope of it. Ever yours, GREY."

On his return to town he received the thanks of his colleagues in the following notes:

"It is impossible to appreciate too highly the sacrifice which Lord Grey has consented to make, which nothing but a paramount sense of duty could have warranted us in calling upon him to incur, in a case where it was so indescribably painful to him. RIPON."

"I consider this as a most eminent act of public virtue and self-denial in every way in which it can be regarded, and that, great as his claims were before on the gratitude of the country, this carries them farther. I also feel that we, as individuals and as a party rescued from the extremity of embarrassment (to say no more), are under the greatest obligations to him. H. BROUGHAM.

"The strictest secrecy is absolutely necessary."

"I entirely agree with the chancellor in all that he has expressed. J. RUSSELL."

"I entirely concur in the expressions used by the chancellor. They could not be too strong. Lord Grey must give us credit now for what we must all feel as to the sacrifice he has made to avert incalculable embarrassment and confusion; and I agree with Lord Holland, that we can *best show* it by omitting nothing that is possible hereafter to make it easy to him. LANSDOWNE."

"I most cordially agree with the chancellor. Should not we all, who signed the other paper, address now a paper to Lord Grey, expressing the sentiments we must all feel?

"CH. GRANT.

"January 17, 1834."

"I do not think that a paper such as suggested by Mr. Grant can be necessary, but I certainly feel it incumbent on us all to show on every occasion that we are impressed with the truth of all the chancellor observes upon Lord Grey's conduct, and anxious to render the position in which he is placed by the sacrifices he has made as little irksome and uneasy to him as we can. HOLLAND."

"I entirely concur in the opinion expressed by the chancellor. MELBOURNE."

"I entirely concur in the sentiments expressed by my colleagues as to the greatness and importance of the service which Lord Grey has rendered to the public, and as to the extent and painfulness of the sacrifice which he has made of personal feeling, as a minister and a man, in deference to the opinion of others as to what was most essential for the interests of the country; and I can not entertain a doubt that we shall all endeavor to manifest our sense of his conduct in the manner suggested by Lord Holland. PALMERSTON.

"January 17, 1834."

On receiving these, with a letter to the same effect from myself, he wrote as follows:

[*Private.*] FROM EARL GREY.

"Downing Street, January 18, 1834.

"MY DEAR CHANCELLOR,—Nothing can be more kind or more gratifying to my feelings than the note which you have transmitted to me, with those from the rest of my colleagues.

"It has been a painful conflict, but I feel that what I have done was what an indispensable duty prescribed. I perceive, however, great difficulties before me, from which I can only hope to extricate myself by the cordial and determined support which you all have promised me.

"Ever yours, GREY."

Lord Grey notified the king's approval as follows:

"The king approved highly of the decision of the Cabinet, and expressed again, in the strongest terms, his anxiety to prevent any change in the Government.

"Ever yours, G.

"Monday."

On the subject of the dinner proposed to be given to him at Edinburgh, I wrote to him as follows:

TO EARL GREY.

[*Private.*] "Wednesday.

"MY DEAR LORD GREY,—Don't think me troublesome if I beg and entreat of you to *reconsider* the Scotch dinner, for this reason—the whole Scotch people are really attached to you *upon principle.* They are *reformers* and improvers, but with a great deal of caution and considerateness, being so according to their character and habits, both of thinking and acting. Your liberality, therefore, is exactly of the kind that suits them, because it is of a *really* safe and conservative kind, and not rash and heedless. This being the case, not only they deserve at your hands (and I say ours, for we most of us agree with you in this) any gratification you can give them; but your meeting them tends to encourage and promote that very wholesome kind of opinion, and also to give them the thing they want and you have (and certainly it constitutes a *defect* in you both)—viz., a contempt of place. Their failing is to like too much, and yours to hate too much, being in office.

"I assure you I feel this very strongly, or I should not plague you with it. What signifies ninety miles' journey in September? You should attend the scientific assemblage, Oxford, Cambridge, Dublin, and at Edinburgh, 8th September, at any rate, even if you had no banquet to go to. I went from York Assizes (two hundred miles), and gave up my briefs in 1825, and I *know* my going did (though dinners are a sad bore) much good.

"I assure you the sacrifice you make by attending is nothing to mine. Edinburgh is certainly the place in all the world I shall be most hurt by seeing. I never intended to go there again while I lived. The misery I have been in these last nine months will be revived just when it is beginning to give way to time; for since I lost both my brothers I have not been in the place we were born and bred in. You may suppose how this hangs on me when I am unable even to go to Brougham but for a day. However, I have told them at Edinburgh that if the dinner takes place I will preside, as they desire it.

"Pray, then, reconsider this; you may finally decide when you get to Howick, and find how you feel.

"Yours ever, H. BROUGHAM.

"P.S.—The Scotch are also with us in the war I am waging with the London press, and for which that body never will forgive me—I mean the political society formed for emancipating the people from its insolence. The Scotch *to a man* adhere, and despise the bullies, just as the reformed House of Commons does."

TO EARL GREY.

[*Private.*] "Monday, 1834.

"MY DEAR LORD GREY,—I have had no opportunity of speaking to you about a thing I really begin to feel the necessity of more and more—namely, Denman having a peerage, if he will take it, which, from something he said at the beginning of last term, I think on the cards, but I have never come upon the subject with him. The want of a lawyer and judge in the Lords you know as well as I do. But you don't quite know how I am worked, for I don't talk of these things, because people bore me by saying how hard I work, and they *exaggerate*, of course. However, at present, and for once, I assure you they are not far wrong. In order to keep down the arrear in Chancery, and also to prevent appeals to the House of Lords (where I have no kind of help), I am forced to write all my judgments at great length. I never go out, except to a Cabinet dinner, having since Christmas only dined out once — namely, yesterday, because Miss Spalding would not go without me to Sefton's. I am never in bed till two, and sometimes three, and I am up again early, with a man copying while I'm correcting what I wrote overnight. I dine at half-past five or a quarter before six, and am at work sometimes in half an hour, and never am a whole hour at table, *during which* time I have letters to write.

"If I relax, there is an arrear gets up in Chancery, as there did when I was unwell two years ago, and also when I was kept last summer in the House of Lords; and unless I take this kind of pains, the appeals get crowded in the Lords.

"I have not been able to sit there one day this session for appeals. Eldon and Lyndhurst had Leach to sit for them half a session at a time—for us he will not sit a day. Indeed I can hardly ask Denman to sit there as *deputy speaker*, for it is putting a chief-justice in a very absurd position, as he is not allowed to open his mouth except to put the questions. Besides, it is not satisfactory to parties, because he can not give reasons; and it is bad for the law, because the courts below see their judgments reversed, and don't know on what ground they went wrong.

"If he were a peer (to give you an illustration), his circuit being over ten days before term, he could easily sit all that time in the Lords, and do exactly what I ought to have been doing this session had I been able to leave the Court of Chancery (where I have sat seven and sometimes eight hours a day).

"This is my case, and I should add that the present is a very favorable moment for making the attempt (which would imply, of course, a great honor and favor, even though his private reasons should prevent his accepting), because he is just yielding to a very urgent and very disagreeable petition of mine (which I went to Bedford yesterday morning to enforce personally)—namely, to give up *Parke* in order that I may put the Exchequer upon a complete footing, and so remedy the great difficulty Horne's business has got us into. Lyndhurst does not object, but rather approves my scheme.

"Yours ever sincerely, H. BROUGHAM."

TO EARL GREY.

[*Private.*] "Friday.

"My dear Lord Grey,—Denman writes to me that he has written to you, and desired you *not* to *press* it if you find it against the grain. This is great nonsense, and you ought on no account to attend to it; for Denman distinctly not only agrees, *but wishes it,* and this is a piece of ultra delicacy, as indeed he admits. It is founded on the recollection of the obstacles to his being made C. J.; but the king has quite come off that, and has once or twice spoken to me most favorably of Denman. The title he wishes to take is Denman of Dovedale, county Derbyshire (he having a very good estate there which his brother bought, and he has extended considerably).

"My belief is that this will be one of the most popular things you ever did. Yours ever, H. Brougham.

"I am to see the king at half-past two, when I shall propose the peerage. I have not the least expectation of any objection to it. If there shall be one, what I shall do must depend upon the circumstance attending it; but I shall not willingly give way. Yours ever, H. Brougham."

TO EARL GREY.

"January 23, 1834.

"My dear Lord Grey,—The dispatches to-day from Mulgrave are most satisfactory, and redound to his honor in the very highest degree. But so does all he has done. His administration has been brilliant and successful, and I feel that we are bound by any principle, and clearly by our interest as a Government, to distinguish him in all ways.* He has carried through our greatest and most difficult measure, and justice to him, and still more our own credit, require us to reward him. We ought to treat him like an officer who has rendered a great service, for we shall reap the honor of it as well as he. For this reason I am clearly of opinion that in any arrangements made now he should be borne in mind.

* He was Governor of Jamaica during the crisis of the slave emancipation. Created Marquis of Normanby in 1838.

His not being in sight is a reason the more for this. I mean arrangements diplomatic as well as at home.

"Yours ever, H. BROUGHAM."

I had long contemplated effecting an important change in the Court of Exchequer. This mainly depended upon a vacancy occurring in that court which would enable us to place there a good Equity man, than whom I knew none more fit than Horne, if he could be persuaded to accept the place. I was aware, also, that such an arrangement would be approved of by some of my colleagues, particularly Althorp and John Russell, who were desirous of having Horne removed from the office of attorney-general, while I myself would have been well pleased to see Campbell placed there, with Pepys as solicitor, he, next to Sugden, being by far the best man of the Chancery Bar.

When therefore I heard, early in February, 1834, that Sir John Bayley had determined to resign, as this would make the desired vacancy, I brought the whole question before the Cabinet. While it was under discussion I saw Campbell, and mentioned to him in general terms the proposed arrangement, but told him that there were many and great difficulties — among others, the concurrence of the chief baron (Lyndhurst) was indispensable. After we discussed the question in the Cabinet, Lord Grey and my other colleagues heartily approving, it was agreed that I should see Lyndhurst, and if he consented to the plan, that I should offer the place of Baron of the Exchequer to Horne. I had much correspondence afterwards with Horne, and the negotiation ended at length in his declining.

While all this was going on, and while I was really using my utmost efforts on behalf of Campbell, he commenced a proceeding which, I will venture to say, was never equalled for wrong-headedness and absurdity. So extraordinary was it, that I can not avoid detailing it. A day or two after I had seen him, and told him as far as I could without impropriety what was then going on, I received from him the following letter:

FROM THE SOLICITOR-GENERAL.

"New Street, February 6, 1834.

"My dear Lord Chancellor,—As I understood from you that the arrangement on Baron Bayley's retiring was discussed in the Cabinet, and as this arrangement seems to me *to be unjust to my fair pretensions*, I have thought it right to address a protest to the head of the Government, of which I inclose your lordship a copy.

"I own it strikes me as *rather hard*, after the *prospect* I had, that I should be *permanently condemned to the office of solicitor-general with its scanty emoluments*, and the great labors cast upon me; at the same time having *to find an independent seat in Parliament.*

"But I shall always retain a most grateful recollection of the uniform personal kindness I have always experienced from your lordship. I remain, yours very faithfully,

"J. Campbell.

"The Lord Chancellor."

The italics are Campbell's. The inclosure referred to was as follows:

[*Copy.*]

TO EARL GREY.

"New Street, Spring Gardens, February 6, 1834.

"My dear Lord,—I beg leave to state to you, with *manly sincerity*, the disappointment I feel at the arrangement which has been announced to me by the lord chancellor as about to take place upon the retirement of Baron Bayley.

"When I had the honor to be appointed solicitor-general in November, 1832, it was intimated to me that as soon as a vacancy occurred on the bench of the Court of Exchequer I should be promoted to the office of attorney-general. *In this expectation* I cheerfully, during the whole of the last session, exerted myself *to the utmost* in the House of Commons as an English law officer, and likewise acted as Attorney-General for Ireland, there being no Irish law officer in Parliament. From time to time I received very flattering testimonies of approbation from several members of the Government for my zeal and assiduity; and certainly, in attending to the Coercion Bill and other measures which passed last session, my labors and *sacrifices* were considerable.

"A vacancy has occurred on the bench of the Court of Exchequer; and, *without any change of circumstances* that I am aware of, I find that I am to *continue in my present* irksome position *indefinitely, without any reasonable hope of any promotion of any sort.*

"I should be willing to make any effort, or to submit to any sacrifice, for the advantage or convenience of your lordship's Government; but I think I should be unworthy of your good opinion, which I am most desirous to enjoy, if I were without a protest to acquiesce in an arrangement which seems to me, without any just reason, to show an entire disregard of my feelings and *interests.* I remain, my dear lord, yours most faithfully, J. CAMPBELL.

"To EARL GREY, etc., etc., etc."

After reading the above—the italics are Campbell's own—I thus wrote to him, as follows:

[*Private.*] TO SIR JOHN CAMPBELL.

"Stanhope Street, Thursday evening, February 6, 1834.

"MY DEAR SOLICITOR-GENERAL,—I assure you that few things have ever given me greater pain and surprised me more than your letter to Lord Grey. The surprise is, that you should have understood me to say yesterday that the arrangement was *completed,* when I had, as I thought, described it to you as full of difficulties, through which I did not see my way. The pain arises from your supposing that you had any one member of the Government more disposed to stand your friend and do you justice than myself. I will again remind you, that if I had allowed the affair to take its usual course, it would have been this: I should have made up my own mind, without consulting any one, and taken the king's pleasure on the new baron's appointment. I *might* have mentioned it to Lord Grey and Lord Melbourne, before going to the king, but that would have been accidental and out of the common course, unless they had spoken to me on the subject; and so Lord Eldon always, except on occasions of interference from higher quarters, acted. In truth, the *undivided* responsibility of judicial appointments ought, for obvious reasons, to rest on the chancellor, and I know of only two exceptions—Chief-justice of the King's Bench and Common Pleas. But I was so anxious to have the present appointment fully considered in all its relations, that I departed from the rule, and almost treated it as a Cabinet question.

"Your appeal to Lord Grey, therefore, is sufficiently embarrassing, if I were a person to mind etiquette. If it were an appeal against another being made a judge, and claiming the appointment for yourself, it would still be embarrassing. But it is not this—it is of a still more unusual nature; it is an appeal, or at least a protest in the nature of an appeal, against my not making the attorney-general a judge, and thereby preventing you being made attorney-general in his room. The ground of the protest is, that in November, 1832, it was intimated that on a vacancy in the Exchequer you were to be promoted to the office of attorney-general. It would certainly be more accurate to say that every effort was made by me, *at that time*, to facilitate such an arrangement; and you can not entertain the least doubt that, had such a vacancy then occurred, no pains would have been spared to make the consequent vacancy in the attorney-general's office available, so that you might at once have been attorney-general. Indeed I may appeal to your own recollection if the office of solicitor-general was not offered to you quite as a matter of course, not to say tendered to you, as the means of your obliging us by accepting it. I so felt it, and never dreamed of conferring a favor by your promotion to it. At the same time it would be the height of absurdity in me to suppose for a moment that I had made a bargain with you, and prevailed upon you to be solicitor-general, to which you had consented, upon condition, not only of succeeding to the attorney-general's place, when vacant (which would be of course), but upon the condition of a vacancy in that place being made, *at all hazards*, as soon as a judge retired. Suppose you had then been distinctly told that at some future time the attorney-general was not to be promoted to the bench on a vacancy happening, but was to be asked to continue a little while longer attorney-general, can it be stated that you would on that ground have refused to be solicitor-general?

"All the negotiation that took place respecting Mr. Baron Bayley's retiring, was principally with a view to the vacancy happening in November instead of February, to avoid two elections, and enable you at once to come in as attorney-general. It is clear that nothing which then passed could bind me, at all events and in all circumstances, to make the attorney-general a judge on the first vacancy. The baron's present retirement is wholly unconnected with any thing which took place at that time.

"I do assure you that the desire I had in November, 1832, to see you attorney-general is, to the full, as strong now—indeed your important services to the Government are well calculated to make it stronger, but that it could hardly be so. Nevertheless, I do feel extremely uneasy, in the prospect of consequences which I know MUST ensue from *judicial* arrangements unsatisfactory in themselves, as well as to others connected with them; and this feeling is greatly increased by the knowledge which I *think* I have now, and to which, in November, 1832, I certainly never could have looked forward, that other arrangements of the most beneficial kind to the whole Equity side of Westminster Hall are within our reach. I shall therefore abandon a prospect so highly, and I may add unexpectedly, beneficial to the public service, and so honorable to the Government, with much reluctance, if I find the many difficulties which surround it insuperable. But I believe *that* will be the only disappointment experienced; for, first, all my *personal* predilections will be much more gratified by the other course; next (which I ought to have reckoned under the first head), you will be better satisfied; and, lastly, your new coadjutor will be (as he will have every reason to be) infinitely better pleased, to say nothing of the satisfaction of the Government.

"Yours most sincerely, H. BROUGHAM."

My letter seemed to bring Campbell in some degree to his senses, for on the night of the same day he wrote to me as follows:

FROM SIR JOHN CAMPBELL.

"New Street, Thursday night.

"MY DEAR LORD CHANCELLOR,—I am anxious to assure you that I meant no offense to you in writing to Lord Grey. Understanding that the matter had been arranged in the Cabinet, and thinking (whether justly or not) that I was aggrieved, I thought that my protest would most properly be addressed to him. No one can feel more deeply than I do that the puisne judges should be appointed upon the responsibility of the lord chancellor.

"When I was made solicitor-general, there was no bargain whatever for my promotion; and I shall always recollect, with the most lively gratitude, the exertions which your lordship made that I might at once be attorney-general. But, as Bayley's continuing was considered the only obstacle, I certainly thought it was understood that as soon as he retired I should be promoted; and, until the interview with which you favored me on Tuesday, I had no doubt that this understanding would be acted upon. I might be wrong in forming this expectation; but some allowance may be made for what I must necessarily have felt in supposing that I was *condemned* to remain in my present very irksome official position, till by some political change I am turned out of office altogether.

"I again say I should be most exceedingly grieved if it were supposed that I had shown you any disrespect. It would be most ungrateful in me to forget the uniform and repeated kindnesses I have experienced from you for many years. I remain yours most faithfully, J. CAMPBELL.

"I may perhaps be excused for adding this single observation, that if you should now be pleased to recommend to his majesty that Sir William Horne should be elevated to the bench, I do not see how this appointment can be considered as at all treading on the prerogative of the lord chancellor, as it would only be carrying into effect an intention before expressed by your lordship, *ex mero motû et certæ scientiæ.*

Thus Campbell was determined to leave no stone unturned. After what had now happened, it appeared to me that a man who had acted as Campbell had done—urged by the insane desire to better himself—might, on some future occasion, press unreasonable claims, or, worse still, embarrass the Government by insisting that a judicial vacancy should be made for his behoof. It will be seen that in the following autumn, when the Rolls became vacant by Leach's death, my February anticipations had been tolerably accurate, and that I had then formed a pretty correct estimate of Campbell's readiness to urge, *quocunque modo,* his claim for promotion.

Thus reflecting, I considered it a duty to place before my colleagues an exact account of what had recently taken place. This I did in the following memorandum:

MEMORANDUM.

"After the strange, and, as all feel it, wholly unreasonable claim set up by the solicitor-general, who converts my kindness towards him in November, 1832, when I tried to make a vacancy of attorney-general that he might *at once* get it and avoid two elections, into a pledge (which no human being *could* give except Sir William Horne) that, whensoever a vacancy happened on the bench, he should be made attorney-general, it seemed quite necessary to explain distinctly the footing he was to be on with respect to Equity appointments. Therefore, when I saw him to discuss the general subject for the third time, I observed that the complaints urged in his letters (of remaining always solicitor-general) really meant to refer to the little chance there was of chiefships falling vacant, owing to Tindal, Copley, and Denman being such good lives. He said that was the fortune of war; and after much other conversation (which was only the substance of my letters and former conversations), I said he gained nothing by being attorney-general, except a step of rank and some increase of income, neither of which could very much signify to him in his station as head of the Common Law bar; and that, as for promotion, whether he were attorney or solicitor-general could make no difference at all, as he would have the *law* chiefships that fell, and his colleague, being an Equity man, would of course have the *Equity* places—and I took the Rolls for an instance of the latter—adding that he must feel that a common lawyer, both on the Wool-sack and Rolls, was a thing wholly out of the question, especially now, when by the new Act motions were to be heard there. (Leach had indeed before the Lords' Committee stated himself to be unfit to hear them, after being five or six years out of the practice.) Campbell distinctly assented to this statement, but said nothing when by a general remark I extended it to Ireland. We had much other talk on the subject generally, and I never saw a man have so little argument to urge, or even plausible statement to make, of his case. It is certainly one of unexampled absurdity, and would not be credited if stated. For a man to maintain seriously, and with a grave face, that he is ill-used, because when a judge resigns, the Government won't *force* the attorney-general to go on the bench in order to let *him* be attorney-general, seems incredible. Horne was no party to any kind of understanding whatever. Besides, what possible remedy could Campbell have (suppose Government had given him any thing like a pledge) but to resign the solicitor-generalship, because the *condition subsequent* had not been performed? He would not have done *that*, 'I guess,' whatever had happened.

"First. The utmost that can be said is, that I, out of an excess of kindness and delicacy to the solicitor-general, treated his taking that office in November, 1832, as no favor bestowed by the Government, and then did all I could to make him attorney-general *per saltum*, and that he then expected the attorney-general to be pushed out of his way, not only if Baron Bayley had *then* retired, but at whatsoever time he should go, and in what circumstances soever.

"Second. *No such promise was made*, nor any thing like it; and if it had, like all such promises, circumstances must be allowed to affect its performance.

"Third. He is quite wrong in saying that no change of circumstances has happened. The Exchequer *is* changed; it is to have a new Equity court separated from the Law court, and the circuits are to be changed to suit this arrangement. In November, 1832, no Equity lawyer of any eminence would hear of going there, very much on account of circuits, but also for other reasons. Unexpectedly we have *now* the prospect of the best man at the Equity bar taking it.

"Fourth. It is strange to see any man avowing that he has *exerted himself to do his duty*, merely in the expectation that room would be made for his promotion.

"Fifth. It is to be apprehended that, without a very clear explanation when he becomes attorney-general, he will complain if others are not shifted to let him move onward."

I now take leave of this unpleasant subject, and proceed with my narrative.

FROM EARL GREY.

"March 26, 1834.

"MY DEAR CHANCELLOR,—Nothing would give me greater pleasure than to find it in my power to do any thing that might be agreeable to Horne, or serve to alleviate his wounded feelings. But the place of comptroller is quite impossible.* If given to Horne, Ripon would certainly have a right to think himself ill-used in its not being given to Henry Ellis,† whose pretensions would be in every way equal, if not superior, from his connection with the office, and his appointment would save £1400 a year to the public. I am inclined to think that now this will be the best arrangement.

"Ever yours, GREY."

To this I at once answered:

"I see the *full force* of your difficulty. Indeed there is no way of getting over it. But *pray*, as to Ellis, let every means be tried to avoid that. It really will create much annoyance to our House of Commons friends. Althorp says it was more this feeling against Ellis than love of Poulett Thomson that kept them favorable to the Auckland arrangement. I hope you will fight this of Ellis, and not make it necessary for *me* to object—for this reason, that Arthur Eden's interest would be much promoted by Ellis getting it, and it is putting me in a very invidious position to be objecting to any thing which is useful to *him* (Eden). I was extremely glad that the Auckland clause went off without my being at all accessory to it, for the same reason, as Eden as well as Auckland would, I understand, though I don't know how, have been benefited by it. Yours ever, H. B."

---

* Comptroller of the Exchequer, vacant by the death of Lord Grenville. The office was given to Sir John Newport, Bart.

† Sir Henry Ellis, one of the tellers of the Exchequer.

CHAPTER XXVI.

Memorandum on the Position of the Grey Cabinet.—Interview with the King.—Divisions in the Ministry on the Irish Church Question.—The Chancellor's Memorandum to his Colleagues. — The Secession. — The Progress of the Irish Church Measure.—Tithe Adjustment and Appropriation of Surplus.—Sketches of the Seceders.—Lord Stanley (afterwards Lord Derby).—The Duke of Richmond.—Episode on the proper Conduct of Public Business.—Sir James Graham.—The filling of the Vacancies.—The Irish Coercion Bill. — O'Connell. — The Disclosures. — Lord Grey's Resignation.

INTENTLY occupied as I was at this time in well considering all the circumstances of our position as a Ministry, and all the great difficulties and dangers which surrounded us, I deemed it to be my bounden duty to lay before the Cabinet my opinion at some length upon the state of affairs, impressed too as I then was with the belief, amounting to a conviction, that some of the most valued of our colleagues were likely to leave us, and that, on such a catastrophe occurring, Grey would to a certainty attempt to follow them. With these feelings and anticipations I wrote the following paper:

MEMORANDUM.

"April 30, 1834.

"The chancellor feels so deep an anxiety upon the present state of the Government and the country, that he considers it his indispensable duty to state his views to his colleagues, and to assure them, first of all, that he has no feeling whatever but that of the most entire confidence in their integrity and good intentions, and the most earnest desire to continue as heretofore, acting with them for the benefit of the public service. He trusts, then, that they will not misconstrue the motives of this memorandum, and he ventures to hope that they will give it a candid consideration, and that if there be any of its suggestions which strike them as worthy of attention, and of being acted on, they will treat them rather with the regard due to their own importance, than with that which their author can justly claim.

"It is the result of the best consideration which the chancellor can give to the state of the country, whether England, Ireland, or Scotland—and whether the counties be regarded or the towns, but especially the latter—that a Government formed of the Conservative party would be found utterly unable to carry on the public business, unless something befalls their opponents which shall entirely destroy their credit—some great failure or signal disgrace; and even if they are so crippled as to be incapable of retaining power, as the unpopular party would gain hardly any credit by the misfortunes or disgrace of their adversaries, they would be but little the better able to take and hold the helm. On the contrary, all public character would be lowered, and the projects of the Radical leaders, rather than of any regular and respectable party, would be furthered.

"Could, then, these Conservative leaders form a junction with any portion of their adversaries? With the Radical leaders? This seems impossible: but even with any of the present Government is a course eminently beset with difficulties; for any such arrangement would irreparably injure both the parties to it, unless the course of events should lead naturally to it. We need not say it may never do so; all we need assert is, that neither party dares risk the loss of all public confidence by listening to any such plans now. If, then, the present Government were dissolved (things remaining as now or not materially otherwise), to whom could the king or country look? The Radicals must be plainly put out of view. They have neither pieces nor pawns for the game. Their leaders are tried and found wanting; but they are manifestly a small minority in the country of property and even of numbers, and they are more incapable than the Conservatives of undertaking the task. That they may be rendered more strong in every way, both in and out of Parliament, is not to be denied. The errors of the regular parties have this direct tendency, and may unhappily in time render recourse to that quarter not only practicable but necessary. The question is, in what state parties are now? and one object of this memorandum is to show how so great a calamity is inevitable, unless pains be taken to arrest it, and by what means this can be effected.

"On any question of individual conduct or feeling, surely each of the ministers should keep steadily in view the end to which every thing tends that endangers this Administration. To submit to many things—to bear and forbear—to undertake tasks alien to his inclinations—*to do all but abandon principles*—appears to be every minister's duty, until a better prospect shall open of replacing this Government. No one of its members has, perhaps, more reason personally to desire the ease which such an event would bestow on him than the writer of these pages. The labor which he undergoes and can not escape, and which, since the 2d of November last, with the interruption of a fortnight far more painfully passed, must be continued three months longer—he feels it every hour more irksome, and looks forward to its becoming unbearable. When he says that, besides sitting daily in court seven hours, he is never in bed before two, and that he has since November written with his own hand above seventy long judgments, some of which took an hour, and some two, to read, and all of which would fill two very large printed volumes, he is far from desiring to boast of hard work; but he makes the statement as an irrefragable proof that he must have a singular taste to love such an existence. And to what does he prefer it? To a state which he has all his life deemed the perfection of happiness, and never enjoyed for a week—namely, being free from all care and all occupation, and at liberty to devote himself to his public and Parliamentary duty as an independent member of Parliament, upon the side of the question most congenial to his habits. But he does not hesitate an instant in abandoning all such schemes of enjoyment, and continuing a drudge. Neither does he hesitate in postponing or suppressing any opinion, how deeply soever he may feel it, which could by possibility raise any difference with any one colleague, and thereby in any degree weaken the Government. Then what other recourse can his majesty have than this, that part of the present Government remain and form a new Administration? But this implies that others should join them who are neither of the Conservative nor Radical persuasion. The chancellor knows of none such, at least none who would lend the Government the requisite strength to support itself after losing such men as may be supposed to retire upon unfortunate differences of opinion respecting Ireland. For the mere alteration would be the source of great weakness in both houses and in the country, and those who had left the Ministry would in a very short time be more or less unfriendly to those who remained. This is almost unavoidable, even among the best and the most friendly men; and as a pointed discrepancy of opinion on important matters will have secured their disunion, the breach will be the more apt to widen.

"To such a result the chancellor looks forward as most lamentable. The successive formation of ephemeral ministries is fatal to all unity of design, and to all power of execution in policy, whether foreign or domestic, and would also prove the sure forerunner of a popular crisis. He is, therefore, deeply impressed with alarm at such a contemplation, and yet it is by far the best that can possibly result from any change in the construction of the present Cabinet.

"For let the only other alternative be considered. If the Cabinet entirely breaks up (and this unfortunately is far more likely to happen than the other alternative just discussed), we are driven back to the formation of a Conservative Government.

"This the chancellor verily believes would be attended with the most imminent hazard to the country, and speedily.

"He desires to speak with all the respect and gratitude which he sincerely feels towards the first Reformed Parliament, whose wisdom and honesty he thinks would have done honor to any Senate in any times. But he can not avoid perceiving that the moderate courses pursued by the Government, and the influence of the Government over the members, have alone restrained them from adopting much stronger measures than the safety of the country and the stability of some of its institutions will at all allow. Friend to Reform and improvement as he is, and always has been, and even disappointed at some measures having been postponed so long, he infinitely prefers the disappointment, the sickness arising from hope deferred, to the perils of too rapid changes—to sweeping reforms; and he is quite assured that, had this

Ministry been in opposition during these two sessions, there would have been a far more swift and more extensive change effected in our establishments than is at all consistent with their stability.

"Suppose a Conservative Cabinet in power, and the Radical party reinforced with all those who only through the influence of the Government have been restrained from joining them, it is almost certain that too strong measures would be adopted, both with respect to the civil and ecclesiastical constitution of the country. The House of Lords would in vain attempt to stem the tide, *for the votes of money would certainly be refused. It is a fact wholly undeniable, that the repugnance exists no longer which even in the most factious times used formerly to make men refuse to stop supplies who would vote for every thing else.*

"That an immediate or almost immediate dissolution would take place is inevitable. Then the new Parliament must of course contain more Conservatives than this, chosen under the influence of the Reform Bill; but another party would gain, at the least, as much—the Radical, or if not the Radical, the high popular party, and both would unhappily gain at the expense of the moderate Liberals. A new Parliament would certainly place the Government in the position which really broke up the same Cabinet in 1830—namely, at the mercy of their enemies, and relying on their forbearance or even support for every vote.

"There can not be a question that in this state of things parties must run very high, and men will pledge themselves in the contest to high popular courses. The speedy downfall of the Government will be by far the most probable result—long delayed it can not be. But though the Parliament will be far too little Conservative to support such a Ministry, it will be too little Liberal to sustain their adversaries with a House of Lords always hostile to them. A second dissolution will then be inevitable, and a new Parliament will be chosen under the most violent popular excitement, and whoever is their minister will be an instrument in the hands of the more violent portion of the people. It is to this result that the chancellor looks forward—it is this that he dreads as leading to the most fatal catastrophe; and he does entreat all who are apprehensive of it to act as if they felt each to be responsible for bringing it about, should he not use his utmost efforts to prevent the premature dissolution of the present Government."

By Grey's desire I went to the king for the purpose of letting him know what our feelings and apprehensions were. On my return I immediately wrote to Grey.

[*Private.*] TO EARL GREY.

"May 2, 1834.

"I have just seen the king.

"The king is in the strongest and fullest sense of the word cordial with the Government, and as warm and hearty in his wish to support us as any one man can be. I can not tell you half the things he said of you—of your honor—*your being incapable of deceiving him*, or of any change NOW, except the filling up the two or three vacant places. He really reviewed all our measures, foreign and domestic, and all those now pending, in a very distinct and friendly manner, and said, 'Never man had better cause to like a Ministry, though he once or twice had differed, and once only on foreign politics, when he luckily proved wrong.'

"In short, I never saw him half so cordial and so naturally cordial. It is not merely as fearing a change, but from confidence and good-will. He expressed himself about you in a way that (from regal pride) he may make less strong to yourself. But to me it was very strong indeed. I must insist on your not trying to mar all this (which will be *followed by House of Commons*) by any speculative or prospective idea, as in your letter. When the time comes we can find your successor. H. BROUGHAM."

Before the end of May there were indications which satisfied me that some of our most valued colleagues had made up their minds to leave us. The evil of this secession was so great, that I made an attempt to avert it by circulating the following paper:

"Some weeks ago the chancellor took the liberty of entreating the attention of his colleagues to a memorandum which he laid before the Cabinet.

"It appears to him that the time is now arrived when the substance of that paper is of more pressing and practical importance than ever, and he must be excused for now presenting to the Cabinet, rather, he fears, as a 'protest' than for any other purpose, that which he before tendered by way of advice and of warning. He perceives that some of his colleagues are bent upon a course which must break up the Government, unless a firmness is shown by the rest, and a self-denial which he hardly dares hope to find prevail.

"He is still altogether at a loss to understand how any one can possibly think that a vote of the Commons, which he resists, and which all his colleagues, though on different grounds, refuse to join in, can render it dishonorable to remain in office, when it produces no one practical effect, calls upon nobody to do or submit to any one thing, and leaves every one entirely free to act as he pleases in all respects.

"The chancellor has ascertained that the movement has its origin altogether in the language held by two or three of the Cabinet within the last ten days, that it was to break up in July. The chancellor ventures to think that the history of human affairs affords no instance of equal indiscretion. He had believed that the intention, or rather possibility, alluded to, would have remained a profound secret. That any ministers could have spread a report, the truth of which *must of necessity* always have been uncertain until the last moment—a report which, coming from authority, was enough to destroy any Ministry—he never could have supposed possible. The chancellor can not even now bring himself to believe it. But sure he is that those who have so far implicated the Government and the public safety, are of all men the most imperatively called upon to assist in saving the country from the effects of such a proceeding.

"To that proceeding it is owing that Ireland is about to be left in the hands of agitators without a Coercion Bill, the Church to be deprived of its last chance, the Tithe Bill; the Poor Law, and other great measures, to be left in every hazard of failing, and the whole empire abandoned without a Government, to be scrambled for by factions and mobs, and fanatics, religious and political.

"There is no personal sacrifice which the chancellor is not

prepared to make in order to see his principles triumphant and the progress of improvement sped, both at home and abroad. But he deems its acceleration far too dearly purchased by the extreme dangers to the peace of the country and the stability of its best institutions, which he apprehends will arise from the change which he sees some of his colleagues are bent upon having made."

"Saturday evening, May 24, 1834.

"The chancellor omitted to state, what he has since distinctly told his colleagues in Cabinet, that though a reluctant supporter of the Coercion Bill, as a measure of hard necessity, he could only bring himself to consent to it from the confidence he felt in those whose hands were to be armed with its extraordinary powers. To the Orange party, or a Government connected with that faction, he could never think of intrusting its authority; and if the present Government proposes its renewal, there will of course be material omissions in it, especially as regards courts-martial."

In the above paper I referred to what had been said by some of the ministers (particularly Graham). But that things were continually told out of doors as having been said by members of the Cabinet, and not only thus told, but sent to newspapers, there can be no doubt. Some of these reports we traced, and found them to be pure inventions; others were misunderstandings of the words spoken; but *all* were traced to *Cabinet dinners*—tales carried by the servants, who were in the habit, no matter at what house we were dining, of seizing every pretense for remaining in the room; then some of our colleagues would go on talking as if none but ourselves were present. Then, again, dinner was no sooner over, and one hoped the door was closed against the liveried watchers for Cabinet secrets, than some one—generally Holland—would ring for a cup, or, as he called it, after the fashion of his uncle, a *dish*, of tea; when in again rushed the servants with all their ears open. Our more important matters were really kept secret, because they were always discussed at councils held in the day-time; or, at all events, at meetings unaccompanied by eating, drinking, and attendants.

Next day I wrote to Grey as follows:

TO EARL GREY.

[*Private.*]

"May 25, 1834.

"MY DEAR LORD GREY,—I am sure no one who was at our Cabinets yesterday and to-day, and who read the strong paper which I circulated, or my private and friendly letter to Stanley, can have the least doubt of my regarding the possibility of Graham and Stanley going out as a great calamity, and that there is nothing I would not do to prevent it. But that point being, I much fear, decided by their very foolish views, although I make a very great distinction between them, it remains for us, and, above all, for you, Althorp, and myself, to do our duty firmly and like rational men, not like children throwing all up and every thing into confusion because we have not our own way.

"I begin by saying that *now* I have demonstrative proof of Graham's resolution to go out at all events, and that he only is seeking a pretext, or rather (for I wish to say nothing harsh) a ground. With Stanley it is not so clear; he behaves quite fairly and above-board. But I am informed, and believe it, that some people have been to him and Graham to suggest their going out, in order that the Church question may be settled and the Government relieved. This has not unnaturally irritated them, and I fear is the real cause of both their determinations. But they are very silly in so doing, I admit. However, we can not hope now to prevent it, and the next thing to be considered is, the consequences.

"It will materially strengthen the Government in the country and in the House of Commons; and although their places may not be very easily supplied, yet we have quite debaters enough, besides the great favor the Government will have, for some time at least. Stanley is quite honest and open, and will part friends and give nothing but support to the Government. In the Lords we may be a little injured by the change. But really and truly we are so ill there already, that this can do us no harm. In every other quarter we are stronger by the change.

"As for you and Althorp or me dreaming, in these circumstances, of throwing up the Government, rather than take the trouble of putting in Spring Rice and Radnor, or any other two you please, it is too absurd. We really could not face the country after such an abandonment of all duty. What! can we not carry on the Government in peace and with such a majority and such support out-of-doors, and a plain dealing king, when Addington did so against you all—Pitt, Fox, Windham included? Really the thing is too absurd to deserve a moment's refutation. Surely no one can be serious in taking this view. As for your going out at the end of the session, I must say *alors comme alors;* but at any rate this is no time for it.

"I further say, that suppose *even you* were to go out, which on every account I should consider as the greatest calamity to the country and to myself, and *to yourself also* (with your leave be it spoken), my firm determination is to join the remains of your Cabinet in forming a new Government, or rather continuing your own—even if so it must be without you; and I am clearly of opinion—how desperately annoying for us and bad for the country it may be, and no one can feel it more than I do—yet that it can and ought to succeed. The king may refuse—probably he will—but he must do so with the full knowledge that the thing is within his power, and that it is quite practicable. This must be left undoubted and plain; because if he refuses, and prefers Wellington and Peel, all the Liberal party will do what their bounden duty requires, and oppose the new Government by every fair means, in Parliament and out. Of these I avow myself among the most determined and strenuous, and my avowed object will be to turn out the Government, and to take their place, for the sake of the measures and the principles I feel devoted to. Don't say I am ambitious or want to be in power because I have not had enough of it. But I owe it as a duty to those who have so gallantly supported us these four years. Also, don't say I am using inconsistent arguments, when I at *one* and the same time tell you that another Government could be made, and that my chief object is to induce you to remain, and keep every thing as it is. That is the main point with us all, except two, and those are exceptions only for the present. But I must also say, that if in that we fail, my deliberate opinion is that, though with infinitely less power to do good in all ways, yet a Government *could* be made.

"However, with that we have nothing *now* to do, happily. My present object is to remind you that Graham and Stanley going gives no one even the shadow of a pretext for not closing the session well, and carrying through the bills.

"Yours ever truly, H. BROUGHAM."

At this time Lansdowne was making a terrific push to get Auckland into the Cabinet. Much as I really liked Auckland as a friend and connection, I felt it my duty thus to express to Grey my opinion of the proposal and its probable consequences.*

TO EARL GREY.

[*Private.*] "May 29, 1834.

"MY DEAR LORD GREY,—I am very sorry, indeed, to say that I entirely and widely differ about Auckland. I consider him another name for Lord Lansdowne as a wet blanket. He is quite a tool of Lansdowne's. It is no accession of character—no weight with the country—no speaker in the House—and merely puts him in the place where, if he remains a week, he retires on a pension of £2000, or, I believe, £3000 a year. It is a very unseemly thing, and will be a source of infinite feebleness, and make our Cabinet as uncomfortable a place as I ever was in, and only please Thomson.

"Yours ever, H. B."

In spite of all our efforts, and the undoubted friendliness of the king, Grey still harped upon resigning, as will appear from the following:

TO EARL GREY.

"House of Lords, 30th May.

"I am here till the House meets. Can't you come over for five minutes? As to *not* going on after all that has passed, it is absolutely ridiculous. *Nothing can* justify it either to king, Parliament, or country.

"Abercromby is *quite appeased.* I have written to him, and had his answer. Ellice coming in is a good thing."

* In reference to the appointment of Lord Auckland to succeed Sir James Graham as First Lord of the Admiralty.

Early in the session it had become necessary seriously to consider the tithe question in Ireland, and the probable necessity of continuing the Coercion Bill of the previous session, or of renewing it with certain modifications.

The compulsory payment of tithes by the Catholic population towards the support of a Protestant Church was one of the great grievances, and, more than any thing else, was the cause of the disorganization that existed in almost every part of that distracted country. It became, therefore, with us a serious question whether a new appropriation of Church property was not inevitable and unavoidable. On this question it is not to be denied that there were great differences of opinion in the Cabinet.

Many members of the Commons who voted for the second reading of the Irish Church Bill in 1833, announced their intention of opposing it in the next stage, unless the whole fund derived from Church property was applied to ecclesiastical purposes. The O'Connell party, of course, took a very opposite view, their hope being, through means of the Church Bill, to strike a blow at the Established religion. Even Joseph Hume went so far as to declare, in his place in Parliament, that the future peace of Ireland depended upon the destruction of the Protestant Church.

When we came to consider whether the funds derived from Church property, and calculated to amount to something like three millions, should, after duly providing for the just and fair expenses of the Establishment, be appropriated to State purposes, we felt quite assured that such a measure would be rejected by the Lords, and therefore we determined to withdraw the clause in the Commons. Accordingly, in June, 1833, Stanley moved its omission. As might be expected, unmeasured abuse was heaped upon the Government, its defense being that the application of Church property to State purposes had never been a principle of the bill—the right of Parliament to apply or not to apply the property of the Church to secular purposes having throughout been left untouched. The bill then passed with the omitted clause; and now (1834) we had to consider whether, in the existing state of things in Ireland, it had not become necessary and unavoidable to admit that the Church revenue ought to be reduced to a sum only sufficient to support the Church Establishment, and that the surplus, if any, should be applicable to secular purposes.

Further discussions in Cabinet on this difficult question took place about the end of May, at which time a debate was going on in the Commons on a motion affirming that the Protestant Establishment was excessive, regard being had to the spiritual wants of its members, and that therefore the temporal possessions of the Irish Church ought to be reduced. It was avowed that this motion was only a step to the resumption by the State of the surplus, whatever it might amount to. Thus it became necessary to decide what our future course should be on this question.

We had agreed, without any exception, on the necessity of remodelling the Irish Church Establishment, considering that the question of the application of surplus revenue would not come before us until the amount required for the due support of the Establishment had been decided; but the motion in the Commons made it manifest that this matter could be no longer delayed; and accordingly, when we met about the end of May, four members of the Government, differing from the majority, resigned—these were, Stanley, Richmond, Graham, and Ripon.

And here I think I may appropriately say a few words upon the public character and distinguishing attributes of the four colleagues who had thus separated from us.

Stanley, like John Russell, came into the Cabinet some time after it was formed. His talents were of a very high, though not of the highest, order. He was a perfectly ready and a very able debater, with great powers of clear and distinct statement, with a high-pitched voice, far from musical, but clearly heard in every part of the House. He argued closely, but he required much backing and cheering, and never could fight an up-hill battle. In debate, he, like Canning, stuck at nothing in order to snatch an advantage. With the gravest face, he would invent what he assumed his adversary to have said, but what he notoriously never did say. His judgment was *nil*, or nearly so. He would make a statement, well aware it would be answered; and committed the most unpardonable of all errors, that of suppressing a fact or ignoring a paper, which he knew must be produced against him. He would have invariably lost his verdict at the bar by such blunders as these, which all proceeded from the desire to gain a momentary triumph.

He was quite reformer enough naturally to take to the Reform Bill, having on that subject nothing to unsay; but he helped it very little, being so fully engaged in his own—the Irish department—which he most ably represented against O'Connell & Co.

I believe he made but a moderate colonial minister, judging from some I have seen and others I have heard of his errors.

The Duke of Richmond is and always has been a high Tory of the old school, and was, like his father (an honest but inferior man), a hot Orangeman and ultra Protestant; hence his union with the Whigs. For when the Duke and Peel emancipated the Catholics in spring, 1829, Richmond and others never could forgive it, and they almost all joined us in punishing them by turning them out, just as they afterwards did to revenge themselves on Free Trade. Knatchbull was to have been of our Cabinet, but accidental circumstances prevented it, so Richmond was taken as representing that party, through whose aid we had turned out the duke's Government, November, 1830. We had no very full explanation with him on Reform, only it was quite understood by all of us that some Parliamentary Reform was made an indispensable condition of our taking office, and this was so stated to the king.

I have already stated that, in pursuance of a pledge given in Yorkshire, I had explained my plan of Reform at a meeting at Althorp's chambers.

How far Richmond would have agreed with this had its details been laid before him at their joining our Government, I can not tell; but little by little he came into the great plan.

Richmond was an admirable colleague. Full of courage, clear-headed, very good-humored, very quick, very candid—uneducated, except as a soldier; and who would with education have done considerable, perhaps great things.

He was an excellent speaker—few better, that did not profess the art.

In Cabinet he was frank, open, and honest, despising all

intrigue—we were always sure of him. He agreed with us who urged the dissolution in April, 1831, half friendly as the king was. He refused joining in the peer-creation the following year, and was the only one who did refuse.

Ripon was one of the moderate Tory converts to the Whig Government. But he was always much esteemed by us, while we had been in opposition to him. He had been an *élève* of Castlereagh; and nothing could exceed the bitterness of Castlereagh's family, as shown through his brother Londonderry, at finding him one of us. However, it was not new, for in 1827 he led the junction Government in the Lords; and after Canning's death, in August, he was prime minister till January. His nerves failed him, and he could not stand the expected session. There never was a more upright or amiable man. His abilities were very respectable—indeed more. In the House of Commons he had greatly distinguished himself. His free-trade operations are the origin of that policy. He and my friend Wallace (afterwards Lord Wallace) were the earliest and most important of Huskisson's converts. His joining us on Parliamentary Reform was more difficult. But he, Palmerston, and Glenelg, all come within the same description; and if they were to be reformers at all, then, like Melbourne and Richmond (more stout anti-reformers than themselves), they did right to take a large and efficient measure.

Nothing could be more honest, open, and ingenuous than Ripon's conduct on all occasions. His scrapes came from this amiable quality. His "prosperity" and his "godsend" (repayment of Austrian Loan) are instances.* In the Lords he sometimes did admirably; sometimes his nerves failed him. But he was always a person of weight there, by his character, his talents, and his experience. The Duke of Wellington always valued him highly.

His business-like habits were invaluable to the inexperienced and unofficial Whigs—the Whigs who never learned the lesson—the first in business of all kinds—that a chief in a department must delegate as much as possible to the best

---

* In allusion to the name of "Prosperity Robinson," fixed on him for his sanguine speeches in times of depression. He died in 1851.

agents possible, else he will be tormented to death and do his work ill. The best man of business is he who does least with his own hands and most through good agents. This is a cardinal rule. My principle always was to be most careful in my selection, and then to give the persons chosen my entire confidence, calling on them to do the same each in his own branch. It was thus I got through the Boundary Bill in 1831 and 1832. That the Reform Bill would be carried, no one doubted; and all that was done. Yet the greatest of the difficulties remained—the boundaries. Grey and others told me I never should do it in three years. I did it in three months, and did it well. I chose Lieutenant Drummond, known to me in the Useful Knowledge Society, where he was an important workman, though he wrote little or nothing; but I knew him to be a good mathematician. I made him take half a dozen more of the Useful Knowledge Committee. I went over the heads of the plan fully, and showed him how he was to operate. I scarcely even saw him again, except that I once had all the committee under him to a great dinner. Durham insisted upon attending it; he came too late, and found us at table, and was sulky all the evening.

When Stanley was to become a secretary of state, Ripon was to be pushed up to the Privy Seal. He was much annoyed, even to tears, but it was done by Grey as differently as possible from Glenelg's case. He also had an earldom, and promise of the Garter.

Although Graham was certainly raised out of his turn to a very high place—first lord of the Admiralty—and perhaps would have done better if he had risen more gradually, yet all admitted that his administration of that great department was as good as possible.

I believe the Admiralty and the Foreign Office were the best administered, though indeed Melbourne at the Home Office was excellent. But I mark Graham and Palmerston, because they showed the least defect in the routine and bureaucratic faculties in which the placeless life of the Whigs had, generally speaking, made them so deficient. Graham was also to be highly commended for his staunch virtue in refusing all jobbery. Nothing of nepotism (so rife elsewhere) could be charged upon him. The defects charged on Graham were of a totally different class, but they were not light ones. He was supposed to be somewhat intriguing, and we found him to be somewhat hurried in Council. The prejudices of Durham, who had hoped to have him as a kind of pocket-vote, and was very angry when he found he had thrown him entirely off, no doubt made him more talk about this than the facts warranted; yet I believe he (Graham) did addict himself to Stanley. But nothing could be more natural, and without any job in view, or without any intriguing spirit in working it out.

I do not at all wonder at Graham and Stanley joining; but had it been otherwise, what blame was there? Stanley was to the full as good a Whig as Graham, and was the representative of an old Foxite Whig family, Graham being the first of his people who ever was any thing but a staunch Tory. Was there, then, the least blame in singling out Stanley for his associate, or, if you will, his leader?

Graham was a modest as well as a moderate man, and did not set up for a party chief. He owed much to Grey; but was he to stick to him when he really agreed more with Stanley?

As for want of nerve, I really think this too has been unfairly stated — at least greatly exaggerated. He was quite wrong, once or twice, in not debating when the Government was in great straits in the Commons. But he was not the only one who failed in this respect. The timber-duties, on which Peel put us in a minority, came far more under Poulett Thomson, Vice-president of the Board of Trade, and HE said not one word. Graham was quite wrong in the fear he had of Campbell going against them should he fail in thrusting out Horne from the attorney-generalship. Never was fear more groundless. Nothing would have driven Campbell into opposition. He was far too anxious for promotion (like a true Scotchman as he was) ever to have gone into opposition.

Graham was one of those who forced Grey and me to yield; but in this he did not stand alone, for Althorp and John Russell equally desired to get rid of Horne. The constant wish of Lord Grey to retire before this period, appears in all our correspondence; but when the above secession happened, he considered the Government so shaken by it that it could not go on. Our colleagues and myself were of a different opinion, and I exerted myself to overcome the resolution which he had taken to retire.

I wrote him a very urgent remonstrance, reminding him how often I had regarded my retirement as not only justifiable, but indispensable, from the state of my health; entering into some details, but reminding him how I had consented to remain, that the Government might not be broken up, which it certainly would be if he went out.

The answer was as follows:

[*Private.*] "Downing Street, May 25, 1834.

"MY DEAR CHANCELLOR,—I received last night your most kind and affectionate letter. You may be assured that it shall not go beyond myself, and that I never can reflect upon such a proof of confidence without feelings of the most sincere regard and gratitude — feelings, indeed, so strong that it is most painful to me to find myself deprived of the power of acquiescing at once in the wish which you so strongly express.

"But there are points upon which every man must judge for himself; your case is very different from mine: you are nearly twenty years younger than I am, and however serious your sufferings may have been, and however painful the exertion to overcome them, you still had time before you; you still possessed all the renovating powers of youth, and might hope to recover the strength which had been temporarily impaired. I am descended far into the vale of years—past the age of man. I enjoy, thank God, strength and health not often possessed by a person of my years, or, I should rather say, freedom from complaint. But I feel my moral and physical energies much impaired, and that I am totally unequal to the performance of duties which, even in a season of calmness, would be above my powers; judge what must be my feelings amidst the difficulties and dangers which surround us, and which would require the highest qualities in their full vigor to surmount them. You say nobody else perceives the decay of which I complain. But I myself feel it, and I am sure you would not wish to see me *ad extremum ridendus*, breaking down under a burden which I can not support. It is as if, seeing me walking along a gravel-walk, you should say, you are upright, your step is firm, there can be no want of sufficient strength, therefore; a great and urgent interest requires it, set out immediately on foot for Windsor, to discharge a duty for which it is necessary that you should undergo this fatigue. My answer would be, the appearances, as you see me, are as you state, but I feel and know that I can not do what you require; I should break down by the way, and you would have the proof, in a way which would be most painful to yourself, of what you will not now believe, and more detrimental to the very object for which you urge me to expose myself to a fatigue to which I am unequal.

"I really feel, therefore, if the Cabinet is to break up, as I think it must, that I have no choice—that my public life is closed. My endeavor will be to reconstruct it on the same principles, under another head. In this I do not expect to succeed; but I shall not fail for want of exertion in doing my best. There is one way in which I might continue *a little* longer—viz., by filling up the vacancies now, with an understanding that another who must now be agreed upon should succeed, at a convenient time, to my place. I think it would be much better on all accounts to make a final settlement now. But if this could not be done, and an arrangement might be effected in the way I have stated, to this I could consent. But there are two things indispensable: first, that the Government should be permanently settled, with the alteration only of the person at its head; and, secondly, that the public and Parliament should in the arrangement itself have proof of this assurance.

"If the king could be brought to consent to this, it must be our desire, indeed it would be our duty, to introduce persons into the vacant offices, who with right principles would be personally acceptable to him.

"I am to see him to-day on this subject, and shall take the earliest opportunity afterwards of talking with you further upon it. Ever yours, GREY.

"I return Murray's letter. It does not impress one with confidence."

The difficulties in the way of either course suggested by him, and the agreement of us all that no other person could be put in his place, at length prevailed upon him to remain.

When Grey saw the king upon the question of filling up the vacancies, and announced to him that the Government intended to go on, I was rather surprised to hear that his majesty had been really cordial, and had even expressed himself to the effect that, "so long as Lord Grey and I remained, he would stand by us and give the Government his firm and hearty support." Such were the words which Grey stated to me had been used by the king. And so we went on. The secession strengthened us in the Commons and in the country. And now came the question of the necessity of renewing the Irish Coercion Bill. I ought first, however, to state that the vacancies in the Cabinet were filled by Spring Rice succeeding Stanley as Colonial Secretary; Auckland as first Lord of the Admiralty, instead of Graham; Lord Conyngham, Post-office; Lord Carlisle, Privy Seal. The other changes were: Abercromby coming into the Cabinet as Master of the Mint; Cutlar Fergusson was made Judge-Advocate; Poulett Thomson became President of the Board of Trade; and Robert Grant went out as Governor of Bombay.

TO EARL GREY.

[*Private.*] "May 30, 1834.

"MY DEAR LORD GREY,—It is a GREAT MISTAKE, into which I wonder Auckland should have fallen, to fancy I have the LEAST personal objection to him. I wanted a man who would have—and, on being better known to the public, given—greater pledge of firmness and stoutness in difficult times; and I was aware that the House of Commons wished those known as such. *I* don't doubt Auckland's nerves, and I don't fear any crotchets; so that, as far as *my own* opinions and feelings go, I have nothing at all to complain of, and I am doing and have done all I can to satisfy others. His own conduct must do the rest. Let him imitate his predecessor in his *official* conduct, and let him exactly be the reverse of him in his leaning on all occasions towards Tories. Patronage the Liberals will and must have, and they must not see it go among their base and spiteful adversaries. Auckland will be well or ill viewed three months hence—perhaps three weeks—as he does so or not. Yours ever, H. BROUGHAM."

FROM EARL GREY.

[*Private.*]

"Downing Street, June 1, 1834.

"MY DEAR CHANCELLOR,—* * * But I feel more and more doubtful as to the possibility of our going on. The whole press and the high popular party against us on one side, the Tories on the other, and our friends, notwithstanding their parting solicitations to me to go on—instead of showing confidence and giving us support, even if in some instances they may think us wrong—full of complaint, and assisting the attacks of our enemies;—what have we to expect but that, on the very first occasion, we should be exposed to a new difficulty like that which has brought on the present crisis? We may stagger on for a while, but we must strike at last under circumstances much more disadvantageous both to ourselves and to the public.

"I feel greatly inclined, therefore, to give the thing up at once, stating both to the king and the country that we were willing and desirous to do every thing in our power to avert the consequences of a change, but that we have found it impossible to form an Administration sufficiently strong in public confidence to conduct the affairs of the country with advantage.

"This is the result of my reflections during the last twenty-four hours. I really believe it to be the only course that is creditable or safe. For myself personally, how am I to hope to get through in the conflict that awaits us, when I am already so harassed and oppressed that I really hardly know what I am doing? Ever yours, GREY."

FROM EARL GREY.

[*Private.*]

"Downing Street, June 2, 1834.

"MY DEAR CHANCELLOR,—I had no motive for desiring you not to say any thing about Radnor till I saw you again, but that of preventing the thing being talked of before it was done; and it had occurred to me that I could not at the moment when I told the king that every thing must be suspended for preparing other appointments. I wished also to talk with you on another point, which only occurred to me at the moment—viz., whether by taking Radnor away, as it were, from Durham's side, a more marked character might not be given to the exclusion of the latter. This, perhaps, was more a matter of personal feeling, but it was deserving of some consideration with respect to the public.

"I have also a great and increasing dislike to the appearance of every thing being done under duresse; and therefore my feeling is just the contrary, in one respect, of yours—viz., that the thing should be done before the meeting, and as a sort of sop to them. We must know whether they give us confidence or not; and for all these reasons I am decidedly against taking any step in this matter before the result of the meeting is known.

"From all I hear, things do not look well. My answer to the letter, I am told, has created dissatisfaction. In short, it comes to this: we must submit to be the agents of a certain number of persons in the House of Commons, or forfeit their support. To this condition I can not submit.

"But there is a more serious matter behind. Althorp is nearly overpowered by the difficulties of his situation, and I doubt very much whether he will be able to go on in any case. But his continuance in the House of Commons is more precarious than ever. Lord Spencer is, as it appears to me, in a most alarming state. The physicians think so, not having been able to get his pulse—which has been as low as twenty-six—above thirty-four; and this without any apparent affection of his health to account for it. In short, it appears to me impossible that the Government should go on.

"Ever yours, GREY."

FROM EARL GREY.

[*Private.*]

"Downing Street, June 4, 1834.

"MY DEAR CHANCELLOR,—I have just received your note, and hope you will believe that I am sensible, as I ought to be, of all its kindness.

"Upon talking over the matter since I saw you with Althorp, we agreed that, upon the whole, it would be best to offer the Privy Seal to Radnor; and, as an old and intimate friend and school-fellow, he has undertaken to say to him that I wished to make the offer, but to be assured previously that it would not be disagreeable to him. I did not hesitate in this, as I was sure you could not dislike it. If Radnor refuses, I shall of course offer it to Dacre.

"I have a very good account from Rice of Cambridge. I am just getting into my carriage for Windsor.

"Ever yours, GREY."

TO EARL GREY.

[*Private.*] "June 6, 1834.

"MY DEAR LORD GREY,—I am very sorry at seeing that there is some *hitch* about Radnor; because my firm belief is, that the declaration to-morrow morning that he was Privy Seal would at once remove all kind of difficulty, and do away with the very bad effects of Auckland's appointment. This opinion is confirmed by the following anecdote:

"I met Sefton, and asked him if he had altered his opinion (which I know he entertained on Thursday and Friday), as you had heard of his grumbling at Brookes's. He utterly denied the charge, and says there never was any thing so unfounded; that he praised the whole heartily, though he could not deny he felt hurt at finding Auckland's appointment so generally disapproved. He added, that he felt confident that it might all be set right by other good nominations, and thought Ellice's was one that helped it much. I asked whom he and others would have had instead of Auckland, and I said that there was a reason personal to Abercromby, which would plainly have made his taking it liable to any misconstruction. He said he did not mean Abercromby, but Radnor; and that he really thought if Radnor had been named, all the world would have been highly satisfied, and still would be so.

"This is very strong confirmation of our opinion, and I heartily hope you may still be able to name him.

"By-the-way, why not give Sefton himself the post-office? —of course *without* Cabinet. It is a just punishment to others, and he would do it admirably.

"Yours very truly, H. BROUGHAM."

TO EARL GREY.

[*Private.*] "June 7, 1834.

"MY DEAR LORD GREY,—I never like to plague you, but you know I never have but *one* object, and *always* give up my own crotchets and adopt *yours*.

"It strikes me that it would greatly help us all, and be of infinite service to us in the Commons, if we had Abercromby among us as Master of Mint or Post-office, and Radnor Privy Seal. He is extremely liked in and out of Parliament; his name is very popular, and has great weight with all the army, as Abercromby's has with all Scotch people.

"As for his repining and fanciful disposition, I can take on myself to keep that under. He is firm, and very honest. Pray think of this, and also tell me if Lady Grey and Lady Georgiana and you can meet the Levesons next Friday to dinner with only a small party.

"Ever yours, H. BROUGHAM.

"I could dream of nothing but your speech; it was perfect in all respects. I thought Sefton would have *kept up*. I fasted fifteen hours!"

It soon became necessary to consider the question of the Irish Coercion Bill. The act of last session had undoubtedly been successful. Under its provisions, districts in Westmeath and Galway had been proclaimed; the number of offenses had thereupon greatly diminished. When the question of continuing or renewing the act was placed before Lord Wellesley, he recommended that the whole act should be renewed, with the exception only of the court-martial clauses; and soon afterwards he further confirmed this advice by sending us the opinions of the inspectors-general of provinces, all of whom unanimously recommended a renewal of the act.

In the Cabinet there was much discussion on the subject, and I fear I must admit, much difference of opinion. Durham showed a strong tendency to O'Connell's view of the question, and went so far as to oppose on the second reading the clauses in the bill which related to public meetings.

The ministers who in Cabinet agreed with Durham's objection to these clauses were Althorp, Charles Grant, Spring

Rice, and Abercromby; but these yielded to the majority, which supported Grey's view that these clauses were indispensable.

On the 1st of July, Lord Grey introduced the bill in an admirable speech. He stated, from Lord Wellesley's dispatch of the 18th of April, the grounds for strongly recommending the renewal of the bill; and he made out a case quite sufficient to convince me of the necessity, even if I had not, after a perusal of the papers sent by Lord Wellesley, fully made up my mind to support Grey. On the second reading, Durham, as I have said, objected to the public meetings clauses. I answered him, strongly supporting Grey, and arguing that it would be most unjust to curb the peasantry by those clauses relating to agrarian disturbances, which Durham did not object to, and to leave agitators like O'Connell free to get up meetings in all the towns of Ireland, professedly for the redress of grievances, but in reality for the repeal of the union. I stated that my consent to the measure was wrung from me by the hard necessity of the case, and that I could agree to its continuance only for the further period of one year. The House approved of the view we took, and the bill was read a second time without further opposition.

In the course of this debate, some observations were made to the effect that negotiations were going on out-of-doors between a member of the Irish Government and the very men who were the cause of all the mischief. Lord Grey being asked if he knew of, or had originated, any such negotiations, at once indignantly denied all knowledge of any thing of the kind, and stated that, had he been spoken to on the subject, he should not only have expressed his marked disapprobation, but have done all in his power to prevent such proceedings. To Lord Grey's statement I added my belief that no such negotiations had taken place; although I admitted that the Irish Secretary (Littleton) *might* have, unknown to Government, held some communications with parties interested in the subject of the Coercion Bill, just as I myself had done when, sitting on the wool-sack, I had discussed some of the clauses with a noble friend to whom I had gone so far as to express my objection to some parts of the bill as unconstitutional, and only to be tolerated in a case of the most urgent necessity; of which necessity I had become entirely convinced, after a perusal of the papers which had been quoted by Lord Grey when he introduced the bill.

The bill was ordered to be committed on an early day, and now came out in the House of Commons disclosures which had important consequences. It was there stated by Littleton, the Irish Secretary—and this was afterwards confirmed by Althorp—that a communication had been made by Littleton to O'Connell, to the effect that certain clauses of the bill were under the consideration of the Cabinet; that Littleton had expressed a hope that such clauses would be omitted in the new bill, but had by no means stated that such was the decision of ministers; that this communication had been made in confidence, and on a promise of absolute secrecy. Littleton himself, in his place, admitted, in so many words, that "he had committed a gross indiscretion," but added that such indiscretion could in no respect justify O'Connell's breach of faith in telling others what had taken place in confidence and secrecy.

O'Connell, when he first heard that the bill was to be renewed in all its parts, had written a letter to Wexford, abusing the Ministry as "a base Whig faction which threatened to enslave Ireland;" and he forthwith started a repealer as candidate at the coming election.

O'Connell's defense to Littleton's charge of breach of confidence was, that upon the faith of Littleton's assurance that the objectionable clauses were to be omitted, he had at once withdrawn "the repealer," and had prepared his Irish friends in Parliament to support the Government; that, finding Lord Grey had, in the very teeth of Littleton's assurance, brought in the bill without the omissions, he considered that he had been tricked, and that he and his friends had been so grossly deceived by Littleton, that he regarded the confidence in which the communication had been made as at an end; that such confidence never would have been broken by him, if he had not been thus tricked and deceived.

Littleton stated afterwards in the House that he had not communicated with O'Connell till after consulting friends upon whose judgment he could rely, and that in all he had done he had acted under what he considered a sufficient authority.

This was supposed to refer to Althorp; and undoubtedly, when the effect all these circumstances had upon the Ministry was discussed in the Commons, Althorp stated that when Littleton suggested to him the expediency of telling O'Connell, he had strongly warned him to use the most extreme caution in any communication he might make, and on no account to commit himself.

When all the questions connected with the Coercion Bill were discussed in the Cabinet, Lord Grey, at one of our meetings held shortly before he introduced the bill in the Lords, laid before us a letter from Lord Wellesley, which he had received on the 23d of June. In this letter Lord Wellesley stated his opinion that the public meeting clauses might be safely omitted, remarking that the change of circumstances since he had written his letters of the 18th of April and 11th of June to Lord Melbourne, were sufficient to justify this change in his opinion. Althorp quite agreed with this view, so also did Charles Grant, Spring Rice, Abercromby, and Edward Ellice. But the majority of the Cabinet decided to adopt Lord Grey's view, which was that, notwithstanding Lord Wellesley's letter, the bill must be renewed, omitting only the court-martial clauses.

Grey considered this letter so strictly private, that he thought he was scarcely justified in showing it to the Cabinet, and that nothing but the peculiar circumstances in which he was placed could have permitted him to refer to it in the House of Lords, as he did on the 9th of July, when he stated the grounds of his resignation.

CHAPTER XXVII.

Incidents of the Situation on Lord Grey's Retirement.—The Chancellor and Wellesley.—Lord Althorp.—The King and his Predilections.—Lord Melbourne's Premiership.—How accomplished.—Personal Feeling of the King.—Lord Durham.—The English Poor-law Bill.—The "Grey Festival" in Edinburgh.—Biographical Sketches of Lord Grey.—Campbell's Attempt at the Rolls.—Correspondence with Lord Grey continued.—Personal Position towards him.—How it had been misunderstood.—Lord Lyndhurst.—Estimate of his Character and Capacity.—Proposed Register of Land Rights.—Dismissal of the Melbourne Cabinet.—Winding up of the Chancellor's Business.—Conclusion of Autobiography.

In consequence of what had passed in the House of Commons, Althorp felt that the grounds upon which the renewal of the bill had been originally urged by Lord Wellesley, and on which he himself was to have carried the bill through the Commons, had been cut away by Lord Wellesley's letter of the 21st of June, and the change of opinion he therein expressed; and therefore, feeling that he could no longer act usefully to the Government or satisfactorily to himself, he wrote a letter to Lord Grey tendering his resignation. He adhered to this in a subsequent interview, and this determined Lord Grey himself to resign, which he accordingly did, and announced it in the Lords on the 9th of July, in a speech in which he was very greatly affected.

In referring to the communication made to O'Connell, Grey only designated this as the height of imprudence. Like a true gentleman as he was, he accused no one, but put the grounds of his resignation on the loss of Althorp, as the leader of the Government in the Commons, and as the man on whom he placed his chief confidence. But *I knew* that he felt most severely the proceedings of those who had influenced Lord Wellesley, and had dealt with O'Connell. The letter which Littleton had written to Lord Wellesley, and which had produced Lord Wellesley's letter to Grey of the 21st of June, was concocted, as Grey entirely believed, by Edward

Ellice. Certainly he blamed him more than he blamed Durham or any one else; and afterwards, in referring to this painful subject, he exclaimed to me, "But to think of Ellice, 'mine own familiar friend, who did eat of my bread'—to think of him of all men thus conspiring against me!"

At this period of wranglings and disputes and charges against every body, more or less well founded, the mischief-makers attempted to get up a case against me, founded upon a letter I had written to Lord Wellesley. A letter was in fact written about this period, but it was of a purely private nature, and could not at any time have exercised the smallest influence on his mind. How should it? It was a letter about some verses of Lord Wellesley's, and about other gossip, too private to be here quoted. But the sentence I have referred to was as follows: "You have done yourself much credit, in my opinion, in recommending the giving up the court-martial clauses in the bill. If things were in such a state as to justify you in recommending the omission of the unconstitutional clauses about meetings also, you would be on a pinnacle." That was the exact sentence, and contained every word I wrote to Lord Wellesley on the subject.

On Grey's resignation I went to the king, and assured him that I believed I could persuade Althorp to retract his resignation, and that I hoped Grey would return also, as we all most anxiously desired his continuance; and all must be aware how severe a blow on the Government his retirement would inflict. His majesty seemed puzzled, and repeated his former assertion of some weeks before, that while Grey and I remained together he was firm in our support. He expressed great doubt of our being able to go on, and left on my mind the very distinct impression that he was disposed to accept *all* our resignations, and try a Tory Government.

The king's situation and ours, then, was this, according to my observation—and all which followed has demonstrated that I was right in my estimate of it: Sick of a Government that was urged on to make changes, of which he had had quite enough—still more sick of being urged on by that Government to consent to fresh changes; panting for the quiet of a Tory Ministry, the natural favorite of all kings; not relishing a set of ministers who looked to popular support rather than to Court favor—still less liking a Ministry which almost every month spoke of breaking up (as under Lord Grey had been too often the case), and leaving him in the position of all others to all kings the most hateful and even alarming, that of being left for a time without a Government, and so feeling all responsibility thrown on themselves; sighing almost equally for a restoration of the peers to his standard, and a cessation of their opposition and that of the Church, the irksomeness of which he had lately shown by his closet speech to the bishops, so very different from his rating letter to them in June, 1833—he, in short, sighed to have a regular Tory Administration. But this he never could have with the present House of Commons, unless the Liberal Government voluntarily broke itself up, when, from their resigning, and the necessity of there being *some* Government, the Commons would support any one that could be formed, at least for the remainder of the session, when a dissolution would strengthen their hands. All his chance, then, of getting rid of us, and getting hold of a Conservative Ministry that could stand, depended on one of two events—either our resigning and refusing to carry on his affairs, or a vacation coming and enabling him to dissolve. Perceiving this, I acted accordingly, and forever lost his favor till he was on his death-bed.

I addressed a letter to him offering to go on, and assuring him that all my colleagues were firmly determined to stand by his majesty with myself, stating that, even should Lord Grey's lamented retirement be unavoidable, Althorp was ready to return to his service; and further stating that, if Melbourne were placed in Grey's situation, all would be easy and certain, with the continuance of his majesty's countenance and support.

The king's constant plan for relieving the Ministry from their embarrassment, and himself from the constraint of any party, was by a coalition of all but the extreme popular members, whom he regarded as representing the Radicals, and what he considered the destructives. When I had proposed Melbourne to succeed Grey, and prevent the Government being changed, his answer, that he took Melbourne, was accompanied with an objection to my proposal as being narrowed to one political class; and this he followed up by strongly recommending a coalition Ministry—a recommendation often repeated in subsequent letters.

FROM SIR HERBERT TAYLOR.

[*Private.*]

"Windsor Castle, July 10, 1834.

"MY DEAR LORD,—I had not the opportunity of submitting your lordship's letter of yesterday afternoon to the king until shortly before his majesty left St. James's, and therefore could not reply to it, as directed by him, until I returned here.

"His majesty having given due consideration to its contents, has honored me with his commands to acquaint your lordship that he did not expect you to hasten to resign the Great Seal into his hands, and that it was not his wish or his intention to have called for that resignation any more than for that of Lord Grey or any other member of the Administration; but that it was impossible for him to view the circumstances under which the Administration was placed by the resignations which had been tendered to him, and which he considered himself under the necessity of accepting, as involving any thing short of its dissolution. It has, in his majesty's opinion, fallen to pieces; and that event has been produced, not by any irresistible or overbearing opposition to the measures of the Government, but by the operation of internal causes, against the wearing effects of which, the high character and influence and the irreproachable conduct of Lord Grey, and the unqualified and undeviating support which the Government over which his lordship so ably presides, received from his majesty, have proved unavailing.

"Under this impression and this view, which have not been removed, his majesty felt it to be his duty not to delay taking such steps as appeared to him best calculated to extricate himself and the country over which he has been called to rule from the difficulties in which both are placed; and the instructions with which his majesty has thought fit to intrust Lord Melbourne resulted from a conviction on his mind that the safety of the country, its dearest interests, and the maintenance of the blessings which it has so long enjoyed under its present admirable constitution and valuable institutions, would be best promoted by a union of the most respectable and influential individuals of those parties which have shown any solicitude for the preservation of those advantages, and from the hope that, with the aid and the support of these, his majesty might be able to check the designs of lawless agitators and the progress of violent changes.

"His majesty orders me to observe to your lordship, as he has stated to Lord Melbourne, that in the pursuit of an object which he considers reasonable and legitimate, and consistent with his duty and with the welfare of the country, he is not actuated by predilection for any political party, or by any prejudice which can have the effect of circumscribing the sphere from which the selection shall be made, or of excluding from his councils, or from the service of the country, those whose integrity, abilities, and experience entitle them to consideration and confidence. But, in proportion as he values the peace and the prosperity of the country, its general security, and the protection of property against spoliation, he must be anxious to resist the admission into places of trust and authority of those who aim at the destruction of those blessings, and who would not only readily yield to, but might feel disposed to invite and encourage, constant and active pressure from without, tending to violent changes and the introduction of frightful differences and collisions between the various classes of society.

"His majesty is confident that your lordship's sentiments must accord with his own in this respect; and he flatters himself that, upon further consideration, you may feel disposed to admit that in the endeavor to accomplish an object so consistent with the duty of the sovereign (who would be unfit for his station if he were influenced by party-feeling and prejudice) his majesty is justified in seeking a broader basis than that to which your lordship would seem disposed to confine him.

"His majesty is indeed sensible of the difficulties to be encountered, and that they may disappoint his hopes of success. But his majesty attaches much value to even the possibility of reconciling in some degree those jarring feelings and political differences among the most estimable of his subjects, which have so long produced embarrassment and mischief to the affairs of the State and to the best interests of the country, that he can not and will not lightly abandon the attempt; and his majesty estimates too highly your lordship's talents, the extraordinary resources of your mind, and your indefatigable zeal in the pursuit of all that you undertake, and in the discharge of most arduous and important duties—he is too well assured of your lordship's solicitude for the welfare of this great country, and too sensible of the value of your influence on the public and in society—not to feel most anxious to obtain your concurrence in views which, as a patriot and a faithful servant of the Crown, you can not but approve. I have the honor to be, with the highest regard, my dear lord, your lordship's most obedient and faithful servant,

"H. TAYLOR.*

"THE LORD HIGH CHANCELLOR."

Nothing could be more manifest than that the king and those about him, except Sir Herbert Taylor, had hoped that first the retirement of Stanley, Graham, and the others, followed by Grey's wish then to go, and then his actual resignation, with Althorp's, would have rendered a continuance of our Government impossible, and would have led to a union of parties. The disappointment was great when, having sent the proposal of Melbourne, I went to the House at once, and declared that we could, and probably should, go on—a declaration caught up and acted upon in the Commons. He complained much of these proceedings, as in the following letter; and he never forgave me for the sudden declaration, which he considered as having destroyed all chance of ending the Whig Ministry, and putting a combined one in its place. We, quite as much as he, desired to have our Ministry extended, and made many attempts to effect this, all of which failed.

FROM SIR HERBERT TAYLOR.

[*Private.*] "Windsor Castle, July 12, 1834.

"MY DEAR LORD,—I do not delay acknowledging the receipt of your lordship's letters of this day, which I have had

* Sir Herbert Taylor's name will not be found in the usual biographical dictionaries. He was born in 1775, and died in 1839.—See *Memoir* ("Gentleman's Magazine"), June, 1839, p. 654.

the honor of submitting to the king, who was very glad to learn from them that he had misconceived your expression of a disposition in certain members of the House of Commons to urge upon Lord Althorp their desire that he should resume his situation in the Government into a desire or an intention to force a minister upon his majesty; and that their language could not be construed into disregard of the most constitutional views of the royal prerogative, which his majesty considers it due to the interests of the State, as well as to his own honor, that he should jealously guard.

"The king is quite willing to admit your lordship's construction of his rights, and he does not doubt your doing justice to the principle on which he asserts them.

"It is also satisfactory to his majesty to be assured by your lordship and by others that there is a friendly feeling in many, even popular, quarters towards himself, and a disposition to consider the difficulties in which he is placed, and to give him credit for an honest desire to consult the peace and the welfare of the country. His majesty would be glad, however, to know that there is allied to those sentiments a more conciliatory feeling towards the aristocracy, of which he considers the existence, and the maintenance with unimpaired influence, to be clearly connected with that of the monarchy, and essential to the character and the credit of the country.

"The king can not but approve of the good taste and the good sense of those who have exerted themselves to prevent the presentation of an address to Lord Althorp, calling upon him to resume, or rather to retain, office, for he is still in the exercise of the functions of his office. It must, indeed, be satisfactory to Lord Althorp to know that his exemplary services are justly appreciated; and his majesty has no doubt that, whenever he shall feel that they have again become indispensable, he will not hesitate, any more than your lordship has done, to sacrifice ease and comfort and more agreeable pursuits to the service of this country.

"His majesty rejoices to gather, from your lordship's expression on the subject, that you approve of his not abandoning the attempt to effect a union of parties until it fail; and although he has ceased to entertain much hope of success, he will not regret having made the trial. Mr. Stanley's answer to Lord Melbourne appears to him, as it does to you, extremely creditable to him; and his majesty has learned with sincere pleasure that he has so well redeemed, by his letter to Lord Grey, the error he committed in attacking so violently his late colleagues and friends in his speech on Friday week last.

"I have the honor to be, with my best regards, my dear lord, your lordship's most obedient and faithful friend,

"H. TAYLOR.

"P.S.—I have this moment received and communicated to the king your lordship's third letter, of this date; and not wishing to detain your messenger until after dinner, I have only time to say that his majesty gives you full credit for the zealous motive which produced your communication to Lord Rosslyn (of whom his majesty entertains, as you do, a very high opinion), and that he must derive satisfaction from any thing that may offer a hope of reconciling jarring feelings and views."

Althorp made some difficulty in retracting his resignation, because he felt great scruple in separating himself from Littleton, who had resigned; but this was all set right by Littleton consenting to return to the Irish office. Before the end of July the Irish Bill was withdrawn, and another brought in, omitting the public meetings clauses, and became law before August.

My reason for suggesting Melbourne rather than Althorp was obvious, and was entirely approved by Sefton and others whom I consulted. Althorp could not have come back to take Grey's place, after his resignation had been stated as the cause—and it was, in fact, the main cause—of Grey's own resignation. This was too clear to admit of a doubt. As for my proposing Melbourne because he was my intimate friend, as some suggested, Althorp was to the full as much so. The sole reason was what I have above stated, and a sufficient one. I felt all the evils of Melbourne's unpopularity; and of all the former known parts of his public life—his ratting from Grey, his support of the six Acts and Manchester massacre, his opposing Reform till it became lucrative, his joining the Tories upon the occasion of their affronting his uncle and borough patron (Lord Fitzwilliam), under whom he was actually then sitting in Parliament. I also felt the evils of his bad personal habits as a man of business, his inefficiency in debate, his careless temper. All this I saw staring me in the face; but against it all I had to set the evils that any other course was liable to. Then I also knew that Melbourne had many valuable and even brilliant qualities, and I hoped that both would become unfolded to the world, and remove in some degree the king's extreme prejudice against him—a prejudice he inherited from George III., who always looked upon Melbourne House as a kind of second Carlton House, and hated it as he hated every thing that belonged to his eldest son. William IV. saw, or at least always tried to see, with his father's eyes, and they were accordingly jaundiced when looking at Melbourne.

Before receiving the king's answer I repaired to the House of Lords, and announced that the Government had not resigned, nor had any intention of doing so. I made "a most powerful and affecting speech" on the loss of Lord Grey, utterly denying his age being any reason, as he had alleged, for his retirement—extolling all his great and good qualities; and received his and Lady Grey's most hearty acknowledgments for that speech. I quote above the description given by themselves of it. I have seldom in all my life exerted myself more, or been more touched with my subject.

This speech decided the affair, for the Commons and the country rallied round me; and any thing we chose was voted by the one and backed by the other. But the king never forgave it. I pardon him—the measure was a strong one, but it was necessary. The letter to himself prevented him from dismissing us, except at the peril of being opposed in and out of Parliament. My speech prevented any relaxation of support in Parliament. If I had deferred it, even for twenty-four hours, I should have given him time for intriguing with other parties, and accomplishing his favorite object of turning us off and taking in the Tories. Both steps were necessary, but that could not well make either step agreeable to him. He yielded a sullen compliance, wrote me a letter that he accepted Melbourne for minister, and never more smiled on me while he lived.

Durham entertained great hopes of joining the Government, now that Grey was out. I never had the least objection to act with him, unless when his father-in-law was there also—*that* we had found to be utterly impossible, because in Durham's presence, whatever was the subject, the fear of a violent personal explosion from him precluded Grey from being any thing like a free agent; but Durham was quiet and tractable enough with others. To have a prime minister thus fettered was quite out of the question. But Grey, unhappily, being now removed by his own resignation, I for one never objected to Durham. I believe, however, all the others did, and Melbourne certainly would not have taken the Government with him for a colleague. Durham showed his chagrin by sending an excuse to me, instead of coming to dinner, the day our changes were fixed.

The Poor-Law Bill, which had been brought in by Althorp in April, after much interruption and much opposition, passed the second reading by a very large majority, and in July was brought up to the House of Lords. Hard worked as I was in every way, I nevertheless took charge of it, and made a long and carefully-prepared speech on introducing it on the 21st of July. Although opposed by some peers, it was well supported by Wellington, Richmond, and Winchelsea, and passed through the different stages without much difficulty, but with amendments, to some of which the Commons refused to agree. The Lords did not insist, and so this important measure became law. The whole weight of carrying it through the Lords fell upon me, and I was not sorry when the session closed in the middle of August, and I prepared to leave town.

The Cabinet met for the last time before the recess, and no men could be more cordial together. Before we separated, we arranged all our measures and new improvements for next session, and distributed among ourselves the different plans in contemplation: thus, one took municipal reform; others took Church reform; others law reform, including local courts; and so forth.

Lord Grey had at this time resolved to decline the public dinner proposed to be given to him at Edinburgh, and thus announced to me his determination:

[*Private.*] FROM EARL GREY.

"Downing Street, August 12, 1834.

"DEAR CHANCELLOR,—The lord advocate spoke to me about the dinner. I am most grateful for the kindness and honor intended me, but I felt myself obliged to decline it. Had I been living near Edinburgh, or passing that way, the case might have been different, but there are many objections to going so far.

"I return George III.'s correspondence, having in the mean time read Holland's copy. The king was very full of it when I was at Windsor. Ever yours, GREY."

I then saw him, but did not succeed in persuading him to relent and to accept the proffered honor; but when I got to Brougham I heard he had yielded, and I thus wrote to him, in answer to a letter urging me to attend the dinner without fail:

[*Private.*] TO EARL GREY.

"Brougham, August 22, 1834.

"MY DEAR LORD GREY,—Pray let me know as soon as you fix the day for the Edinburgh banquet, as I shall contrive my journey to the North accordingly. They first asked me to preside, but as I told them a Scotch grandee [would be] better, they took the Duke of Hamilton. I said if they preferred me, I cheerfully would. They must judge. I conclude *you* have no choice.

"I am, I see, abused by the press about '*my order*' by all sides, as much as you used to be, and with as good reason. They lyingly leave out the fact of Radnor saying, 'I agree in every one word the chancellor has said, and I second his motion for reading the Warwick Bill this day six months.' And after willfully suppressing this, they charge me with *counteracting* the friends of the bill. They also leave out Harrison's admission, that, suppose you believed all his witnesses had said, he could only affect 19 voters out of 1200. Can any one living pretend to say this was a ground for any act?

"Yours ever, H. BROUGHAM."

And he answered thus:

[*Private.*] FROM EARL GREY.

"Howick, August 24, 1834.

"MY DEAR CHANCELLOR,—I received your letter this morning. I found it impossible to resist the invitation to the dinner which the Lord Provost of Edinburgh and Sir James Gibson-Craig brought to me yesterday. They wished it to be on some day in the week beginning the 15th September—the day being left to be settled by the Duke of Hamilton, who, they told me, had been invited to take the chair. As all days are alike to me, I left it to be settled by them as they please. I understand the duke made it a condition that there were to be no lights! Are we to dine at twelve, or to be in the dark after seven?"

"I can not be otherwise than highly gratified by your thinking me worthy to have your speech on the Poor Laws dedicated to me. You know I was actually up to move it when Londonderry stopped me; and the reason of my not attending that or any other question afterwards was the desire of avoiding the eternal references that I foresaw would be made to my resignation.

"The only way with newspaper attacks is, as the Irish say, 'to keep never minding.' This has been my practice through life. There is nothing that answers the purpose of those who attack more than to answer them, which brings a controversy. Time and conduct set these things right.

"Ever yours, GREY."

In August I went to visit the Duke of Hamilton, and while there I wrote to Grey on the subject of the Edinburgh dinner.

[*Private.*] TO EARL GREY.

"Hamilton Palace, August 30, 1834.

"MY DEAR LORD GREY,—The duke of this place has graciously condescended to take the 15th instead of 17th, at the joint request of some Edinburgh people and of myself. It makes a great difference to me; and the Edinburgh scientific meeting being over on the 13th (Saturday), it would have been hard on them to keep them assembled beyond Monday.

"From your letter it was plain *you* did not care which was the day. I met the Woods (quite well) at the Falls of the Clyde yesterday. They are gone on towards Ellice's.

"In haste, yours ever, H. B."

FROM EARL GREY.

[*Private.*]

"Howick, August 31, 1834.

"MY DEAR CHANCELLOR,—I really don't see how it was possible for any man to do more than I did in my speech on Wharncliffe's motion, to counteract any unfavorable impression that my resignation might produce. I will not deny, however, that I felt that I had great reason to complain, as I stated more than once in the Cabinet, of the communications which produced Lord Wellesley's strange contradiction of every thing he had before said and written, and still more of the communication to O'Connell; but I never suspected that they were meant injuriously to *me*, or that they proceeded from any other than, in my opinion, a very false imputation of creating facilities for carrying the Tithe Bill. For the purpose of removing me nothing could be more useless, for my intention of retiring was well known; and had only been suspended by the representations of my colleagues, of which those made by you were perhaps the strongest, and of a character to remove all doubt of their sincerity.

"As to my sons, they felt, not unnaturally, angry at what had occurred. But you do them injustice in believing that they wished the Government to be broken up to give greater *éclat* to my resignation. How could they wish it to take place under circumstances more advantageous to me personally?

"As to any thing that has passed lately there can be no imputation attached to *them*. Howick left England for Germany some time before the prorogation, and there he still is; and Charles soon afterwards for the Highlands, where he now is, thinking of nothing but killing his twenty brace a day.

"Howick was provoked, as well he might be, at Littleton's taking credit to himself for preventing the unpopular clauses, instead of showing shame and contrition for his most unjustifiable conduct. This was the cause of his speaking, and of the question he put, which, if it did harm, it was because Littleton did not answer it.

"As to the newspapers, what public man has not reason to complain of them? If I thought it worth while to make a grievance of the daily tone of the ministerial papers, in holding out expectations of more effective reforms now that the chief obstacle to them is removed, I should have ample cause to do so.

"I shall be at Edinburgh on the morning of the 15th, which is, as Sir James Gibson-Craig informs me, the day fixed for the dinner. Ever yours, GREY."

This letter refers to Wharncliffe's motion, on the 18th of July, for the production of the correspondence with Lord Wellesley. In making his motion, he entered into all the questions of the resignations and the conduct of every body concerned in the transaction, especially attacking Littleton for communicating with the lord lieutenant. Grey, while he admitted that Wharncliffe had stated the case with sufficient accuracy, objected to any inference that he had been betrayed by a member of his Cabinet. He stated distinctly that he made no complaint of any body, that he accused nobody, that he complained of no ill-treatment, because none had been intended. He repeated, as he had done on a former occasion, that a communication had certainly been made to the lord lieutenant without his knowledge; but he blamed no one, because he was convinced that such communication had been made with the best and most honorable intentions. The motion was withdrawn, and thus the subject was forever ended.

Of Lord Grey, who that values high spirit and perfect honor, combined with great abilities, can speak but in terms of affection and admiration? He had virtues and defects, both great, for Government, and for hard times. Of his virtues, honesty, openness, courage were striking. His business-like talents were perfect; no better man of business ever tied with red tape.

Grey retained his faculties entire, and his temper got mellowed by age. I had known him in opposition intimately for twenty-five years. We had once or twice nearly split on account of his Whig-like adherence to that vile Whig principle, "The party every thing, the country little or nothing, unless seen through party eyes." Then came 1827, the junction with Canning, which I advocated and helped to form, and which junction broke up the old Tory party, and made a rent in it that enabled us to carry Catholic Emancipation and Reform.

Grey's talents as a debater were of a very high, but not of the highest, order. His reply in October, 1831, on the Reform Bill was wonderful, considering his age—68—and his having, after sitting five nights in debate, spoken at six in the morning.

His manner was excellent, both in person and in delivery; but he wanted clear argument combined with powerful declamation — the most difficult of all — and he could not *prepare.* His *forte* was a very lucid and seductive statement, and sometimes powerful appeals to the feelings—powerful, because evidently sincere. Canning's appeals were all from the mouth, never from the heart. But Canning had talents which Grey wanted. He could open a question far better than most people. His reply was generally less able.

Grey valued himself highly on being able to speak on evidence, and he justly so valued himself. But in the queen's case he constantly fell into the error of criticising *us* (the counsel) as missing points, etc., when it was his own want of professional experience and knowledge that made him unable to perceive our play, and his utter ignorance of what was in our briefs. So he would set up for a cross-examiner, and as long as he succeeded, or fancied he succeeded, he would play the advocate (often, quite unconsciously, damaging our case); then the moment he failed, he drew up and put on the judge, and professed that he had not been cross-examining, but only endeavoring to get at the truth!

In Cabinet, Grey was the best of all colleagues—modest, unsparing of himself, firm when put up to it, perfectly free from all vanity, full of resources—next to Palmerston the fullest, perhaps—and perfectly fair and above-board.

But his weakness for his family was grievous, and produced the not unfounded charge of nepotism. He once even sounded me on making his nephew, Sir George Grey, *solicitor-general,* knowing that he scarcely ever had held a brief, and that few in or out of the profession knew he belonged to it. Of course I would not hear of it seriously. He complained most of the attacks of the "Times" on this score of nepotism.

But his great vice as a minister and party chief was the low fit he was periodically seized with; once a month he was for resigning, and insisting on the Government being broken up. Lansdowne, Dover, and I frequently kept him in by main force. This love of resigning was always during the first half of the session. Towards the end he was more willing to stay in, because then he had the long vacation before him.

These were little weaknesses in my friend, all more or less allied to his most kind and amiable nature, and all made apparent in him; while others, having none of his frank and open honesty, but having the same flaws in character, would have kept them concealed. But no one can tell how very much they increased the difficulty of acting with him in governing the country. Foreign affairs was what he took most pleasure in, and understood by far the best. His education was on the old system, and he hated all finance, all colonial, all East Indian questions most profoundly, and would not give his mind to them. On military matters he thought he had a great knowledge and much skill, and in this he was perhaps right; but here his easily-conceived impressions, not always unprejudiced, marred his judgment on both men and measures. At one time he undervalued the Duke of Wellington to a degree quite unaccountable, but the candor of his honest nature at last prevailed. The duke's dispatches converted him entirely, and he ever after regarded him as something above human, both as a captain and as a statesman.

The subject on which Grey had most interested himself was Reform, owing to his having belonged to the Society of Friends of the People with Lauderdale and others, but not with Fox, who never would be of it; and next, that he had made the motion in 1797, on which the absurd, and indeed improper, measure of secession was announced by Fox.*

In 1830 and 1831 it became clear that Grey must redeem his pledges, though his Reform zeal had somewhat abated.

* In the third-best speech he ever made, and the second-best reported. The best was on the war in 1803; the second on the Scrutiny, 1784, when the extempore burst of many moments' duration, at an unexpected interruption, exceeds all, perhaps, that he ever did.

He would have preferred a more moderate measure, but he, like others, yielded to the consideration that it was better to push a large measure at once; besides the obvious argument that if you give little you gain no great support, and are as much, or nearly as much, opposed as if you gave a great deal; also, he felt that the existence of the Government depended on the acceptance of the Reform measure with the people.

He had always great frankness of nature, and in age it never lessened. Many who loved and respected him, and admired his brilliant qualities, yet undervalued his sagacity and his judgment. Fitzpatrick held it very low, and Thanet, one of the very ablest of the party, used to say he never saw a man more overrated; and as he would only regard the very first-rate speakers as worth considering, for mere oratory, so he placed Grey, as the jockeys say, nowhere in the race for the prize of rhetoric. This is, indeed, so far true, that many a man speaks below his capacity; but inasmuch as I have consulted infinitely more with Grey, and on graver matters, and in more trying circumstances, than I ever did with any other man, I take upon myself to assert that his quickness and sense were great, and his counsel excellent.

In the middle of September, 1834, Leach died at Edinburgh. Almost as soon as this could be known, I found that Campbell had written to Melbourne urging his claim as attorney-general, for the Rolls. Now this was rather too bad, because I had taken an opportunity, on his being appointed attorney, to tell him *most distinctly* that, in the event of a vacancy, an Equity man would probably be selected by the Government, because, to have a common lawyer at the Rolls as well as on the wool-sack was a thing not to be thought of. To all this Campbell fully assented. Great, then, was my surprise, when I found that the moment the breath was out of Leach's body Melbourne had been written to. I presume no notice was taken of the application, because it was followed up by an immediate attack upon *me* in the following letter:

[*Private.*] "Taymouth Castle, September 22, 1834.

"MY DEAR LORD CHANCELLOR,—I am rather surprised that I have not yet heard a syllable from any quarter about the

Rolls. I presume that no arrangement would be concluded without *my* being consulted.

"As your lordship has now gained such an ascendency in the Court of Chancery, I hope you will no longer consider that there is any objection to the attorney-general, though a common lawyer, succeeding to the vacancy according to the usual course. When Lord Lyndhurst, a common lawyer, was chancellor, and Leach was supposed to be dying, Scarlett, a common lawyer, had notice that he was to succeed him.

"I certainly feel that by devoting myself to the duties of the office, I could discharge them satisfactorily.

"As Edinburgh now stands, I could be again returned without even showing myself, so that I might still assist you as effectually as at present in carrying through any measures of legal reform; and, if it were thought expedient, I might sit, as Alexander did, and relieve you from a good many of the Scotch appeals.

"Upon the whole, I believe that, all things considered, no other arrangement will be found more advisable.

"Yours very faithfully, J. CAMPBELL.

"I am going to-morrow to Inverary, where I shall remain eight days.

"THE LORD CHANCELLOR."

I had never for one moment doubted that Pepys was the right man, and so he was appointed and sworn in before the end of January.* As soon as this was settled, I got Melbourne's concurrence to open a communication with Bickersteth, in the hope that he would consent to be solicitor-general.† He declined. Anxious that he should accept this office, I went out of my way to ascertain why he had refused. So Le Marchant, by my desire, went to see him on the subject. On asking him his reason for refusing, Bickersteth said that he could not accept it, "because no political relationship existed between him and the Government; and even had there been no such objection, he should have refused to accept it from *me*, because the appointment belonged to the prime min-

* Charles Christopher Pepys, afterwards Lord Chancellor Cottenham.

† Henry Bickersteth, afterwards Lord Langdale and Master of the Rolls.

ister and not to the chancellor, consequently it was impossible to receive it from him." Melbourne afterwards saw Bickersteth, and explained to him that the original offer had been made with his entire concurrence. At all events, he then repeated it, saying it might *now* be considered as coming *direct* from him. The matter ended in Bickersteth suffering this bit of temper to prevail, and ultimately Rolfe was appointed.

"On a previous occasion, when very great pressure had been put on Lord Grey by Lady Holland, who had a diseased notion that Bickersteth was a first-rate man, I so far interfered that, in writing to Grey, I told him that I considered Bickersteth far from being a first-rate man in any sense of the word —certainly any thing but a profound lawyer; and besides, he had always been a political enemy, and at times offensively so; and that if we went out of our own camp, it should be to take a first-rate man; that, in such a case, I should not hesitate to take Sugden or Scarlett, for their eminence would justify their appointment in the eyes of our friends, none of whom could have any right to complain, if, in making a judge, we obtained for the public so great a benefit as Sugden or Scarlett would have conferred.

I certainly had no grudge against Bickersteth, for in 1831, after his conduct had been extremely offensive to me personally, I offered to appoint him chief judge in Bankruptcy, which he declined, pleading his own unfitness and his great objection to the court of review; which, he said, he felt himself incapable of ever making work satisfactorily.

Enough about Bickersteth. To return to Campbell. As soon as I found what he was about, I wrote to Lord Grey as follows:

[*Private.*] "September 24, 1834.

"MY DEAR LORD GREY,—The attorney-general has laid claim to the Rolls, notwithstanding my distinct notice! He never whispered a syllable to me, but the very moment Leach died he wrote to Melbourne. Of course it was scouted. According to Campbell—attorney-general or even solicitor-general, like the Crown, is endowed with a general prerogative. I told him that if attorney-general had any *right*, *Horne* would have been the man, and not he; and that 'you as well as others were so much of this mind, that you did not see how Horne could be passed over even to take in Pepys.' To say the truth, Horne's claim is so great, and one feels his abominable treatment so strongly, and his admirable and truly unexampled behavior so much, that I never did any thing with more pain than in now passing him over. But it was a matter of necessity, as we must all allow. Your offer of Comptroller of the Exchequer, and mine of arranging so as to make him accountant-general (£5000 a year), either of which he so immensely deserved, rather lessens his right to complain.

"Bickersteth wrote refusing the solicitor-generalship; and although Melbourne was to see him yesterday, I don't believe he will take it. Yours ever, H. B."

I need scarcely say that I had many more letters from Campbell on the subject of the Rolls.

[*Private.*] "Stanhope Street, September 30, 1834.

"My dear Attorney,—The letter I wrote you on arriving in town on Monday answered by anticipation yours which I got yesterday on my return from Brighton, when I came here to swear in the Master of the Rolls (Chancery writs of all kinds being stopped till he is in office). I am very sorry you should fancy there is any breach of precedent in passing you over, for I venture to say no one ever supposed attorney-general had any claim to the Rolls, as he is allowed to have to his 'pillow,' the Common Pleas.

"Were it as you say, attorney-general would truly be not only Master of the Rolls, but master of the Government and of the law, and of all we have of discretion in judicial appointments.

"Every one knows that Chief Baron of the Exchequer is the peculiar patronage of the Great Seal. In December, 1830, Alexander came to me from Lord Eldon to let me know that the chancellor never even spoke to his colleagues upon the appointment.

"According to your doctrine, the 'prerogative' (for I can call it nothing else) of attorney-general overrules Lord Eldon, and makes the patronage of the Great Seal in chief baron a mere name. The cases of attorney-general going to the Rolls are very few—only one in our day. Leach, Plumer, Grant, are all the other way, and even Gifford's case would only prove that *Horne* had the right now; for assuredly Horne could never in common justice, or even in common sense, be said to forfeit any right because he refused to go to the bench, any more than Gifford* forfeited by taking the Common Pleas. Even Shadwell is an instance against you.† For how can a distinction be taken between Rolls and vice-chancellor? If attorney-general has any claim, it is as first law officer of the Crown, and this applies to one vacancy as well as to another. As to Copley and Scarlett, whom you mentioned in your letter of the 22d, I never heard the circumstance before, and I feel certain you must have been misinformed. I know that Sugden knew nothing of this, because, when I appointed William Adam accountant-general, Sugden came to me with a representation from the Equity bar against a common lawyer going to that office, and in the course of the very proper and altogether fair and candid remarks which he made on that occasion, he spoke of the office of *chancellor* as quite well adapted to a common lawyer, and said expressly that the Equity bar never objected to *that;* but that the others (and he expressly specified Rolls and vice-chancellor) were at all times held to belong to the Equity bar, and he complained that no Equity baron had been made; on which I said there should be one next vacancy; and accordingly, as you know, Bickersteth and Sugden had the refusal. Now, however, when motions are to go to the Exchequer, and the Master of the Rolls and vice-chancellor are to have an entirely concurrent jurisdiction, it becomes a thousand times more out of the question to put in common lawyers. In fact, your doctrine would lead constantly to this — that Equity men would be chief-justices, and common lawyers Equity judges.

"Then how long do you hold that the attorney-general's prerogative is to last? If you were Master of the Rolls, and

* Sir Robert Gifford, Solicitor-general, 1817; Attorney-general, 1819; Chief-justice of the Common Pleas, 1824; and then created Baron Gifford of St. Leonards, County Devon, Master of the Rolls, and Deputy-speaker of the House of Lords, April, 1825.

† Sir Lancelot Shadwell, Master of the Rolls at his death, 1850.

Pepys succeeded you as attorney-general, and Denman died, Pepys, of course, would have a right to be Chief-justice of the King's Bench, unless you add to the claim this other, that any one who *had been attorney-general* has a right to the chief-justiceship, as well as the actual attorney-general; but then that principle would exclude *you*, and let in *Horne*.

"I believe I mentioned to you on Thursday that Leach had stated before the Lords' Committee, as one reason for introducing the clause suspending the act during his lifetime, that, having been so many years out of the practice of hearing motions, he could not do so satisfactorily, and yet Leach was not behind *you* in the confidence he had in himself.

"As for appeals, you could not be deputy-speaker of the Lords and member for Edinburgh.

"Yours ever, H. B."

The following letter from Campbell closed our correspondence upon this most disagreeable transaction:

FROM SIR JOHN CAMPBELL.

"Edinburgh, October 3, 1834.

"My dear Lord Chancellor,—The arrangement with respect to the Rolls being put upon the ground of public expediency, I must be contented. I hope I should be the last person to press any claim for my own advantage which could interfere with the best administration of justice in the country. I own I thought I could have filled the office as satisfactorily as Plumer, Gifford, or Copley, and that even its new duties did not absolutely disqualify a common lawyer from aspiring to it. However, *dis aliter visum*, I am far from supposing that any personal slight to me was intended, and I am sure it was not forgotten that I had made rather greater exertions and sacrifices in the Liberal cause than his honor Sir Charles Christopher, for whom, be it understood, I have a sincere regard, and indeed I have never known in the profession a more honorable or respectable individual.

"The office of solicitor-general being vacant, I am afraid my presence may be necessary in London, and I shall be there in eight or ten days. Yours faithfully,

"J. Campbell."

The following letter from Grey followed me to London:

"Howick, September 29, 1834.

"MY DEAR BROUGHAM,—I think there is a great deal of truth in what you say of the present state of things. From the time I left office, the tone taken by the Government papers, as well as by the Radicals, and continued to the present moment, was to represent me as the real obstacle to popular measures, and to contrast the more liberal views of the present Government with mine. But all this I have borne not only without complaint, but without notice, being certain that Melbourne and all those of my late colleagues, for whom I have the greatest esteem, would be as much or rather more amazed by it than I could be; and being confident, besides—and in this expectation I have not been disappointed—that I should not suffer by it in the public opinion. I shall, therefore, persevere in the same course. But I am much more annoyed at the new system of agitation on which O'Connell is now acting, and upon which it appears to me to be necessary that the ministers should declare themselves plainly and unequivocally. Ever yours, GREY."

Before I left Brougham I had written as follows to a friend in London:

"Brougham, September 22, 1834.

"MY DEAR P.,—When I come up to prorogue Parliament on the 25th, I shall hope to see you, if Denman is in town; if not, there is no need to give you the trouble of coming to Stanhope Street.

"I see by some extracts in our county papers that your able and candid friend of the 'Standard,' whose proceedings generally are as fair as his ability is unquestionable, has fallen into the absurd mistake committed by several others, such as the 'Times,' of asserting (what is almost too ridiculous for me to contradict) that I wanted to be prime minister, and turned out Lord Grey with that design. There never was so wild a fiction invented by poet or madman, or even newspaper provider.

"My whole object for the past four years was to keep Lord Grey in, knowing he was anxious every six weeks to retire; and also knowing that his going would break up the Government, *I myself personally* kept him from resigning, both at the end of the session of 1833, and afterwards in December, when there was a difference among us on Portuguese interference; and again, when Stanley and the others went, when all I could prevail on him to do was to promise he would stay till autumn. When Althorp resigned, I moved heaven and earth to keep Lord Grey in. On one of these occasions I went so far as to make all my colleagues sign a joint remonstrance and petition to him not to retire. All this, and much more which I can't mention (but which Lord Grey and my colleagues well know), was done by me with but one view —to keep Lord Grey in; and the king uniformly and earnestly seconded all my efforts down to the last.

"If, indeed, I had ever for a moment differed with Lord Grey, and deemed his leaving the Government an advantage either to the Ministry or to the State, I should at once have said so, and openly refused to continue with him. On two occasions I had refused to remain in office unless the measures I had proposed were agreed to, and on both my colleagues had agreed to what I proposed. But any dream so wild as my turning out Lord Grey never was invented. The fancy that I wished to succeed him is as absurd to the full; for every one of my colleagues always knew that nothing could induce me so to act. I always refused this when Lord Grey was anxious to go out, and my reason is plain. I could not afford it without getting into debt (the end of a public man's independence). I could not have lived in Downing Street a single year. My retiring pension is equal to the prime minister's whole salary, and with it (the pension) I shall not be able to live in town above half the year, owing to the pressure of large family liabilities. All this my colleagues knew full well. As for honor, what greater could I have than the chancellor enjoys? I being chancellor, I assure you there has scarcely been one thing I have wished done these four years that I have found the least difficulty in accomplishing. What possible use could there be, then, in giving up £9000 a year?"*

* Under the act the chancellor's salary was £14,000 a year, his retiring pension, £5000; so the loss on resigning was £9000.

Circumstances which occurred in the following year, but which it is unnecessary that I should now enter into, caused me to write to Grey himself a request that he would give me candidly his own opinion and feelings on the subject.

His answer was as follows:

"Howick, September 15, 1835.

"MY DEAR BROUGHAM,—I yesterday received your letter, with the accompanying inclosures, which I return you in this and another cover.

* * * * * * *

"Into the other matters of your letter I will not now enter, farther than to express to you how very sensible I am of all its kindness to me, and to repeat to you that *I never for one moment believed* that you had entered into any intrigue, and least of all with Althorp, to remove me from office.

"Independently of all the other considerations which would repel such an idea, the reasons which you state, both public and private, to show the impossibility of such a design, would be quite conclusive to any body who gave one moment's consideration to such a charge. I am, my dear Brougham, yours very faithfully, GREY."

When in November I saw Lyndhurst, I told him of Campbell's attempt upon the Rolls, and entered fully into all the circumstances. He said I could not possibly have acted otherwise, but added, that for one reason he rather regretted what had happened, because it would to a certainty make Campbell my enemy for life. I could not see the matter in that light, but he insisted. "Depend upon it," said he, "Campbell will never forgive you. In process of time Pepys may be chancellor, and vacate the Rolls; and then what has just happened will be a reason for passing Campbell over again. He will be furious, and lay the whole blame upon you. And I'll tell how he will pay you off. You remember Wetherell said, when the 'Lives of the Deceased Chancellors' came out, 'Campbell has added a new sting to death.' I predict that he will take his revenge on you by describing you with all the gall of his nature. He will write of you, and perhaps of me too, with envy, hatred, malice, and all uncharitableness, for such is his nature."

I always thought Copley was much too hard upon Campbell; yet the judgment he formed of men was generally as accurate as it was sagacious; so perhaps he was right and I wrong.

Let me try to pass an unbiased judgment upon my excellent friend Lyndhurst. I must begin by asserting that he was not gifted with very great tenacity of political opinions. How far he ever was a *Jacobin*, I am unable to say; although Denman used to charge him with having had that tendency in early life; but after long and certainly very great intimacy, my opinion of him is, that he looked up to nobody, or rather, I should say, he held all men very cheap. In truth, he was so immeasurably superior to his contemporaries, and indeed to almost all who had gone before him, that he might well be pardoned for looking down rather than praising. Nevertheless he was tolerably fair in the estimate he formed of character; and being perfectly free from all jealousy or petty spite, he was always ready to admit merit where it existed. Whatever he may have thought or said of his contemporaries, whether in politics or at the bar, I do not think his manners were ever offensive to any body, for he was kind and genial. His good-nature was perfect, and he had neither nonsense nor cant, any more than he had littleness or spite, in his composition.

He was a most effective adversary in the lords. His legal learning and reputation, his former official experience and character, his admirable power of clear condensed statement, far exceeding that of any man I ever knew; his firm courage, his handsome presence, his musical voice, his power of labor, *when he chose*, though generally hating work—made him a most formidable antagonist.

No one can better speak of his great resources and powers than I can. We alone fought the Municipal Bill in 1835. No one helped me for it, no one helped him against it; he beat me on some important points, but I succeeded upon the whole.

I recollect that while I was doing this inestimable service to the Whigs, their slander-mongers attacked me as if I had destroyed the bill, which I alone saved; their whole ground of attack being, that after I had defeated Lyndhurst and carried it, I had expressed my sense of the ability and courtesy with which he had fought the battle.

I don't believe, in the whole history of party slander and ingratitude, the match of this is to be found.

Great as Lyndhurst was as a judge, the common impression was, that on the bench *he was not in earnest;* and I am bound to say this verdict of the public was a just one.

His great excellence was in his statement of a case, which, however obscure or complicated, was thereby made clear to the dullest capacity; so perfect was it that it rendered argument almost unnecessary. He convinced and carried along with him his hearers in a way I never saw equalled. This talent made him very powerful as a Parliamentary speaker, and almost, if not quite, supplied the place of the higher flights of eloquence.

Let me now, in a few words, give my impression of the state of things consequent upon Reform, both as regards measures and men.

The members returned to the first Reformed Parliament were, on the whole, moderate men, neither violent in their opinions nor imbued with extravagant fancies. The greater part were friends of safe and rational reform, and were always ready to give a hearty support to every measure of social improvement.

But the country was unreasonable, and expected too much. That a vast deal *was* accomplished, even during the first session of the Reform Parliament, can not be denied; but to judge from the attacks and the complaints on every side, none of the measures that were carried were treated as of any value, because, as was said, so much still remained to be done. In this way unreasonable expectations were excited, and hopes deferred or unfulfilled created feelings of disappointment, and produced most unjust attacks upon the Government. I need scarcely add that much of the clamor and *all* the injustice came from that most unhappy country, Ireland.

I have not space to detail all that the Government effected during our few years of office. With respect to Ireland, we certainly made a good beginning in our attempts to remedy, if not to cure, a state of things in the Protestant Establishment there that was really monstrous. We successfully attacked the Irish Church, and reduced it to something like moderate proportions. Far be it from me to say that what we did in 1833–'4 was considered by us as a final settlement; but something towards that desirable state of things was at least effected when we abolished eight bishops, two archbishops, relieved the people from Church rates by throwing them on the Church revenues, and appropriated to religious instruction a large portion of the surplus revenues, after duly providing for the expenses of the Establishment. All this was a great step in the right direction, and the time will assuredly come when this branch of reform will be carried very much farther.

Of the other measures completed by the Reform Parliament, not the least was the renewal of the charter of the Bank of England, and the regulation of its monopoly. Another was the renewal of the East India Company's charter, in which the Government had to deal with the monopoly of the China trade, so much and so properly objected to. The Company were to retain the political administration of India for a limited period, but without any privileges as a trading company; and in consideration of surrendering all privileges, to be paid an amount equal to the dividends annually received by its proprietors. But beyond, and incomparably more important than, the introduction of a large and liberal policy in the East, was the great measure abolishing West Indian slavery.

Then, great and important were the changes in almost every department of the law; vast improvements in pleading and procedure were introduced, not in the common law courts only, but largely in the Court of Chancery, in which department alone offices were abolished effecting a saving of not less than £100,000 a year.

By the issue of commissions, the way was paved for an entire reform of the municipal corporations; and although I mention it last, not the least important of the beneficial measures we carried was the Poor-Law Act.

To Lyndhurst's mischievous opposition we owed the loss of my Local Courts Bill. But that could only be postponed; a measure so obviously for the benefit of the whole community must pass some day, in spite of attorneys or future Copleys. I wish I could look forward with the same hope to an act for the registration of deeds and titles. But that, I fear me, is too improbable, for, as Cromwell said on a similar occasion, "the sons of Zeruiah are too strong for us."*

I have little more to say.

Having taken to the Great Seal and to the Government, I set about discharging the duties of the former and keeping the latter together. I have already stated that in one year, when I rose on the first of September, I had got rid of all the arrears in the Court of Chancery. During the four years I was chancellor, I decided between seven and eight hundred matters and causes. Of these not more than half a dozen were appealed, and of these the very few reversed were cases in which either the vice-chancellor or the Master of Rolls had agreed with me. One of these I myself reversed on full consideration, thinking the vice-chancellor wrong, whom I had at first affirmed. But there never was yet an instance of so few decisions in any court being appealed from or changed, or of so much business being disposed of in the time. All parties, even the Tories, have concurred in this testimony, both publicly in Parliament and privately.

Nay, this testimony was given in an attack on my ministerial character by a bitter enemy in the 'Quarterly Review,' quoting Dryden's lines on Shaftesbury, who is praised as a judge, but cried down as a minister. I also got rid of all arrears in the House of Lords. I ought to add that my judgments, except during the first year, were always reduced to writing, and carefully prepared—so that they are at this day

---

* This is told by Edmund Ludlow: "Upon the debate of registering deeds in each county, for want of which within a certain time fixed after the sale such sales should be void, and being so registered that land should not be subject to any incumbrance—this word 'incumbrance' was so managed by the lawyers, that it took up three months' time before it could be ascertained by the Committee." And again, in reference to this and the other reforms contemplated by him: "That it was his intention to contribute the utmost of his endeavors to make a thorough reformation of the clergy and the law. But, said he, the sons of Zeruiah are yet too strong for us, and we can not mention the reformating of the law but they presently cry out we design to destroy property; whereas the law, as it is now constituted, serves only to maintain the lawyers, and to encourage the rich to oppress the poor." —*Mem. of Edmund Ludlow* (1751), i., 275.

cited by the bar and bench in favorable terms, as expounding the law on some points, and making it on others.

As for the Government, it is not to be denied that I kept them together. They would have been out again and again, had I not interfered and prevented the catastrophe. There was hardly any difficulty, great or small, that I was not called in upon, and Lord Grey never was satisfied with any debate in which I did not come forward.

When we were turned out in November, 1834, I took leave of the Court of Chancery with these words: "I have now disposed of all the cases which have been heard before me up to the last, and it is with great satisfaction that I quit this court without putting any one party to the expense and delay of having his cause reheard before another judge. I have equal gratification in observing that, beside one cause which stands over by consent, and on the application of parties for a common law judge, there are only two cases which remain to be heard, that were set down before the last long vacation. As I had no right to press the parties closer than this, it was my intention, if I had remained here, to adjourn the court on the last day of term, early next week, until next term, the 11th January, as I was obliged to do last June, for the like reason that the business was all disposed of.

"I have the utmost satisfaction in reflecting that this court, represented by its enemies as the temple of discord, delay, and expense, has thus been twice closed within the space of five months, and I ascribe this singular felicity very much to the great ability and indefatigable industry of my most learned and excellent coadjutors, the present vice-chancellor and the late Master of the Rolls, but greatly, also, to the industry and talent of the bar. That the same good-fortune will follow my successor I confidently expect, for he too will have the aid of the vice-chancellor, and the further aid of the present Master of the Rolls, whose high accomplishments as a lawyer, and whose consummate fitness for the judicial office, render his elevation the greatest benefit to the public, and is my own best title to the gratitude of the profession."

"* * * longæ finis chartæque viæque."

And now my task is ended, and my last words to the public are written.

I have in this autobiography endeavored to recall some of the chief interests and events of my long life.

If I have imperfectly performed my work—if I have appeared to dwell too diffusely on some subjects, while others of equal importance have been passed over—if many statements have been feebly, and some inaccurately, rendered—let it be recollected that I began this attempt after I was eighty-three years of age, with enfeebled intellect, failing memory, and but slight materials by me, to assist it. Above all, that there was not left one single friend or associate of my earlier days whose recollections might have aided mine. All were dead. I alone survived of those who had acted in the scenes I have here faintly endeavored to retrace.

CHAPTER XXVIII.

Personal Sketches of Eminent Contemporaries—viz., Lord Holland, Lord Palmerston, Lord John Russell, Scarlett (Lord Abinger), Plunkett, Croker, Lord Grenville, Lord Ellenborough, Lord Durham, and Louis Philippe.

I AM unwilling to close these Memoirs without a slight notice of some of my most valued contemporaries. Among these I recollect no one with more affectionate regard than Lord Holland; and my wish to take this opportunity of paying a just tribute to his various excellent qualities tempts me to repeat in some measure what I have already written on this subject in my "Sketches of Statesmen of the Time of George III." I endeavored to rewrite the original sketch, but in vain. To change was to destroy the resemblance, and any merit the former composition might have had. I therefore crave forgiveness for in some measure repeating myself.

LORD HOLLAND.*

Lord Holland, both at school and at Oxford, where he was the companion of Canning, Granville-Leveson, and Carlisle, had laid the foundation of his classical learning, which was extensive and sound, and which, when I knew him in 1805 and after, he continued to cultivate, and with success. He used to say that the only Greek he knew was Homer, but that was a great exaggeration. He knew the other poets and the orators also. One proof of his familiarity with Homer was given in the happy selection of the lines from the "Odyssey" as an inscription on the column supporting the bust of Napoleon, of whom he, and especially Lady Holland, were great admirers. She received a legacy from him of the snuff-box given him by the Pope, Pius VI., after the signature of the peace of Tolentino, and there was a constant interchange of kindness while he was at St. Helena. The inscription was

* Henry Richard Vassall Fox, third Lord Holland, born 1773, died 1840.

as follows, and of course the happiness of the selection was much admired:

> * "Οὐ γάρ πω τέθνηκεν ἐπὶ χθονὶ δῖος Ὀδυσσεὺς,
> Ἀλλ' ἔτι που ζωὸς κατερύκεται εὐρέϊ πόντῳ,
> Νήσῳ ἐν ἀμφιρύτῃ· χαλεποὶ δέ μιν ἄνδρες ἔχουσιν."†

But in the admiration of Napoleon we could never concur, and this difference between us lasted throughout Holland's life.

He succeeded to the peerage at so early an age that he never sat in the House of Commons, and thus was prevented from passing through the best school of English statesmen. When he entered the House of Lords, the prospects of the Whig party were as gloomy as it is possible to imagine. There could hardly be said to exist even the name of an Opposition party. He joined himself, however, to the few supporters of his uncle's principles still to be found there.

Lord Holland's course, throughout his whole public life, was one which did equal honor to his head and to his heart. The vigilant enemy of abuses; the staunch supporter of the constitution as established in 1688; the friend of peace abroad and of liberty all over the world; the champion especially of religious liberty and the sacred rights of conscience, and that upon sound principles of universal freedom, not from any tinge of fanaticism, from which no man, not even his illustrious kinsman, was more exempt—he soon obtained that respect in Parliament, and that general esteem among reflecting men in the country, which the mere exhibition of great talents can never command, and which is only to be earned by honest consistency in pursuing a course commendable for its wisdom, or by its sincerity extorting applause from those who disapprove it. During the period of above five-and-forty years that he continued before the eyes of his countrymen, sometimes filling high offices, but more frequently engaged in opposition to the Court and the Ministry of the day, it is certain that whensover any occasion arose of peril to the great cause of toleration, the alarmed eye instinctively turned first of all

---

* Ὀδυσσειας, A. 197.

† "Not yet is dead on earth God-like Ulysses,
But still lives, in mid-ocean kept
On sea-washed isle."

to Lord Holland, as the refuge of the persecuted; and as often as the constitution in any other respect was endangered, or any bad, exclusive, illiberal policy placed in jeopardy our character abroad and the interests of peace, to him among the foremost did the supporters of a wise and catholic policy look for countenance and comfort in their efforts to arrest the course of evil.

How continually have I known him, on occasions the most various, support these his rooted opinions and fixed principles! In addition to this, he was a most disinterested advocate for the abolition both of the slave-trade and slavery. I say disinterested, because, in right of Lady Holland, a great Jamaica heiress, he was the owner of extensive possessions cultivated by slave-labor.

During Christmas, 1831, when I was detained by illness at Brougham, I had much correspondence with Holland on the affairs of Belgium and the treaty respecting the fortresses of Tournay, Philippeville, and Luxemburg. How much he felt on this matter is plain, from his allowing it to interfere with the great subject of that time—viz., our preparations for enabling us to carry the Reform Bill, and, as connected with that, the creation of peers.

FROM LORD HOLLAND.

"December 26, 1831.

"Dear Brougham,—I have little, or rather I have too much, to say to you in a letter. Next week, I think, the great question about the Lords will come before the Cabinet, and I hope you will be there. "Le bon Dieu est toujours pour les gros bataillons." Grey is, I think, uncommonly well, and more than ever amiable, reasonable, and wise.

"We have to-day a Cabinet about the fortresses; a sad hubbub has arisen on that matter, and I am accused somewhat wrongly of the accelerating it by a premature disclosure to Talleyrand, of what I never knew to be the least secret—namely, the treaty about the fortresses.* I only knew that

* In reference to the negotiations for the revocation of "The Barrier Treaties," for the support of frontier fortresses to protect Northern Europe from French aggression. The revocation was concluded by the convention of London in 1832.

it was going on from Talleyrand himself, till Palmerston told us at the Admiralty that it was concluded. But on the substance of the business I am still more uneasy. The French, both in substance and form, make an unreasonable clatter about it, and before we knew any thing of it, the treaty was too far advanced to make it either convenient or honorable to retract; but, at the same time, would it not be madness to quarrel, and is it not dangerous to get even out of humor, about the fortresses in the weak and neutral country of Belgium? No considerate man relied upon them much when in the hands of the King of the Netherlands; but now, as a means of defense, they are nothing, or worse than nothing. The notion of a treaty conducted in secret with four of the powers to keep them up as a security against French perfidy and aggression, is in my judgment preposterous in the extreme. It savors of a confederacy against France, the most unwise and unjustifiable of all possible measures. Palmerston says that if we hold rough language, the French will yield, for their present anger is all *bluster*. He may be right —and if we can not now retract, as I fear we can not, I hope he is; but, at the same time, I must say our *high language*, as far as I am a party to it, would be *bluster* too; nor do I believe any of our friends, the Commons, or the country would consent to spend a shilling about the fortresses, or to place them under the superintendence of Austria, Prussia, or Russia. Figure to yourself the case: before our papers were presented or our statement could be made, the French would be in possession of the very fortresses we were bound to prove were necessary to the defense of Europe! We must justify the war by proving it was hopeless. I wish you were here. Do not write on this matter, but when you come be peaceable, and let them feel how utterly untenable a warlike system would be. I will send you a letter I wrote to Palmerston. Yours, VASSALL HOLLAND."

FROM LORD HOLLAND.

"December 31, 1831.

"MY DEAR BROUGHAM,—I quite agree with Wilberforce, and will write to tell him so; but I do not see what further steps than the treaty are to be taken to prevent the trade.

There are now no neutral flags that I hear of, and if the English and French cruisers do their duty the trade will be entirely stopped: at least such was the opinion of the commodore and the Admiralty before we had obtained and while we were negotiating the treaty.

"Nothing could have terminated better than the awkward position into which we had got about those foolish fortresses, at least if it be, as I trust it is, terminated altogether. The fear of Aberdeen and Wellington here, and of Lamarque and Mauquin at Paris, drove both Governments, in my opinion, to language and conduct that had more the appearance than the reality of springing from unfriendly disposition or suspicion, and which it is best now to forget, and henceforth to avoid. We had a Cabinet yesterday, and resolved to hold strong language to Prussia, to urge immediate ratification to Austria, and to communicate our proceedings to France, with whom, both in substance and form, we avow co-operation in the matter of the treaty of independence with Belgium. Prussia, or rather Ancillon (who is a doctrinaire and a coxcomb), affects to consider the hesitation of Prussia to ratify the treaty as a final disavowal of her plenipotentiaries and *refusal* to ratify; and, moreover, maintained most preposterously that the non-ratification of one party vitiated and annulled the whole transaction, and more than hinted that by this notable piece of sophistry they were released from all engagements themselves, and could not ratify a treaty *which now was not in existence.* Our instructions to Chad are peremptory, and conveyed in an admirable paper, in which Palmerston proves that such conduct would in Prussia be irreconcilable with good faith and honor, as well as contrary to public law; and that the consequences would lead inevitably either to the undoing of all that had been done in Belgium, or to the separation of the ratifying parties (which would probably consist of the other three Powers, but certainly of England and France) from Prussia and Russia. In either hypothesis, war would probably ensue; and the entire dissolution and separation of the conference would leave the respective parties both at liberty, and inclined, to take their respective parts in all other European questions without concert or consultation with those from whom they were separated. Palmerston thinks, and so do Bulow and Esterhazy, who are naturally anxious on the subject, that Prussia will acquiesce and Austria agree without delay. As I wrote to Granville*—'In that case I shall not regret the hesitation of Prussia. Indeed five horses might take us to our journey's end, but I do not despair of reaching it with four, or three, or even two; and I am not quite sure that in my heart I should not prefer a *limonière*, though I acknowledge a *berline* to be the safest and most commodious conveyance.' I knew we should agree about the fortresses; and in our views of the necessity of peace we are nearly alike, though I may be a little less *Quakerish and non-interfering* than you, from a persuasion that seasonable interference, and even the attitude of war, sometimes is the best method of preventing it; for instance, I do not believe that the profession of Quakerism in the British Cabinet just now is half so likely to avert the certainty of Continental war as a persuasion in foreign Cabinets that England, albeit anxious for peace, is determined, if war were to occur, to side with France and Liberalism, and not with Russia and ultraism. Estrangement between France and England is a necessary preliminary to all *real* wars. It is, therefore, the one object which those in whose hearts

'Sævit amor ferri, et scelerata insania belli,'

promote; and nothing but the possibility, and perhaps probability, of an alliance between France and England, if they should drive matters to extremity, will deter them from pursuing that policy. Sebastiani, who thought his *constitutional* vigor a match for Carlist, Bonapartist, or Republican Pozzo, has been cruelly reminded of his inadequacy to such engagements by an attack which I believe was apoplexy, and will keep him from council for a month. If Perrier acts for him we are no losers, for he and Talleyrand, by whose advice he will steer, are perhaps yet more pacific, and certainly more direct and pleasant to deal with, than our friend the Corsican.†

"Grey has an arrangement, but I know not what, not only

* Then our ambassador at Paris.

† Pozzo de Borgo was a native of Corsica.

in view, but ready for Macaulay; but, alas! Calne can not be vacated. I have strongly recommended Grey to speak to Macaulay himself on the subject, and to make him understand that Government has been and is employed in procuring or reserving such arrangements as would secure his services and suit his views. I will take care to let Grey know Macdonald's handsome offer, but I do not think it is necessary, and if it were, should yet be sorry it were accepted. In all you say of Mackintosh I entirely concur, and I am quite happy and grateful for the word you drop about old Scotch Foxites, for I feel that by death or defection they have lost their natural protectors and allies. As I am in such a land of thistles, they have a right to lean on me for such support as I can afford them. *Pour trancher le mot*, Jeffrey, whose general fault is good-nature, seems to me to lose that quality where they are concerned. He enforces with the sternness of Cato or Joseph Hume the full reduction of Charley Ross's place to £100; seems half to grudge even that, and to overlook the circumstance of the public gaining £500, even if the miserable £200 asked for by Ross's friends, and not by him, were left during his life and the existence of the office, neither of which can be very long.

"The postscript of your letter gives me as much pain as the letter did pleasure. I wish, for many reasons, and among them for your health, that you were well out of those regions of frost, cholera, and typhus. We shall feel the want of you on Monday. Our dukes and marquesses are scared at a fresh herd of barons. I conclude you have written your opinion at length to Grey. I wish you had done so to Lansdowne. And if Abercromby and Macdonald agree with us, I hope they have said as much in that quarter. It is a strange quirk to prefer the danger of having no House of Lords to a temporary enlargement of it. For my part, I am for a game of tennis, where one reckons fifteen, thirty, forty — game; and where one often has a *bisque** in one's sleeve to boot. That *bisque* the king must give us, and I agree with you in thinking that if it be known we have it, our adversaries' game will

* A *bisque* at tennis is the privilege to score one point at *any part of the game.*

be checked, and we may win without taking it; but I am writing in one of the few metaphors you do not understand. I dare say, however, you will contrive before the sun sets to comprehend the whole craft and progress of tennis, chases and all, better than Masson himself. It is difficult to find an unknown tongue that you can not talk at twenty-four hours' notice. Good-bye; but, seriously, take care of yourself.

"Yours truly, VASSALL HOLLAND."

FROM LORD HOLLAND.

"January 2, 1832.

"DEAR BROUGHAM,—Grey has no, and I have little, time to write, but Althorp has engaged to let you know what passed in Cabinet, and on me devolves the more disagreeable task of urging you, if your health will anywise permit it, to be in the Cabinet on Saturday, when, Grey says, your presence will be most necessary. Indeed, exclusive of the great question of bill and peer making, there are topics about prosecutions, coercive laws, and other matters in Ireland, discussed, or rather broached, to-day, on which we want you sadly to set us quite right. On the main business of the day, we, on the whole, did well, and went some way to an active agreement in your plan—

'Est quodam prodire tenus.'

"Grey goes down to-morrow to state to the king that some demonstration of a power to create peers, and that some callings-up and some creations immediately, are deemed necessary by his advisers. The exact number he is not yet quite prepared, as from the Cabinet, to suggest, but he would gladly take your suggestion of ten or twelve; and I think the Cabinet, with a little squeamishness, and under distinctions which I do not understand, almost authorized him to name the smaller number to the king. Your letters, which were read before Lansdowne came in late from Bowood, did great execution with the wavering; and Grey conducted the whole business with such candor, temper, and ability, that it was impossible he should not greatly disarm resistance; but Richmond, Palmerston, Melbourne, and Lansdowne are hostile, and Stanley somewhat averse to the measure. You should write to Melbourne and Lansdowne. The former dreads the precedent, and magnifies the extreme permanent importance of the measure; and the latter would, I think, be swayed a little if some of his great worthies, such as Whishaw or Minto, could with truth be quoted in favor of it.

"Melbourne's dread that if once resorted to it will be frequently repeated, should, if you write, be contradicted. In addition to the manifold reasons which will occur to you, arising from the great necessity and peculiar nature of this case, you may with truth observe that the example of Queen Anne was not followed for many years, and that, so far from lowering or degrading the House of Lords, or impairing its powers, it is a common remark that it never was so powerful as during George I.'s reign.

"I am much more sanguine of success since the Cabinet than I was before. Durham read a clear and able paper in favor of a large and immediate creation, and he was more temperate and conciliatory in manner than usual, and better satisfied with the result, though so far short of what he recommended, than I expected. I save the post.

"Yours, VASSALL HOLLAND.

"If you don't come (but do come), write to the king and Sir Herbert Taylor on the state of the country, and the necessity of overcoming all lesser inconveniences for the purpose of speedily passing the bill."

He was so anxious to lose no time that he wrote to me on the journey, so as to give me an opportunity of communicating again with him and the rest of the Cabinet immediately.

"January 7, 1832.

"DEAR BROUGHAM,—I hope you may have got as safely and comfortably to Scarthing Moor as we have got to a point full as advanced on our journey. The king's conversation and his written answer to Lord Grey were as favorable as, and more favorable than, we could expect—full of compliments and confidence in Grey and his ministers, reluctant to grant peerages to any great extent, but willing to overcome his reluctance if the loss of the bill and its consequences are really the alternative. He acknowledges that the hopes of passing the bill without having recourse to such expedients had become fainter, and is disposed to defer to the opinion of his advisers upon the necessity, from a conviction that nothing but a well-founded persuasion that such necessity existed would induce them to urge such a measure. His expressions of confidence and regard for Grey and his colleagues were most unqualified; and his avowal that he did not think any men could or would replace them, together with an acknowledgment that the loss of the bill must be the downfall of the Ministry, amount to a full admission that whatever is necessary to secure the bill must be done. He wishes, however, that on so very important a subject he should have *written* advice of the Cabinet; and for that purpose, but particularly with a view to the advantage of *your* presence and sanction, we settled to meet next Wednesday. In the mean while, a minute of Cabinet, acknowledging with becoming gratitude his gracious communication, and deferring our written answer till we had the advantage of consulting you, was unanimously agreed upon and sent; and there is every prospect of all acquiescing, though with shades of difference, in the result of advising the king to create, either by installments or by one payment, such as may be found necessary to pass the bill in the Lords. The king himself prefers creating all necessary at once. As I foresaw, when once he determines his course, he is against slackening sail and taking Lord Grey's calculation of twenty majority against us. He urges one or two conditions with great earnestness — all, except the two or three actually promised, must be either eldest sons or collateral heirs of childless peers; or, if the number must be eked out by others, Scotch or Irish peers; and nobody who has been active in agitating the people is to be recommended. On this latter point he is very earnest, though without any individuals in his eye; and in general there is in his letter and in his conversation an anxious exhortation to the Government to guard against the press, and the democratical spirit which is afloat, and to protect the institutions, and the Lords and the Crown in particular, from encroachment and clamor, direct and indirect control. His substantial acquiescence in the measure, and his unexpected (except by me), and I think wise, disdain of diluting it, if resorted to, by not giving us a sufficient number, has, I hope, reconciled, and I am sure surprised, some of the more timid among us. My opinion is, we shall have no more trouble about it. The report of the conversation with the king, and the whole of Grey's demeanor in the Cabinet, brought to my mind your just and warm eulogium of him. Nothing could be more perfect, nothing more able, amiable, and judicious. He told us, in *great confidence*, that Chandos had written a letter to Sir Herbert Taylor, lamenting the discontinuance of all negotiation about modifying the bill, laying the blame on Lord Grey, and then expressing the dread felt at the reported creation of peers, hinting at the danger to which hereditary authority was exposed, with allusions to the abolition of hereditary legislature in France, and a variety of other matters, calculated to prepare the king to resist any such proposal from his ministers. Sir Herbert's answer was most masterly, and most handsome and proper. He concluded the letter was intended to be communicated to Lord Grey! He had done so before showing it to the king, and he proceeded to repeat Lord Grey's remarks on what had passed at the interview with Harrowby and Wharncliffe, and he then with very civil language glanced at the impropriety of making him the channel of such communications, and suggested the propriety of selecting some one who had a responsible situation for any such correspondence.

"I write after my four o'clock dinner, and am half asleep, but not quite so dead asleep as when I wrote yesterday. We are all, I think, in high good-humor, and more nearly agreeing on this thorny question than I ventured to hope. The Irish agitators, the unions, and, above all, the press, continue to annoy the king exceedingly. I trust our reforming measures may allay some of these symptoms, but it is good to be upon one's guard against the proposal of any coercive laws, and to divert those who might be brought to approve of them to other methods of contending with the evils they deplore.

"I really am ashamed of seeing poor Goodwin. It is so strange and so wrong that nothing is done for his son. The consulship of Madeira, which he longed for, is restored to the man formerly recalled. My place (*d'ailleurs* not vacant) would not have suited Goodwin; it has no salary or profit.

"Yours, VASSALL HOLLAND.

"Lansdowne goes to Bowood, and does *not* return for Wednesday. One is always sorry he should absent himself, but the exchange of the president for the chancellor will not be particularly injurious this time for the matter in hand. You must come and *keep us up to it.* There is loose talk of converts; but Lauderdale, Lowther, Duke of Rutland, and sundry other anti-reformers, were more sanguine than ever, till they began to smell what we might be at about peers. They then will take, and indeed have taken, to railing."

Like his uncle, he was always desirous of bringing forward the "young one," and the whispering against any one did not at all weigh upon him any more than on his uncle. Here is an instance: On George Lamb's death, and Howick's appointment to succeed him as under-secretary, not being in the House of Commons, Holland had heard some impression respecting Howick, probably from persons also not in that House, and wanted me to counteract it, which he seemed to think a far more difficult thing than it really was.

"January 6, 1834.

"Dear Brougham,—I was sincerely rejoiced to see your letter to Grey. It proves your application to business, which is good for *you*—your agreement in my opinion, which is good for *me*—and your authority to us to proceed before your return to town, which is good for the country. There are other matters that press not a little, but yet they admit of deliberation; and I hope you and Melbourne will be able, and others willing, to be present time enough to prepare all matters for Parliament. Melbourne has already signified his readiness to place Howick in the situation of poor George. I own I rejoice and approve: I rejoice, because it relieves Grey—but I approve, because, in spite of any clamor it may occasion, I think it a very good though unpopular appointment. It would not be very easy to find many young ones ready to work hard in an office, equally able to represent it and fight its battle in debate; and with the chief in the Lords this is an indispensable requisite in an under-secretary. I believe, by what I hear, that he will be pleased, and that he will not be disposed, as assuredly he would not be able, to assume so much in the office under Melbourne, as he was really tempted and half invited to do elsewhere. At any rate, as I say of worse bargains, such as Pedro and others, make the best of it; and from that inexhaustible store of reasons which you have at all times in your quiver, pray select such as inspire love for, not estrangement from, the measure. I am sure I have persuaded myself it is a good one, and I hope and believe that those who consider it dispassionately will allow it to be so. I have not seen poor Melbourne. He is, I understand, terribly cut up, and yet it did not take *him* altogether by surprise—he had long suspected mischief.

"Yours most truly, VASSALL HOLLAND."

Holland's power as a speaker was of a very high order, and never was sufficiently esteemed. He was full of argument, which he could pursue with great vigor and perfect closeness; copious in illustration; with a chaste and pure diction, like his uncle, shunning every thing extravagant in figure and unusual in phrase; often, like him, led away by his ingenuity; and, like him, not unfrequently taking a trivial view of his subject, and dwelling upon small matters which did not much help on the business in hand, nevertheless always keeping that in view, and making no sacrifices to mere effect. Declamation was the forte of neither, although occasionally the uncle would show that he could excel in that also; neither made any the least pretense to gracefulness of action, and both were exceedingly deficient in voice, the nephew especially, as he had little of the redeeming quality by which his uncle occasionally penetrated and thrilled his audience, with those high and shrill notes that proceeded from him when, heated with his argument, he overpowered both his own natural hesitation and the faculties of his hearers. In Lord Holland the hesitation was so great as to be often painful; and instead of yielding to the increased volume of his matter, it often made him breathless in the midst of his most vehement discourse. He wanted command of himself and, seeming to be run away with, he was apt to lose the command over his audience. The same delicate sense of humor which distinguished Mr. Fox, he also showed, and much of the exquisite Attic wit which formed so large and so effective a portion of that great orator's argumentation, never uselessly introduced, always adapted nicely to the occasion, always aiding, and, as it were, clinching the reasoning.

After all, it was in his private and domestic capacity that Lord Holland's principal charm lay. No man's conversation was more delightful. It was varied, animated, full of information, checkered with the most admirable vein of anecdote, but also with deep remark, and aided by a rare power of mimicry, never indulged in a way to offend by its harshness. Whoever had heard him represent Lord Thurlow, or the late Lord Lansdowne,* or the famous Duke of Brunswick, or George Selwyn, little needed to lament not having seen those celebrated personages. His advice was excellent: he viewed with perfect calmness the whole circumstances of the friend who consulted him; he foresaw all difficulties and consequences with intuitive perception and never-failing sagacity; he threw his whole soul into the discussion, and he was entirely free from the bias, as well of selfishness as of prejudice, in the counsels which he gave. But the great delight of those who approached him was certainly in the amiable disposition of his heart, and in a temper so perfectly sweet, so perseveringly mild, that nothing could ruffle it for an instant, nor any person, nor any passing event, make the least impression upon its even surface. Many tempers are equal and placid constitutionally, but then this calm results from their being cold; the waters are not troubled because their surface is frozen. Lord Holland's temper, on the contrary, like his uncle's, was warm, excitable, lively, animated. Yet, though I knew him intimately for five-and-thirty years, during a portion of which we had political and even party differences, and I had during the most of these years almost daily intercourse with him, I can positively assert, that though I saw him often sorely tried —and fear me I was now and then among those who tried him—I never for one moment perceived that there was in his composition the least element of anger, spite, peevishness, or revenge. In my whole experience of our race, I never saw such a temper, nor any thing that nearly resembled it.

Both uncle and nephew had the genuine Whig predilection for the kind of support given by the union of great families,

* William, second Earl of Shelbourne, and first Marquess of Lansdowne.

considering this as absolutely necessary to maintain the popular cause against the Court. But Mr. Fox went somewhat farther, and showed more complacency in naming high-born supporters than seemed consistent with the tenets of a philosophical statesman. They both had, with the simplicity, the defects of children; their feelings were strong but not deep; the impression made on their hearts was soon effaced. I have often rallied Holland for regarding men with the eye of a naturalist rather than of a brother, and interesting himself in observing their habits, rather than regarding them as their relation to us required. This was no doubt an exaggeration. The kindly feeling towards his friends was shown in the care he took to leave some little memorial to all with whom he was most intimate. To me he left a portrait of Romilly, well knowing how much more I should value that than any thing else he could give. He had for Romilly the greatest veneration. I recollect he one day showed much acuteness in at once guessing that he was the author of an article in the "Edinburgh Review" upon Bentham, from a single phrase which I used in referring to it. At once he said, "Then I am certain it is Romilly's." Romilly's esteem for him was great, and he often expressed to me his grateful sense of Holland's taking charge of his bills in the Lords, and of the ability with which he supported them, and his vexation on the single occasion of his voting against one of them, as Lansdowne also did. He considered him as a person whose advice was entirely to be taken as, what the French call, *de fort bon conseil,* and most justly. When General Savary sent Romilly a long paper on the treatment he had met with on board the Bellerophon, and on the grievances of Napoleon, begging him to make use of it in their behalf, and authorizing him to publish it, he considered Holland the fittest person to consult on the subject, because he had the greatest confidence in his judgment, and was quite certain that all his prejudice in favor of Napoleon would never warp it. The result was that, acting on Holland's advice, he neither published the paper nor made any use of it.

LORD PALMERSTON.*

Lord Palmerston was a man of great ability, and one of those who, having all their lives been in office, was invaluable in such a Government as ours, which chiefly failed in men accustomed to business.

Palmerston had been a member of almost all Ministries since 1804, and his talents for office were of the highest order. He became from mere accident a Reformer and a Whig, having joined Canning, and continued with Huskisson when the duke got rid of the Canning remains. I never knew a man whom it was more agreeable to act with; for he was firm, and even bold; quite steady to his friends; indifferent to abuse; full of resources; using his pen better and more quickly than almost any body; and not punctilious or vain, or standing upon trifles and personalities. He is by far the most important accession the Whigs ever made from the Tory ranks. I highly disapprove his foreign meddling; but I speak of his general talents. Yet Melbourne was as near as possible losing him in 1835, and only on the usual Whig principle, because he was the object of abuse, and especially of newspaper attack. I have no doubt that Holland joined in this mistaken view of the "interests of our party." Melbourne confessed to me while it was going on that he had great difficulties; and the answers Palmerston made to them I could plainly perceive were given to Melbourne through his sister, now married to Palmerston, and who fought his battle ably and stoutly with her brother.

The want of such able men of business was a grievous evil to the Whigs. They had no habit of business, as ministers of the first class. Their immediate subordinates were as useless as such men could well be. Then the permanent ones—under-secretaries and clerks—who really knew their trade, were all extremely hostile; and on any vacancy in the latter occurring by death or superannuation, a retired host of adversaries was ready out of which must be taken those to fill up the blank when a pension could be saved.

To such a Government a man like Palmerston was invaluable.

* Henry John Temple, Viscount Palmerston, born 1784; died 1865.

He gave universal satisfaction to all of us except Durham, who wanted to turn him out, in order to get his place. With foreign ministers and with his official under-secretaries, I have always heard he was unpopular. But as his temper was excellent, I think this must have been accidental.

LORD JOHN RUSSELL.*

Lord John Russell was not in the Cabinet when our Government was formed in November, 1830; therefore his being intrusted with the honor of bringing in the Reform Bill gave much surprise to some, much offense to others, and was openly assailed by Wetherell as indicating our being divided on the measure.

Grey, and I believe Holland, proposed giving him this charge, to please the Duke of Bedford, who was dissatisfied because John was not in the Cabinet.

John Russell is a most excellent man, of great firmness, amounting even to obstinacy; of sufficient quickness; and has read, and also written, a great deal. He has the family love of freedom and jealousy of the Crown; but he has also their love of a party, as if it were a religion. This leads to many an error, both in conduct and opinion.

As a speaker he is very good—clear and distinct, if not always forcible; as a debater, he is quite first-rate. In Cabinet he was always firm, straightforward, and wholly to be relied on.

He possesses such self-confidence, that he would fearlessly try his hand at any thing whatsoever. There really was some foundation for Sydney Smith's joke, that "Lord John would take the command of the Channel Fleet, or cut for the stone." This saying showed a true appreciation of his character.

His attachment to the Liberal party and devotion to its interests was constant and unwavering. His strong feelings, as well as fixed opinions on all that regarded religious liberty, need hardly be cited. He was as much wrapped up in the Catholic question as in the Dissenters' disabilities; and he did a great service to the party by his able conduct of the test question.

---

* Now Earl Russell, born 1784.

Upon all measures for the amendment of the law and the improvement of legislation, Lord John's attention was constantly awake, and he generally took very sound views.

The great fault of Lord John Russell, in his official capacity, is the disposition to do rash things without consulting any of his colleagues. It is in the family.

I may cite as illustrations of this tendency his, to my mind, ill-advised corn-law letter, published the instant he perceived what Peel's game was; his flying visit to Ireland during Lord Clarendon's vice-royalty; above all, his making Hampden a bishop in defiance of public opinion. But how insignificant are such errors compared with his great merits as a judicious leader of his party; his perfect honesty, his singleness of purpose, and the inestimable services that, very much owing to these qualities, he has rendered, and continues to render, the Liberal cause!

SCARLETT.*

Of the three great advocates, chiefs of the bar, who flourished in my time, Scarlett, Erskine, and Berryer† (in France), I must here say a few words.

Scarlett (afterwards Lord Abinger) rose to the highest place among the advocates of his time.

He had all the mastery of the conduct of a cause—that self-devotion to his client, and that skill, readiness, and fertility of resource, which long and varied experience can alone give.

His success at the bar was, in one respect, almost unexampled in the courts of common law: he retained his leading practice for above forty years—in short, all the time he continued in the profession—a piece of good-fortune that even Erskine himself had not.

Scarlett took a most liberal and enlightened view of all professional questions in Parliament, making Romilly his guide in this department, as he did Erskine in the legal profession. Romilly's measures of law amendment had his hearty concurrence; and on one occasion he urged a great improvement on his bill for diminishing the number of capital punishments,

* James Scarlett, Lord Abinger, born in Jamaica 1769; died 1844.

† Antoine Pierre Berryer, a distinguished French barrister and political orator. Born in Paris in 1790; died 1868.

and confining them to such cases as were attended with violence. However, he found the objections to this change so strong and unceasing, especially from the judges, that he was induced to prefer attempting the improvement by successive measures applied to different offenses.

In 1818, Scarlett was returned by Lord Fitzwilliam for the borough of Peterborough. Soon after he took his seat, he distinguished himself by one of the most able speeches that any professional man ever made,* and proved that his great eminence at the bar would in all likelihood have been equalled by his success in Parliament, if, like others, he had been placed there before he rose to the head of his profession.

The speech I have referred to was made upon the discussion of the most extraordinary proposal of the Government to give an allowance from the Civil List to the Duke of York for taking care of his royal father. I well recollect the impression which that speech made upon those who were least inclined to expect much from lawyers. The common talk of the House was that we were all distanced by him, and that he more than balanced the loss just sustained in Romilly.

This first success of Scarlett in Parliament was very great, but it was fated to be almost his last. This was owing to his besetting weakness, vanity, which greatly injured him on many occasions, and never more than in the House of Commons, unless, indeed, it be on the bench. He always took for granted that he knew what it was quite impossible he should know, from utter want of experience; and this made him as a judge, though with all the qualities required for the office, yet inferior to men of far less talent, and nothing like his acquaintance with business.

In like manner, with every requisite to make him a great debater, he was far outshone by others in all respects inferior to him, except in giving their minds wholly to the matter in hand.

Scarlett had a decided objection to our Reform Bill in its most popular portion, Schedule A. I had several discussions with him on the subject, and I found it vain to attempt to alter his opinion.

---

* Hansard, xxxix., 600.

But that he was a friend to Reform is certain, and he had communicated to me the conditions which he made with the duke, of taking his own course upon the question of Reform, without regard to that of the Government under which he was attorney-general.

Much has been said against Scarlett for his separation from the Whig party and taking office under the Wellington Administration. This was treated as an act of apostasy, although both his and Rosslyn's junction with the duke had been entirely approved of by us at the time; and the treatment he met with from the Whigs could hardly have been justified if he had been under the greatest obligation to the party, instead of the obligation being on the other side.

The cry raised against him because he differed irreconcilably with us on the great question of our Reform Bill, was utterly absurd, and reminded one of the same clamor raised against Burke, who always held that his party had deserted him, not he them, for that his principles always were and had been those of the constitutional Whigs.

When he came in 1834 to the House of Lords, he took a part entirely becoming his judicial station, avoiding all party conflicts, and rendering great assistance in the proceedings before us.

We derived important help from his constant watchfulness and his great acuteness and professional experience, as well as the attention he had at all times given to political questions. In debate he did not so constantly take a part, but this arose from his very proper indisposition to mix himself in party disputes.

It is impossible to forget his just and generally accurate observation of what passed in debate. Both I and others who conversed with him saw how his sagacity and good taste were shown in his remarks, and we often benefited by them. So great confidence had I in his tact and quickness of perception in discovering a fault committed, or an advantage missed, that on several important occasions I used to watch his expression of countenance, and in some sort be guided by what I observed of his opinion and feelings as I went on.

Though a West Indian by birth, and of a great Jamaica family, he always was most firmly an adversary of the West

Indian interest, taking a strong part in favor of the abolition of the slave-trade and slavery.

It was only after four-and-twenty years that Scarlett attained the rank that he had been fairly entitled to, at the very least, fourteen years before. His intimate friendship with Perceval would, in all probability, but for his Whig principles, have secured his promotion to the chief-justiceship on Ellenborough's death in 1818; and that nothing else kept him from the place of attorney-general long before, is proved by his great lead, not only on the northern circuit, but at Westminster and Guildhall. Though the party in power was chiefly answerable for the injustice done to him, their adversaries were really little less blamable than those for whom his sacrifices had been made and the penalty incurred. The conduct of the party to him who had made such sacrifices, compared with their treatment of others who had made few or none, has always appeared to me one of the worst parts of its history.

LORD PLUNKETT.*

Whoever has cultivated a pure and classical taste for the oratorical art, must feel at the mention of Plunkett's name somewhat of the thrill which the illustrious Greek's never fail to cause. For assuredly the modern orator is unsurpassed, if he has ever been equalled, since Attic voices were mute. It is to be lamented that no perfect collection of his speeches has ever been made; although partly from the deliberate as well as very distinct manner of his utterance, partly from the deep impression of his discourse, the ordinary channels render them with an almost unexampled fidelity.

It was in the debates upon the change of Ministry, March, 1807, that Mr. Plunkett, already high among the speakers of his own country, first burst forth upon the world at large as an orator of the first class. His subject was the Catholic question, and it becomes, perhaps, the only doubt whether or no he shall be placed at the head of all the eloquent, that his fame should have been almost entirely confined to this one subject. The novelty, the almost wholly unexpected appear-

---

* William Conyngham Plunkett, born 1764; died 1854.

ance, of so brilliant a luminary above the political horizon, attracted all eyes, and fixed the most earnest attention. It formed none of the least striking circumstances in this phenomenon, that there was no resemblance at all in any portion of its phasis with either of the great luminaries which had recently set, or with the lesser lights which still shone. There was nothing of the majestic declamation of Pitt; nothing of the fierce vehemence of Fox; nothing of Canning's sparkling fancy, nor of Wyndham's Attic graces: it was strong, cogent argument—plain, but deep sense—and earnest rather than impassioned feeling; happy, because most appropriate, imagery, sparingly introduced, and never without close bearing upon the subject, and only to illustrate or to press home the reasoning, never to dazzle or amuse. This, in truth, is the perfection of such ornaments. They should never be employed as a display of fire-works; they should rather be as the sparks thrown off by the friction of the machine, lending, peradventure, a light, but the result of the useful movement, and never for an instant interfering with it, by requiring any the least waste of power for their production. That the success of this, his first speech, was prodigious, may easily be imagined. But it seemed to be also his last; he quitted Parliament for six years. Returning in 1813, he took hardly any part in its debates, speaking but twice in the sessions of 1813 and 1814. The Catholic question formed the subject of both speeches, and each was of the highest order, especially the first upon Mr. Grattan's motion. The second was upon the speaker (Abbot's) speech to the throne, stigmatizing the question, and boasting that the Commons had rejected it. See how, with the fierce and indignant eloquence of Demosthenes, and nearly in his words, he tears to tatters the arguments, and scatters to the wind the alarms, of those who would exclude the Catholics by tests and securities:

"You accept his word as proof that he has abjured his religious tenets, but you will not receive his oath as long as he abides by them. Is it that he is insincere in his oath? Then why trust his declaration? Has the oath a negative power? Is it not merely that his oath is not binding, but that what shall be full evidence if he merely assert it by implication, shall become utterly incredible if he swear it directly?

Why, this is worse than transubstantiation; it is as flagrant a rebellion against the rules of demonstration as the other is against the testimony of sense."*

Another fine passage is less remarkable for the close texture of the argument than the perfect felicity of the diction. Speaking of the penal laws—"Those mighty instruments, why are they hung up like rusty armor? Does not every man know that they are endured only because they are not executed; and that they never are referred to in any discussion whatever, without pleading their inactivity as the only apology for their existence? The taste and sense of the public is in this respect a reproach to the tardy liberality of the Legislature."

In the speech of April, 1814, on the speaker's address, we find among other beauties the following brilliant passage, which must have been painful to the personage it was addressed to. After referring to the usage at a Roman triumph of having a whispered humiliation to lower the victor's pride, and the speech containing an allusion to the Duke of Wellington's victories, he goes on—"But you, sir, while you were binding the wreath round the brow of the conqueror, assured him that his victorious followers must never expect to participate in the fruits of their valor, but that they who shed their blood in arduous conquests were the only persons who were never to share, by the profits of success, in the rights of citizens."

The speech of 28th February, 1821, is by many described as finer than any they ever heard in the House of Commons. It is a model of cogent and profound reasoning, impassioned declamation, and happy allusions to historical facts. But it affords little opportunity of selection and citation. One passage may be referred to, and it produced more impression than any thing in the whole oration. After referring, in terms singularly appropriate, to the merits of the great men who had in former days borne a part in discussing the question, he thus closes the magnificent passage: "Walking before the sacred images of the illustrious dead as in a public

* For the whole of this speech, see the "Life and Speeches of Lord Plunkett," by his grandson the Hon. David Plunkett, i., 319.

and solemn procession, shall we not dismiss all party feeling, all angry passion and unworthy prejudices? I will not talk of triumph—I will not mingle in this act of national justice any thing than can awaken personal animosity."

Great as has always been my admiration of Plunkett, both from intimacy with him in private, and from many years' experience in both Houses, I have always reckoned it a great misfortune never to have seen him in his other and original capacity of a great advocate, his high excellence as the head of the Irish bar having been described to me by many members of the profession, and by none more strikingly than Chief-justice Bushe, whose acquaintance I had the great pleasure of making when he came over to be examined before the Irish Committee of the Lords.

Of all I have ever heard of Plunkett's greatness at the bar, nothing made a more lasting impression on me than a passage in an address of his to a jury on the evidence of usage and the principle of prescription where deeds could no longer be produced to support a title acquired by long possession. Thus he spoke: "But how stands the case at present? Witnesses have died; evidence has been lost; but possession has matured into a statutable title. Time is ever mowing down with his scythe in one hand the evidence of title. Wherefore, the humane and considerate wisdom of the law places in his other hand an hour-glass, by which he metes out the periods that shall supply the place of muniments destroyed."

It was often said that, on removing to the House of Lords, the spirit had departed from him; but this is untrue, though he certainly made no speech which could be compared with the great exhibitions of former years. Yet that he retained his peculiar genius was plain. The faculty, so rare, of striking at the root and heart of a subject with a single blow—the fervid imagery, never ornamental in its purpose, how much soever in its incidental and collateral effect—the power of embodying in an allusion or a simile the whole argument by a comparison at once unexpected and felicitous, and marvellously appropriate—was still his, and in perfect preservation. On the Reform Bill in 1831, he had to reconcile his support of it with his ancient enmity to such changes; and how admirably did he effect this explanation!

"In those days Reform came like a felon, and was only to be resisted. It now comes as a debtor; you admit the justice of the demand, you confess the debt, and only haggle on the installments by which it shall be paid." Surely this reminds us of the comparison, perhaps the happiest in all the history of rhetorical art, which I have just referred to, where the image, like the one last cited, is taken from the most commonly known form under which time is figured to us, as the old man with a scythe and hour-glass. Of such ordinary, such homely materials, is magnificent imagery composed.

He had some inclination himself towards the opinion that he was no longer the man he had been, and I have more than once combated this with him.

On the occasion of the House of Lords speech I resumed the subject, as I drove him home after the debate, saying, "Now you will admit that I am right, for never was any thing more perfect or more in your best style."

The report of that speech, though meagre, and in most points unsatisfactory, gives the famous passage that has been referred to tolerably well, and I have always been confident in my recollection of it. But of the other I had received different accounts, and some doubts had been raised by my friend Mr. Napier as to its existence, at least in the form which has always been given. I was anxious to learn from Plunkett himself his own recollection; and I wrote to him, inclosing an extract from my judgment in the case of the Irish marriages, in which I had quoted the passage, and I added that, as it was the only good thing in that judgment, I would fain know if I had quoted him correctly.

The extract to which my letter referred, was from my judgment in the case of the Irish marriages, Queen *vs.* Millis. "Human legislation is exposed, is necessarily liable, to three great imperfections. The lawgiver can not foresee and provide for all possible cases; his provisions may in their application become inoperative, or frustrated by the destructive operations of Time, the powerful and sleepless enemy of all human works; and his commands, how carefully soever framed, may be erroneously interpreted. There is no good or safe remedy for the first of these evils, but a resort to the legislative power for new provisions. For the second there is a remedy, and human wisdom has applied it. "Time"—(as was most eloquently said by Lord Plunkett) then followed the quotation in the words I have stated above.

Napier's version was so entirely different in the very material particular, that it omitted the scythe and the hour-glass. Lord Plunkett, in his answer to my letter, entirely approved of my wording of the passage; indeed there could be no doubt that the scythe and the hour-glass could not have been omitted; for without them, the figure would have been wholly defective; with them, the beauty is surpassing.

A most groundless statement, as it afterwards appeared, having been made in a letter to some one in Dublin, that Lord Grey had accused Plunkett, in 1819, of "acting with more than the zeal of an apostate" in the support he gave to the repressive measures of the Government after the Manchester outbreak (the "six Acts"), he was extremely incensed at the supposition of the account being correct, as indeed he had a good right to be, he never having belonged to Lord Grey's party, but to the Grenville section, and Lord Grenville was almost as much complained of for the same course which Plunkett took. Under the influence of this indignation, he wrote a long letter to Sir John Newport, tracing his whole conduct from his entrance into public life. It is dated Old Connaught, Jan., 1821. The following is an extract from it:

"Without going into the question of the queen's guilt or innocence (which, as a subject of *direct* Parliamentary discussion, I consider as finally disposed of), it appears to me that great blame attaches to almost the entire course of proceeding of the Government, as well abroad as at home, and perhaps to the originating such a proceeding on such grounds. That ministers have shaken themselves in public confidence (and especially in the opinion of the sober and intelligent portion of the community, whom I consider as truly and substantially constituting the people of England) appears to me, with such means as I have of forming a judgment, very manifest. If common prudence were allowed to be taken into consideration by their opponents, I think there could be little doubt of their being displaced; and even as it is, the chances appear to me rather against them. But if they are doing much to put themselves down, there seems to be a noble emulation kindled in the minds of their adversaries to keep them up. Is it true that the British public are divided into two classes —the enjoyers or expectants of the Crown's patronage on the one hand, and the enemies of the Crown and of the State on the other? I mean not those merely whose direct object is to pull down both, but those who, in pursuit of their object or under the influence of their passions, would not scruple to endanger them. That there is a portion of honesty and firmness which might steer the country through its difficulties, I fully believe; but will it, or can it, be brought into action? My expectations, I confess, grow every day more faint. The folly and frenzy which have been displayed in various quarters, high and low, may subside or be forgotten; but ought those who in any change would naturally be looked to by the country, and who, independent of any change, ought to give wholesome direction to the public sentiments—ought they, I say, to make themselves parties to such proceedings?"

He then refers to Lord Grey's attending the Durham meeting, and to other indiscretions, as he calls them, and concludes that in such a state of things, and with his opinions and feelings, his making the great sacrifice of going over to attend Parliament would really be of no use, as he should in all probability give offense to all parties.

Full explanation having put an end to the difference, though, like Lord Grenville, Plunkett took a different view from the Whigs of the means resorted to, there was no want of cordiality during the following years; and though he agreed with those who supported the junction in 1827, and was himself both promoted to the bench and to the House of Lords, there was really no more difference between him and Lord Grey than in my own case; and when the Government of 1830 was formed, the Catholic question having been carried the year before, no hesitation could be felt in offering him the Great Seal of Ireland, provided he had no objection himself to give up his chief-justiceship for a very precarious office. He accepted it, and was, of course, one of our most effectual supports in the days when we stood most in need of assistance, from our position in the House of Lords. When we left office in 1834, the duke and Peel would gladly have retained him as Irish chancellor, but he peremptorily declined to quit his political friends, and was only restored the April following, when the Melbourne Cabinet was formed. He was a most effectual support of that Government, and his attendance in the House of Lords was most important, both on judicial and general business. So it went on until 1839, when the ministers were in great straits, and, as always happens in such cases, were sorely pressed by their more considerable supporters. It never has been publicly owned, but no one could entertain a doubt that Campbell, the attorney-general, was most anxious for promotion, and as neither Cottenham nor Langdale was disposed to resign, he set his mind on the Irish chancellorship. What *is* known is, that the lord lieutenant (Ebrington) was desired by Melbourne to sound Plunkett. His letter expressed great kindness as well as respect, and his sense of the loss the country would sustain if the reports were well founded that he intended to resign, but confessing that his retirement would be a great accommodation to the Government, as it would give the Irish Seal to the attorney-general. His answer to this question was a distinct negative; but he coupled it with an expression of gratitude to Ebrington for having given his son a bishopric; and this expression was the ground of their rejecting him a year and a half after.

"October 18, 1839.

"MY DEAR LORD,—I received your letter of the 15th last night, too late to answer it by return of the post. At my time of life, the wish to retire would be a very natural one, but I *never* expressed such a wish to any person; nor, at present, should I have thought it becoming, either with respect to myself or to the Government from whom I have received so many marks of regard and confidence, to intimate a desire or intention to withdraw myself from the discharge of public duty, either here or in Parliament. At the same time it is quite clear that, after the communication of Lord Melbourne's wishes on the subject, I can not continue in office, but it is merely for that reason that I come to such a conclusion. I have to request, therefore, that you will be so good as to communicate to him my readiness to comply with the wishes of the Government, and with an assurance that I am very sensible of the kind manner in which he has expressed himself with respect to me, and that my retirement shall not in the slightest degree interfere with my cordial support to the queen's Government, and to the principles on which it is founded. And now, my dear lord, in conclusion, let me express to you my grateful sense of the uniform kindness and confidence with which you have honored me, and most particularly for the important obligations conferred on my son and myself in the appointment to the bishopric.

"I am always, with sincere respect and regard, your excellency's faithful servant, PLUNKETT."

It is needless to pursue this farther. As was inevitable, Plunkett was turned out to make room for Campbell "the insatiable."

"Finis coronat opus"—

there is nothing more to be said.

LORD GRENVILLE.*

My very sincere admiration of Lord Grenville's character and his great qualities, have always made me regard it as peculiarly fortunate that I was not in Parliament either during the time of the first war with France, and the unconstitutional measures which grew out of it, or after the return of Bonaparte from Elba gave rise to a difference between the Liberal party and Lord Grenville, in which I, though with some hesitation, joined in opposing the Government, but joined in company with Lord Wellesley, and I have always suspected that the duke had his doubts upon it. I have since been convinced that in this supposition I was entirely mistaken, and also that Lord Wellesley and myself were quite wrong in our belief that Napoleon's nature had suffered such a change, or that circumstances were so altered, as to give a reasonable prospect of peace being safely maintained with him.

Of Grenville's public virtues, it is enough to say that he voluntarily abandoned place and power for his principles; and though desirous of the authority which office gives, for the promotion of those measures to which he was sincerely and

* Born 1755; died 1834.

upon full consideration attached, he continued during twenty years in the same exclusion from power, almost all parties being desirous that he should possess it. But his high character was supported by great capacity and ample acquirements. He had studied history with great diligence and mature reflection; and with the history of his own country, and of the parties that have at all times prevailed in it, he was peculiarly familiar. He accompanied his eldest brother (Lord Temple, afterwards Marquess of Buckingham) to Ireland as secretary, the year he entered Parliament, when not more than twenty-two; he was thus early introduced into business, and formed early official habits. No one had a more thorough acquaintance with political business, both in its principles and details; and he became well versed in the doctrines of political economy, like his kinsman Pitt, who had ever cultivated the acquaintance of Adam Smith. There was nothing in his life that he regretted more than his giving way to Pitt in 1797 on the currency question. His oratory was of a masculine caste, avoiding all ornament, and was, like all his talents, for use, and practical use. I remember Dumont telling us one day at Bentham's, that he had watched a long speech of Grenville's which he heard, and could not find a single metaphorical expression—not even such phrases bordering on the figurative as are constantly used. But the great staple of his discourse was argument, and this, as well as his statement, was clear and impressive, and, I may say, authoritative. His declamation was powerful, and his attacks hard to be borne. The industry with which he mastered a subject previously unknown to him, may be judged from his making a clear and impressive speech upon the change proposed in 1807 in the Court of Session; and no lawyer could detect a slip on any of the points of Scotch law which he had to handle. But his love of labor, for labor's sake, indicated a pleasure in mere work, without regard to the object in view, or the fame to be gained. His opinions being adopted on full consideration, were adhered to with a decision which sometimes savored of obstinacy, but his mind was ever open to conviction. He considered any reasons offered by intelligent and impartial persons with the greatest attention, and his candor was truly exemplary, in abandoning what he was satisfied had been a prejudice. Of this my experience was frequent; though in some cases of great moment, when he retained his own opinion, my mortification was considerable. On matters of ecclesiastical policy, his strong early opinions — it may be said, prejudices — were very much strengthened by his becoming Chancellor of Oxford. Upon all secular questions he had the views and the feelings of a reformer. The French Revolution, and the horrors of the Reign of Terror, had impressed him very strongly with strong feelings of alarm at the prospect of Jacobinical principles extending to this country; and his position at the Foreign Office had made him in a peculiar way the antagonist of France, insomuch that he approached much more the views of Burke than Pitt did, and resisted the attempts at negotiation which his kinsman made, both in 1796 and 1797; and in 1800 he went much more decidedly against entertaining the offer of Napoleon. With honest and conscientious persistence in the same views, he joined Wyndham in opposing Addington's negotiation, which Pitt supported, and strongly united with him in his general opposition and coalition with the Whigs to overturn the Addington Ministry. Nothing could be more noble than his conduct on the change thus effected, whether we regard it on the more narrow view of party honor towards his Whig allies or on the larger and more important ground of the necessities in which the country stood, and the conduct of the war requiring a strong Administration. But all that had happened for the last fourteen years gave him a tendency towards vigorous and unpopular measures at home, as well as against French influence abroad, and made him, contrary to his natural disposition, adverse to measures of a popular cast and a pacific policy.

It must be observed that the accident which in 1801 threw him into opposition, greatly mitigated some of his prejudices, and he became generally less disinclined to popular courses. Many of his speeches during the junction of parties against the Addington Government were appeals to the prevailing popular opinion, and even feelings. The Peace of Amiens, which Wyndham and he opposed, presented no ground for popular attacks; but the alarm of invasion which followed the rupture of that peace made the whole country hostile to the Ministry, whose qualifications for conducting the public defense, and indeed for carrying on the war, were the ground of attacks as well of statesmen as of the people. I well recollect that, when Lord Grenville for many days kept one of the defense bills from passing in the House of Lords, by his unsupported exertions, and was in all respects the Opposition in his own person. For weeks, on that occasion, it was remarkable how he always faced to the bar as often as he spoke, seemingly conscious that he was in a small minority of the Lords, and that his arguments were rather addressed to persons out of the House. This habit he retained afterwards, when for a short time he was at the head of the Government, and still more when the change of ministers, in spring, 1807, once more restored him to his place on the Opposition benches. My personal acquaintance with him began during his Ministry, but was rendered more intimate by his noble conduct on the abolition of the slave-trade, and his gallant stand against the Court on the Catholic question, and the king's unconstitutional demand of a pledge never again to bring it forward. I very soon after found the clearest proofs that he had changed his opinion on some of the most important subjects connected with Pitt's Administration; of these, the fatal tampering with the currency in 1797 was the most prominent. The depreciation of the bank paper, which had been discussed with great doubts by Henry Thornton and Horner in 1802, and by Lord King the year after as admitting of demonstration, became with all political economists an opinion which they held admitted of no doubt. In the beginning of 1810, Horner moved for the appointment of the Bullion Committee; that his progress in the inquiry gave Lord Grenville entire satisfaction, may be inferred from what passed in the following year, when it was believed that the regent intended to change his ministers and recall Lord Grenville; in expectation of this, he applied to Horner to beg that in this event, which was then deemed quite certain, he would consent to be one of the Secretaries of the Treasury—he being First Lord, and Tierney Chancellor of the Exchequer; but Horner declined it, being, as he said, resolved not to take a political place until he had fortune enough to live independent of office. I had not been on the Bullion Committee, having come into Parliament the week it was appointed; but Henry Thornton pressed me to be added, on my being returned. The Walcheren inquiry and the spring circuit made it impossible for me to undertake it, but I warmly supported all its proceedings, and next year took an active part in opposing the most absurd bill that was perhaps ever introduced into Parliament—which declared that the bank-note was not to be depreciated, and which punished as a misdemeanor any one who sold or bought it for less than twenty shillings, at a time when it was certainly worth little more than thirteen in the market.

Some years after, Lord Grenville published a very able pamphlet on the subject, when Peel's bill put an end to the bank restriction; the motto referred in a striking manner to his change of opinion since 1797. It was, *γηράσκω δ' αἰεὶ πολλὰ διδασκόμενος* (I grow old, learning many things). He sent me a copy of this work, and I, knowing his love of literary curiosities, such as rare copies of books, had one copy printed of my anti-slavery pamphlet, just published, with a quotation from Cicero's "Brutus" of the character of L. Torquatus,* and sent it to him as *unicum exemplar*. He warmly thanked me; but he did more. Some years afterwards he sent me his "Essay on the Sinking Fund," with a very beautiful dedication in Latin verse, as follows:

CLARISSIMO VIRO.

HENRICO BROUGHAM.

Suavem spirat odorem, atque inviolata colores
  Servat adhuc vivo flore corolla micans,
Quam memori curâ Torquato† texuit olim
  Tullius, æternum pignus amicitiæ.
Hanc, decus ipse fori, Henricus, lumenque senatûs
  Angliaci, in nostrum transtulit esse caput;
Egregiosque suos inter grandesque labores
  Vult aliquem et nostris laudibus esse locum.
Hoc proprium ingenii est, fovet has quibus eminet artes,
  Immeritisque etiam dat decus esse suum.
Ergo iterum et scripto huic faveas, seniique benigno
  Accipias animo dona suprema mei.

---

* "Etiam L. Torquatus, elegans in dicendo, in existimando admodum prudens, toto genere perurbanus."—*Cicero in Bruto*, 68.

† L. Torquatus a Cicerone laudatus in Bruto.

Upon the Orders in Council, and all the questions connected with the subject, Lord Grenville had not, as on the bank question, been hampered by any measures of former times; for the first armed neutrality was before his day, and the second was during the Addington Ministry. But one of these very Orders in Council had been issued in July, 1807, just before the end of his own Government, and it was beyond any doubt in principle exposed to the same objections urged against the famous orders of November following—the orders of Stephen and Perceval. Attacked, Lord Grenville gallantly threw himself into the controversy, just as if there had been no Orders in Council before those of Stephen and Perceval. He had a perfect right to do so, because, even if the principles of both measures were allowed to be the same, the second carried those principles to so extravagant a length, that he had a right to regard them as a *reductio ad absurdum* of the claim grounded thereon. And whether such right was admitted or not, was indifferent to him; he fearlessly encountered any charge of inconsistency in the discharge of what he deemed an imperative duty. The weight of his authority was most important with the rest of the party in both its branches, and contributed much to the undivided support which was given to Baring and myself in our whole operations.

Upon questions connected with Parliamentary Reform, Grenville was entirely free from the prejudices which might be supposed to remain after the hostility arising out of the French Revolution had made Pitt and him anti-reformers. In 1810, when the question was revived in consequence of the conduct of the Commons on the Walcheren inquiry, my impression was that our friends took an injudicious course by going for extensive measures, wholly impossible to be carried; whereas there existed a favorable opportunity of obtaining most important practical, though partial, reforms, and I circulated a letter strongly recommending this course.

When the Reform Bill of 1831 was brought in, Charles Williams Wynn, Lord Grenville's favorite nephew, and in whom he had great confidence, was in office, and continued with us for some time; but on further consideration, he found that he could not go along with the measure unless some material alterations were made in it, and this being impossible, he left us, to our very great regret—to no one's more than my own; and his subsequent conduct was as fair as possible towards both us and our bill. It was supposed, from this difference, that Lord Grenville was against us. That he disliked the extent of the reform is undeniable; but he never showed the least indisposition towards our Government generally; and I recollect Lord Holland assuring us, when, after Wynn's resignation, some one was expressing apprehensions of Grenville being against us, "You may depend on it he has great confidence in the chancellor." I had certainly endeavored to overcome his objections to certain parts of the measure, and had failed; but I had no reason whatever to believe that he had a general distrust of our Government. That he entirely approved of our foreign policy I am absolutely certain; and I am as well assured, indeed still more so from his own words, that the excess in the Reform Bill which he greatly lamented, and in a friendly spirit, was by him ascribed to the refusal by Wellington's Government of all moderate measures —so friendly a spirit that he excused us for the excess by referring to that refusal. I can not recollect the expressions which he used, but they led me to believe that he rather regretted Pitt and himself having been driven to regard all reform as pernicious, by the events of the French Revolution and war, and the conduct of some parties in England connected with it.

I have often thought of Grenville's course in life, and his having given up the profession for which he had been originally intended, like his cousin-german Pitt, of the same age, and like himself a younger son. I have had too much experience, both of Parliament and of our profession, to pronounce with any confidence what man, when taken from the bar, will make a good judge or will succeed in Parliament. But I have no fear of the converse as regards Parliament, and of saying what man would have made a good leader of causes, and even ultimately a good judge, had he devoted himself to his profession, and not, through impatience, exchanged it for what is no profession at all. Such is politics. A man can not earn his subsistence unless his party is in power; and if he takes a line to obtain place, or to keep it, he acts without regard to his principles. So long as members of Parliament receive no pay, this must always be the case; and a person who looks to his exertions in the House for his support is like a barrister working on the principle of no cure no pay, which is regarded not merely as unprofessional, but as infamous. It has always appeared to me that Canning's favorite doctrine of a person being unable to serve the country effectually, unless in office, was more or less mixed up with this view of political life. However, a man like Pitt or Grenville, with a younger son's fortune, might not regard politics as a profession, and might not have his conduct influenced, as Canning's was, by the love of place for its emoluments as well as its power. Nevertheless, when Pitt expected to be excluded from office in 1788, he took steps for returning to the profession which he quitted, with the surest prospects of success; and, had he stuck to it, would not have died insolvent, as he did, after having been twenty years in lucrative places. And when Fox's circumstances reduced him to depend upon the contributions of his friends, it was his intention to have tried his chance at the bar, as I know from an intimate friend of his, my kinsman Adam (afterwards chief baron in Scotland), who had a commission from him to look out for chambers. But Fox's chance of success at the bar was as desperate as Pitt's was assured. He had no power of cool and prepared statement—no command of temper—no eloquence, except in contest and reply—no sustained discretion and calm judgment — none, in short, of the qualities that distinguish the great advocate, and are far more essential than the power of speaking.

That Lord Grenville's success both at the bar and on the bench must have been signal, seems abundantly manifest. He was certain to have had, and speedily, a foremost place among barristers, and to have reached the highest place among judges. As he probably would have deemed himself above what he might term the trick of *nisi prius*, it was reserved for him to have been perhaps the greatest chancellor whom we have ever known, in all the essential qualities of that high office, judicial, legal, and political, even to the graces of a manner at once dignified and courteous.

CROKER.*

Croker was a most important person in opposition. Nothing could exceed his ability and his thorough knowledge of his subject. He made but one error—committing all his objections to writing and print, in the form of a motion, and by this we largely profited. Althorp's knowledge of the Reform Bill, and Croker's, were the two wonders of the day; but Croker debated far better, though with less weight. Althorp muzzled all his party on finding that they, being unacquainted with the details, were perpetually getting him and themselves into scrapes, Croker watching the sight of the Whig officials unable to explain their own bill!

Croker's pen was almost as important an ally as his debating powers. Indeed, to him and his articles in the "Quarterly Review," Peel's and the party's obligations are not to be overrated. He was ill repaid by Peel's keeping him in the dark, till all the world knew every thing about his plans. For this, Peel suffered most seriously, and Croker had just cause of complaint. I was never more disgusted with any act of injustice in my life than when Peel answered Croker's letter, beginning "Dear Sir Robert," with "Sir." It was most unbecoming.

Croker's talents were of a very high class, and have not, I think, been sufficiently allowed. He also was a man of great personal kindness to his friends, though a good hater of his enemies, and so much devoted to his opinions, that he voluntarily retired from Parliament as soon as the Reform Bill passed, and he never returned.

ELLENBOROUGH.†

Ellenborough was another formidable adversary. He was one of the best speakers I ever heard—clever, nervous, short, *incisive*, with such a voice as few have for sonorous and penetrating force.

It was to me one of the highest gratifications to hear him. He worked hard, too, and argued almost as powerfully as he

---

* John Wilson Croker, born 1780; died 1857.

† Edward Law, Earl of Ellenborough, born 1780.

declaimed. His judgment was not so remarkable. He committed one of the greatest errors I ever knew when he showed his cards on our resigning in 1832.

In his East India Government he was most successful; but Peel, as usual, did not well defend him, and he always said he owed his defense to the Duke of Wellington and myself. His error in India was not treating the directors with sufficient respect and flummery. Lord Wellesley, like Ellenborough, had refused to do their jobs; but he had refused with great politeness.

DURHAM.*

Durham had many good and some great qualities, but all were much obscured, and even perverted, by his temper, which was greatly affected by the painful liver disease under which he labored all his life. He was in the best sense of the word high-spirited. He was generous, open, and incapable of falsehood or meanness of any kind. His abilities were great, though not cultivated by instruction, for his education had been much neglected. When he spoke in Parliament, which he did very rarely, he distinguished himself much; and when he spoke at public meetings, more than almost any body. He was very modest respecting his own merits, and favorable towards those of others, with even an enthusiasm that was exceedingly touching and amiable. Instead of pluming himself on his talents, he really was chiefly fond of exalting his wealth and family.

Durham had an object in view, and pursued it steadily. He desired an earldom, but was wholly incapable of making any sacrifice of his principles to the attainment of it, though the wish often blinded him to obvious considerations. He had warmly supported the junction of 1827, and on that subject differed with Grey widely. But his support was purely upon the ground of disuniting the Tory party, and he had been, both before and afterwards, as desirous of a union with the duke from the same motives, at which time Grey entirely agreed with him.

The Junction Government, after Canning's death, most

* John George Lambton, Earl of Durham, born 1792; died 1840.

properly gave him a peerage, and while this was being arranged, I had this letter from him:

"Paris, December 7, 1827.

"MY DEAR BROUGHAM,—I have had no official notification, therefore I can not imagine the event will take place until after that has occurred. However, I am now prepared, and, come when it may, things can not be made 'too bad' in the country; neither have I heard as to the rank, and I tell you fairly I shall be much annoyed if my representations on that point are not attended to. I shall, it is true, if I accept it, become possessed of a seat in the Upper House, but not with that degree of consideration which would enable me to retain for the benefit of the ministers that influence in the North, which you well know I am now 'seized of,' as you lawyers would say.

"I know very well that many persons think, by accepting any peerage whatever, I shall descend from the prominent position I now occupy. Certainly, if it is an inferior rank, they are right, as the situation of the first commoner is more marked and honorable than that of the last baron.

"Coke in 1806 was offered an earldom; he refused it. His son-in-law, Mr. Anson, was made a viscount. The present Lord Londonderry was given an earldom for his son by Lady Frances Vane; and in 1784 Sir James Lowther was created Earl of Lonsdale and Viscount Lowther. The latter is an unanswerable precedent; his situation was exactly like mine —large landed possession, and great influence in the North, added to a most ancient family, were his claims. They are mine, without taking into account my own situation in the political world.

"My grandfather was offered a peerage when the Duke of Portland joined Pitt in 1793. He refused it, because his principles would not allow him to abandon Mr. Fox. I have a fair right, therefore, to be placed in that situation which I should have occupied by a promotion, supposing him to have been made a peer.

"Pray reassure me on this point, which is one to which I attach great importance. From the first period of our friendship you have always found me indefatigably attached to your interests. I am pleased in knowing that the world thinks so.

I am sure Canning did, by the step he took, of which I informed you. I therefore rely with confidence on your active support of my interests, in the same degree that I know I never lose sight of yours. Adieu.

"Ever yours, J. G. LAMBTON."

I answered him thus:

"MY DEAR LAMBTON,—There are great difficulties in the way of an earldom; and the cases you refer to are by no means similar to yours. Coke was offered the earldom of Leicester in 1806, which, with another peerage given to the family a hundred years ago,* had been in the family more than half a century before. The family of our friend came through the female line, from the great chief-justice.†

"The Londonderry earldom was given, by *special limitation*, to the second son of Lady Frances Vane, who was daughter of the Countess of Antrim.

"As to the Lonsdale earldom, you seem to have forgotten that Sir James Lowther had nine borough members (of whom Pitt himself was one, having been brought first into Parliament by Sir James for Appleby), and had, besides this great borough interest, vast estates in Westmorland and Cumberland. Moreover, there had been a viscounty in the family in William III.'s time.‡

"You can not doubt my readiness to do whatever is *possible*, in your case; but I really feel that there is a fair answer to your demand. I have entered into the above minute particulars, to prove to you that your letter has been fully considered. I hope soon to see you, and we can then discuss the matter further. Kindest regards to Lady Louisa, and believe me most affectionately yours, H. BROUGHAM."

---

* The barony of Lovel, of Minster Lovel, Co. Oxford, May, 1728. Viscount Coke of Holkham, and Earl of Leicester, May, 1744.

† Thomas William Coke, who was offered the earldom in 1806, which he refused, was the son of Wenman Roberts, nephew of the Earl of Leicester, of 1744. Mr. Roberts succeeded to the estates, and took the name of Coke. His grandson, Thomas William Coke, of Holkham, was created Earl of Leicester in 1837.

‡ Sir John Lowther, created Viscount Lonsdale, May, 1696. Extinct on the death, without issue, of his grandson Henry.

I had another letter insisting on this point, and when we met he resumed the discussion; for I well remember his complaining that he was to be put on the footing of Abbott, a barber's son, who had been made a baron. I reminded him that Abbott was Chief-justice of England, and said that Wilberforce and others had always objected, on constitutional grounds, to a chief-justice not being at once made a peer. I also referred to Lord Eldon's case, who remained a baron for twenty-two years, while he was chancellor, before he got his earldom. Among other things, I remember telling him how he exaggerated in this discussion. He had a way of reckoning his income by some great years of the yield of his coal-mines, and then he would say his property was so many thousands a year; but I said, "My dear fellow, I can assure you that the Darlingtons, Fitzwilliams, Thanets, Lonsdales, only reckon by *surface*, and reduce mere coal-owners, like Curwen, to a low figure." He also overrated greatly his Parliamentary weight in Durham, where even his own single seat was contested; though for one member it was, on the whole, safe. The city was always a matter of doubt, as the college had great influence there.

Durham was very active in political matters all his life, and very much misunderstood. Having been always a strong party man, he had violent personal prejudices, and strong likings and dislikings. At one time he took part against the regular leaders of the Whig party, calling them "*The mock Opposition*," and siding with the *mountain*, as it was called, or the ultra-Liberal, half-Radical parties.

But his connection, by marriage, with Lord Grey in 1816, made him afterwards strongly opposed to that set. Nevertheless he was always quite rational, and felt the shortcomings of the regular leaders, which he often helped to prevent or to remedy. At different times the Radicals found they had got hold of him from his accidental and temporary opposition to the regular party, and from his taking strong and even violent courses at public meetings and at elections.

At the general election in 1820, when he supported Bell in Northumberland, a quarrel took place with Beaumont, and nothing could be more triumphant than the refutation which Lambton gave to the attack that had been most foully made, but most ridiculously, in the eyes of all who knew him, as to his personal courage. Such attacks ceased from that moment. Here is his letter on the occasion:

"Howick, July 2, 1820.

"My dear Brougham,—I fear I have no chance of getting over to you. Our election is still going on. The coalition between Liddell and Beaumont has put us out of the field as far as success goes; but we remain to defeat the sting of the tail, which is the defeat of Bell, in which case Mr. Beaumont's lead would have returned the two members. I have no doubt Bell will come in, though it will be very near. If we had resigned, he would have been beaten, as our splits with Liddell were to have been transferred to Beaumont.

"Beaumont at last, on Friday, broke out against me, and used, on the hustings, language that I was compelled to notice. He seems to have been long seeking an opportunity, and he certainly could not have chosen a worse (as you will see by the report), of quarrelling with me.

"A meeting was appointed for the same evening at nine. We arrived on the ground (General Grey and I) at the time; Beaumont's second came after us, and said that so many people had assembled at the skirts of the town, three miles from which we were to go, that he feared we should be interrupted, and had sent Beaumont back. He then appointed four o'clock the next morning (yesterday) to be on the same ground. I got out of the town a back way, and reached the place. Again Beaumont was interrupted in the main street, and his second said he had mounted his horse to get out of the way of the constables and Sir David Smith, the magistrate, who was scouring the country in a carriage-and-four to arrest us.

"We then settled to meet in the neighborhood of Belford, and at four o'clock we at last overcame all interruptions, and met near Bamburgh Castle. We exchanged shots without any injury—the seconds interfered, and the affair terminated.

"So much for this little adventure. It was peculiarly annoying from the obstacles thrown in our way by the magistrates, who, if they had succeeded in preventing our meeting, would only have forced us to go to France.

"Your prospects don't appear very bright,* but I tell every one what you desired me.

"Beaumont swears he will keep the poll open until Thursday next. Ever yours, J. G. LAMBTON.

"If Hedworth is with you, show him this letter."

Lambton's anxiety about the Catholic question was untiring; and his expectation, or at least hope, varying from day to day, that the duke would bring it forward, was much increased by the impression that if this obstacle were removed, a junction with him, which he always had so much at heart, might be effected. This, after Rosslyn's taking office with him, and other similar indications on the duke's part, had been a prevailing idea both of Lord Grey and those immediately connected with him. Many letters which I received from Lambton and from Grey show how entirely all notion of Peel giving in to the measure was out of the question, and further show what a surprise his disclosure was, at the meeting of Parliament.

"January 29, 1829.

"MY DEAR DURHAM,—I should have written to Lord Grey or you before, but there has been nothing worth communicating since I came to town, till within the last day or two. Whether it be that I had been locked up chiefly and seen few people, or that there is within so short a time a great alteration in the tone of the ultras, I know not; but I am confident there is the greatest alteration since I left town, about three weeks ago. They are all alive and triumphant; they think Peel has beat the Duke of Wellington—at least that there is an end of all risk of his doing any thing for the Catholics. This recall of Lord Anglesey is a most fatal step for the said duke; it unites all who were half separated, and makes those who were wavering as steady and even violent as can be. Of course you have heard that it had nothing to do with the letter (of Lord Anglesey) to Curtis;† the date made that *physically* impossible: the recall was communicated by the duke to him (Lord Anglesey being sent the 24th to Drogheda) in

* I was then standing for Westmorland.

† Dr. Curtis, Catholic Primate of Ireland.

a letter 28th of December. Then comes a dispatch from Peel, formally directing him to hand over the Government to the lord-justices. And coupling *this* with the letter to Curtis, is it conceivable that Peel did not know of Wellington's letter of the 28th? But if he did, is it conceivable that he can mean to quibble and say, when the dispatch is moved for, that the recall is the official and not the private letter? As for the duke keeping him in ignorance, it would not be very wonderful, for he does things in a way quite new in this country. Parke received the announcement of his appointment as judge, in a letter from him, and not from the chancellor—a thing quite unexampled; still, on the recall, it is quite impossible Peel should have been ignorant, especially if the ultras be right in saying he has beat the duke; indeed, the letter of the 28th states, as I understand, that he had consulted his colleagues upon it. The session, then, as far as one can see, will be most stormy and very disagreeable on many accounts; but it can't be helped. I hear that the joy is exceeding great at Middleton* over Lord Anglesey's recall. Milady says the Duke of Wellington will now have fair play; that Lord Anglesey was throwing the country into a flame, etc., etc. I suppose it was in no flame before. I have not heard from herself, but they say this is her language. *He* writes very rationally and sensibly, as he is always sure to do when he exercises his own most excellent understanding.

"What will our old friend Jack Calcraft do? I suppose he must go out. I don't think we ought to entangle ourselves in O'Connell's question as to his seat, unless it really is found to be *with him*—which I have no idea of—or unless the Government do something violent.

"After all, till the very eve of the meeting, the duke has it in his power to pour oil on the waters, and half a word would do it. Yours ever, H. BROUGHAM."

In all measures, both before our taking office and while in office together, we had almost always agreed. In the great question of creating peers to carry the bill, he had taken somewhat prematurely a very strong view of its necessity,

* Lord Jersey's place in Oxfordshire.

and wrote the long letter to Lord Grey which I have already given *verbatim*, and which was read in the Cabinet in January, 1832, when the bill had passed the Commons. It contained all the arguments stated in a very distinct and indeed luminous form; but it does not grapple with the most important of all the difficulties—namely, that such a creation, in whatever way made, must render a similar proceeding necessary on every certain change of Ministry; and on this ground both Grey and I have always felt that we were saved from the greatest calamities by the timely yielding of the Tory Opposition. Durham went greatly beyond this, and his views were those of the somewhat rash and unreflecting parties, not few in number, who regarded the creation as a good in itself, as laying the foundation of permanent influence over the House of Lords. Although I strongly opposed the act under which Durham was sent to Canada, I not only defended his appointment, but on all occasions supported his able and useful report, to which we really owed the establishment of constitutional and responsible government there, and perhaps the preservation of the colony.* But it was wholly impossible to defend his ordinances, which were altogether illegal, and were the more inexcusable as the act had given him almost dictatorial power, and an excess was not to be endured. After the part I had taken against the Canada act, there was no course open to me but to declare against these ordinances; and in consequence of the part I had taken, I was called upon by the leading authorities in the House of Lords, including the duke, Ellenborough, and Lyndhurst, to proceed against them. In this matter I rendered the best service in my power to Durham, by bringing in a bill to indemnify him for his utterly illegal acts. John Russell attacked my bill, and would have thrown it out, but refrained on the lawyers satisfying him that Durham was a ruined man unless it passed; for actions to an enormous amount would have been brought against him, and must have succeeded.

---

* After the insurrection in Canada in 1838, Lord Durham was sent as governor with special powers to reorganize the administration of the province.

LOUIS PHILIPPE.*

When at Paris, I used to go in the evenings to the receptions at the Tuileries, which were very easy, and without any ceremony or etiquette, the queen, and Madame Adelaide, her sister, with their ladies, sitting round a table working or conversing, and the king receiving all that came, and walking about the room to converse with them.

He constantly made me come with him into the next room, where, as well as in his room in the morning when I had an audience, we had conversation on all subjects, political as well as personal. In 1834, when I first saw him as king, I took with me Cutlar Fergusson, an old acquaintance of mine and a member of the Jacobin Club; and when I left Paris in autumn, 1836, for Cannes, which I then saw for the first time, and where I made a purchase, the king always gave Fergusson the reports of the telegraph by which he learned my motions. Louis Philippe's intimacy with Fergusson broke off after his marriage with a lady whom he very improperly presented at Court without permission, or even notice, and this the king and queen never forgave.

Before this, nothing could be more kind than he was to him. I recollect one day at dinner he desired Fergusson to tell the queen an East Indian anecdote which had amused him much.

A native prince against whom Fergusson had gained an important lawsuit asked him to his palace in the country, and gave him a great entertainment. But after dinner he proposed to him to ride out, and required him to get upon an elephant. Fergusson, when told to get upon the front seat, suspected some trick, and declined, to the great fury of the rajah; and the cause of it was soon seen, for the animal sprang forward with violence, and got under a portico, against which, whoever had sat where Fergusson had been desired to sit, would have been dashed to pieces. In relating this, Fergusson said, "Si au lieu d'avoir gagné le procès j'avais trahi mon client, et il avait perdu, il n'y a pas de grace qu'il ne m'aurait pas faite. Il aurait." But the king, interrupting him, said,

* King of the French, born 1773; died 1850.

"Vous voulez dire il aurait fraternisé avec vous. Pourquoi avez-vous oublié notre language des Jacobins?"

Nothing could be more perfectly amiable than the queen and the rest of the family, but Madame Adelaide was the person of greatest capacity, and she was much relied on by the king, who communicated every thing to her, having entire confidence in her opinion. It was generally believed that she it was who strongly advised the king to give a favorable answer to the address in 1830, calling upon him to take the crown. For the queen he had the most sincere affection, and even a kind of superstitious belief that she was his good genius. The young princesses were both amiable and well-informed. I recollect one of their ladies practicing a trick upon me at a time when they had seen very little of me. They introduced me to the Princess Clementine, since Queen of the Belgians, without naming her, but leading me to suppose she was a young lady of rank dining at the table, and I was to lead her out. I had a great deal of conversation with her upon every kind of subject, and in the drawing-room, after dinner, Madame de Montesquieu (I think it was) asked me, "Comment avez-vous trouvé la Princesse Clementine?" I said I had not conversed with her at all. She then let me know that it was her I had handed out to dinner; and when I was very angry at the risk she had exposed me to, of talking with a person whose name I did not know, she said she had done so by the princess's particular order, as she wished to converse with me under no restraint. This is that princess, afterwards Queen of the Belgians, whose death created, I really believe, more real sorrow than any royal demise ever did, always excepting the Princess Charlotte's.

The king himself was as good company as possible, wholly independent of his conversation upon important subjects. He was perfectly free from affectation of every kind; his manners were easy and natural, and he had no unnecessary state, though maintaining fully the dignity of his station. His good-nature was unruffled, and he bore contradiction with perfect ease, and without any thing like condescension. He was *bon conteur*, full of anecdote, related well, and had a great talent for imitation (mimicry), insomuch that on my observing to one who had been his minister, and giving him an instance of it, "Voyez vous que s'il n'était pas grand roi, il serait grand comédien," the answer was, "L'un n'empêche pas l'autre. Il peut bien être tous les deux." He was always very desirous to learn both our opinions in England of French affairs, and our mode of proceeding on occasions like those existing in France—both because he reckoned our authority of great importance and wished to profit by our experience and follow our example, and because he was most anxious for a cordial good understanding with us. Nor do I ever recollect his expressing himself with greater regret, even indignation, than on the publication of De Joinville's letter on the state of our navy, which was intended to pay court to the Napoleon party by the profession of anti-English feelings. He said he had made him leave Paris for a whole year and go to Spain.

I may mention one instance of his good-nature, when he was really not a little vexed. He had formed a Ministry which he thought sufficiently able, and the members of which, though very respectable, were for the most part inferior and little known men. He had heard that I had given it the name of a "Ministère poisson d'Avril," the 1st of April being the day of its birth. This enraged him, and he broke out upon me the day after, and added a warm panegyric of the Ministry, to which I could not assent, but said I only hoped he might find I was wrong. "Oh," he said, "I will punish you by introducing you to Marshal Bugeaud, 'fameux sabreur,' because I know you undervalue such artists." I said I only hoped he may not have me roasted as he had the Arabs in Algeria. I think he answered, "It was not he but another (Pelissier) of whom that was said, probably without foundation." The truth is that the Ministry pleased him beyond any other he ever had, just because it had little or no will of its own.

He had the failings of most kings of great capacity, and of consequent self-reliance. He wished to have ministers of sufficient ability to perform their official duties, but not of sufficient weight to have a will of their own; and the greatest evil which he committed in this respect was his being somewhat impatient of the one in whose integrity he had the most entire confidence, and whose character, as well as abilities and information, were of the highest order—Duc de Broglie.

Among other matters on which he consulted me, or asked information as to England, one was the king with us, sitting in Cabinet: "Does William IV. ever attend the meetings of the Cabinet?" I said it was more fit to inquire what William III. did, whose position more resembled that of his majesty; and I told him that William IV. never did on any occasion, but William III. very often; and I said that the king never sitting in the French Cabinet could be reckoned no departure from the spirit of our Government, regard being had to his peculiar circumstances.

He often consulted me on such matters as the riots, amounting to insurrection—for example, the one at Lyons, and the sentences passed on the offenders, as well as the means taken to quell them, about which he always felt great anxiety.

In all these instances I saw two excellent qualities—great humanity, and perfect firmness, not to be unduly led away by humane feelings. The Lyons insurrection seemed to have given him the greatest pain, both for the consequences of the outrage itself and for the loss of life occasioned in putting it down. On judicial sentences he was the same. One case I recollect—a case of an atrocious murder, where the jury had found extenuating circumstances, thus avoiding a capital punishment. I said that the circumstances would in England be reckoned an aggravation, and I believed everywhere, even in Paris, where the addition was most probably made as a compromise to bring in dissentient voices. It was a murder of a father by his daughter, because he had refused his consent to her marrying a man whom she was in love with. He at once agreed. There were other sentences which I thought would have been more severe in England. He had no sentimental crotchets on any such subjects.

On the great evils of the infinite subdivision of property, from its tendency to prevent the foundation of an aristocracy, so necessary to a constitutional monarchy, we entirely agreed. When I mentioned having seen a small field near Cannes, which he always good-humoredly called "ma bonne ville de Cannes" (the jest was on account of this title being only given to great towns or cities), divided into four small lots, in each of which stood a single olive-tree, because the four sons could not agree—he said that was nothing to what they had near Paris, where a person often had a right of property in one-twentieth of a single tree; and he mentioned that, beside the political or constitutional objection, there was the legal; and he explained, as accurately as any conveyancer could have done, the insuperable difficulties thence arising, often amounting to an impossibility of tracing title. I was not then aware of another great evil—the setting members of the same family against each other. On the parents' decease, the course is to have an arbitration and division, frequently ending in a lawsuit. And there were constant instances of brothers not on speaking terms, from discontent with the division.

Nearly the longest interview I had with him was one evening when, as usual, he took me into the private room adjoining that where the reception was. We had a long discussion upon the state of things in England—the Ministry and Lord Aberdeen, for whom he always had the greatest regard. But we had considerable differences as to some matters in France. He talked much of his own position, and I recollect his saying, "Savez-vous qu'il est bon pour nos Français d'avoir un roi qui a ciré ses bottes." This led to my remark that they had what was still better for them—a king who had been a school-master. He said, "Yes, but he found them not always as good pupils as he had often had."

He spoke of his travels in America, and his astonishment when he now read accounts of great towns, and even cities, on spots where, when he and Alexander Baring travelled together, they had been obliged to sleep under a tent in the forest. He expressed the greatest regard for Baring, and the highest opinion of his judgment, and of his capacity generally, in which I fully agreed. After a long-continued conversation, he said, "I fear we must now go back to the queen, for I dare say the reception has been over a great while," and desired me to go, and he would follow me. I was on the point of acting on Lord Stair's example, whom Louis XV. praised for his politeness in getting, as he desired, into the carriage before him, when I recollected another way of obeying him. I took two candles to light him on the way, which was strictly according to etiquette, and went in. I instantly perceived why he had made me go first. I could have sworn that Alexander Baring was behind, so perfectly did he imitate him; and turning round to express my astonishment, he said it was not Alexander Baring only that he could give me, but others whom, happily for myself, I had not known as I did him. However, he said I might judge of the correctness of his representation by what I had seen of it in Baring's case. He then gave me Robespierre, and lowered his voice, and seemed to contract his features into the form of that wretch; next, he puffed himself out with the gross form of Danton, of whom and of Robespierre he spoke nearly in the same terms Carnot had used when speaking of him to me in 1814. But his imitation gave me a most lively impression of them both; and such as I was well prepared for, by all the descriptions I had heard of their style of speaking.

The scene of Robespierre he laid in the last struggle of the Convention, when Danton and others* had been denounced and arrested, and it was proposed that the accused should be heard at the bar, especially Danton, who had in September, 1792, saved France, although now arrested as a traitor. Robespierre, on this, rushed to the tribune, exclaiming, "Au trouble depuis long-temps inconnu, qui règne dans cette Assemblée, on voit bien qu'il est question ici, d'un grand intérêt, qu'il s'agit de savoir si quelques hommes l'emporteront aujourd'hui sur la patrie. Mais comment pouvez-vous oublier vos principes, jusqu'à vouloir accorder aujourd'hui à certains individus, ce que vous avez naguère refusé à Chabot, Delaunay, et Fabre d'Eglantine? Pourquoi cette différence en faveur de quelques hommes? Que m'importent à moi les éloges qu'on se donne à soi et à ses amis? Une trop grande expérience nous a appris à nous défier de ces éloges.

"Legendre paraît ignorer les noms de ceux qui sont arrêtés. Toute la Convention les connait; son ami Lacroix est du nombre des détenus; pourquoi Legendre feint-il de l'ignorer? Parcequ'il sait bien qu'on ne peut, sans impudeur, défendre Lacroix. Il a parlé de Danton, parcequ'il croit qu'à ce nom sans doute est attaché un privilège—

* Desmoulins, Philippeau, and Lacroix.

non, nous ne voulons pas de privilèges; nous ne voulons pas d'idoles!"

Robespierre, he added, had all the audacity and power to say all he wished; and on no other occasion had he shown himself so clever and so false. To talk of a sacrifice in deserting Danton, and to take credit to himself for this, was, as the king said, the highest flight of hypocrisy and baseness.

It was decided that the arrested Deputies should not be heard before the Convention. When they came to Danton, Saint-Just accused him of avarice, treachery, deceit, and cowardice, and of having conspired with Mirabeau, with Dumourier, with the Girondins, with d'Orleans, and with the party for restoring Louis XVII.

Here he gave an imitation of Danton, delivering his famous speech "L'audace."—"Que les lâches qui m'accusent, paraissent, et je les couvrirai d'ignominie;—Qu'ils paraissent! Au reste, peu m'importe vous et votre jugement."

Calling on his accusers to appear produced a great effect, and drew upon him the remark of the president: "Danton, l'audace est le propre du crime; le calme est celui de l'innocence." On which Danton shouted out, "L'audace!—l'audace individuelle est réprimable, sans doute; mais l'audace nationale, dont j'ai tant de fois donné l'exemple, que j'ai tant de fois mise au service de la liberté, est la plus méritoire de toutes les vertus. Cette audace est la mienne!"

The king said he had chosen these speeches because I knew them, having read them. He considered that of Danton was in his own character; Robespierre's was not; it was animated, and deserving of great praise. On almost all other occasions his manner was as bad as possible, and even his utterance was defective in a great degree.

He spoke of Danton as having been very kind to him when he first came to Paris, after Dumouriez's revolt and flight, on whose staff he had been, and had distinguished himself in commands given him by Dumouriez, in some of his greatest battles. He ventured to disclose himself, knowing that Danton had been a friend of his father's, but saying at the same time that, both on his father's account and Dumouriez's, he was certain to be sacrificed if known. "Don't be too sure of that, my young man; I can protect you." He did so, and,

I rather think, recommended him to Montesquieu, then commanding in Switzerland. This conversation with Danton he gave with the most lively representation of Danton's voice, manner, and even figure.

He then told me how delighted he had been at his father's conduct on the trial of Louis XVI., and said he was perfectly certain that, had he been with him, he could have prevented the fatal vote. He spoke with the warmest affection of him, and said there was no man who had been less understood, or more the victim of party and mob violence. In this I could not agree; though I admit that there has been great exaggeration, especially in concealing his few good qualities. He said he was determined to make an attempt at doing justice to his memory, if his own life was spared, which seemed exposed to endless attacks.

APPENDIX A.

In May, 1832, I had an interview with the Duke of Buckingham. Of what then occurred I made at the time the following memorandum:

Having had a singular kind of conversation a day or two ago with the Duke of Buckingham, in consequence of a note asking a private interview on matters of moment, he came to the House of Lords and began by saying how much he and those he acted with approved my principles of *safe* reform, and referred to the phrases I used, of steering on a lee-shore among unknown shoals, with the lead in hand. But I said I was decidedly for the bill as now in the House of Commons, admitting I had not intended, when I should move on Tuesday, 18th November, to propose so much, especially in one direction; and admitting my doubts as to at once doing away *all* close boroughs. But I added that the more Schedule A was considered, the more difficult it was to draw the line, and that this was in principle the most indefensible. I also said I was for *all* householders voting; and that three years were long enough for a Parliament; so that my plan was really as sweeping and as odious to his people. He again said that in the turns and changes which were sure to come, they felt much satisfaction in thinking that my aversion to violent wholesale change would probably lead me to act with them, and they felt greatly so disposed. I said, "All this goes upon a complete mistake—namely, that I am not cordially agreed with my colleagues, especially on the bill; and nothing can be more entirely untrue." He said he only supposed there might, in the course of the measure, differences arise. I said, of this I could say nothing, and added, "Alors comme alors," saying that nothing could be less likely, but that no man could beforehand say either one way or another how he should be obliged to act in unknown cases. He desired this to be confidential, and should mention it to none but Wharncliffe and Harrowby, adding the bill was sure to be lost by fifty or so, which I entirely denied.

I mentioned this generally to Lord Lansdowne, who said Wharncliffe would not be consulted if a change took place.

NOTE TO VOL. II., Pages 122, 166.

A LETTER from Lord Stanhope, published in "The Times" of June 12, 1871, renders necessary an explanation of the circumstances under which the letter beginning "Georgius Rex," page 122, was printed. This letter, together with that from Queen Charlotte, page 166, was sent to Lord Brougham in an envelope indorsed thus:

"*Original Letter of Geo. III. to the Prince (Regent) of Wales.*

"*Also Queen Charlotte to the Pss. of Wales.*"

Lord Brougham himself wrote on the envelope the following words:

"*Sent to me by Pss. of W.*—1810."

The letter in question is wholly in the handwriting of George II., and must have been given to the Princess of Wales by George III. Hence it is most probable that the extraordinary similarity of the circumstances in Frederick's treatment of the mother of George III. before and after the birth of the Princess Augusta, and the regent's treatment of his wife before and after the birth of the Princess Charlotte, led the Princess of Wales to believe that the letter had been written by George III.

Hence the indorsement. Hence Lord Brougham took for granted that the letter was what it professed to be, and therefore introduced a full copy of it in his narrative.

This copy was sent to press exactly as Lord Brougham left it, and, following his precise instructions in that behalf, without examination or comment.

BROUGHAM & VAUX.

Brougham, November 12, 1871.

THE END.

VALUABLE STANDARD WORKS

FOR PUBLIC AND PRIVATE LIBRARIES,

PUBLISHED BY HARPER & BROTHERS, NEW YORK.

☞ *For a full List of Books suitable for Libraries, see* HARPER & BROTHERS' TRADE-LIST *and* CATALOGUE, *which may be had gratuitously on application to the Publishers personally, or by letter enclosing Five Cents.*

☞ HARPER & BROTHERS *will send any of the following works by mail, postage prepaid, to any part of the United States, on receipt of the price.*

MOTLEY'S DUTCH REPUBLIC. The Rise of the Dutch Republic. By JOHN LOTHROP MOTLEY, LL.D., D.C.L. With a Portrait of William of Orange. 3 vols., 8vo, Cloth, $10 50.

MOTLEY'S UNITED NETHERLANDS. History of the United Netherlands: from the Death of William the Silent to the Twelve Years' Truce—1609. With a full View of the English-Dutch Struggle against Spain, and of the Origin and Destruction of the Spanish Armada. By JOHN LOTHROP MOTLEY, LL.D., D.C.L. Portraits. 4 vols., 8vo, Cloth, $14 00.

NAPOLEON'S LIFE OF CÆSAR. The History of Julius Cæsar. By His Imperial Majesty NAPOLEON III. Two Volumes ready. Library Edition, 8vo, Cloth, $3 50 per vol.

Maps to Vols. I. and II. sold separately. Price $1 50 *each*, NET.

HAYDN'S DICTIONARY OF DATES, relating to all Ages and Nations. For Universal Reference. Edited by BENJAMIN VINCENT, Assistant Secretary and Keeper of the Library of the Royal Institution of Great Britain; and Revised for the Use of American Readers. 8vo, Cloth, $5 00; Sheep, $6 00.

MACGREGOR'S ROB ROY ON THE JORDAN. The Rob Roy on the Jordan, Nile, Red Sea, and Gennesareth, &c. A Canoe Cruise in Palestine and Egypt, and the Waters of Damascus. By J. MACGREGOR, M.A. With Maps and Illustrations. Crown 8vo, Cloth, $2 50.

WALLACE'S MALAY ARCHIPELAGO. The Malay Archipelago: the Land of the Orang-Utan and the Bird of Paradise. A Narrative of Travel, 1854–1862. With Studies of Man and Nature. By ALFRED RUSSEL WALLACE. With Ten Maps and Fifty-one Elegant Illustrations. Crown 8vo, Cloth, $3 50.

WHYMPER'S ALASKA. Travel and Adventure in the Territory of Alaska, formerly Russian America—now Ceded to the United States—and in various other parts of the North Pacific. By FREDERICK WHYMPER. With Map and Illustrations. Crown 8vo, Cloth, $2 50.

ORTON'S ANDES AND THE AMAZON. The Andes and the Amazon; or, Across the Continent of South America. By JAMES ORTON, M.A., Professor of Natural History in Vassar College, Poughkeepsie, N. Y., and Corresponding Member of the Academy of Natural Sciences, Philadelphia. With a New Map of Equatorial America and numerous Illustrations. Crown 8vo, Cloth, $2 00.

WINCHELL'S SKETCHES OF CREATION. Sketches of Creation: a Popular View of some of the Grand Conclusions of the Sciences in reference to the History of Matter and of Life. Together with a Statement of the Intimations of Science respecting the Primordial Condition and the Ultimate Destiny of the Earth and the Solar System. By ALEXANDER WINCHELL, LL.D., Professor of Geology, Zoology, and Botany in the University of Michigan, and Director of the State Geological Survey. With Illustrations. 12mo, Cloth, $2 00.

WHITE'S MASSACRE OF ST. BARTHOLOMEW. The Massacre of St. Bartholomew: Preceded by a History of the Religious Wars in the Reign of Charles IX. By HENRY WHITE, M.A. With Illustrations. 8vo, Cloth, $1 75.

LOSSING'S FIELD-BOOK OF THE REVOLUTION. Pictorial Field-Book of the Revolution; or, Illustrations, by Pen and Pencil, of the History, Biography, Scenery, Relics, and Traditions of the War for Independence. By Benson J. Lossing. 2 vols., 8vo, Cloth, $14 00; Sheep, $15 00; Half Calf, $18 00; Full Turkey Morocco, $22 00.

LOSSING'S FIELD-BOOK OF THE WAR OF 1812. Pictorial Field-Book of the War of 1812; or, Illustrations, by Pen and Pencil, of the History, Biography, Scenery, Relics, and Traditions of the Last War for American Independence. By Benson J. Lossing. With several hundred Engravings on Wood, by Lossing and Barritt, chiefly from Original Sketches by the Author. 1088 pages, 8vo, Cloth, $7 00; Sheep, $8 50; Half Calf, $10 00.

ALFORD'S GREEK TESTAMENT. The Greek Testament: with a critically revised Text; a Digest of Various Readings; Marginal References to Verbal and Idiomatic Usage; Prolegomena; and a Critical and Exegetical Commentary. For the Use of Theological Students and Ministers. By Henry Alford, D.D., Dean of Canterbury. Vol. I., containing the Four Gospels. 944 pages, 8vo, Cloth, $6 00; Sheep, $6 50.

ABBOTT'S FREDERICK THE GREAT. The History of Frederick the Second, called Frederick the Great. By John S. C. Abbott. Elegantly Illustrated. 8vo, Cloth, $5 00.

ABBOTT'S HISTORY OF THE FRENCH REVOLUTION. The French Revolution of 1789, as viewed in the Light of Republican Institutions. By John S. C. Abbott. With 100 Engravings. 8vo, Cloth, $5 00.

ABBOTT'S NAPOLEON BONAPARTE. The History of Napoleon Bonaparte. By John S. C. Abbott. With Maps, Woodcuts, and Portraits on Steel. 2 vols., 8vo, Cloth, $10 00.

ABBOTT'S NAPOLEON AT ST. HELENA; or, Interesting Anecdotes and Remarkable Conversations of the Emperor during the Five and a Half Years of his Captivity. Collected from the Memorials of Las Casas, O'Meara, Montholon, Antommarchi, and others. By John S. C. Abbott. With Illustrations. 8vo, Cloth, $5 00.

ADDISON'S COMPLETE WORKS. The Works of Joseph Addison, embracing the whole of the "Spectator." Complete in 3 vols., 8vo, Cloth, $6 00.

ALCOCK'S JAPAN. The Capital of the Tycoon: a Narrative of a Three Years' Residence in Japan. By Sir Rutherford Alcock, K.C.B., Her Majesty's Envoy Extraordinary and Minister Plenipotentiary in Japan. With Maps and Engravings. 2 vols., 12mo, Cloth, $3 50.

ALISON'S HISTORY OF EUROPE. First Series: From the Commencement of the French Revolution, in 1789, to the Restoration of the Bourbons, in 1815. [In addition to the Notes on Chapter LXXVI., which correct the errors of the original work concerning the United States, a copious Analytical Index has been appended to this American edition.] Second Series: From the Fall of Napoleon, in 1815, to the Accession of Louis Napoleon, in 1852. 8 vols., 8vo, Cloth, $16 00.

BALDWIN'S PRE-HISTORIC NATIONS. Pre-Historic Nations; or, Inquiries concerning some of the Great Peoples and Civilizations of Antiquity, and their Probable Relation to a still Older Civilization of the Ethiopians or Cushites of Arabia. By John D. Baldwin, Member of the American Oriental Society. 12mo, Cloth, $1 75.

BARTH'S NORTH AND CENTRAL AFRICA. Travels and Discoveries in North and Central Africa: being a Journal of an Expedition undertaken under the Auspices of H. B. M.'s Government, in the Years 1849–1855. By Henry Barth, Ph.D., D.C.L. Illustrated. 3 vols., 8vo, Cloth, $12 00.

HENRY WARD BEECHER'S SERMONS. Sermons by Henry Ward Beecher, Plymouth Church, Brooklyn. Selected from Published and Unpublished Discourses, and Revised by their Author. With Steel Portrait. Complete in 2 vols., 8vo, Cloth, $5 00.

LYMAN BEECHER'S AUTOBIOGRAPHY, &c. Autobiography, Correspondence, &c., of Lyman Beecher, D.D. Edited by his Son, Charles Beecher. With Three Steel Portraits, and Engravings on Wood. In 2 vols., 12mo, Cloth, $5 00.

BOSWELL'S JOHNSON. The Life of Samuel Johnson, LL.D. Including a Journey to the Hebrides. By James Boswell, Esq. A New Edition, with numerous Additions and Notes. By John Wilson Croker, LL.D., F.R.S. Portrait of Boswell. 2 vols., 8vo, Cloth, $4 00.

DRAPER'S CIVIL WAR. History of the American Civil War. By JOHN W. DRAPER, M.D., LL.D., Professor of Chemistry and Physiology in the University of New York. In Three Vols. 8vo, Cloth, $3 50 per vol.

DRAPER'S INTELLECTUAL DEVELOPMENT OF EUROPE. A History of the Intellectual Development of Europe. By JOHN W. DRAPER, M.D., LL.D., Professor of Chemistry and Physiology in the University of New York. 8vo, Cloth, $5 00.

DRAPER'S AMERICAN CIVIL POLICY. Thoughts on the Future Civil Policy of America. By JOHN W. DRAPER, M.D., LL.D., Professor of Chemistry and Physiology in the University of New York. Crown 8vo, Cloth, $2 50.

DU CHAILLU'S AFRICA. Explorations and Adventures in Equatorial Africa: with Accounts of the Manners and Customs of the People, and of the Chase of the Gorilla, the Crocodile, Leopard, Elephant, Hippopotamus, and other Animals. By PAUL B. DU CHAILLU. Numerous Illustrations. 8vo, Cloth, $5 00.

BELLOWS'S OLD WORLD. The Old World in its New Face: Impressions of Europe in 1867–1868. By HENRY W. BELLOWS. 2 vols., 12mo, Cloth, $3 50.

BRODHEAD'S HISTORY OF NEW YORK. History of the State of New York. By JOHN ROMEYN BRODHEAD. 1609–1691. 2 vols. 8vo, Cloth, $3 00 per vol.

BROUGHAM'S AUTOBIOGRAPHY. Life and Times of HENRY, LORD BROUGHAM. Written by Himself. In Three Volumes. 12mo, Cloth, $2 00 per vol.

BULWER'S PROSE WORKS. Miscellaneous Prose Works of Edward Bulwer, Lord Lytton. 2 vols., 12mo, Cloth, $3 50.

BULWER'S HORACE. The Odes and Epodes of Horace. A Metrical Translation into English. With Introduction and Commentaries. By LORD LYTTON. With Latin Text from the Editions of Orelli, Macleane, and Yonge. 12mo, Cloth, $1 75.

BULWER'S KING ARTHUR. A Poem. By EARL LYTTON. New Edition. 12mo, Cloth, $1 75.

BURNS'S LIFE AND WORKS. The Life and Works of Robert Burns. Edited by ROBERT CHAMBERS. 4 vols., 12mo, Cloth, $6 00.

REINDEER, DOGS, AND SNOW-SHOES. A Journal of Siberian Travel and Explorations made in the Years 1865–'67. By RICHARD J. BUSH, late of the Russo-American Telegraph Expedition. Illustrated. Crown 8vo, Cloth, $3 00.

CARLYLE'S FREDERICK THE GREAT. History of Friedrich II., called Frederick the Great. By THOMAS CARLYLE. Portraits, Maps, Plans, &c. 6 vols., 12mo, Cloth, $12 00.

CARLYLE'S FRENCH REVOLUTION. History of the French Revolution. Newly Revised by the Author, with Index, &c. 2 vols., 12mo, Cloth, $3 50.

CARLYLE'S OLIVER CROMWELL. Letters and Speeches of Oliver Cromwell. With Elucidations and Connecting Narrative. 2 vols., 12mo, Cloth, $3 50.

CHALMERS'S POSTHUMOUS WORKS. The Posthumous Works of Dr. Chalmers. Edited by his Son-in-Law, Rev. WILLIAM HANNA, LL.D. Complete in 9 vols., 12mo, Cloth, $13 50.

COLERIDGE'S COMPLETE WORKS. The Complete Works of Samuel Taylor Coleridge. With an Introductory Essay upon his Philosophical and Theological Opinions. Edited by Professor SHEDD. Complete in Seven Vols. With a fine Portrait. Small 8vo, Cloth, $10 50.

CURTIS'S HISTORY OF THE CONSTITUTION. History of the Origin, Formation, and Adoption of the Constitution of the United States. By GEORGE TICKNOR CURTIS. 2 vols., 8vo, Cloth, $6 00.

DOOLITTLE'S CHINA. Social Life of the Chinese: with some Account of their Religious, Governmental, Educational, and Business Customs and Opinions. With special but not exclusive Reference to Fuhchau. By Rev. JUSTUS DOOLITTLE, Fourteen Years Member of the Fuhchau Mission of the American Board. Illustrated with more than 150 characteristic Engravings on Wood. 2 vols., 12mo, Cloth, $5 00.

GIBBON'S ROME. History of the Decline and Fall of the Roman Empire. By EDWARD GIBBON. With Notes by Rev. H. H. MILMAN and M. GUIZOT. A new cheap Edition. To which is added a complete Index of the whole Work, and a Portrait of the Author. 6 vols., 12mo, Cloth, $9 00.

HARPER'S NEW CLASSICAL LIBRARY. Literal Translations.
The following Volumes are now ready. Portraits. 12mo, Cloth, $1 50 each.
CÆSAR.—VIRGIL.—SALLUST.—HORACE.—CICERO'S ORATIONS.—CICERO'S OFFICES, &c.—CICERO ON ORATORY AND ORATORS.—TACITUS (2 vols.).—TERENCE.—SOPHOCLES.—JUVENAL.—XENOPHON.—HOMER'S ILIAD.—HOMER'S ODYSSEY.—HERODOTUS.—DEMOSTHENES.—THUCYDIDES.—ÆSCHYLUS.—EURIPIDES (2 vols.).—LIVY (2 vols.).

DAVIS'S CARTHAGE. Carthage and her Remains: being an Account of the Excavations and Researches on the Site of the Phœnician Metropolis in Africa and other adjacent Places. Conducted under the Auspices of Her Majesty's Government. By Dr. DAVIS, F.R.G.S. Profusely Illustrated with Maps, Woodcuts, Chromo-Lithographs, &c. 8vo, Cloth, $4 00.

EDGEWORTH'S (MISS) NOVELS. With Engravings. 10 vols., 12mo, Cloth, $15 00.

GROTE'S HISTORY OF GREECE. 12 vols., 12mo, Cloth, $18 00.

HELPS'S SPANISH CONQUEST. The Spanish Conquest in America, and its Relation to the History of Slavery and to the Government of Colonies. By ARTHUR HELPS. 4 vols., 12mo, Cloth, $6 00.

HALE'S (MRS.) WOMAN'S RECORD. Woman's Record; or, Biographical Sketches of all Distinguished Women, from the Creation to the Present Time. Arranged in Four Eras, with Selections from Female Writers of each Era. By Mrs. SARAH JOSEPHA HALE. Illustrated with more than 200 Portraits. 8vo, Cloth, $5 00.

HALL'S ARCTIC RESEARCHES. Arctic Researches and Life among the Esquimaux: being the Narrative of an Expedition in Search of Sir John Franklin, in the Years 1860, 1861, and 1862. By CHARLES FRANCIS HALL. With Maps and 100 Illustrations. The Illustrations are from Original Drawings by Charles Parsons, Henry L. Stephens, Solomon Eytinge, W. S. L. Jewett, and Granville Perkins, after Sketches by Captain Hall. 8vo, Cloth, $5 00.

HALLAM'S CONSTITUTIONAL HISTORY OF ENGLAND, from the Accession of Henry VII. to the Death of George II. 8vo, Cloth, $2 00.

HALLAM'S LITERATURE. Introduction to the Literature of Europe during the Fifteenth, Sixteenth, and Seventeenth Centuries. By HENRY HALLAM. 2 vols., 8vo, Cloth, $4 00.

HALLAM'S MIDDLE AGES. State of Europe during the Middle Ages. By HENRY HALLAM. 8vo, Cloth, $2 00.

HILDRETH'S HISTORY OF THE UNITED STATES. FIRST SERIES: From the First Settlement of the Country to the Adoption of the Federal Constitution. SECOND SERIES: From the Adoption of the Federal Constitution to the End of the Sixteenth Congress. 6 vols., 8vo, Cloth, $18 00.

HUME'S HISTORY OF ENGLAND. History of England, from the Invasion of Julius Cæsar to the Abdication of James II., 1688. By DAVID HUME. A new Edition, with the Author's last Corrections and Improvements. To which is Prefixed a short Account of his Life, written by Himself. With a Portrait of the Author. 6 vols., 12mo, Cloth, $9 00.

JAY'S WORKS. Complete Works of Rev. William Jay: comprising his Sermons, Family Discourses, Morning and Evening Exercises for every Day in the Year, Family Prayers, &c. Author's enlarged Edition, revised. 3 vols., 8vo, Cloth, $6 00.

JEFFERSON'S DOMESTIC LIFE. The Domestic Life of Thomas Jefferson: compiled from Family Letters and Reminiscences by his Great-Granddaughter, SARAH N. RANDOLPH. With Illustrations. Crown 8vo, Illuminated Cloth, Beveled Edges, $2 50.

JOHNSON'S COMPLETE WORKS. The Works of Samuel Johnson, LL.D. With an Essay on his Life and Genius, by ARTHUR MURPHY, Esq. Portrait of Johnson. 2 vols., 8vo, Cloth, $4 00.

KINGLAKE'S CRIMEAN WAR. The Invasion of the Crimea, and an Account of its Progress down to the Death of Lord Raglan. By ALEXANDER WILLIAM KINGLAKE. With Maps and Plans. Two Vols. ready. 12mo, Cloth, $2 00 per vol.

KINGSLEY'S WEST INDIES. At Last: A Christmas in the West Indies. By CHARLES KINGSLEY. Illustrated. 12mo, Cloth, $1 50.

KRUMMACHER'S DAVID, KING OF ISRAEL. David, the King of Israel: a Portrait drawn from Bible History and the Book of Psalms. By FREDERICK WILLIAM KRUMMACHER, D.D., Author of "Elijah the Tishbite," &c. Translated under the express Sanction of the Author by the Rev. M. G. EASTON, M.A. With a Letter from Dr. Krummacher to his American Readers, and a Portrait. 12mo, Cloth, $1 75.

LAMB'S COMPLETE WORKS. The Works of Charles Lamb. Comprising his Letters, Poems, Essays of Elia, Essays upon Shakspeare, Hogarth, &c., and a Sketch of his Life, with the Final Memorials, by T. NOON TALFOURD. Portrait. 2 vols., 12mo, Cloth, $3 00.

LIVINGSTONE'S SOUTH AFRICA. Missionary Travels and Researches in South Africa; including a Sketch of Sixteen Years' Residence in the Interior of Africa, and a Journey from the Cape of Good Hope to Loando on the West Coast; thence across the Continent, down the River Zambesi, to the Eastern Ocean. By DAVID LIVINGSTONE, LL.D., D.C.L. With Portrait, Maps by Arrowsmith, and numerous Illustrations. 8vo, Cloth, $4 50.

LIVINGSTONES' ZAMBESI. Narrative of an Expedition to the Zambesi and its Tributaries, and of the Discovery of the Lakes Shirwa and Nyassa. 1858-1864. By DAVID and CHARLES LIVINGSTONE. With Map and Illustrations. 8vo, Cloth, $5 00.

M'CLINTOCK & STRONG'S CYCLOPÆDIA. Cyclopædia of Biblical, Theological, and Ecclesiastical Literature. Prepared by the Rev. JOHN M'CLINTOCK, D.D., and JAMES STRONG, S.T.D. *3 vols. now ready.* Royal 8vo. Price per vol., Cloth, $5 00; Sheep, $6 00; Half Morocco, $8 00.

MARCY'S ARMY LIFE ON THE BORDER. Thirty Years of Army Life on the Border. Comprising Descriptions of the Indian Nomads of the Plains; Explorations of New Territory; a Trip across the Rocky Mountains in the Winter; Descriptions of the Habits of Different Animals found in the West, and the Methods of Hunting them; with Incidents in the Life of Different Frontier Men, &c., &c. By Brevet Brigadier-General R. B. MARCY, U.S.A., Author of "The Prairie Traveller." With numerous Illustrations. 8vo, Cloth, Beveled Edges, $3 00.

MACAULAY'S HISTORY OF ENGLAND. The History of England from the Accession of James II. By THOMAS BABINGTON MACAULAY. With an Original Portrait of the Author. 5 vols., 8vo, Cloth, $10 00; 12mo, Cloth, $7 50.

MOSHEIM'S ECCLESIASTICAL HISTORY, Ancient and Modern; in which the Rise, Progress, and Variation of Church Power are considered in their Connection with the State of Learning and Philosophy, and the Political History of Europe during that Period. Translated, with Notes, &c., by A. MACLAINE, D.D. A new Edition, continued to 1826, by C. COOTE, LL.D. 2 vols., 8vo, Cloth, $4 00.

NEVIUS'S CHINA. China and the Chinese: a General Description of the Country and its Inhabitants; its Civilization and Form of Government; its Religious and Social Institutions; its Intercourse with other Nations; and its Present Condition and Prospects. By the Rev. JOHN L. NEVIUS, Ten Years a Missionary in China. With a Map and Illustrations. 12mo, Cloth, $1 75.

OLIN'S (DR.) LIFE AND LETTERS. 2 vols., 12mo, Cloth, $3 00.

OLIN'S (DR.) TRAVELS. Travels in Egypt, Arabia Petræa, and the Holy Land. Engravings. 2 vols., 8vo, Cloth, $3 00.

OLIN'S (DR.) WORKS. The Works of Stephen Olin, D.D., late President of the Wesleyan University. 2 vols., 12mo, Cloth, $3 00.

OLIPHANT'S CHINA AND JAPAN. Narrative of the Earl of Elgin's Mission to China and Japan, in the Years 1857, '58, '59. By LAURENCE OLIPHANT, Private Secretary to Lord Elgin. Illustrations. 8vo, Cloth, $3 50.

OLIPHANT'S (MRS.) LIFE OF EDWARD IRVING. The Life of Edward Irving, Minister of the National Scotch Church, London. Illustrated by his Journals and Correspondence. By Mrs. OLIPHANT. Portrait. 8vo, Cloth, $3 50.

RAWLINSON'S MANUAL OF ANCIENT HISTORY. A Manual of Ancient History, from the Earliest Times to the Fall of the Western Empire. Comprising the History of Chaldæa, Assyria, Media, Babylonia, Lydia, Phœnicia, Syria, Judæa, Egypt, Carthage, Persia, Greece, Macedonia, Parthia, and Rome. By GEORGE RAWLINSON, M.A., Camden Professor of Ancient History in the University of Oxford. 12mo, Cloth, $2 50.

RECLUS'S THE EARTH. The Earth: a Descriptive History of the Phenomena and Life of the Globe. By ELISÉE RECLUS. Translated by the late B. B. Woodward, and Edited by Henry Woodward. With 234 Maps and Illustrations, and 23 Page Maps printed in Colors. 8vo, Cloth, $5 00.

POETS OF THE NINETEENTH CENTURY. The Poets of the Nineteenth Century. Selected and Edited by the Rev. ROBERT ARIS WILLMOTT. With English and American Additions, arranged by EVERT A. DUYCKINCK, Editor of "Cyclopædia of American Literature." Comprising Selections from the Greatest Authors of the Age. Superbly Illustrated with 132 Engravings from Designs by the most Eminent Artists. In elegant small 4to form, printed on Superfine Tinted Paper, richly bound in extra Cloth, Beveled, Gilt Edges, $6 00; Half Calf, $6 00; Full Turkey Morocco, $10 00.

SHAKSPEARE. The Dramatic Works of William Shakspeare, with the Corrections and Illustrations of Dr. JOHNSON, G. STEEVENS, and others. Revised by ISAAC REED. Engravings. 6 vols., Royal 12mo, Cloth, $9 00.

SMILES'S LIFE OF THE STEPHENSONS. The Life of George Stephenson, and of his Son, Robert Stephenson; comprising, also, a History of the Invention and Introduction of the Railway Locomotive. By SAMUEL SMILES, Author of "Self-Help," &c. With Steel Portraits and numerous Illustrations. 8vo, Cloth, $3 00.

SMILES'S HISTORY OF THE HUGUENOTS. The Huguenots: their Settlements, Churches, and Industries in England and Ireland. By SAMUEL SMILES. With an Appendix relating to the Huguenots in America. Crown 8vo, Cloth, $1 75.

SPEKE'S AFRICA. Journal of the Discovery of the Source of the Nile. By Captain JOHN HANNING SPEKE, Captain H. M. Indian Army, Fellow and Gold Medalist of the Royal Geographical Society, Hon. Corresponding Member and Gold Medalist of the French Geographical Society, &c. With Maps and Portraits and numerous Illustrations, chiefly from Drawings by Captain GRANT. 8vo, Cloth, uniform with Livingstone, Barth, Burton, &c., $4 00.

STRICKLAND'S (MISS) QUEENS OF SCOTLAND. Lives of the Queens of Scotland and English Princesses connected with the Regal Succession of Great Britain. By AGNES STRICKLAND. 8 vols., 12mo, Cloth, $12 00.

THE STUDENT'S SERIES.

France. Engravings. 12mo, Cloth, $2 00.
Gibbon. Engravings. 12mo, Cloth, $2 00.
Greece. Engravings. 12mo, Cloth, $2 00.
Hume. Engravings. 12mo, Cloth, $2 00.
Rome. By Liddell. Engravings. 12mo, Cloth, $2 00.
Old Testament History. Engravings. 12mo, Cloth, $2 00.
New Testament History. Engravings. 12mo, Cloth, $2 00.
Strickland's Queens of England. Abridged. Engravings. 12mo, Cloth, $2 00.
Ancient History of the East. 12mo, Cloth, $2 00.
Hallam's Middle Ages. 12mo, Cloth, $2 00.
Lyell's Elements of Geology. 12mo, Cloth, $2 00.

TENNYSON'S COMPLETE POEMS. The Complete Poems of Alfred Tennyson, Poet Laureate. With numerous Illustrations by Eminent Artists, and Three Characteristic Portraits. 8vo, Paper, 75 cents; Cloth, $1 25.

THOMSON'S LAND AND THE BOOK. The Land and the Book; or, Biblical Illustrations drawn from the Manners and Customs, the Scenes and the Scenery of the Holy Land. By W. M. THOMSON, D.D., Twenty-five Years a Missionary of the A.B.C.F.M. in Syria and Palestine. With two elaborate Maps of Palestine, an accurate Plan of Jerusalem, and several hundred Engravings, representing the Scenery, Topography, and Productions of the Holy Land, and the Costumes, Manners, and Habits of the People. 2 large 12mo vols., Cloth, $5 00.

TYERMAN'S WESLEY. The Life and Times of the Rev. John Wesley, M.A., Founder of the Methodists. By the Rev. LUKE TYERMAN, Author of "The Life of Rev. Samuel Wesley." Portraits. 3 vols., Crown 8vo.

VÁMBÉRY'S CENTRAL ASIA. Travels in Central Asia. Being the Account of a Journey from Teheran across the Turkoman Desert, on the Eastern Shore of the Caspian, to Khiva, Bokhara, and Samarcand, performed in the Year 1863. By ARMINIUS VÁMBÉRY, Member of the Hungarian Academy of Pesth, by whom he was sent on this Scientific Mission. With Map and Woodcuts. 8vo, Cloth, $4 50.

WOOD'S HOMES WITHOUT HANDS. Homes Without Hands: being a Description of the Habitations of Animals, classed according to their Principle of Construction. By J. G. WOOD, M.A., F.L.S. With about 140 Illustrations. 8vo, Cloth, Beveled Edges, $4 50.